MATHEMATICAL
SOFTWARE III

Publication No. 39
of the Mathematics Research Center
The University of Wisconsin—Madison

Mathematical Software III

Edited by John R. Rice

Proceedings of a Symposium
Conducted by the Mathematics Research Center
The University of Wisconsin—Madison
March 28–30, 1977

Academic Press
New York • San Francisco • London   1977

A Subsidiary of Harcourt Brace Jovanovich, Publishers

ACADEMIC PRESS, INC.
111 Fifth Avenue, New York, New York 10003

United Kingdom Edition published by
ACADEMIC PRESS, INC. (LONDON) LTD.
24/28 Oval Road, London NW1

Library of Congress Cataloging in Publication Data

Mathematical Software Symposium, University of Wisconsin—
        Madison, 1977.

        Mathematical software III.

        (Publication of the Mathematics Reserch Center, the
University of Wisconsin—Madison ; no. 39)
        Includes bibliographies and index.
        1.   Numerical analysis—Data processing—Congresses.
2.   Mathematics—Data processing—Congresses. I. Rice,
John Rischard. II. Wisconsin. University—Madison.
Mathematics Research Center. III. Title. IV. Series:
Wisconsin. University—Madison. Mathematics Research
Center. Publication ; no. 39
QA3.U45   no. 39   [QA297]   510'.8s   [519.4]   77-22192
ISBN 0-12-587260-7

PRINTED IN THE UNITED STATES OF AMERICA

Contents

Contributors   vii

Preface   ix

Research, Development, and LINPACK   1
   G. W. Stewart

A Technique that Gains Speed and Accuracy in the Minimax Solution
of Overdetermined Linear Equations   15
   M. J. Hopper and M. J. D. Powell

Infallible Calculation of Polynomial Zeros to Specified Precision   35
   G. E. Collins

Representation and Approximation of Surfaces   69
   Robert E. Barnhill

Simulation: Conflicts between Real-Time and Software   121
   C. W. Gear

Mathematical Software and Exploratory Data Analysis   139
   David C. Hoaglin

Software for C^1 Surface Interpolation   161
   C. L. Lawson

Mathematical Software Production   195
   W. R. Cowell and L. D. Fosdick

Computational Aspects of the Finite Element Method   225
   I. Babuška and W. Rheinboldt

The Art of Writing a Runge-Kutta Code, Part I   257
   L. F. Shampine and H. A. Watts

Multi-Level Adaptive Techniques (MLAT) for Partial Differential Equations: Ideas and Software   277
  Achi Brandt

ELLPACK: A Research Tool for Elliptic Partial Differential Equations Software   319
  John R. Rice

A Realistic Model of Floating-Point Computation   343
  W. S. Brown

The Block Lanczos Method for Computing Eigenvalues   361
  G. H. Golub and R. Underwood

Index   379

Contributors

I. Babuška, Institute for Physical Science and Technology, University of Maryland, College Park, Maryland 20742

Robert E. Barnhill, Department of Mathematics, The University of Utah, Salt Lake City, Utah 84112

Achi Brandt, Department of Mathematics, The Weizmann Institute of Science, Rehovot, Israel

W. S. Brown, Bell Laboratories, Murray Hill, New Jersey 07974

G. E. Collins, Computer Sciences Department, The University of Wisconsin, Madison, Wisconsin 53706

W. R. Cowell, Applied Mathematics Division, Argonne National Laboratory, Argonne, Illinois 60439

L. D. Fosdick, Department of Computer Science, University of Colorado, Boulder, Colorado 80302

C. W. Gear, Department of Computer Science, University of Illinois, Urbana, Illinois 61801

G. H. Golub, Computer Science Department, Stanford University, Stanford, California 94305

David C. Hoaglin, Department of Statistics, Harvard University, Cambridge, Massachusetts 02138

M. J. Hopper, Computer Science and Systems Division, Atomic Energy Research Establishment, Harwell, Oxfordshire, England

C. L. Lawson, Information Systems Division, Jet Propulsion Laboratory, California Institute of Technology, Pasadena, California 91103

M. J. D. Powell, Department of Applied Mathematics and Theoretical Physics, Cambridge University, Cambridge, England

W. Rheinboldt, Computer Science Center, University of Maryland, College Park, Maryland 20742

John R. Rice, Mathematical Sciences, Purdue University, West Lafayette, Indiana 47907

L. F. Shampine, Numerical Mathematics Division, Applied Mathematics Division, Sandia Laboratories, Albuquerque, New Mexico 87115

G. W. Stewart, Department of Computer Science, University of Maryland, College Park, Maryland 20742

R. Underwood, Nuclear Energy Division, General Electric Company, San Jose, California 95127

H. A. Watts, Numerical Mathematics Division, Applied Mathematics Division, Sandia Laboratories, Albuquerque, New Mexico 87115

Preface

This volume contains the proceedings of the Symposium on Mathematical Software held in Madison, Wisconsin, March 28–30, 1977, sponsored by the Mathematics Research Center, University of Wisconsin—Madison, with financial support from the United States Army under Contract No. DAAG29-75-C-0024 and the National Science Foundation under Grant No. MCS7700887. The five sessions were chaired by

D. B. Moler, *University of New Mexico*
J. H. Griesmer, *IBM Research, Yorktown Heights*
W. J. Cody, *Argonne National Laboratory*
W. Kahan, *University of California, Berkeley*
T. E. Hull, *University of Toronto*

The program committee consisted of C. W. de Boor, J. R. Rice, and J. M. Yohe, with the editor as chairman.

All of the papers presented at the symposium are included plus an additional paper by the editor. While 14 papers are necessarily a small sampling from the field of mathematical software, these papers do exhibit the diversity of its directions for research, its richnesses in connections with mathematics, and its delicate combination of art and science.

It is with sincere gratitude that I thank Gladys Moran for her efficiency as administrator of the symposium affairs and Sally Ross for aid in preparing these proceedings.

Research, Development, and LINPACK
G. W. Stewart

ABSTRACT

LINPACK is a software package for the solution of linear systems and least squares problems that is currently under development. Although the purpose of the LINPACK project, aside from the production of the package itself, is to investigate the problems involved in the development of high quality mathematical software, the design and implementation of the package has revealed a number of research problems in numerical linear algebra. This talk surveys some of these problems.

1. INTRODUCTION

LINPACK is a cooperative effort to produce a software package for the solution of linear systems of equations and linear least squares problems. The project is funded by the National Science Foundation and will be completed at the end of June 1978. The organization of the project is unusual in that responsibility for various parts of the project is divided among three principal investigators at separate universities and a group in the Applied Mathematics Division of Argonne National Laboratory. The university participants are responsible for designing algorithms, producing code, and writing documentation. The group at Argonne is responsible for collecting the code, translating between various versions of the same algorithm (e.g. real and complex versions), and distributing the code to test sites, which are funded by separate NSF grants.

In producing the package we are striving for quality in a number of areas.

1. Algorithms. Every attempt is being made to select the best algorithms for a given task or, where there are several alternatives, to make a justifiable choice.

2. Code. We are attempting to make the code highly legible, and, as far as the FORTRAN language will permit, well structured.

3. Verification. The LINPACK programs will be tested extensively on several different computers at different test sites. As much care is being taken in the design of test drivers as in the design of the programs themselves.

4. Transportability. The programs are being coded in such a way that it will be relatively easy to get them working on a new system.

5. Documentation. This starts with a common nomenclature for all the programs and extensive internal comments. We hope to produce written documentation at two levels: technical documentation on a level of that found in the handbook series [13] and a guide explaining to the casual user what problems LINPACK can solve and giving code for typical applications.

Although the immediate goal of the participants in LINPACK is to produce quality software, the final package is not the reason the project is being funded by the NSF, which regards it as research in the methodology of software production. No one has built a package from scratch in quite the way we are doing it, and it is important to find out if a decentralized organization such as we have elected can really be effective. It is easy to see why such a rationale is considered necessary for funding. Whatever the case for public support of software development (and I believe it is a strong one), organizations like the NSF are responsible for research in the sciences, and to divert funds to development projects would be to fail their charge.

The argument has a convincing ring, and I certainly believed it when we were preparing our proposals. But now, a year into the project, I am no longer as certain. What has caused me to doubt is that a number of interesting research problems have emerged from the purely developmental aspects of LINPACK, and I am now coming to believe that funding software development is an excellent way to stimulate research. I do not wish to argue this point; rather I should like to take this opportunity to describe five research problems that have cropped up in the course of our labors, after which the reader may judge for himself.

2. ESTIMATION OF CONDITION NUMBERS

In choosing algorithms for incorporation into LINPACK, we have been guided by considerations of numerical stability, in the backward sense of the term. For example, an algorithm for solving the linear system

(2.1) $$Ax = b$$

is deemed stable if the computed solution $\bar{x}$ satisfies an equation of the form

(2.2) $$(A+E)\bar{x} = b,$$

where the elements of the matrix E are a modest multiple of the computer's rounding unit times some reasonable norm of A. The reason for requiring stability is that in many applications the errors already present in the matrix A are greater than those represented by the perturbation E. In this case, any inaccuracies in the computed solution may be attributed to the errors in A and not to the algorithm itself. Of course, this line of reasoning does not apply when the elements of A are known exactly; but such problems arise relatively infrequently, and there are specialized techniques, such as iterative refinement, for dealing with them. For more on backward error analysis, see the work of J. H. Wilkinson [11,12], who was the first to exploit the idea systematically.

    The existence of a backward error analysis of the form (2.2) does not guarantee the accuracy of the computed solution $\bar{x}$; it merely suggests that if a user gets an inaccurate solution, he should look to his original problem for a remedy. The difficulty from the user's point of view is that it is not easy to recognize an inaccurate solution. For example, the residual r = b - A$\bar{x}$ tells far more about stability than accuracy (cf. §3), and its computation requires that the user allocate storage to save the matrix A. One way of estimating the accuracy of solutions is provided by the following theorem, in which $\|\cdot\|$ represents a suitable vector norm and a subordinate matrix norm.

THEOREM 1.1 [11]. Let

(2.3)
$$\kappa(A) = \|A\| \|A^{-1}\| .$$

If

(2.4)
$$\kappa(A) \frac{\|E\|}{\|A\|} < 1 ,$$

then

(2.5)
$$\frac{\|x-\bar{x}\|}{\|x\|} \leq \frac{\kappa(A)\|E\|/\|A\|}{1-\kappa(A)\|E\|/\|A\|} .$$

If the left-hand side of (2.4) is reasonably less than unity, say less than 1/10, then the denominator in the right-hand side of (2.5) can be ignored, in which case the bound states that the relative error in the solution may be as large as $\kappa(A)$ times the relative error in A. Thus the number $\kappa(A)$, called the condition number of A with respect to inversion, will tell a user whether to expect an inaccurate solution.

    Unfortunately the definition (2.3) of $\kappa(A)$ involves A^{-1}, which is not available. It can of course be computed, but at considerable additional cost. Instead, in designing the LINPACK codes, we have chosen to estimate $\|A^{-1}\|$. The procedure is based on the observation that for most vectors   u, if

(2.6)   Aw = u

then $\|w\|/\|u\|$ will be a fair estimate of $\|A^{-1}\|$. Since the computation
of   w   only involves the solution of the linear system (2.1), it can be
accomplished with little more work than was required for the initial
reduction of   A   to triangular form.

   In developing a condition estimator, we have included two safeguards.
The first is a systematic method for choosing u. Specifically, the
original matrix A is reduced as usual to LU form:

$$A = LU ,$$

where L is lower triangular and U is upper triangular. The calculation of w can then proceed via the solution of two triangular systems:

   1. Lv = u ,
   2. Uw = v .

Because L is lower triangular, the components of u can be chosen
adaptively as the equation Lv = u is solved in such a way that the
growth of v is enhanced. The actual algorithm for doing this has
changed considerably as our friends have submitted counter-examples to
our earlier proposals.

   The second safeguard is to make a second pass with A, or rather
A^T. Specifically, once w has been computed, a new vector x is
computed as the solution of the system

$$A^Tx = w ,$$

and the actual estimate of $\|A^{-1}\|$ is taken to be $\|x\|/\|w\|$. The justifi-
cation of this step, which involves the singular value decomposition, is
too long to reproduce here.

   The details of the condition estimator will be published elsehwere.
The actual coding is nontrivial. For example, care must be taken to
deal properly with overflows and underflows (we report the reciprocal
of $\kappa(A)$ so that an exactly singular matrix can be signaled by zero).
The algorithm has been extensively tested and has been found to give a
very reliable estimate of $\kappa(A)$. Its cost compared to that of the
original LU decomposition is significant for matrices of order ten or
less, but with increasing order the cost becomes relatively less significant.

3. STABILITY OF LEAST SQUARES SOLUTIONS

The assessment of the stability of a computation may be easy or difficult. For example, if one has used Gaussian elimination to compute the LU factorization of a matrix A, all that is necessary is to form the product $\bar{L}\bar{U}$ of the computed factors and compare it with A. The problem is more difficult when the factorization is used to solve the linear system (2.1); for the computation of x involves calculations beyond those required to factor A. Fortunately, the stability of a computed solution $\bar{x}$ can be determined from the residual vector

$$r = b - A\bar{x} .$$

Specifically, we have the following theorem, in which $\|\cdot\|_2$ denotes the usual spectral norm.

THEOREM 3.1. Let

(3.1)
$$\frac{\|r\|_2}{\|A\|_2\|\bar{x}\|_2} = \varepsilon .$$

Then there is a matrix E with $\|E\|_2/\|A\|_2 = \varepsilon$ such that

(3.2)
$$(A+E)\bar{x} = b .$$

Conversely if $\bar{x}$ satisfies (3.2), then

$$\frac{\|r\|_2}{\|A\|_2\|\bar{x}\|_2} \leq \frac{\|E\|_2}{\|A\|_2} .$$

PROOF: The matrix E is $r\bar{x}^T/\|x\|_2^2$. The converse follows from taking norms in the equation $r = E\bar{x}$.□

The theorem has important implications for software testing. Given a computed solution, one can calculate the number ε. If it is a modest multiple of the rounding unit for the computer in question, then the computation has proceeded stably. Note that the converse is equally important in this application. It says that if the reduction has proceeded stably then ε will be satisfactorily small. Thus the theorem provides a very convenient way of testing the stability of an algorithm. It is particularly useful for detecting malperformance of an algorithm as it is transported across systems. One merely reports the number $\rho = \varepsilon/\varepsilon_m$, where ε_m is the rounding unit for the machine in question; if ρ is large, say greater than 100, something has almost certainly gone wrong.

When one considers the problem of assessing the stability of least squares solutions, one encounters difficulties. It is not difficult to find readily computed numbers whose smallness will guarantee the stability of the computation; the problem is the lack of a converse.

Specifically, let x be the solution of the least squares problem of minimizing

$$\|b-Ax\|_2$$

and let $r = b - Ax$ be the associated residual. Let $\bar{x}$ be a purported solution and let $\bar{r} = b - A\bar{x}$. Then we have the following theorem.

THEOREM 3.2. The vector $\bar{x}$ exactly minimizes

$$\|b-(A+E_i)\bar{x}\|_2 \qquad (i=1,2)$$

where

$$E_1 = -\frac{\bar{r}\bar{r}^T A}{\|\bar{r}\|_2^2},$$

and

$$E_2 = \frac{(\bar{r}-r)\bar{x}^T}{\|\bar{x}\|_2^2}.$$

PROOF: The proof for E_2 may be found in [9]. The proof for E_1 is accomplished by verifying that $\bar{x}$ satisfies the normal equations $(A+E_2)^T[b-(A+E_2)\bar{x}]$. □

The norms of the matrices in Theorem 2.2 are given by

$$\|E_1\|_2 = \frac{\|A^T\bar{r}\|_2}{\|\bar{r}\|_2}$$

and

$$\|E_2\|_2 = \frac{\sqrt{\|\bar{r}\|_2^2-\|r\|_2^2}}{\|x\|_2} = \frac{\|\bar{r}-r\|_2}{\|x\|_2}.$$

The first is small when the residual $\bar{r}$ is almost orthogonal to the column space of A. The second is small when $\|\bar{r}\|_2$ is almost equal to $\|r\|_2$. Both can be used to derive a statistic for software testing, although the second requires that the test problem be contrived so that the norm of the true minimizing residual is known.

Unfortunately the statistics are not necessary for stability. It is quite possible for $\bar{x}$ to be a solution of a slightly perturbed least squares problem yet for both $\|E_1\|_2$ and $\|E_2\|_2$ to be orders of magnitude larger than the norm of perturbation. Thus, although a small statistic guarantees stability, a large one tells nothing. A great deal of thought, both by myself and by J. H. Wilkinson, has not solved this problem, and I therefore pass it on to you: find easily computable

statistics that are both necessary and sufficient for the stability
of a least squares solution.

4.   SCALING AND COLUMN ELIMINATION

LINPACK includes no subroutines to prescale the coefficients of a
linear system. This is partly because the problem of how to scale the
elements of a matrix preliminary to reducing it by Gaussian elimination
is not at all well understood, in spite of a number of papers that have
appeared on the problem [1,2,4,5]. However, a second reason is that,
if the informal arguments I am about to present are correct, it is not
possible to construct a satisfactory scaling scheme that does not require the user to supply estimates of the uncertainty in the elements
of his matrix.

The effect of scaling on the behavior of a linear systems solver
can only be understood if three factors are taken into account. They
are

1.   The effect of rounding errors,

2.   The role of pivoting in the elimination algorithm,

3.   Errors in the original matrix.

We shall discuss these factors as they apply to the usual Gaussian
elimination routine in which the original matrix A is factored into
the product LU of a lower and an upper triangular matrix.

The effect of rounding errors is described by a now classical
theorem [11,12].

THEOREM 4.1.   Suppose that in the presence of rounding error the algorithm of Gaussian elimination can be carried to completion on the matrix
A of order n. Let $\bar{L}$ and $\bar{U}$ be the computed factors. Then

$$\bar{L}\bar{U} = A + E$$

where

(4.1) $|e_{ij}| \leq f(n) \cdot g \cdot \alpha \cdot \varepsilon_m$,

with

$f(n)$ a low degree function of n   that depends
on the details of the arithmetic used,

g the ratio of the magnitude of the largest
element encountered in the reduction to the
magnitude of the largest element of A,

α the magnitude of the largest element of A,

ε_m the rounding unit for the arithmetic used.

The theorem is proved by a typical backwards rounding-error analysis.

The role of a pivoting strategy in Gaussian elimination is to control the size of the error matrix E, which is accomplished by limiting the size of the growth factor g in (4.1). With complete pivoting, g is bounded by a very slowly growing function of n; with partial pivoting g can become as large as 2^n. However, it has been observed that in practice, with either strategy, g seldom exceeds unity by much (the latest "big" value of g is 23, which was produced by C. B. Moler in some experiments with random matrices), and the simpler partial pivoting strategy is customarily the one used.

The rationale (already mention in §2) for performing a backwards rounding-error analysis is that in many applications the original matrix A is already contaminated by errors, say $A = \tilde{A} + F$, where $\tilde{A}$ is the "true" matrix. If the rounding errors e_{ij} are less than the initial errors f_{ij}, then errors in the final solution are the responsibility of the user, not of the algorithm. If in the bound (4.1) we ignore the factor g, which with partial pivoting will be small and practically unaffected by scaling, we are left with the requirement that

(4.2)
$$f(n) \cdot \alpha \cdot \varepsilon_m \leq |f_{ij}| .$$

Now the inequality (4.2) is not invariant under scaling, as the following example with $f(n) = 1$ and $\varepsilon_m = 10^{-4}$ shows. The matrices

$$A = \begin{pmatrix} 0.002 & 1.234 \\ 1.571 & 5.872 \end{pmatrix} \qquad F = \begin{pmatrix} .001 & .001 \\ .001 & .001 \end{pmatrix}$$

clearly satisfy (4.2). If the first rows of A and F are multiplied by the factor 100 to give the matrices

$$A' = \begin{pmatrix} 2.000 & 1234 \\ 1.571 & 5.872 \end{pmatrix} \qquad F' = \begin{pmatrix} 1.000 & 1.000 \\ 0.001 & 0.001 \end{pmatrix},$$

then A' and F' will not satisfy (4.2).

One heuristic scheme for insuring that (4.2) is satisfied is <u>to scale the rows and columns of</u> A <u>so that the magnitudes of all the initial errors</u> f_{ij} <u>are approximately equal to a common value</u> φ. If this is done, the relative error in any element will be greater than a quantity of the order φ/α. Now φ/α will almost always be larger than ε_m, for the elements of A will generally have to be rounded to be represented in the computer; and in practice φ/α will be significantly larger. In particular, if $\varphi/\alpha \geq f(n) \cdot \varepsilon_m$, then (4.2) will be satisfied.

A particularly attractive feature of this analysis is that it separates the roles of pivoting and scaling. Specifically, pivoting serves the purpose of keeping the bound (4.1) reasonably small, whatever the scaling; on the other hand, scaling makes it possible for (4.2) to be satisfied, so that the backward error analysis has significance. The fact that one must look at the actual errors in the matrix to determine the proper scaling seems first to have been suggested by Wilkinson [12,p. 193].

When partial pivoting is used, the scaling criterion suggested above may be relaxed somewhat; for the rounding errors generated by Guassian elimination with partial pivoting are essentially unaffected by column scaling. In fact, the bound (4.1) can be replaced by

$$|e_{ij}| \leq f(n) \cdot g_j \cdot \alpha_j \cdot \mu_m$$

where α_j is the magnitude of the largest element of the j-th column of A and g_j is the growth factor for the j-th column. In consequence, it is only necessary to scale the rows of A so that the errors in each column are approximately equal.

The above analysis was inspired by a programming problem that arose in the design of the LINPACK subroutines for solving banded systems by Gaussian elimination. For technical reasons, which are irrelevant here, it was necessary to eliminate by column operations in these subroutines. The thought naturally occurred to us that we might, for consistency's sake, use column elimination throughout the entire package. It was only after some reflection that it occurred to us that column scaling merely amounts to a change of scale in the unknowns and that an unfortunate choice of units in one of them, say parsecs instead of inches, could elevate an unacceptable element into the role of pivot. The highly conventional nature of the units used in any particular science makes this not at all unlikely.

However, this suggests yet another problem, whose solution must necessarily be empirical. Most people who use Gaussian elimination with partial pivoting do not scale their matrices. Yet they seem to be generally satisfied with the results. Therefore, I leave you with the following questions: <u>does the row scaling of matrices arising naturally tend to be better than the column scaling</u>; <u>and if so, why</u>?

5. DOWNDATING

LINPACK has subroutines for computing the QR factorization of an n × p matrix X, usually as a preliminary to solving least squares problems involving X. The factorization has the form

$$X = QR$$

where Q has orthonormal columns and R is upper triangular. From the fact that $Q^TQ = I$ it follows that

(5.1) $X^TX = R^TR$;

in other words R is the Cholesky factor of the matrix X^TX of the normal equations of the associated least squares problems. In LINPACK the factorization is computed by the Householder-Golub method of ortho-gonal triangularization [3,6].

When n is very large, so that X cannot be contained in main storage, alternative means must be found to compute the factorization. This is usually done by reducing X a row at a time [6]. Specifically, if the QR factorization of X is known, it is possible to compute the QR factorization of the augmented matrix

(5.2) $\tilde{X} = \begin{pmatrix} X \\ x^T \end{pmatrix}$.

This process is referred to as "updating" the QR factorization. It has the particular advantage that the matrix Q, which requires as much storage as X, need not be saved. The algorithm is very stable.

In some applications it is necessary to remove a row from the matrix $\tilde{X}$ and compute the resulting QR factorization, a process which we will call "downdating". It has long been recognized that this process is subject to numerical instabilities. What has emerged from our LINPACK efforts is a fact that I believe is not widely known; namely the insta-bilities in downdating are intrinsic to the problem itself and no amount of algorithmic tinkering can get around this hard fact.

Let us begin by considering the relation of the downdated QR factor-ization to the QR factorization of $\tilde{X}$, which we will write in the form

$$\tilde{X} = \tilde{Q}\tilde{R} .$$

It follows from (5.1) and (5.2) that

$$\tilde{R}^T\tilde{R} = \tilde{X}^T\tilde{X} = X^TX + xx^T$$
$$= R^TR + xx^T$$

or

(5.3) $R^TR = \tilde{R}^T\tilde{R} - xx^T$.

What we shall show is that R can be an ill-conditioned function of $\tilde{R}$

and x; that is, small perturbations in $\tilde{R}$ and x can induce large changes in R.

It turns out that the difficulties are quite well illustrated by the case where R, $\tilde{R}$, and x are scalars. This case is equivalent to recomputing the norm of a vector from which a single component has been removed, a calculation that occurs in practice. In scalar form, (5.3) may be written

$$r^2 = \tilde{r}^2 - x^2 .$$

Now suppose that a small relative error of size ε is introduced in $\tilde{r}$. The effect on r is to produce a new quantity

$$\bar{r}^2 = \tilde{r}^2(1+\varepsilon)^2 - x^2$$

which can be written in the form

$$\bar{r}^2 = r^2 + \tilde{r}^2\varepsilon(2+\varepsilon) .$$

From this it is seen that if

$$r \cong \tilde{r}\sqrt{\varepsilon}$$

then $\bar{r}^2$ will be a completely inaccurate approximation to r^2; in fact $\bar{r}^2$ may even be negative. For a specific example, take $\tilde{r} = O(1)$ and $\varepsilon = O(10^{-10})$. Then if $r = O(10^{-5})$ it cannot be computed; perturbations of order 10^{-10} in $\tilde{r}$ will introduce perturbations of order 10^{-5} in r.

The situation is much the same for matrices [10]. The important quantities in this case are the singular values, $\tilde{\sigma}_1 \geq \tilde{\sigma}_2 \geq \ldots \geq \tilde{\sigma}_n$ of $\tilde{R}$. Any attempt to reduce the smallest singular value $\tilde{\sigma}_n$ below $\sqrt{\varepsilon}\tilde{\sigma}_1$, where ε is the spectral norm of the perturbation in $\tilde{R}$ may fail entirely. However, there is one important difference between the scalar case and the matrix case. In the scalar case the failure of the downdating can be readily detected; in the matrix case it is conceivable that a failure could go undetected, since the size of the smallest singular value need not be apparent from examining the matrices $\tilde{R}$ and R. For this reason we have not yet decided whether to include a downdating algorithm in LINPACK.

6. TIMING THE BLAS

The Basic Linear Algebra Subroutines are a collection of programs to perform basic vector operations that have been proposed for general use by C. Lawson, R. Hanson, D. Kincaid, and F. Krogh [8]. Although the subroutines are defined in FORTRAN, efficient machine language versions have been produced for several widely used computers.

The BLAS SAXPY is typical. To simplify the following exposition, we shall work with a modified version SAXPY1, whose definition is as follows:

```
        SUBRØUTINE SAXPY1(N,X,Y,A)
        INTEGER N
        REAL X(N),Y(N),A
(6.1)   DØ 10 I=1,N
          Y(I) = Y(I)+A*X(I)
     10 CØNTINUE
        RETURN
        END.
```

From this definition it is seen that SAXPY1 adds a constant multiple of the vector X to the vector Y.

The BLAS can be used to simplify code for matrix operations. For example, the call

(6.2)   CALL SAXPY1(N,X(1,J1),X(1,J2),A)

is equivalent to the in-line code

```
        DØ 10 I=1,N
(6.3)     X(I,J2) = X(I,J2)+A*X(I,J1)
     10 CØNTINUE
```

which adds A times column J1 of the matrix X to column J2. Our experience in LINPACK has been that the use of the BLAS results in programs that are at once more legible and easier to debug. One quickly becomes accustomed to the shorthand represented by (6.2), and the writing of the single statement (6.2) is less error prone than the writing of the longer code (6.3).

However, a price must be paid for these advantages in the form of the overhead for the subroutine call in (6.2). For this reason we have been careful not to commit ourselves to the BLAS; although our programs have been coded using them, we have automatic facilities to translate calls to the BLAS into in-line code. At the same time we are undertaking timing tests to determine the relative merits of various versions of the BLAS, and here I should like to describe the results of two of the tests.

The first set of tests, which were performed by Jack Dongarra, Cleve Moler, and myself at the start of the project, indicates that on a nonoptimizing compiler the use of the BLAS can actually speed up matrix computations. To see how this may come about, suppose that in the code (6.3), the array X has been dimensioned by the statement

```
              REAL X(NN,N) ,
```

and that a singly subscripted array XX has been equivalenced to X.
Then a reference to X(I,J) is equivalent to a reference to
XX(I+NN*(J-1)). Thus, in slightly nonstandard FORTRAN, the code (6.3)
can be written as

```
           DØ 10 I=1,N
(6.4)        XX(I+NN*(J2-1)) = XX(I+NN*(J2-1))+A*XX(I+NN*(J1-1))
           10 CØNTINUE
```

Now a nonoptimizing compiler will produce code that is very close
to (6.4). The computations to make an array reference will be performed
inside the loop separately for each reference. The compiler will not
recognize that it is computing I+NN*(J2-1) twice. Nor will it recognize
that the quantities NN*(J1-1) and NN*(J2-1) are independent of I,
so that their computation can be lifted outside the loop. On the other
hand, the call (6.2) to SAXPY1 forces the computations NN*(J1-1) and
NN*(J2-1) to be made right away when the addresses of X(1,J1) and X(1,J2)
are passed. The code inside SAXPY1 refers to singly subscripted arrays,
which even nonoptimizing compilers know how to handle via index registers.

The timings we have made confirm the above arguments. For example,
on the IBM G-level compiler, a QR decomposition coded with the BLAS is
more efficient than one with in-line code for all matrices of order
greater than ten. The BLAS themselves were coded in FORTRAN and
compiled on the G-level compiler. With the optimizing H-level compiler,
the use of the BLAS did not significantly degrade performance for larger
matrices. The reason for this is that the overhead for the subroutine
calls increases as N^2 whereas the total work increases as N^3.

An extensive series of timing runs at the LINPACK test sites that
have been initiated by Jack Dongarra have yielded surprising results
on the unrolling of loops. In this device the increment of the loop is
increased and the body of the loop is repeated a corresponding number
of times with its indices adjusted accordingly. For example, the inner
loop in (6.1) might be replaced by

```
              DØ 10 I=1,N,3
                Y(I) = Y(I)+A*X(I)
                Y(I+1) = Y(I+1)+A*X(I+1)
                Y(I+2) = Y(I+2)+A*X(I+2)
           10   CØNTINUE
```

Of course additional code is necessary to handle boundary conditions

when N is not a multiple of 3. Owing to the complexity and length
of the code generated, it is impractical to unroll loops in line.

The results of comparing several different versions of the BLAS on
several different computers indicate that BLAS with unrolled loops are
far and away the most efficient. Because the architectures of the
computers in question are quite different, we are far from understanding
this phenomenon. It is probably composite, depending in varying degrees on such factors as reduction of loop overhead, more efficient
index calculation, and better use of parallel and pipelined registers.
However, we can say nothing for sure until we have had a chance to
examine the compiler-generated machine codes in detail.

REFERENCES

1. F. L. Bauer (1963), Optimally scaled matrices, Numer. Math., 8,
       pp. 73-87.
2. P. A. Businger (1968), Matrices which can be optimally scaled,
       Numer. Math., 12, pp. 346-348.
3. _____ and G. H. Golub (1965), Linear least squares solu-
       tions by Householder transformations, Numer. Math., 7,
       pp. 269-276.
4. A. Curtis and J. K. Reid (1974), On the automatic scaling of matrices
       for Gaussian elimination, J. Inst. Math. Appl., 10, pp. 118-124.
5. D. R. Fulkerson and P. Wilfe (1962), An algorithm for scaling
       matrices, SIAM Rev., 4, pp. 142-146.
6. G. H. Golub (1965), Numerical methods for solving least squares
       problems, Numer. Math., 7, pp. 206-216.
7. A. S. Householder (1958), Unitary triangularization of a nonsymmetric
       matrix, J. Assoc. Comput. Mach., 5, pp. 339-342.
8. C. L. Lawson, R. J. Hanson, D. Kincaid, F. T. Krogh (1976), Basic
       linear algebra subprograms for FORTRAN usage, to appear ACM
       Trans. Math. Software.
9. G. W. Stewart (1977), On the perturbation of pseudo-inverses, pro-
       jections, and linear least squares problems, to appear SIAM
       Rev.
10. _____ (1976), An observation on downdating Cholesky and QR
       decompositions, Univ. Maryland Computer Science Tech. Rep. 488.
11. J. H. Wilkinson (1963), Rounding Errors in Algebraic Processes,
       Prentice-Hall.
12. _____ (1965), The Algebraic Eigenvalue Problem, Oxford Univ.
       Press.
13. _____ and C. Reinsch, eds. (1971), Handbook for Automatic
       Computation, Vol. II, Linear Algebra, Springer Verlag.

This work was supported in part by the National Science Foundation under
Grant No. MCS76-03297.

Department of Computer Science
University of Maryland
College Park, Maryland 20742

A Technique that Gains Speed
and Accuracy in the Minimax Solution
of Overdetermined Linear Equations
M. J. Hopper
M. J. D. Powell

ABSTRACT

An extension to the exchange algorithm for solving overdetermined linear equations is proposed. The new technique chooses
the equation to leave the reference on each iteration in a way that
often reduces the total number of iterations and that lessens the
danger of having to solve a square system of linear equations with a
nearly singular matrix. In other words it keeps the pivots of a linear
programming calculation away from zero. It can help most of the
computer algorithms that are available for the minimax solution of
overdetermined equations.

1. INTRODUCTION

Many approximation and data fitting problems can be expressed as
the solution of the overdetermined system of linear equations

$$(1.1) \qquad r_i(\underline{x}) \equiv \sum_{j=1}^{n} a_{ij}x_j + b_i = 0, \qquad i=1,2,\ldots,m,$$

where $m > n$ and where $\underline{x}$ is the column vector whose components are $(x_1, x_2, \ldots, x_n)$. A minimax solution is a vector $\underline{x}$ that minimizes the piecewise linear function

$$(1.2) \qquad F(\underline{x}) = \max_{1 \leq i \leq m} |r_i(\underline{x})|.$$

It is usually calculated by a linear programming method, the exchange algorithm (Stiefel, 1963) being particularly suitable. The solution need not be unique, but non-uniqueness is not a difficulty to most linear programming procedures.

The exchange algorithm is iterative and before each iteration a "reference" is chosen, which is a selection of $(n+1)$ of the equations (1.1). We let I be the set of integers that number the equations in the reference. The vector, $\underline{x}\{I\}$ say, that minimizes the function

$$(1.3) \qquad F(\underline{x}, I) = \max_{i \in I} |r_i(\underline{x})|$$

is calculated. We let $h(I)$ be the value of $F(\underline{x}\{I\}, I)$. The procedure finishes if the inequalities

$$(1.4) \qquad |r_i(\underline{x}\{I\})| \leq h(I), \qquad i = 1, 2, \ldots, m,$$

are obtained, because then $\underline{x}\{I\}$ minimizes the function (1.2). Otherwise we let p be an integer that satisfies the condition

$$(1.5) \qquad |r_p(\underline{x}\{I\})| > h(I).$$

Usually $r_p(\underline{x}\{I\})$ is the residual whose modulus is largest. The integer p replaces one of the members of I, the equation that is removed from the reference being chosen so that $h(I)$ increases monotonically as the iterations proceed. Then another iteration is begun. We define q to be the integer that leaves I to make room for p.

The linear programming method fixes the value of q automatically, but sometimes the choice that is made causes near-singularity in the linear equations that define the next value of $x\{I\}$. An example is given in Section 2. Therefore the main purpose of this paper is to consider whether other choices of q are suitable and whether there are advantages in using them. The "optimal exchange algorithm" uses the value of q that

maximizes the next value of h(I). We give an extension to this procedure that helps to avoid the occurrence of nearly singular matrices.
Also we give a method of applying the Optimal Exchange algorithm that
requires less work than the algorithm proposed by Anselone and Taylor (1973).

    A very important feature in practice is to carry forward information
from one iteration to the next in order to reduce the total amount of
work. The $(n+1)\times(n+1)$ matrix $A(I)$ whose rows have the components

(1.6) $(a_{i1}\ a_{i2}\ \cdots\ a_{in}\ s_i),\ i\epsilon I,$

is important, because $\underline{x}(I)$ and $h(I)$ are defined by the linear equations

(1.7) $$A(I)\left(\begin{array}{c} \underline{x}(I) \\ -\overline{h}(I) \end{array}\right) + \underline{b}(I) = 0$$

(Stiefel, 1963), where the values of $s_i(i\epsilon I)$ are known and where the
components of $\underline{b}(I)$ are $b_i(i\epsilon I)$. Each iteration of the exchange
algorithm changes only one row of A(I), which allows the system (1.7) to
be solved in only of order n^2 computer operations by using one of the
following two methods.

    Either a factorization of A(I) is calculated and revised as the
iterations proceed (see Gill and Murray, 1973, for instance) or the
inverse of the matrix A(I) is modified on each iteration. The second
method was a standard technique in linear programming but now
factorizations have become more popular. One reason for this change is
to take advantage of sparsity. Another reason is that, if the matrix
A(I) becomes nearly singular, then $[A(I)]^{-1}$ has large elements and hence
larger errors than usual. Some of these errors are inherited by the
matrices $[A(I)]^{-1}$ of future iterations, even though the later matrices
A(I) may be well-conditioned. On the other hand the elements of a
factorization of A(I) usually remain of a moderate size throughout the
calculation.

    However a disadvantage of factorizations is that changing the scale
of the variables of the calculation can make a substantial difference to
the final accuracy, even though it is only a trivial change to the
original problem in floating point arithmetic. Here we have in mind
that the rules for choosing pivots in the current methods for obtaining
and revising factorizations do depend on row and column scaling. On the
other hand such a change to the problem only causes a corresponding
change of scale to the rows of $[A(I)]^{-1}$, which can be made perfectly

satisfactorily in floating point arithmetic.   Therefore it is sometimes
better to use inverse matrices instead of factorizations.

We find that the new technique for choosing the equation that
leaves the reference on each iteration helps to avoid singularity in
A(I).   Therefore we recommend the use of inverse matrices for the
minimax solution of overdetermined linear equations.   To strengthen
this point of view a theorem is given that shows that there is some
suppression of accumulated rounding errors when inverse matrices are
updated.   This result applies to most linear programming calculations, but
the rest of the theory is special to the new technique for choosing q.
One theorem gives an a priori bound on the number of iterations that are
needed to achieve limited accuracy in function approximation.

2.   NUMERICAL INSTABILITY IN THE EXCHANGE ALGORITHM

In order to study and extend the iteration of the exchange algorithm
we refer frequently to two vectors which we call $\underline{\sigma}$ and $\underline{\tau}$.   We let the
components of $\underline{\sigma}$ be σ_i (i$\in$I) for there is one component for each equation
in the reference.   They must satisfy the conditions

(2.1) $$\sum_{i\in I} \sigma_i a_{ij} = 0, \quad j=1,2,\ldots,n,$$

(2.2) $$\sum_{i\in I} |\sigma_i| = 1$$

and

(2.3) $$\sum_{i\in I} \sigma_i b_i \geq 0.$$

The element s_i of the row vector (1.6) has modulus one and the same sign
as σ_i.   It follows that the components of $\underline{\sigma}$ are the elements of the last
row of the matrix $[A(I)]^{-1}$.   It also follows from equation (1.7) that
h(I) has the value

(2.4) $$h(I) = \sum_{i\in I} \sigma_i b_i$$

(Stiefel,1963). We let σ_p be zero, where p was defined in Section 1 to be
the integer that is brought into the reference.

If a zero value of σ_i(i$\in$I) occurs we have what linear programmers
call "degeneracy".   This situation can be treated robustly by the
technique due to Wolfe (1963).   However we suppose that every σ_i (i$\in$I)
is non-zero, because this simplifies greatly the description of the new
technique.

The vector $\underline{\tau}$ has $(n+2)$ elements, one for each equation in the reference and the component

(2.5) $$\tau_p = \text{sign}[r_p(\underline{x}\{I\})] \ .$$

They are defined by equation (2.5) and the conditions

(2.6) $$\sum_{i \in I} \tau_i a_{ij} + \tau_p a_{pj} = 0, \quad j=1,2,\ldots,n,$$

and

(2.7) $$\sum_{i \in I} \tau_i s_i + 1 = 0.$$

In the original exchange algorithm the integer q, that numbers the equation that leaves the reference, is chosen so that $-\sigma_q/\tau_q$ is the least positive number in the set $\{-\sigma_i/\tau_i, \ i \in I\}$.

One consequence of this choice of q is that the equation

(2.8) $$|\det\{A(I^*)\}| = |\tau_q| \ |\det\{A(I)\}|$$

is obtained, where I^* is the reference of the next iteration.   Therefore the matrix $A(I^*)$ is nearly singular when $|\tau_q|$ is very small.

An example of ill-conditioning occurs if we apply the original exchange algorithm to the overdetermined system of linear equations

(2.9) $$\begin{cases} r_1(\underline{x}) \equiv x_1+1 = 0 \\ r_2(\underline{x}) \equiv x_1+(1-\varepsilon)x_2+2 = 0 \\ r_3(\underline{x}) \equiv x_1+x_2+3 = 0 \\ r_4(\underline{x}) \equiv x_1+(1-2\varepsilon)x_2+4 = 0 \end{cases},$$

where ε is a very small positive number. We let the initial reference be $I = \{1,2,3\}$.

We find that three iterations are needed, that the references are $\{1,2,3\},\{2,3,4\}$ and $\{1,2,4\}$ and that the values of x_1,x_2,h and $|r_p(\underline{x}\{I\})|$ are the ones given in Table 1. A feature of the exchange algorithm that enables convergence to be proved is that h increases monotonically as the iterations proceed.   This property is shown in the table, but we find also that the second reference gives a maximum residual of $(2+5\varepsilon)/(4\varepsilon)$ which is much worse than on the first iteration. Also we note that the components of $\underline{x}(I)$ are large on the second iteration.   These unwelcome things happen because on the second iteration the matrix

$$(2.10) \qquad A(I) = \begin{pmatrix} 1 & 1-\varepsilon & -1 \\ 1 & 1 & 1 \\ 1 & 1-2\varepsilon & 1 \end{pmatrix}$$

is almost singular.   The difficulty is signalled on the first iteration by the very small value $|\tau_q|=2\varepsilon$.

This calculation gives a good example of the kind of difficulty that a robust algorithm should avoid completely. When the initial reference {1,2,3} and the final reference {1,2,4} are used, then the matrices of the equations that are solved are well-conditioned.   Therefore there is no instability in the given initial reference or in the calculation of the final solution.   However the exchange algorithm itself generates unstable intermediate calculations, even though we have a well-conditioned problem.

We claim that the technique described in Section 3 gives a worthwhile improvement to the exchange algorithm by avoiding values of q that make $|\tau_q|$ small unnecessarily.   On the example (2.9) it finds the reference that gives the minimax solution to the linear equations on the first iteration.

3.   <u>THE NEW TECHNIQUE</u>

It has been mentioned that convergence of the exchange algorithm is obtained by ensuring that the quantity h(I) increases monotonically as the iterations proceed, and that the original algorithm has this property.   Therefore we are interested in the numbers $h(I_s)$($s\varepsilon I$), where I_s is the reference that is formed by deleting s from I to make room for p. We require the new choice of q to satisfy the condition

$$(3.1) \qquad h(I_q) > h(I) .$$

Because the definitions of $\underline{\sigma}$ and $\underline{\tau}$ imply that the equations

$$(3.2) \qquad \sum_{i\varepsilon I} (\sigma_i+\theta\tau_i)a_{ij}+(\sigma_p+\theta\tau_p)a_{pj}=0, \quad j=1,2,\ldots,n ,$$

hold for all values of the parameter θ, it can be shown that $h(I_s)$ has the value

$$(3.3) \qquad h(I_s) = \frac{\left| \sum_{i\varepsilon I_s} (\sigma_i+\theta\tau_i)b_i \right|}{\sum_{i\varepsilon I_s} |\sigma_i+\theta\tau_i|} ,$$

where θ is equal to $-\sigma_s/\tau_s$ (Rice, 1964). Therefore the quantities $h(I_s)(s\epsilon I)$ can be found by considering the function of one variable

$$(3.4) \qquad \phi(\theta) = \frac{|\sum_{i\epsilon I}(\sigma_i+\theta\tau_i)b_i + \theta\tau_p b_p|}{\sum_{i\epsilon I}|\sigma_i+\theta\tau_i| + |\theta\tau_p|} .$$

This function allows the following description of the new technique.

We let the variable θ increase from zero to infinity and then from minus infinity back to zero until $\phi(\theta)$ starts to decrease. The values of i ($i\epsilon I$) such that $-\sigma_i/\tau_i$ is in the range of θ that is obtained are collected into a set which we call I^+. We let η be the number

$$(3.5) \qquad \eta = \max_{i\epsilon I^+} |\tau_i|$$

and we choose q to be the integer in I^+ that maximizes $h(I_q)$ subject to the condition

$$(3.6) \qquad |\tau_q| \geq \tfrac{1}{4}\eta .$$

Most of the rest of the paper shows that this method can be applied very easily and that it has some nice properties. In particular we note that $|\tau_q|$ is not small unless $|r_p(\underline{x}\{I\})|$ is close to the least maximum residual of the system of linear equations.

In the example (2.9) when the initial reference is $I = \{1,2,3\}$ and when $\epsilon = 0.2$ we find that the vectors $\underline{\sigma}$ and $\underline{\tau}$ have the components

$$(3.7) \qquad \underline{\sigma} = \begin{pmatrix} 0.1 \\ -0.5 \\ 0.4 \\ 0 \end{pmatrix} \qquad \underline{\tau} = \begin{pmatrix} -0.4 \\ 0 \\ -0.6 \\ 1 \end{pmatrix} .$$

Hence $\phi(\theta)$ is the function

$$(3.8) \qquad \phi(\theta) = \frac{|0.3+1.8\theta|}{|0.1-0.4\theta|+0.5+|0.4-0.6\theta|+|\theta|}$$

which is composed of the following pieces

$$\phi(\theta) = 0.3+1.8\theta, \qquad 0\leq\theta\leq\tfrac{1}{4},$$

$$\phi(\theta) = (0.3+1.8\theta)/(0.8+0.8\theta), \qquad \tfrac{1}{4}\leq\theta\leq\tfrac{2}{3},$$

$$\phi(\theta) = (0.3+1.8\theta)/2\theta, \qquad \tfrac{2}{3}\leq\theta\leq\infty,$$

and

$$\phi(\theta) = |0.3+1.8\theta|/(1-2\theta), \qquad -\infty\leq\theta\leq0.$$

Therefore, because $\phi(\theta)$ increases monotonically in the range $0\leq\theta\leq\tfrac{1}{4}$, the new technique first places the integer 1 in the set I^+. Then the integer 3 is added to the set I^+ because $\phi(\theta)$ also increases monotonically in the range $\tfrac{1}{4}\leq\theta\leq\tfrac{2}{3}$. However we find that $\phi(\theta)$ decreases for $\theta>\tfrac{2}{3}$. Therefore the set I^+ is complete. Because $\phi(-\sigma_3/\tau_3)$ is greater than $\phi(-\sigma_1/\tau_1)$ we let q=3 provided that condition (3.6) is satisfied. This condition is obtained. Hence the new procedure calculates the required reference {1,2,4} on the first iteration, which is an improvement over the linear programming method.

The nice properties of $\phi(\theta)$ that are shown in this example are obtained generally. The function is composed of sections of the form

$$(3.9) \qquad\qquad \phi(\theta) = (a+b\theta)/(c+d\theta).$$

The joins of the sections occur when θ is in the set $\{-\sigma_i/\tau_i, i\epsilon I\}$, when $\theta=0$ and when the numerator of expression (3.4) is zero. On the first section that is reached by increasing θ from zero, the function $\phi(\theta)$ is the linear function

$$(3.10) \qquad\qquad \phi(\theta) = h(I) + \theta[|r_p(\underline{x}\{I\})|-h(I)].$$

This result is obtained from the definitions of $\underline{\sigma},\tau$ and the signs $s_i(i\epsilon I)$. Hence $\phi(\theta)$ increases initially. Note also that, because each function of the form (3.9) is monotonic, the point where $\phi(\theta)$ begins to decrease is in the set $\{-\sigma_i/\tau_i; i\epsilon I\}$.

We show later that $\phi(\theta)$ begins to decrease at only one point of the range $-\infty\leq\theta\leq\infty$. Hence the set I^+ that is formed always includes the integer s that gives the maximum value of $h(I_s)(s\epsilon I)$. This property is advantageous because $\underline{x}\{I\}$ is the required vector of variables only if the reference I gives the maximum value of $h(I)$ over all possible references. When the new technique chooses a value of q that is different from the one that is calculated by the linear programming method, then $h(I_q)$ is greater than before. In this case the new technique usually gains speed by saving one or more iterations.

However more work than before is required on each iteration that chooses the value of q to be different from the one that is given by the linear programming algorithm. In the linear programming calculation the signs of the residuals $r_i(\underline{x})$ ($i\epsilon I, i\neq q$) remain the same on the next iteration but in the new method some of these signs may alter. Specifically the sign of $r_i(\underline{x})$ ($i\epsilon I, i\neq q$) changes if and only if the number $-\sigma_i/\tau_i$ is in the range that is obtained by increasing θ from zero to infinity and then from minus infinity to zero until the point $-\sigma_q/\tau_q$ is reached. The corresponding signs s_i that occur in the last column of the matrix $A(I)$ must be switched. Hence, in order to prepare for the next iteration, not only is the q-th row of $A(I)$ altered, but also the last column of $A(I)$ is changed, which about doubles the amount of computation that is needed to revise either a factorization of $A(I)$ or the matrix $[A(I)]^{-1}$. The extra work is well justified because it is much less than half of the total calculation of an iteration and usually at least one iteration is saved. Because of the new choice of q we must replace equation (2.8) by the inequality

$$(3.11) \qquad |\det\{A(I^*)\}| \geq |\tau_q| \, |\det\{A(I)\}| \; .$$

The result, mentioned earlier, that $\phi(\theta)$ begins to decrease at only one point of the range $-\infty \leq \theta \leq \infty$, and also an excellent method of programming the new technique, are obtained by considering the sign of $\phi'(\theta)$. We make use of the fact that, where $\phi(\theta)$ is equal to expression (3.9), the sign of $\phi'(\theta)$ is the sign of the number $(bc-ad)$. However this number changes when θ passes through a point of the set $\{-\sigma_i/\tau_i; \; i\epsilon I\}$. We calculate the change from the definition (3.4) in the usual case when the numerator of $\phi(\theta)$ is non-zero at $\theta=-\sigma_i/\tau_i$. In this case the values of a and b do not alter when θ passes through $-\sigma_i/\tau_i$ and the inequality

$$(3.12) \qquad a + (-\sigma_i/\tau_i)b > 0$$

holds. We find, therefore, that the change in $(bc-ad)$ is the quantity

$$2b \, \sigma_i \, \text{sign}(\tau_i) - 2a|\tau_i|$$
$$(3.13) \qquad = -2|\tau_i|\{a+b(-\sigma_i/\tau_i)\}.$$

The fact that this expression is negative is important.

One reason is that, if one considers the values $\theta=0$ and $\theta=\pm\infty$ also, it follows that the only point of the range $-\infty \leq \theta \leq \infty$ where $(bc-ad)$ increases is where the numerator of $\phi(\theta)$ is zero. Hence $(bc-ad)$ becomes negative at most once as θ is increased from zero to infinity and then from minus infinity back to zero. Such a point does exist because $\phi'(0)$ is positive.

The procedure that we recommend in practice for choosing the new value of q avoids all calculations of the function $\phi(\theta)$. Instead we use the changes that occur in the number (bc-ad) as θ varies. Because $\phi(\theta)$ has the form (3.10) initially, we begin by setting the value

(3.14)
$$bc-ad = |r_p(\underline{x}\{I\})| - h(I).$$

Each time an index i is added to the set that we called I^+ in the earlier description of the method, we subtract the number

(3.15)
$$2|h(I)\tau_i - [|r_p(\underline{x}\{I\})| - h(I)]\sigma_i|$$

from (bc-ad), which gives the change (3.13). The set I^+ is complete when (bc-ad) becomes negative. Then expressions (3.5) and (3.6) are used as before.

Apart from the fact that this procedure requires little work, there is another reason why it is advisable not to find the set I^+ by comparing the numbers

(3.16)
$$h(I_i) = \phi(-\sigma_i/\tau_i), \quad i\epsilon I.$$

It follows from the remark that some members of the set $\{-\sigma_i/\tau_i, \ i\epsilon I\}$ may be very close to each other. If this case occurs then the corresponding values of $h(I_i)$ are close also, so it is possible that computer rounding errors cause changes to the calculated values of $h(I_i)$ in a way that suggests erroneously that $\phi(\theta)$ has started to decrease. A wrong decision is inefficient of $\phi'(\theta)$ is still significantly greater than zero. On the other hand (bc-ad) is not small unless $\phi'(\theta)$ is small. Hence the recommended procedure is suitable even in degenerate and nearly degenerate situations.

To apply the new procedure to the example (3.8) we note that we have the values

(3.17)
$$\begin{cases} h(I) = 0.3 \\ |r_p(\underline{x}\{I\})| - h(I) = 1.8 \ , \end{cases}$$

so the initial value of (bc-ad) is equal to 1.8. As before the index i=1 is the first member of I^+. Equations (3.7) and (3.17) show that the corresponding value of expression (3.15) is the number

(3.18) $2|(0.3)(-0.4) - (1.8)(0.1)| = 0.6.$

Therefore (bc-ad) is reduced to 1.2.   Because the value of (bc-ad) is still positive the index i=3 is added to I^+.   Now expression (3.15) has the value

(3.19) $2|(0.3)(-0.6) - (1.8)(0.4)| = 1.8.$

When it is subtracted from (bc-ad) we find that (bc-ad) becomes negative. Therefore the set I^+ is complete.   This example shows that the new procedure for choosing q is very easy in practice.

4.   THEORY

The remarks made so far, in particular inequality (3.11), suggest that it is advantageous if no value of $|\tau_q|$ is small.   The main theorem of this section gives a lower bound on $|\tau_q|$.   From this theorem we deduce a bound on the number of iterations that are required by the new procedure to obtain an approximation whose maximum error is within a certain factor of the least maximum error.   The size of the factor is probably too large to be useful, but the theorem is interesting because the factor is essentially independent of m.   Finally there is the theorem that is relevant to the accuracy of most linear programming algorithms that revise inverse matrices on each iteration.

In order that it is easy for the reader to omit the details of the proofs, we present all the theorems before their proofs.   All discussion of the theorems is deferred to the final section.

Theorem 1   The recommended choice of q causes τ_q to satisfy the inequality

(4.1) $|\tau_q| > \dfrac{1}{24(n+1)} \; \dfrac{|r_p(\underline{x}\{I\})|-h(I)}{h*}$,

where h* is the minimum value of the function (1.2).

Theorem 2   Let W be the number

(4.2) $W = \max_I |\det A(I)|,$

where the maximum is taken over all references, and let w be the value of $|\det A(I)|$ for the initial reference.   Let each choice of p be such that $|r_p(\underline{x}\{I\})|$ is the largest of the numbers $[|r_i(\underline{x}\{I\})|; \; i=1,2,\ldots,m]$. Then, after k iterations of the new procedure, the least calculated value of expression (1.2) is less than the quantity

$$(4.3) \qquad \{24(n+1) (W/w)^{1/k} + 1\} h^*,$$

where h^* is the minimum value of the function (1.2).

Theorem 3 Let B be a nonsingular matrix, let z be a non-zero vector, and let q be any integer such that the q-th component of the vector

$$(4.4) \qquad \underline{\tau} = -\tau_p B^T \underline{z}$$

is non-zero, where τ_p is a constant. Then the inverse of the matrix

$$(4.5) \qquad B^* = B \left(I - \frac{\underline{e}_q (\tau_p \underline{e}_q + \underline{\tau})^T}{\tau_q} \right),$$

where $\underline{e}_q$ is the q-th coordinate vector, is equal to the inverse of B, except that the q-th row of $[B^*]^{-1}$ is the vector $\underline{z}^T$.

Proof of Theorem 1 Without loss of generality we suppose that I is the set of integers $\{1,2,\ldots,n+1\}$ and that the set $\{-\sigma_1/\tau_1, -\sigma_2/\tau_2,\ldots,\sigma_{n+1}/\tau_{n+1}\}$ begins with its positive terms arranged in ascending order followed by its negative terms, also arranged in ascending order. We let s be the number of elements in I^+. Hence I^+ is the set $\{1,2,\ldots,s\}$. The given method for choosing q has the property that, if we sum the terms (3.15) for $i=1,2,\ldots,s$, the result is larger than the initial value of (bc-ad). Hence the inequality

$$|r_p(\underline{x}\{I\})|-h(I)$$

$$(4.6) \qquad\qquad < 2 \sum_{i=1}^{s} |h(I)\tau_i - [|r_p(\underline{x}\{I\})|-h(I)]\sigma_i|$$

is satisfied. A more suitable form of the right hand side is obtained by recalling that the modulus of expression (3.10) is equal to the numerator of $\phi(\theta)$ for all values of θ. Thus the definition (3.4) provides the equation

$$(4.7) \qquad \phi(-\sigma_i/\tau_i) = \frac{|h(I)\tau_i - [|r_p(\underline{x}\{I\})|-h(I)]\sigma_i|}{\sum_{j=1}^{n+1} |\sigma_i\tau_j - \sigma_j\tau_i| + |\sigma_i\tau_p|} .$$

We recall also that $|\tau_p|$ is one and that h^* is an upper bound on $h(I)$ for every reference I. In particular, because $\phi(-\sigma_i/\tau_i)$ is equal to $h(I_i)$, it is an upper bound on expression (4.7). Therefore expressions (4.6) and (4.7) provide the inequality

$$(4.8) \qquad \frac{|r_p(\underline{x}\{I\})|-h(I)}{2h^*} < \sum_{i=1}^{s} \left\{ \sum_{j=1}^{n+1} |\sigma_i\tau_j-\sigma_j\tau_i|+|\sigma_i| \right\} .$$

In order to continue the proof we must remove most of the modulus signs from expression (4.8). Therefore, from the order of the terms $\{-\sigma_1/\tau_1, -\sigma_2/\tau_2, \ldots, -\sigma_{n+1}/\tau_{n+1}\}$ given at the beginning of the proof, we deduce the equation

$$(4.9) \qquad |\sigma_i\tau_j-\sigma_j\tau_i| = \begin{cases} s_i s_j(\sigma_i\tau_j-\sigma_j\tau_i) , & i<j , \\ -s_i s_j(\sigma_i\tau_j-\sigma_j\tau_i), & i>j , \end{cases}$$

where s_i has been defined already to be the sign of σ_i $(i=1,2,\ldots,n+1)$. Hence we obtain the bound

$$\sum_{j=1}^{n+1} |\sigma_i\tau_j-\sigma_j\tau_i|+|\sigma_i|$$

$$(4.10) \qquad \begin{aligned} &= -\sum_{j=1}^{i-1} s_i s_j(\sigma_i\tau_j-\sigma_j\tau_i) + \sum_{j=i+1}^{n+1} s_i s_j(\sigma_i\tau_j-\sigma_j\tau_i) +|\sigma_i| \\ &\leq |\tau_i| \sum_{j=1}^{n+1} |\sigma_j|+|\sigma_i|\left\{ -\sum_{j=1}^{i-1} s_j\tau_j + \sum_{j=i+1}^{n+1} s_j\tau_j + 1 \right\} \\ &\leq |\tau_i| + 2|\sigma_i| \sum_{j=1}^{i} |\tau_j| , \end{aligned}$$

where the last line depends on equations (2.2) and (2.7). By summing over i and using equation (2.2) again we find the inequality

$$(4.11) \qquad \begin{aligned} \sum_{i=1}^{s}&\left\{ \sum_{j=1}^{n+1} |\sigma_i\tau_j-\sigma_j\tau_i|+|\sigma_i| \right\} \\ &\leq \sum_{i=1}^{s} |\tau_i|+ 2 \sum_{i=1}^{s} |\sigma_i| \sum_{j=1}^{s} |\tau_j| \\ &\leq 3 \sum_{i=1}^{s} |\tau_i| . \end{aligned}$$

It follows from inequality (4.8) that the bound

$$(4.12) \qquad \max_{i\epsilon I^+} |\tau_i| > \frac{|r_p(\underline{x}\{I\})|-h(I)}{6(n+1)h^*}$$

is obtained. We recall that the choice of q is subject to the condition (3.6). Therefore Theorem 1 is true.

Proof of Theorem 2   Because h* is an upper bound on h(I), it follows from Theorem 1 and the choice of p that the condition

(4.13)
$$|\tau_q| > \left(\frac{W}{w}\right)^{1/k}$$

is obtained when the inequality

(4.14)
$$\max_{1 \le i \le m} |r_i(\underline{x}\{I\})| \ge \left\{24(n+1) \left(\frac{W}{w}\right)^{1/k} +1\right\} h*$$

is satisfied.   In this case expression (3.11) implies the bound

(4.15)
$$|\det\{A(I*)\}| > \left(\frac{W}{w}\right)^{1/k} |\det\{A(I)\}| .$$

However the definitions of W and w show that this bound does not hold for each of the first k iterations.   Therefore the theorem is true.

Proof of Theorem 3   The identity

(4.16)
$$\left(I - \frac{\underline{e}_q(\tau_p\underline{e}_q + \underline{\tau})^{T}}{\tau_q}\right)^{-1} = I - \underline{e}_q\left(\underline{e}_q + \frac{\underline{\tau}}{\tau_p}\right)^{T}$$

and equation (4.4) imply that the inverse of expression (4.5) is the matrix

(4.17)
$$[B*]^{-1} = \left[I - \underline{e}_q \left(\underline{e}_q + \frac{\underline{\tau}}{\tau_p}\right)^{T}\right] B^{-1}$$

$$= (I-\underline{e}_q\underline{e}_q^{T})B^{-1} + \underline{e}_q\underline{z}^{T} .$$

Therefore Theorem 3 is true.

5.   DISCUSSION

The advantages we have noted so far in the new procedure are as follows.   It is very easy to program and the extra work over the linear programming method for choosing q is neglible, unless the new procedure chooses a different value of q.   In this case the total number of iterations is usually reduced.   However our gains in computer time are seldom as great as the ones that are obtained by the analogous procedure for L_1 calculations (Barrodale and Roberts,1973).   Certainly we cannot find an example of increased efficiency that compares with their calculation of a linear approximation to the exponential function.

On the question of accuracy the new technique avoids the difficulties of the simple example given in Section 2, because the choice of $|\tau_q|$ tends to prevent near-singularity in the matrices A(I).   However the discussion so far of accuracy is not very convincing because of the possibility that a sequence of iterations may cause $A(I)$ to be nearly singular.   In any case the determinant of $A(I)$ is only one of several factors that contribute to the size of the elements of $[A(I)]^{-1}$. Therefore we now look more closely at the relation between $[A(I^*)]^{-1}$ and $[A(I)]^{-1}$.

When $A(I^*)$ is obtained by replacing the q-th row of the matrix $A(I)$ by the row vector $\underline{z}^T$, we have the equation

$$(5.1) \qquad\qquad A(I^*) = (I - \underline{e}_q \underline{e}_q^T) A + \underline{e}_q \underline{z}^T ,$$

which gives the relation

$$(5.2) \qquad\qquad [A(I^*)]^{-1} = [A(I)]^{-1} \left\{ I - \frac{1}{\tau_q} \underline{e}_q (\tau_p \underline{e}_q + \underline{\tau})^T \right\} ,$$

where $\underline{e}_q$ is the q-th coordinate vector, where τ_p is any non-zero number and where $\underline{\tau}$ is the solution of the equation

$$(5.3) \qquad\qquad [A(I)]^T \underline{\tau} + \tau_p \underline{z} = 0.$$

We have used the notation $\underline{\tau}$ and τ_p deliberately, because the system of equations (5.3) is identical to the conditions (2.6) and (2.7) on $\underline{\tau}$ when $\underline{z}$ is the new row of $A(I^*)$ that is required by the exchange algorithm.   In most versions of the algorithm that revise the matrix $[A(I)]^{-1}$ when $A(I)$ is changed, the formula (5.2) is applied because this calculation requires only of order n^2 computer operations.   The vector $\underline{\tau}$ is obtained from the equation

$$(5.4) \qquad\qquad \underline{\tau} = -\tau_p \{[A(I)]^{-1}\}^T \underline{z}$$

before q is chosen.   If q is different from the value that would be chosen by the linear programming method, a further revision of $[A(I)]^{-1}$ is needed to allow for the sign changes in the last column of $A(I)$.   This calculation is similar to the revision (5.2), but it does not possess the danger of ill-conditioning.   Further details are given in Madsen and Powell (1975).

The present purpose of equation (5.2) is to note the actual dependence of the elements of $[A(I^*)]^{-1}$ on the value of τ_q.   We see that the elements of $[A(I^*)]^{-1}$ do not suddenly become much larger than the elements of $[A(I)]^{-1}$ unless τ_q is very small in comparison with the other elements of $\underline{\tau}$.   If we are successful in keeping the matrix $A(I)$ well-conditioned, then equation (5.4) shows that the elements of $\underline{\tau}$ remain moderate in size.   Certainly we have good reasons for avoiding small values of τ_q, so the fact that Theorem 1 shows that τ_q is not small until $|r_p(\underline{x}\{I\})|$ is close to h* is encouraging.

This is a good point at which to explain the importance of Theorem 3. It is relevant to the possible build-up of rounding errors when formula (5.2) is used by a large number of iterations. Because each new inverse matrix inherits some errors from the previous one, we are concerned about the possibility that the accumulation of errors may cause serious loss of accuracy. If this situation occurs then inherited errors become larger than those of the current iteration. Therefore we let B and B* be the approximations to $[A(I)]^{-1}$ and $[A(I*)]^{-1}$ and we consider the errors in B* due to the errors in B, supposing that the formula for calculating B* from B is applied exactly. It is convenient to measure the errors by the matrices

$$(5.5) \qquad \left\{ \begin{array}{l} E \ = A(I) - B^{-1} \\ E* = A(I*) - [B*]^{-1} \end{array} \right. .$$

Theorem 3 states that the elements of E* are equal to the elements of E, except in the q-th row. The q-th row of $[B*]^{-1}$ is equal to $\underline{z}$, which is just the q-th row of A(I*). Hence, except for local errors, the iteration reduces the q-th row of the error matrix to zero and it leaves the other rows unchanged. Thus, if all the integers in the current reference are replaced, the current errors do not contribute to the result of the whole calculation.

This suppression of errors is a special case of the numerical stability of a version of the rank one correction formula that is studied by Powell (1969). It is an important result because the formula (5.2) occurs in many of the early linear programming algorithms. Perhaps it explains why some linear programming calculations are more accurate than is expected by some theoreticians. It suggests also that some of the criticism of the use of inverse matrices may have been overdone. We do not dispute that small pivots in linear programming calculations can cause large errors, but it does seem that, when there is a bound on pivot sizes, for example inequality (4.1), then the use of inverse matrices can be quite satisfactory. It is good to avoid the disadvantage of factorization methods that was mentioned earlier, namely the dependence on the scaling of the variables.

Theorem 2 of Section 4 is included because some readers may find it interesting, not because of the size of the bound that is given but because of its form. We claim that the number W, defined in equation

(4.2), is essentially independent of m because we can find an upper
bound on W from only the value of n and bounds on the coefficients
$\{a_{ij}, i=1,2,\ldots,m;\ \ j=1,2,\ldots,n\}$. In the approximation of functions
on an interval a finite calculation is obtained often by considering the
error of the approximation at only m points of the interval.
Alternatively one can sometimes extend a linear programming algorithm
to treat all points of the interval by considering the method of
calculation in the limit as m tends to infinity.   This can be done
in the present case.   Thus Theorem 2 is an example of an a priori
bound on the number of iterations that are needed to obtain limited
accuracy that keeps some value in the limit as m tends to infinity.

The history of the new technique for choosing q is rather unusual.
It was developed several years ago but a report was not prepared then
because it was thought that similar work was about to be published by
Barrodale and Phillips.   However we discovered later than their research
was on procedures for choosing the initial reference and they
developed an excellent method (Barrodale and Phillips, 1975). At about
the same time Madsen and Powell extended the work that is reported now to
the case when there are simple upper and lower bounds on the variables
x_j, $j=1,2,\ldots,n$.   They published a Fortran subroutine for this
calculation (Powell and Madsen, 1975).   Hence a Fortran program for an
extension of the present work exists already and it gives satisfactory
results.   However the subroutine is rather sophisticated because it
includes many additional features, one of them being Wolfe's (1963)
technique for treating degeneracies and another one being an automatic
method for finishing the calculation when the accuracy seems to be
dominated by computer rounding errors. Some of the theory of the
method of the subroutine is described by Powell (1975), but much of
his paper concerns the bounds on the variables.

The background to our work is explained because we wish to make
clear that this paper is not an extension to the report by Powell and
Madsen (1975).   Instead the report gives an example of the use of the
present technique.   The new procedure for choosing q can be used
without bounds on the variables, it does not require the use of inverse
matrices and it is not dependent on the initial choice of I.   Hence it
can help many of the existing algorithms for the minimax solution
of overdetermined linear equations. We have seen that the new technique
provides some advantages and, except for the lengthening of computer
programs, there seem to be no disadvantages。 We do not expect it to

give large gains in speed, but we do expect it to reduce the occurrence of ill-conditioned equations that are sometimes hard to solve and that can give large residuals, as in the second iteration shown in Table 1.

Acknowledgement   We are very grateful to Ian Barrodale for his comments on the first draft of this paper.   His remarks on the theory led to a substantial reduction in the length of the paper and he helped us to explain more clearly the advantages and limitations of the new technique.

REFERENCES

1. P. M. Anselone and G. D. Taylor (1973)   "The optimal exchange algorithm and comparisons with the generalized Remes algorithm", Applicable Analysis, Vol. 3, pp. 7-27.

2. I. Barrodale and C. Phillips (1975)   "An improved algorithm for discrete Chebyshev linear approximation" in "Proceedings of the Fourth Manitoba Conference on Numerical Mathematics" (Utalitas Mathematica Publishing Inc., Winnipeg).

3. I. Barrodale and F. D. K. Roberts (1973)   "An improved algorithm for discrete L_1 linear approximation", SIAM J. Numer. Anal., Vol. 10, pp. 839-848.

4. P. E. Gill and W. Murray (1973)   "A numerically stable form of the simplex algorithm", Linear Algebra and its Applics., Vol. 7, pp. 99-138.

5. K. Madsen and M. J. D. Powell (1975)   "A Fortran subroutine that calculates the minimax solution of linear equations subject to bounds on the variables", Report R. 7954 (A.E.R.E. Harwell).

6. M. J. D. Powell (1969)   "A theorem on rank one modifications to a matrix and its inverse", Computer Journal, Vol. 12, pp. 288-290.

7. M. J. D. Powell (1975)   "The minimax solution of linear equations subject to bounds on the variables", in "Proceedings of the Fourth Manitoba Conference on Numerical Mathematics" (Utalitas Mathematica Publishing Inc., Winnipeg).

8. J. R. Rice (1964)   "The approximation of functions, Vol. I" (Addison-Wesley Publishing Co., Reading, Mass.).

9. E. L. Stiefel (1963)   "Introduction to numerical mathematics" (Academic Press, London).

10. P. Wolfe (1963)   "A technique for resolving degeneracy in linear programming", SIAM Journal, Vol. 11, pp. 205-211.

Computer Science and Systems
   Division
Atomic Energy Research Establishment
Harwell, Oxfordshire, England

Department of Applied Mathematics
   and Theoretical Physics
University of Cambridge
Cambridge, England

Table 1

The example (2.9)

Iteration	x_1	x_2	h	$|r_p(\underline{x}\{I\})|$
1	$-\frac{1}{2}-\epsilon$	-2	$\frac{1}{2}-\epsilon$	$1\frac{1}{2}+3\epsilon$
2	$\frac{-2-9\epsilon}{4\epsilon}$	$\frac{1}{2\epsilon}$	$\frac{3}{4}$	$\frac{2+5\epsilon}{4\epsilon}$
3	$\frac{-2+1\frac{1}{2}\epsilon}{1-\epsilon}$	$\frac{-1}{1-\epsilon}$	$\frac{1-\frac{1}{2}\epsilon}{1-\epsilon}$	Converged

Infallible Calculation of Polynomial Zeros to Specified Precision

G. E. Collins

ABSTRACT

Let D be a Euclidean domain which is a subring of
the field of complex numbers and in which the arithmetic
operations can be algorithmically performed. Examples of
D are $\underline{Z}$, the integers, $\underline{Q}$, the rational numbers, $\underline{G}$,
the Gaussian integers, and $\underline{P}$, the real algebraic numbers.
We are concerned with algorithms which, given any polynomial
$A(x) \in D[x]$ and any positive rational number ϵ , computes
a sequence of disjoint intervals (rectangles) of length
(width) ϵ or less, each containing exactly one real (complex) zero of A , and together containing all real (complex)
zeros. The algorithms must also compute the multiplicity
of each zero. Any algorithm strictly fulfilling all of these
specification may truly be described as infallible. While
retaining these lofty goals we are nevertheless concerned
with algorithms which are as efficient as possible, in practice as well as theory.

Such infallible algorithms can be derived quite readily
from several diverse mathematical theorems using "exact"
arithmetic in the domain D , but these algorithms may differ
significantly in their time complexities. Also, one may
further improve practical efficiency by appropriate substi-
tution of "approximate" arithmetic (e.g., interval arithmetic) for exact arithmetic in certain contexts without
sacrificing infallibility (using exact arithmetic as backup).

This paper surveys recent progress on this problem, starting from Heindel's 1970 implementation and analysis of Sturm's theorem, including Pinkert's 1973 application of Sturm sequences to complex zeros, the 1975 Collins-Loos algorithm based on Rolle's theorem, the 1976 Collins-Akritas modification of Uspensky's method based on Descartes' theorem, and concluding with a brief report on current research by Collins and Chou relating to use of approximate arithmetic and the "principle of argument". Both theoretical time bounds and empirical times are presented.

1.   INTRODUCTION.

Computing the roots of a polynomial is a classical problem which has been intensively studied from many perspectives. In this paper the problem will be considered in a new perspective. The introduction and widespread use of digital computers has revitalized many mathematical problems and the still more recent emergence of the discipline of algorithm analysis has added its own important contribution to this revitalization. These are important facets of the perspective of this paper. But another equally important facet, though less generally understood and appreciated, is that which derives from the emerging discipline which I prefer to call computer algebra.

I shall not attempt here to define or delineate computer algebra. The name is partly self-explanatory but there are some connotations which are not fully captured by the name. One of the connotations especially pertinent to this paper is that of "exact calculation". "Exact calculation" doesn't have an exact or comprehensive definition either, but the methods discussed in this paper will illustrate several of the senses of this term. In some respects it is the opposite of "numerical analysis"; nevertheless, I hope to show that these "opposites" can be fruitfully combined.

In this paper we will be concerned with algorithms having the following abstract specifications.

Inputs: $A(x)$, a non-zero polynomial with complex coefficients, and ϵ , a non-negative real number.

Outputs: $R=(R_1,\ldots,R_k)$, a list of disjoint rectangles in the complex plane, and $M=(m_1,\ldots,m_k)$, a list of positive integers. Each rectangle R_i contains exactly one root of $A(x)$, say α_i , and m_i is the multiplicity of α_i . $\alpha_1,\ldots,\alpha_k$ are all the distinct roots of $A(x)$. If $\epsilon>0$ then the length of each rectangle is less than ϵ .

We assume that $A(x) = \sum_{i=0}^n a_i x^i$ is given by its list of coefficients, $(a_n,\ldots,a_0)$, $a_n\neq0$, and that the coefficients are given exactly. This implies that for any particular algorithm the coefficients belong to some countable subring R of the field $\underline{C}$ of the complex numbers. For example, R could be the ring $\underline{G}$ of the Gaussian integers or the field $\underline{P}$ of the real algebraic numbers.

There is no loss of generality in assuming that the rectangles have sides parallel to the coordinate axes and that the coordinates of the sides are rational. One could use circles instead of rectangles but rectangles have certain important amenities. In fact, we will assume that the rectangles include only their upper and right boundaries, so that the entire plane can be partitioned into disjoint rectangles. More precisely, each rectangle is to be a Cartesian product $I\times J$ where I and J are non-empty, left-open, right-closed intervals with rational endpoints. I and J will be called standard intervals and R will be called a standard rectangle. It is to be understood throughout that a rational number is to be represented, in lowest terms, by its numerator and denominator, which are arbitrarily large integers, in practice perhaps several hundred decimal digits in length.

We will also be concerned with algorithms of the same kind except that the coefficients a_i are assumed to be real and only the real roots of $A(x)$ are computed. Then the isolating rectangles are replaced by isolating intervals. In fact, since this is a simpler problem, we will consider it first. Also, as we will see, a solution to this simpler problem can be used very effectively in solving the general problem.

We will be concerned with the efficiency of the algorithms we consider, that is, with the maximum, or average,

computing times of the algorithms as functions of the polynomial A(x) and the accuracy ϵ . If, for example, A(x)
has integer coefficients, then in this analysis A will
be characterized by its degree, n , and the number of digits,
d , in its longest coefficient We will see that the problem
we have posed is tractable in the sense that there are algorithms for the problem whose computing times are dominated
by a function of the form $n^h d^k (\log 1/\epsilon)^\ell$ where h, k and
ℓ are fixed positive integers. This was proved by L. E.
Heindel in 1970 for the real case and by J. R. Pinkert in
1973 for the complex case.

But we will also be concerned with the efficiency of
such algorithms in a much more practical sense. Observed
computing times, measured in seconds, for applying the various
algorithms to various examples, will be presented. Through
the repeated improvement of such algorithms during the past
several years, their scope of practical applicability has
broadened tremendously. Thus the tactic has been to begin
with infallible algorithms and make them faster. In the
past, other researchers have sought to make fast algorithms
less fallible.

If, in the abstract specifications, one sets ϵ to
some obvious bound on the absolute values of the roots,
then the condition that the lengths of the rectangles be
less than ϵ is essentially vacuous and the effect of the
algorithm is just to <u>isolate</u> the roots. Alternatively,
we have adopted the convention that when $\epsilon=0$ there is
no restriction on rectangle sizes. It is perhaps rather
surprising that root isolation is a quite difficult problem;
once the roots have been isolated, they can be refined to
the desired accuracy relatively easily and rapidly.

In this paper I will present a survey of the research
on root calculation in which I have participated since 1969.
This begins with an outline of the thesis research of Heindel
(1970) and Pinkert (1973) on real and complex roots, respectively, using Sturm sequences. It continues with more
recent research on the use of Rolle's theorem (in collaboration with Loos, 1975) and Descarte's rule (with Akritas,
1976) for real root isolation. It concludes with some

preliminary results of a current investigation on the use
of interval arithmetic in conjunction with exact arithmetic
and on the application of the new real root isolation algorithms to complex root isolation.

2.   PRELIMINARIES.

     We are assuming that the coefficients of $A(x) =$
$\sum_{i=0}^{n} a_i x^i$ belong to a subring R of the field $\underline{C}$ of complex
numbers. This implies that R is an integral domain, and
we will assume, moreover, that R is a unique factorization domain. Hence we can begin by computing the content
of A, $c = \text{cont}(A) = \gcd(a_n, \ldots, a_0)$, the greatest common
divisor of its coefficients, and dividing A by c to
obtain $\bar{A}$, a primitive polynomial called the primitive
part of A and denoted by $pp(A)$. This doesn't make our
problem easier to solve, but it is a wise tactic computationally since the coefficients of $\bar{A}$ may be smaller. If
R is a field, we adopt the convention that any non-zero
greatest common divisor is 1, in which case $\bar{A}=A$. In
this paper, attention will be focused entirely on the cases
$R=\underline{Z}$, the ring of integers, and $R=\underline{G}$, the ring of Gaussian
integers. If the coefficients belong instead to the field
$\underline{Q}$ of the rational numbers or the field $\underline{Q}(i)$ of the complex
rational numbers, it is probably best in most cases to mul-
tiply A by a suitable constant to obtain a polynomial
in $\underline{Z}[x]$ or $\underline{G}[x]$. SAC-1 and other computer algebra systems contain very efficient algorithms for computing g.c.d.'s
in $\underline{Z}$ and $\underline{G}$; see, for example, [6].

     For simplicity of notation we will henceforth assume
that $A(x)$ is primitive. In the unique factorization domain
R, A has a complete factorization

(1) $$A = \prod_{i=1}^{k} A_i^{e_i},$$

where the A_i are the distinct irreducible factors of A
of positive degrees and the e_i are positive integers.
If we group the A_i according to their multiplicities e_i,
we can rewrite (1) in the form

(2)
$$A = \prod_{i=1}^{h} S_i^{f_i}$$

with $f_1 < f_2 < \ldots < f_h$. This is called the <u>squarefree factor-</u>
<u>ization</u> of A and the S_i are called the <u>squarefree fac-</u>
<u>tors</u> of A . The squarefree factors S_i and their mul-
tiplicities f_i are easily computed by differentiation
and g.c.d. calculations in R[x] as described by Musser
in [20].

Each S_i is squarefree and hence has only simple roots.
Also, the squarefree factors are pairwise relatively prime,
so it suffices to isolate the roots of the S_i individually and then attach to each the proper multiplicity f_i .
An isolating rectangle for a root of S_i may overlap an
isolating rectangle for a root of S_j, $i \neq j$. In this case
we can refine the larger of the two rectangles, bisecting
the rectangle and retaining the half which contains the
root. Repetition of this process will eventually produce
two disjoint isolating rectangles since the two roots are
distinct. We are assuming here that we have at our disposal
an algorithm which decides whether a given standard rectangle
contains at least one root of a given squarefree polynomial.
In the following sections we will discuss alternative algorithms for this purpose; in fact, these algorithms will
compute the number of roots in a given rectangle.

Let $A(x) \in \underline{Z}[x]$, $A(x) = \sum_{i=0}^{n} a_i x_i$. We define $|a_i|_1 = |a_i|$ and

(3)
$$|A|_1 = \sum_{i=0}^{n} |a_i|_1$$

and refer to $|A|_1$ as the <u>sum-norm</u> of A . The sum-norm
is a semi-norm in the sense that

(4)
$$|A+B|_1 \leq |A|_1 + |B|_1 ,$$

(5)
$$|A \cdot B|_1 \leq |A|_1 \cdot |B|_1 .$$

For a Gaussian integer a+bi we define $|a+bi|_1 = |a|+|b|$
and then use definition (3) for $A(x) \in \underline{G}[x]$; (4) and (5)
still hold. In fact, (4) and (5) can be extended to

polynomials in several variables and to matrices and are
generally useful in analysis of algebraic algorithms; see
[12] and [9].

Greatest common divisors in $\underline{Z}[x]$ or $\underline{G}[x]$ are computed using modular algorithms. Such algorithms use the
Chinese remainder theorem together with several g.c.d. calculations in $GF(q_i)[x]$ using the Euclidean algorithm, where
the $GF(q_i)$ are finite fields. The basic ideas are discussed by Knuth in [16]. It is easy to show that if $C =$
$gcd(A,B)$, $\bar{A} = A/C$ and $\bar{B} = B/C$, and if n is the maximum
of the degrees of $\bar{A}, \bar{B}$ and C while d is the maximum
of $|\bar{A}|_1$, $|\bar{B}|_1$ and $|C|_1$, then the computing time of such
a modular algorithm is dominated by $n^3 L(d)^2$. For the
case $\underline{Z}[x]$ this is proved in Pinkert's thesis, [21]; Caviness extends this to $\underline{G}[x]$ in [5]. Here $L(d)$ denotes
the length of the integer d , the number of digits in d
relative to any fixed base. $n^3 L(d)^2$ is a theoretical upper
bound, but Brown shows in [3] that the average computing
time is most likely codominant with $n^2 L(d) + nL(d)^2$.

Using these results, one can show that the maximum time
to compute the squarefree factorization of $A(x)$ is dominated by $n^4 L(d)^2$ if n is the degree of A and d is
a bound for the sum-norm of all factors of A . If B is
a factor of A then one expects that usually $|B|_1 \leq |A|_1$;
however this is not true in general as is illustrated by
the simple example $A(x) = x^3-1$, $B(x) = x^2+x+1$. The best
known bound for $|B|_1$ is due to Mignotte, [17]. His re-
sults imply that if the degree of A is n and $|A|_1 = d$
then $|B|_1 \leq 2^n d$. Hence the maximum computing time for
squarefree factorization of A is $n^4 L(2^n d)^2 \sim n^6 + n^4 L(d)^2$.
This illustrates again the gap between theoretical maximum
computing times and observed average computing times. In
practice, A will often be squarefree. If it is, then
the only g.c.d. computed is $gcd(A,A') = 1$ and in this
case, as shown by Brown in [3], the average computing time
is almost certainly $\sim n^2 + nL(d)$.

In order to make the computing times we are discussing
more concrete, let A, B and C be polynomials of degree
20 with integer coefficients which are eight decimal digits

in length, and suppose these polynomials are pairwise relatively prime. Then the time to compute   gcd(A,B) = 1   on
a UNIVAC 1108 computer using the SAC-1 system, [8], is about
0.15 seconds and the time to compute   gcd(A·C,B·C) = C   is
about 1.35 seconds.

   As we will see, these times are quite negligible relative to the overall times for root calculation. Moreover,
if the squarefree factorization of A is a proper factorization, then it will generally take much less time to compute
the roots of all of the squarefree factors than it would
to compute the roots of their product. For example, if
we assume that the time to isolate the roots of a polynomial
of degree n is proportional to n^3 (an apparently realistic assumption, then it will take $2n^3$ units of time to
isolate the roots of two squarefree factors of degree n ,
but it will take $8n^3$ units to isolate the roots of their
product.

   This suggests that it might even be sound strategy to
compute the complete factorization of A(x) in each case
before computing its roots. A complete factorization algorithm begins by computing the squarefree factorization,
so the question is just whether each squarefree factor should
be subjected to complete factorization. The answer to this
question is somewhat doubtful since complete factorization
is considerably slower than g.c.d. calculation. We would
expect that in most cases the squarefree factors will prove
to be irreducible. In his thesis, [19], Musser recorded
the times required to completely factor five irreducible
polynomials of degree 20 with integer coefficients which
were six decimal digits long. The times varied from 1.92
to 6.51 seconds, with an average of 4.84 seconds. Since
it generally takes much longer to compute all roots of a
polynomial than to compute just the real roots, these figures suggest that perhaps one should usually apply complete
factorization before computing the complex roots, but not
prior to a computation of just the real roots. If one has
any a priori knowledge of the probability of non-real roots
or of reducible squarefree factors, this knowledge should
be used in arriving at a decision. When there are proper

factors, the factorization takes considerably more time.
Musser reported that the time to recover three factors,
with degrees 3, 5 and 7 and with 3-decimal-digit integer
coefficients, from their product of degree 15 averaged about
23 seconds.

Although existing algorithms for complete factoriza-
tion in $\underline{Z}[x]$ or $\underline{G}[x]$ perform well enough to be very
useful for many purposes, there is no known algorithm whose
maximum computing time is known to be dominated by a fixed
power of the degree n of the polynomial to be factored.
The best currently known methods, based on the use of
Berlekamp's algorithms, [1] and [2], for factoring univariate polynomials over finite fields and on the use of Hensel's
lemma, are discussed by Musser in [20]. In the following,
in order to obtain polynomial computing time bounds for
root isolation, we will assume that only squarefree factorization is used.

Let R be an isolating rectangle for a root α of
the squarefree factor S_i, S an isolating rectangle for
a root β of S_j, $i \neq j$. The maximum number of times that
R and S must be bisected before they become disjoint
will depend on the distance between the roots α and β.
If $\alpha_1, \ldots, \alpha_k$ are the distinct roots of a polynomial $A(x)$,
then

$$(6) \qquad \min_{1 \leq i < j \leq k} |\alpha_i - \alpha_j|$$

is called the minimum root separation of A, and denoted
by sep(A). It was proved in [12] that

$$(7) \qquad \text{sep}(A) > \frac{1}{2}(e^{1/2} n^{3/2} d)^{-n}$$

for any squarefree polynomial $A(x)$ with degree n and
$|A|_1 = d$. It follows that

$$(8) \qquad |\log(\text{sep}(A)^{-1})| \leq nL(d) + nL(n),$$

where "$\leq$" is the symbol for dominance (see [9]). Mignotte,
[18], has improved the bound (7), but not enough to improve

the dominance relation (8). Applying (8) with $A = S_i S_j$ yields a bound for the number of bisections required with the proper interpretation of n and d . This same bound applies to the number of bisections required for isolating the roots of a squarefree polynomial in any algorithm which bisects rectangles containing more than one root until they contain only one.

In fact, most of the algorithms we will discuss begin by computing a root bound b such that $|\alpha_i| < b$ for every root α_i of the polynomial $A(x)$. Then the square whose center is the origin of the coordinate axes and whose width is 2b contains all roots. A working list of rectangles is kept, each rectangle containing two or more roots of the squarefree polynomial $A(x)$. A rectangle is removed from the working list and bisected. Each half containing two or more roots is itself placed on the working list. A half containing no roots is discarded, and a half containing one root is put in an output list. In computing real roots, intervals replace rectangles.

Many methods are known for computing root bounds. Some are better in some cases, others are better in other cases. The differences among the known methods are so small in most cases that research on this aspect of root calculation does not appear to be very rewarding. In the algorithms to be described we use throughout the bound

$$(9) \qquad b = 2 \max_{1 \le i \le n} |a_{n-i}/a_n|^{1/i} ,$$

which is given in [16]. Since the terms of (9) are irrational, and since little accuracy is wanted anyway, we compute instead

$$(10) \qquad \ell = \max_{1 \le i \le n \ \& \ a_{n-i} \ne 0} \lceil (\log_2 |a_{n-i}/a_n|)/i \rceil ,$$

and then $\bar{b} = 2^{\ell+1}$. We then have $b \le \bar{b} < 2b$ and we use $\bar{b}$ as a root bound. The terms of (10) are quite easy to compute and, as we will see later, there is a significant advantage in using a power of 2 as a root bound.

It is obvious that $b \le 2d = 2|A|_1$ and hence $\bar{b} < 4d$.

Thus we begin with a square containing all roots whose width
is at most 8d. A rectangle whose length is less than $\frac{1}{2}$
sep(A) cannot contain more than one root. Hence, assuming
that bisections are alternately horizontal and vertical,
a maximal isolating rectangle always results from a sequence
of at most

(11) $$2\lceil \log_2(8d/\tfrac{1}{2} \ \text{sep}(A))\rceil$$

bisections. By (8), the number of bisections in such a
chain is dominated by $nL(d) + nL(n)$.

3.   STURM SEQUENCES FOR REAL ZEROS.

     A polynomial remainder sequence (abbreviated p.r.s.)
over an integral domain D is a sequence of non-zero polynomials $A_1, A_2, \ldots, A_r$ in D[x] such that, for $1 \le i \le r-1$,
A_{i+2} is a remainder of A_i and A_{i+1} with $A_{r+1} = 0$.
To say that A_{i+2} is a remainder of A_i and A_{i+1} means
that there exist non-zero $d_i, e_i \in D$ and $Q_i \in D[x]$ such that

(12) $$d_i A_i = Q_i A_{i+1} + e_i \ A_{i+2}$$

with $A_{i+2} = 0$ or $\deg(A_{i+2}) < \deg(A_{i+1})$. See [7] for a
general discussion of p.r.s.'s and some fundamental theorems
about them. If D is an ordered domain, $d_i e_i < 0$ for all
i and $\deg(A_r) = 0$ then $A_1, A_2, \ldots, A_r$ is called a Sturm
sequence for A_1 and A_2 . If $A_2 = A_1'$, the derivative of
A_1 , then $A_1, A_2, \ldots, A_r$ will be called a Sturm sequence
for A_1 .
     Let $u = (u_1, \ldots, u_s)$ be a sequence of real numbers.
Let $u_1', \ldots, u_t'$ be the subsequence of all non-zero terms of
u . Then var(u) , the number of sign variations in u ,
is the number of i, $1 \le i < t$, such that $u_i' \cdot u_{i+1}' < 0$. Now let
S be the Sturm sequence $(A_1, A_2, \ldots, A_r)$. Then Sturm's
theorem asserts that the number of real roots of A in the
left-open, right-closed interval (a,b], a<b , is equal to
V(S,a)-V(S,b) , where $V(S,u) = \text{var}(A_1(u), \ldots, A_r(u))$.
     Based on our discussion in the preceding section, Sturm's
theorem therefore provides a simple method for isolating

the real roots of any polynomial $A(x) \epsilon R[x]$ for any subring R of the field $\underline{R}$ of real numbers provided R is
a unique factorization domain whose elements can be exactly
represented in such a manner that the arithmetic operations
can be effectively performed and we can decide the order
relation in R . We will restrict our attention to the
case $R=\underline{Z}$; the case in which R is a real algebraic number
field has been considered by Rump, [23]. The resulting
real root isolation algorithm for $\underline{Z}[x]$ was developed,
implemented in the SAC-1 computer algebra system, and analyzed by Heindel in his Ph.D. thesis, [14]; the main results
have been published in [15] and we will only briefly summarize them here, improving his computing time bounds through
the use of (7).

It was proved in [7] that if $A_1, A_2, \ldots, A_r$ is any
p.r.s. over an integral domain then each term A_i , $i \geq 3$,
is similar to some subresultant of A_1 and A_2 . Since
by definition each subresultant coefficient is the determinant of a submatrix of the Sylvester matrix of A_1 and
A_2 , it is easy to show that if $|A_1|_1 \leq d$, $|A_2|_1 \leq d$,
$\deg(A_1) \leq n$ and $\deg(A_2) \leq n$ then d^{2n} is a bound for the
subresultant coefficients. Using this bound and the fundamental theorem of subresultants, [3], Heindel showed that
one could compute a <u>subresultant Sturm sequence</u> for the
squarefree polynomial $A(x)$ in time dominated by $n^4 L(d)^2$

If we replace each term A_i in an arbitrary Sturm
sequence by its primitive part, we obtain a <u>primitive Sturm
sequence</u>, whose coefficients are as small as possible. Although no theorem to the effect is known to me, there is
abundant evidence that d^{2n} is a tight bound for the coefficients of a primitive Sturm sequence; therefore $n^4 L(d)^2$
is also a tight bound for the time required to compute a
Sturm sequence, though I am here excluding asymptotically
faster algorithms which are impractical for existing computers.

The use of Sturm's theorem for real root isolation
also involves the evaluation of the terms of a Sturm sequence at a number of points, the endpoints of intervals.
Since the root bound computed by (10) is a binary rational

number, that is, a rational number whose denominator is a
power of 2, it is easy to see that the endpoints of all intervals arising in the computation will be binary rational numbers. This is important since the evaluation of a polynomial
with integer coefficients at a rational number can be performed significantly faster if the rational number is binary
and the base for large integer representation is a power of
2. It can be shown that under these conditions, if $\deg(B) = m$
and $|B|_1 = b$ then the time to compute the integer
$f^n B(e/f)$ using a version of Horner's method is dominated
by

$$(13) \qquad m^2 L(e)^2 + m^2 L(e) L(f) + m L(b) L(e) .$$

In applying Sturm's theorem we are only interested in the
sign of $B(e/f)$ and, since f is positive, this is the
same as the sign of $f^n B(e/f)$. However, one can also compute $B(e/f)$ without affecting the time bound (13).

    If now B is a term of the Sturm sequence of A with
$\deg(A) = n$ and $|A|_1 = d$, and if e/f is the endpoint
of any interval arising in the real root isolation, then
$m \leq n$, $L(e)$ and $L(f)$ are dominated by $nL(d) + nL(n)$ and
$L(b) \leq nL(d)$. Also the number of polynomial evaluations
will be dominated by $n^2 \{nL(d) + nL(n)\}$. Hence the time for
all evaluations will be dominated by

$$(14) \qquad n^7 L(d)^3 + n^7 L(n)^3 .$$

Since in practical cases n will be small, it is reasonable
to omit the second term of (15). In place of $n^7 L(d)^3$
Heindel obtained the bound $n^{10} L(d)^3$ since he was using an
inferior bound for the minimum root separation.

    The bound $n^7 L(d)^3$ is still unrealistic. It is likely
still subject to improvement. Furthermore, it is likely
that the average time for Sturm sequence evaluations in real
root isolation, as a function of n and d , is substantially
less than the maximum time. In fact, in the cases observed
thus far, the time required for the evaluations is typically
less than the time required to compute the Sturm sequence.

Table 1 shows the times required to isolate all real
roots of polynomials of several kinds and degrees using the
Sturm sequence algorithm. The times are given in seconds
and were obtained using the University of Wisconsin implementation of SAC-1 on a UNIVAC 1110 computer. The three
kinds of polynomials are random (R), product (P) and
Chebyshev (C). The random polynomials have random 33-bit
integer coefficients with random signs. The product polynomials of degree n were obtained as the product of n
linear polynomials with random 8-bit integer coefficients.
After forming the products the coefficients were truncated
to a maximum length of 33 bits. The truncation perturbs
the roots somewhat, but the number of real roots was n
in each case except that the polynomial of degree 20 had
only 18 real roots. The random polynomials had no more
than three real roots in any case. The Chebyshev polynomial
of degree n , of course, has n real roots, and its largest
coefficients are about n bits long.

TABLE 1

Computing Times, in Seconds, for Sturm
Sequence Real Root Isolation

n	R	P	C
5	0.6	0.5	0.4
10	6.8	6.5	1.8
15	28.8	29.1	4.9
20	89.6	89.7	10.8
25	172.5	207.0	19.9

It is surprising that the computing times for Chebyshev
polynomials are much smaller than for the two other kinds.
The reason is that Chebyshev polynomials have unusual primitive Sturm sequences. Normally, the ith term of the primitive Sturm sequence for A will have coefficients which
are about $2id$ digits long, that is, the coefficient lengths
grow linearly. However, in a Chebyshev primitive Sturm
sequence the coefficients actually decrease in size! This
is illustrated in Table 2, which shows the largest coefficient length, in bits, of every fifth term of the primitive

Sturm sequences of the three polynomials of degree 25 used
in Table 1. This peculiarity was not known to Heindel; it
was first observed by Collins and Loos in [13]. This discovery is due in part to G. W. Reitwiesner, who observed
similar behavior for the Sturm sequences of the Stirling
polynomials $S_n(x) = x(x-1)...(x-n+1)$ in correspondence
with Collins in 1972. The Legendre polynomials also have
unusual Sturm sequences. An explanation of unusual Sturm
sequences has not yet been found. The main point to be made
here is that, with a few known exceptions, the usefulness
of Sturm's theorem for real root isolation is limited primarily by the size of the coefficients occurring in Sturm
sequences.

TABLE 2

Coefficient Lengths, in Bits, in the
Sturm Sequences of Polynomials of Degree 25

i	R	P	C
1	33	33	29
5	201	127	24
10	547	394	19
15	899	656	11
20	1254	875	7
25	1595	1037	1

4.   STURM SEQUENCES FOR COMPLEX ZEROS.

Now let $A(x)$ be a squarefree polynomial with complex
coefficients. Let $A(x) = A_1(x) + iA_2(x)$ where A_1 and
A_2 are real polynomials. Let B be the greatest common
divisor of A_1 and A_2, $\bar{A}_1 = A_1/B$, $\bar{A}_2 = A_2/B$ and $\bar{A} = \bar{A}_1 +$
$i\bar{A}_2$. Let $S = (\bar{A}_1, \bar{A}_2, A_3, ..., A_r)$ be a Sturm sequence for
$\bar{A}$. There is a well-known theorem, derived from the principle of argument, which asserts that, since $\bar{A}$ has no real
zeros, the number of zeros of $\bar{A}$ in the upper half-plane
is

(15) $\frac{1}{2} \{m+V(S,\infty)-V(S,-\infty)\}$

where $m = \deg(\bar{A})$. Applying Sturm's theorem to B we can compute the number, k, of real roots of B. Since the non-real roots of B occur in conjugate pairs, we find that the number of roots of A above the real axis is

$$(16) \qquad \frac{1}{2}\{n-k+V(S,\infty)-V(S,-\infty)\} \ .$$

In his Ph.D. thesis, [21], Pinkert showed how to extend this result to determine the number of roots of A in an arbitrary standard rectangle provided that A is a Gaussian polynomial, that is, $A(x)\epsilon\underline{G}[x]$. He further implemented the resulting Sturmian algorithm for complex root isolation in the SAC-1 system and analyzed its maximum computing time. His results are summarized in part in [22].

Let $\hat{A}(x) = A(x)A(-x)$. If

$$(17) \qquad (A(x) = a_n \Pi^n_{i=1} \ (x-\alpha_i)$$

then

$$(18) \qquad \hat{A}(x) = (-1)^n a^2_n \ \Pi^n_{i=1}(x^2-\alpha^2_i) \ ,$$

a polynomial in x^2. Hence if $A*(x) = \hat{A}(x^{1/2})$ then $A*$ is a polynomial whose roots are the squares of the roots of A ; we call $A*$ the root-square of A. The number of roots of $A*$ in the upper half-plane is equal to the number of roots of A in the first and third quadrants plus the number of roots of A on the positive imaginary axis; this last number can be computed using Sturm's theorem. If q_i is the number of roots of A in the ith quadrant and a_i is the number of roots of A on the ith semi-axis then we can compute a_2 hence, also q_1+q_2 and q_1+q_3 . By means of a rotation, $\tilde{A}(x) = A(ix)$, we can similarly compute q_2+q_3 and q_2+q_4 . From q_1+q_2, q_1+q_3 and q_2+q_3 we obtain q_1, q_2 and q_3 , hence also q_4 . So by means of root squaring and rotation the number of roots in each quadrant can be computed. It should be noted that $A*$ may have some double roots, which must be counted twice. Here a simple square-free factorization is required; alternatively one may compute gcd(A(x),A(-x)) .

By means of a translation, $\bar{A}(x) = A(x+a)$, the number
of roots in any translated quadrant can be computed. By
means of four computations of the number of roots in a translated quadrant, the number of roots in any standard rectangle
can be obtained as illustrated in Figure 1. The origins
of the translated third quadrants in Figure 1 are the points
a, b, c and d .

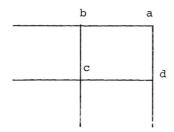

FIG. 1. The Number of Roots in a Standard Rectangle.

Repeated application of this method for the number of
roots in a rectangle during the bisections of root isolation
usually involves many redundant calculations. Accordingly,
Pinkert devised a scheme for moving methodically through
a grid of rectangles using only an algorithm for the number
of roots in a translated quadrant, which scheme is too complex
to be described here.

The analysis of Pinkert's Sturmian algorithm for complex
root isolation is analogous to Heindel's analysis for real
roots and the results are the same in terms of the dominance
relation. Nevertheless, isolation of the complex roots of
a polynomial will entail the construction of numerous Sturm
sequences and the observed computing times are correspondingly
large. Table 3 shows UNIVAC 1110 computing times, in seconds,
for application of Pinkert's root isolation algorithm to random polynomials of various degrees. These random polynomials
have 33-bit rational integer coefficients as in Table 1.

TABLE 3

Computing Times, in Seconds, for Sturm
Sequence Complex Root Isolation

n	time
5	14
8	62
10	262

5. ROLLE'S THEOREM FOR REAL ZEROS.

Rolle's theorem asserts that between two distinct zeros
of a real polynomial $A(x)$ (or other differentiable real
function)   there is at least one zero of its derivative.
An obvious corollary is that if $A(x)$ is a squarefree polynomial and $\alpha_1 < \ldots < \alpha_k$ are the real roots of $A'(x)$ then
each of the intervals $(-\infty, \alpha_1)$, $(\alpha_1, \alpha_2), \ldots, (\alpha_{k-1}, \alpha_k)$,
(α_k, ∞) contains at most one real root of $A(x)$. Since
A is squarefree the α_i are not roots of $A(x)$ and each
interval (α_i, α_{i+1}) , with $\alpha_0 = -\infty$ and $\alpha_{k+1} = \infty$, contains
a root of A just in case $A(\alpha_i)$ and $A(\alpha_{i+1})$ have oppo-
site signs. This suggests the possibility of proceeding
by induction on the degree, obtaining isolating intervals
for the real roots of $A(x)$, being given isolating intervals for the real roots of $A'(x)$.

There are two main problems. One is that $A(x)$ may
be squarefree without $A'(x)$ being squarefree. The other
is to determine the sign of $A(\alpha_i)$ given only an isolating
interval $I_i = (a_i, b_i]$ for α_i as a root of $A'(x)$. Because of the first problem we drop the requirement that $A(x)$
be squarefree, but we insist instead that we be given for
each isolating interval I_i the multiplicity, m_i , of
α_i as a root of $A'(x)$. Because of the second problem
we require moreover that each isolating interval contain
no roots of $A''(x)$ other than α_i , which may be a common
root of $A'(x)$ and $A''(x)$. For convenience we call a list
of intervals and associated multiplicities satisfying these
conditions, together with the condition that the interval
endpoints be binary rational numbers, a strong isolation

list for A' . The problem is now to proceed to a strong
isolation list for A .

Let $J_0, J_1, \ldots, J_k$ be the $k+1$ intervals complementary
to the isolating intervals $I_1, I_2, \ldots, I_k$. We have $J_i =$
$(b_i, a_{i+1}]$ and we can set $b_0 = -b$, $a_{k+1} = b$, where b is
a root bound for $A(x)$. By Rolle's theorem, each inter-
val $J_i \cup I_i \cup J_{i+1} = (b_i, a_{i+2})$ contains at most two roots
of A , and each interval J_i contains at most one. Any
root of A in J_i must be simple and any root of A in
I_i other than α_i must be simple. J_i will contain a root
of A just in case $A(a_{i+1}) = 0$ or $A(b_i)$ and $A(a_{i+1})$
have opposite signs. If J_i and J_{i+1} both contain roots
of A then I_i does not. If just one of J_i and J_{i+1}
contains a root of A then I_i contains at most one root
of A . Let $B = \mathrm{gsfd}(A) = A/\gcd(A, A')$, the greatest squarefree divisor of A . Then α_i is a root of A just in
case B has a simple root in I_i ; B can have at most
one root in I_i , and all roots of B are simple. If α_i
is a root of A then it is a root of multiplicity $m_i + 1$
and there are no other roots of A in I_i .

The only case arising which is not easily disposed of
is that in which neither J_i nor J_{i+1} has a root of A,
α_i is not a root of A, A has the same sign at each endpoint of I_i, m_i is odd, and $A(a_i)A'(a_i) < 0$. In this case
the hypothesis is used that I_i contains no roots of A''
other than α_i . In this case the graph of A behaves as
shown in Figure 2, in case $A(a_i) > 0$, and there are either
two roots of A in I_i or none. By the mentioned hypothesis, the graph of A within the interval lies above the
tangent lines constructed at the endpoints. Hence if the
left tangent line intersects the axis at a point at or to
the right of the intersection with the axis of the right
tangent line, then there are no roots. Otherwise, the problem
remains unresolved. The interval I_i is bisected. Evaluation of A at the bisection point may reveal the existence
of roots of A in I_i and produce isolating intervals for
them. If not, then the process is reapplied to the subinterval of I_i containing α_i .

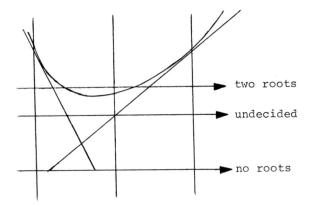

FIG. 2.   Tangent Construction and Bisection.

The real root isolation algorithm which has just been
sketched was devised by Collins and Loos in 1975 and is described more fully in [13].   Also, a computing time analysis
is given which shows that the maximum computing time of the
algorithm is dominated by $n^{10} + n^7 L(d)^3$. This is the same
as the bound for Heindel's algorithm when A is not required
to be squarefree.

In practice, however, the Collins-Loos algorithm is
much faster than the Heindel algorithm except for polynomials,
such as Chebyshev and Legendre, which have "unusual" Sturm
sequences.   Table 4 shows the computing times for real root
isolation using the Collins-Loos algorithm when applied to
the same polynomials as those of Table 1.   For the random
polynomials, the time ratio of the two algorithms increases
with n from about 1 to 7 as n increases from 5 to 25.
For the product polynomials the ratio increases from about
0.4 to 3.2.   For Chebyshev polynomials the ratio remains
near 0.5.   For the random and product polynomials, the
Collins-Loos algorithm times are approximately proportional
to n^3 while for the Heindel algorithm they are approximately
proportional to n^4 .   For both algorithms the times for
Chebyshev polynomials grow just slightly faster than n^2 .

The Collins-Loos algorithm uses the derivative sequence
of A , namely $A^{(0)}$, $A^{(1)}$, $A^{(2)}$,...,$A^{(n-1)}$, in place of
a Sturm sequence for A .   More precisely, it uses the

primitive derivative sequence $\bar{A}^{(0)}$, $\bar{A}^{(1)}$, $\bar{A}^{(2)}$,...,$\bar{A}^{(n-1)}$
where $\bar{A}^{(i)}$ is the primitive part of $A^{(i)}$. Since $A^{(i)}$
is always divisible by i! , every coefficient of $\bar{A}^{(i)}$ is
at most $\binom{n}{i}$ times as large as some coefficient of A .
Hence $|\bar{A}^{(i)}|_1 \leq 2^n |A|_1$ for all i . Thus, for example,
whereas the largest coefficient in the primitive Sturm sequence for the random polynomial of degree 25 was 1595 bits
long, the longest coefficient in the primitive derivative
sequence is only 46 bits long. Thus the problem of Sturm
sequences with very large coefficients is avoided.

The Collins-Loos algorithm has the additional merit
that it computes isolating intervals for all derivatives
of A , and these are wanted in some applications. One such
application is the quantifier elimination algorithm [10].
Another advantage is that it requires much less memory than
the Sturm sequence algorithm.

TABLE 4

Computing Times, in Seconds, for the Collins-Loos
Real Root Isolation Algorithm

n	R	P	C
5	0.8	1.4	0.8
10	3.8	6.8	3.4
15	8.1	17.9	9.0
20	18.4	38.0	18.6
25	25.8	64.0	35.2

6. DESCARTES' THEOREM FOR REAL ZEROS.

In his book Theory of Equations, [24], Uspensky recom-
mends a method based on Descartes' rule of signs for the
isolation of real roots. If we identify A(x) with its
sequence of coefficients $(a_n, a_{n-1}, ..., a_0)$ and write var(A) ,
then Descartes' rule asserts that var(A) minus the number
of positive real roots of A , multiplicities counted, is
an even non-negative integer. This implies, in particular,
that if var(A) = 0 then A has no positive real roots
and if var(A) = 1 then A has exactly one. In fact, only
these two special cases of Descartes' rule are needed for

Uspensky's method.

Suppose $var(A) > 1$. Let $A(x) = A(x+1)$ and $A^*(x) = (x+1)^n A(1/(x+1))$. Under these two transformations, the roots of A in $(0,1)$ are transformed onto the positive roots of A^* and the roots of A in $(1,\infty)$ are transformed onto the positive roots of $\hat{A}$; both root transformations are one-to-one. $A(1) = 0$ if and only if $\hat{A}(0) = 0$. Descartes' rule is then applied to A^* and $\hat{A}$. If either A^* or $\hat{A}$ has more than one variation then the same two transformations are applied to this polynomial. There is a theorem, which Uspensky attributes to an 1836 paper of Vincent, [25], which asserts that every chain of transformations of these two kinds eventually leads to a polynomial with at most one variation provided that the polynomial A is squarefree.

Uspensky, in the pre-computer year of 1947, asserted that this is the "most efficient method" for real root isolation. Collins and Akritas, [11], programmed the algorithm in SAC-1 and indeed found it to be faster than either the Sturmian algorithm or the Collins-Loos algorithm for all the polynomials of the preceding tables except that it was slightly slower for the Chebyshev polynomials of higher degree. However, they also observed that the maximum computing time of the Uspensky algorithm, for every fixed $n \geq 2$, is exponential in the length of $d = |A|_1$. This is rather easily seen if one considers the 2^k subintervals of $(0,\infty)$ corresponding to the transformation chains of length k . As k increases, the lengths of these 2^k subintervals become more and more disparate. For each k , one of these 2^k subintervals is $(1-1/k,1)$. Hence, for example, if A happens to have two real roots which are both just slightly less than 1, then Uspensky's algorithm will require a long time to separate them. This, in fact, explains its relatively poor performance on Chebyshev polynomials.

Collins and Akritas devised a modification of Uspensky's algorithm which eliminates this defect. Let $b = 2^k$ be a root bound for A , and let $\bar{A}(x) = A(2^k x)$ if $k > 0$, $\bar{A}(x) = 2^{-kn} A(2^k x)$ if $k < 0$. Now 1 is a root bound for $\bar{A}$ and it suffices to isolate the roots of $\bar{A}$ in $(0,1)$. If

var($\bar{A}*$) $\leq$ 1   then we are through; otherwise Descartes' rule
is applied, indirectly, to the two transformed polynomials
$\bar{A}'(x) = 2^n \bar{A}(x/2)$ and $\bar{A}''(x) = \bar{A}'(x+1)$.   The roots of $\bar{A}$
in   (0,1/2)   correspond to roots of $\bar{A}'$ in   (0,1)   and the
roots of $\bar{A}$ in   (1/2,1)   correspond to roots of $\bar{A}''$ in
(0,1) .   Hence Descartes' rule is applied to $\bar{A}'*$ and $\bar{A}''*$.
Repeated application of the two transformations ' and " is
tantamount to repeated bisection of a subinterval of   (0,1)
into two parts determined by the midpoint.

    Termination of this modified Uspensky algorithm is as-
sured by consideration of Figure 3.   Under the transforma-
tion $\bar{A} \rightarrow \bar{A}*$, roots of $\bar{A}$ inside the large circle   C , real
or complex, are mapped onto the roots of $\bar{A}*$ in the right
half-plane, roots of $\bar{A}$ on the circle are mapped onto roots
of $\bar{A}*$ on the imaginary axis, and roots of $\bar{A}$ outside the
circle are mapped onto roots of $\bar{A}*$ in the left half-plane.
Likewise, the circles   C'   and   C"   correspond to $\bar{A}'*$ and
$\bar{A}''*$, etc.   A circle containing no roots of $\bar{A}$ corresponds
to a transformed polynomial with no roots in the right half-
plane, and it is easy to prove that in this case the transformed polynomial has no sign variations.   A circle containing exactly one real root and no complex roots corresponds
to a transformed polynomial with exactly one real root and
no complex roots in the right half plane.   Such a transformed
polynomial may have more than one sign variation.   A simple
example is the polynomial $2x^3 - 2x^2 + x - 10 = (x-2)(2x^2 + 2x+5)$.   However, Vincent's theorem can be modified to prove
that if the circle contains exactly one real root and if
there is a larger concentric circle, with radius about n^2
times as large, containing no other roots, real or complex,
then the transformed polynomial will have exactly one variation.   This proves that the modified Uspensky algorithm
terminates.   It appears that, in practice, the outer concentric circle need not be much larger than the inner circle,
but this question has not yet been carefully studied.

    It can be shown that the maximum computing time of the
modified Uspensky algorithm for a squarefree polynomial is
dominated by $n^6 L(d)^2$, an improvement of the $n^7 L(d)^3$ bound
for the Sturmian algorithm.   This reduction in the time bound

may be attributable to the fact that no multiplications are performed in the modified Uspensky algorithm other than multiplications by powers of 2, which are, in effect, performed by shifting. Let $\tilde{A}(x) = x^n A(1/x)$. This transformation merely inverts the order of the coefficients. Then $A^*(x) = \tilde{A}(x+1) = \hat{\tilde{A}}(x)$. Most of the time of the modified Uspensky algorithms is spent performing the transformation $\hat{A}(x) = A(x+1)$, which requires $\binom{n+1}{2}$ coefficient additions.

Observations indicate that the number of translations $A(x+1)$ performed in the modified Uspensky algorithm tends to be proportional to n . If $|A|_1 = d$ then $|A(x+1)|_1 \leq 2^n d$. This suggests that the average computing time of the algorithm may be codominant with $n\binom{n+1}{2}L(2^n d) \sim n^4 + n^3 L(d)$ The observed computing times, which are for relatively small n , do not show the effect of the n^4 term but agree well with the $n^3 L(d)$ term. Table 5 gives the observed computing times for the same polynomials which were used in Tables 1 and 4. For the random polynomials the Collins-Loos to modified Uspensky algorithm time ratios are between 3 and 7, for the product polynomials they are between 1.5 and 3, for Chebyshev polynomials between 1 and 2.

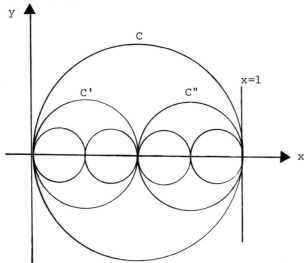

FIG. 3.   The Modified Uspensky Algorithm
and Vincent's Theorem

TABLE 5

Computing Times, in Seconds, for the
Modified Uspensky Real Root Isolation Algorithm

n	R	P	C
5	0.2	0.5	0.4
10	0.7	2.2	2.0
15	1.4	12.5	5.1
20	2.7	17.6	17.0
25	3.5	40.4	31.6

7.   APPLICATION OF INTERVAL ARITHMETIC.

The Collins-Loos algorithm and the modified Uspensky
algorithm are much faster than the Heindel algorithm for real
root isolation because they avoid computing Sturm sequences
with very large coefficients. Nevertheless, some moderately
large integers will emerge in the calculations of the Collins-
Loos and modified Uspensky algorithms, so there is a possibility for further reduction of computing times for real
root isolation if we realize that frequently only the sign
of a number is needed.

In the Collins-Loos algorithm a large rational number
(that is, having a large numerator or denominator) is likely
to result from the evaluation of a polynomial, B , of the
primitive derivative sequence at the endpoint of an isolating
interval. In this algorithm an endpoint will typically be
a small rational number, e/f , with numerator and denominator no more than 5 or 6 bits long. However, if B is
a polynomial of degree n with coefficients h bits long
and if e and f are k bits long, then the integers arising in the calculation of $f^n B(e/f)$ may be as long as about
$\ell = h+nk$ bits long. For example, with $h=50$, $n=25$ and
$k=6$ we have $\ell=200$. In SAC-1 on a UNIVAC 1110 computer,
the time required to add two integers of this size is around
500 microseconds. Hence the time required to compute
$f^n B(e/f)$ may be 10 to 20 milliseconds; this is a large time
investment to decide whether $B(e/f)$ is positive, negative
or zero. If $B(e/f)$ is zero then this much computation
may be necessary to learn that it is zero. But usually

B(e/f) will be non-zero, and indeed large enough that a
rather short approximate calculation will reveal the sign
of B(e/f) . Similarly, in the tangent construction we need
only compute the sign of the difference of the two tangent's
intercepts of the axis.

R. J. Fateman, in a private communication (about June
1976), informed me that he had achieved significant reduc-
tions in the computing time of the Collins-Loos algorithm
by pursuing this idea. His method was to evaluate B(e/f)
approximately using his computer's floating-point arithmetic
instructions and to separately evaluate another formula giving a bound on the error committed in the first evaluation.
If the error bound was not smaller than the approximate value,
then the evaluation would be repeated using exact arithmetic.

An alternative to this approach is to perform the evaluation of B(e/f) using interval arithmetic. If the interval computed does not contain zero, then the sign of B(e/f)
is known; otherwise exact arithmetic is used. This use of
interval arithmetic does not sacrifice the infallibility
of the algorithm whereas in Fateman's approach there is a
chance, however small, that inaccuracy in computing the error
bound results in an incorrect sign.

There are similar opportunities for the use of interval
arithmetic in the modified Uspensky algorithm. We have somewhat arbitrarily chosen to experiment first with its use
in the modified Uspensky algorithm; the methods and some
preliminary results are described below.

In the modified Uspensky algorithm, one isolates the
real roots of a polynomial $A(x) \epsilon Z[x]$ in the open interval
$(0,1)$. For any polynomial $B(x) \epsilon Z[x]$ with $\deg(B) = n > 0$,
let $H(B(x)) = 2^n B(x/2)$, $R(B(x)) = x^n B(1/x)$, $T(B(x)) = B(x+1)$
and $U(B(x)) = T(R(B(x)))$. If $\mathrm{var}(U(A)) \leq 1$ then we are
through; otherwise we compute $A_1 = H(A)$ and $A_2 = T(A_1)$,
corresponding to the intervals $(0,1/2)$ and $(1/2,1)$ respectively, noting that $A(1/2) = 0$ just in case $A_2(0) = 0$.
If $\mathrm{var}(U(A_1)) \geq 2$ then $(0,1/2)$ is bisected by computing
$A_{1,1} = H(A_1)$ and $A_{1,2} = T(A_{1,1})$; similarly for A_2 . In
general, the algorithm performs repeated interval bisections
and for each bisection several polynomial transformations

are carried out, specifically one H transformation, two
R transformations, and three T transformations. For fixed
coefficient size, the H and R transformations take time
proportional to n but the T transformation requires time
proportional to n^2 ; therefore almost all of the time for
the modified Uspensky algorithm is consumed by the T transformations and it is important to make them as fast as possible.

Of the three T transformations, one is used to compute
A_2 , which may be subjected to further transformations, while
the other two are used only to compute $var(U(A_1))$ and
$var(U(A_2))$; $U(A_1)$ and $U(A_2)$ are not then used in any further computations. Therefore, it was decided to continue
to compute A_2 exactly but to compute $U(A_1)$ and $U(A_2)$
using interval arithmetic whenever possible. If any interval coefficient of $U(A_i)$ has indeterminate sign, then
$U(A_i)$ is computed exactly.

The only arithmetic operation occurring in the T transformation is addition. Therefore interval addition was
programmed for SAC-1. For this system of interval arithmetic the interval endpoints are the elements of the set
F which contains zero and those non-zero rational numbers
u which can be expressed in the form $u = a \cdot 2^e$ with a
and e integers, $\beta/2 \leq |a| < \beta$ and $|e| < \beta$. Here β is
the base of the SAC-1 integer arithmetic system. β is
an implementation parameter which is required to be a power
of 2. In the UNIVAC 1110 implementation of SAC-1, $\beta = 2^{33}$.
For every $u \epsilon F$, $u \neq 0$, there is a unique pair (a,e) satisfying the stated conditions, and we say that (a,e) represents u . u=0 is, by convention, represented by (0,0) .

The basic algorithm for interval addition is an algo-
rithm FLSUM which, given $u, v \epsilon F$, computes the largest $w \epsilon F$
such that $w \leq u \cdot v$; if no such w exists then an "overflow"
message results. If now $u = [u_1, u_2]$ and $v = [v_1, v_2]$
are F-intervals then their F-interval sum is $w = [w_1, w_2]$
where $w_1 = FLSUM(u_1, v_1)$ and $w_2 = -FLSUM(-u_2, -v_2)$.

An FLSUM algorithm, which is computer independent,
was written in the ALDES language and translated into Fortran.
Because of its portability this algorithm will be very useful

but its efficiency leaves much to be desired. Therefore
another FLSUM, computer dependent, was programmed in the
UNIVAC assembly language. The execution time of the UNIVAC
FLSUM is highly variable, depending on the dozens of cases
which may occur, but in a sample of over 50,000 executions
its average execution time was 61 microseconds. The UNIVAC
1110 has several instructions for double-precision integer
arithmetic which were very useful for this application.
It is likely that an assembly language FLSUM would be significantly slower on many other computers. On the other
hand it is important to note that if a computer such as
the UNIVAC were equipped with a built-in instruction for
the FLSUM operation, which would be comparable to double-
precision floating-point addition, the time would likely
be reduced to about 10 microseconds.

The one T transformation which is performed exactly
has also been specially programmed for greater speed. Let
$B(x) = \sum_{i=0}^{m} b_i x^i$. Then the coefficients of B are transformed into the coefficients of T(B) by the sequence of
$\binom{m+1}{2}$ additions

(19)   for i=1,2,...,m
          do { for j=m,m-1,...,i do $b_{j-1} \leftarrow b_{j-1} + b_j$ }.

These additions are performed with the coefficients b_i
stored in an array, with k consecutive array positions
for each integer b_i , where β^k is an a priori bound for
all integers arising in the calculation. Then the inner
for-loop of (19) is carried out as if one were adding two
(overlapping) integers each (m-i+1)k β-digits in length,
since it is known in advance that carries across boundaries
between coefficients will not occur. In this way the required time is reduced to approximately 40k microseconds
per coefficient. For k=5 , a typical value, the time for
this "array" version of the T transformation is about
40% of the time for the standard "list processing" version
in which each coefficient is represented as a list of β-
digits and B is represented by a list of these coefficient
lists.

With these changes in the arithmetic of the T transformation we obtain the "improved modified Uspensky algorithm". Table 6 shows the computing times for this algorithm when applied to our same three sets of polynomials.
Since the times for degree 25 have now been again reduced
by a factor of 3 or 4, we now also boldly add polynomials
of degrees 30, 35 and 40.

TABLE 6

Computing Times, in Seconds, for the Improved
Modified Uspensky Real Root Isolation Algorithm

n	R	P	C
5	0.1	0.3	0.3
10	0.3	2.1	1.1
15	0.8	4.9	2.3
20	1.4	6.9	5.0
25	1.9	12.6	7.8
30	2.5	18.5	13.4
35	2.2	22.6	18.6
40	3.4	16.6	29.4

This application of interval arithmetic to computer
algebra has been extremely successful. Among all of the
T transformations performed with interval arithmetic for
the entries in Table 6, estimated at about 1500, only seven
transformations had to be repeated using interval arithmetic. These failures all occurred for the Chebyshev polynomials, one of them for degree 15 and two each for degrees
30, 35 and 40. We expect that other important applications
in computer algebra will soon be found, but it should be
emphasized that such applications must be carefully devised.
An important aspect of the application above is that the
interval arithmetic is interspersed with exact arithmetic
in such a manner that approximation errors do not accumulate indefinitely.

8.   COMPLEX ZEROS WITHOUT STURM SEQUENCES.

By the principle of argument, if A(z) is a non-zero

polynomial in $\underline{C}[z]$ and C is a simple closed curve in
the complex plane on which $A(z)$ does not vanish then the
net change in $\arg(A(z))$ as z traverses C counterclockwise is $2\pi k$ where k is the number of zeros of A inside
C . We can compute the change in $\arg(A(z))$ by observing
each crossing of a coordinate axis by $A(z)$, counting $+1$
for each crossing in the counterclockwise direction, -1
for each crossing in the clockwise direction. Thus if $A(z) =$
$A_1(z) + iA_2(z)$ where A_1 and A_2 are the real and imaginary parts of A , then it suffices to know the quadrant
of A , i.e. to know $\text{sign}(A_1)$ and $\text{sign}(A_2)$, between
each two consecutive crossing points, which crossing points
are the combined zeros of A_1 and A_2 .

We apply this method just in case C is the boundary
of a standard rectangle, and we divide C into its four
edges, counting quadrant changes separately on each edge.
Using the considerations of Section 2, we assume without
loss of generality that A is a squarefree polynomial with
Gaussian integer coefficients. On a horizontal edge, $z =$
$x+si$ with $r_1 \leq x \leq r_2$, where r_1, r_2 and s are binary
rational numbers. Then, for a suitable integer h, $2^h A(z) =$
$2^h A(x+si) = A_1(x) + iA_2(x)$ where A_1 and A_2 are integral
polynomials, and we are interested in the zeros of A_1 and
A_2 in the interval $[r_1, r_2]$. $A(z)$ will have a zero on
this edge just in case $B = \gcd(A_1, A_2)$ has a zero in $[r_1,$
$r_2]$. So we compute B and the cofactors $\bar{A}_1 = A_1/B$ and
$\bar{A}_2 = A_2/B$. The zeros of $\bar{A}_1$, $\bar{A}_2$ and B are all distinct,
and the zeros of B are all simple. The zeros of $\bar{A}_1$,
$\bar{A}_2$ and B in (r_1, r_2) are separately isolated and then,
with further refinement of the isolating intervals as required, the intervals are merged into a single list of disjoint intervals with each interval identified as to the
polynomial to which it belongs. For reasons yet to be explained, the endpoints r_1 and r_2 , which correspond to
vertices of the rectangle, are not included in the real
root isolation.

The quadrant number of $A(z)$ just to the left of a
zero of A_1 or A_2 is determined by computing $\text{sign}(A_1)$
and $\text{sign}(A_2)$ at the left endpoint of its isolating interval.

If the zero is a zero of $\bar{A}_1$ and if we already know the quadrant number to the right of this zero, then we need only compute sign(A_1) ; likewise for $\bar{A}_2$ and A_2 . The quadrant number to the right of the rightmost zero can be obtained using the right endpoint of its isolating interval unless the right endpoint is the zero, in which case the derivatives can be used. In passing through a zero of $\bar{A}_1$ or $\bar{A}_2$ the quadrant change is either +1, -1 or zero, zero just in case the multiplicity of the zero is even. In passing through a zero of B , the quadrant change is ambiguously either +1 (or -3), +2 (or -2), or +3 (or -1) ; it cannot be 0 since A has only simple zeros. A zero of B corresponds to a zero of A on the boundary, and the ambiguity is resolved by deciding whether to count or not count a zero on the boundary. Since we use standard rectangles, we count zeros on the upper and right edges, but not on the lower and left edges.

There remains a problem about zeros at the vertices of a rectangle, but again any ambiguity is resolved by deciding whether to count such a zero; for a standard rectangle only the upper right vertex is included.

This completes, in broad outline, the description of a method for reducing the problem of complex root isolation to that of real root isolation. Any algorithm for isolating the real roots of an integral polynomial in an interval can be used as a subalgorithm, and we have used the improved modified Uspensky algorithm of the preceding section.

Some results, for random polynomials with 33-bit integer coefficients, are shown in Table 7. For purpose of comparison, Table 7 repeats, in the left column, the times from Table 3 which were obtained using Pinkert's Sturm sequence algorithm.

These results indicate a very substantial improvement over the Sturm sequence algorithm and yet leave a great deal to be desired. It is probable that further improvements can still be made in this new algorithm without altering its basic approach. For example, there are transformations of A(z) such as A(x+si) which could be performed within an array, and there are evaluations A(r+si) which could be performed with interval arithmetic. However, such improvements will likely be modest in their effects and so it appears that a different method will be required to achieve the greater improvements which are needed. One possibility might be to use interval arithmetic versions of some combination of Pinkert's Sturm sequence algorithms as a fast means of determining the number of roots in a rectangle in most cases. In case of failure, the algorithm described above would be used as backup.

TABLE 7

Computing Times, in Seconds, for Complex Root Isolation

n	T_1	T_2
5	14	18
8	62	48
10	262	67
15		174

REFERENCES

1. E. R. Berlekamp (1968), Algebraic Coding Theory, Mc-Graw-Hill.

2. E. R. Berlekamp (1970), Factoring Polynomials over Large Finite Fields, Math. Comp., 24, pp. 713-735.

3. W. S. Brown (1971), On Euclid's Algorithm and the Computation of Polynomial Greatest Common Divisors, JACM, 18, pp. 478-504.

4. W. S. Brown and J. F. Traub (1971), On Euclid's Algorithm and the Theory of Subresultants, JACM, 18, pp. 505-514.

5. B. F. Caviness and M. Rothstein (1975), A Modular Greatest Common Divisor Algorithm for Gaussian Polynomials, ACM '75 Conference Proceedings, pp. 270-273.

6. B. F. Caviness and G. E. Collins (1976), Algorithms for Gaussian Integer Arithmetic, Proceedings of the 1976 ACM Symposium on Symbolic and Algebraic Computation, pp. 36-45, ACM.

7. G. E. Collins (1967), Subresultants and Reduced Polynomial Remainder Sequences, JACM, 14, pp. 128-142.

8. G. E. Collins (1972), The SAC-1 Polynomial GCD and Resultant System, Univ. of Wisconsin Computer Sciences Dept. Tech. Report No. 145.

9. G. E. Collins (1973), Computer Algebra of Polynomials and Rational Functions, Am. Math. Monthly, 80, pp. 725-755.

10. G. E. Collins (1975), Quantifier Elimination for Real Closed Fields by Cylindrical Algebraic Decomposition, Lecture Notes in Computer Science, 33, pp. 134-183, Springer Verlag.

11. G. E. Collins and A. G. Akritas (1976), Polynomial Real Root Isolation Using Descartes' Rule of Signs, Proceedings of the 1976 ACM Symposium on Symbolic and Algebraic Computation, pp. 272-275, ACM.

12. G. E. Collins and E. Horowitz (1974), The Minimum Root Separation of a Polynomial, Math. Comp., 28, pp. 589-597.

13. G. E. Collins and R. Loos (1976), Polynomial Real Root Isolation by Differentiation, Proceedings of the 1976 ACM Symposium on Symbolic and Algebraic Computation, pp. 15-25, ACM.

14. L. E. Heindel (1970), Algorithms for Exact Polynomial Root Calculation, Ph.D. Thesis, Computer Sciences Dept., Univ. of Wisconsin.

15. L. E. Heindel (1971), Integer Arithmetic Algorithms for Polynomial Real Zero Determination, JACM, 18, pp. 533-548.

16. D. E. Knuth (1969), The Art of Computer Programming, Vol. 2 (Seminumerical Algorithms), Addison-Wesley.

17. M. Mignotte (1974), An Inequality About Factors of Polynomials, Math. Comp., 28, pp. 1153-1157.

18. M. Mignotte (1976), Some Problems about Polynomials, Proceedings of the 1976 ACM Symposium on Symbolic and Algebraic Computation, pp. 227-228, ACM.

19. D. R. Musser (1971), Algorithms for Polynomial Factorization, Ph.D. Thesis, Computer Sciences Dept., Univ. of Wisconsin.

20. D. R. Musser (1975), Multivariate Polynomial Factorization, JACM, 22, pp. 291-308.

21. J. R. Pinkert (1973), Algebraic Algorithms for Computing the Complex Zeros of Gaussian Polynomials, Ph.D. Thesis, Computer Sciences Dept., Univ. of Wisconsin.

22. J. R. Pinkert (1976), An Exact Method for Finding the Roots of a Complex Polynomial, TOMS, 2, pp. 351-363.

23. S. Rump (1976), Ein Algorithmus zur Isolierung der reelen Nullstellen eines Polynoms mit algebraischen Koeffizienten, Rechenzeitanalyse und Implementierung, Diplomarbeit, Universität Kaiserslautern.

24. J. V. Uspensky (1948), Theory of Equations, McGraw-Hill.

25. M. Vincent (1836), Sur la Résolution des Équationes Numeriques, Jour. de Mathematiques Pures et Appliquees, 1, pp. 341-372.

Acknowledgement. This research was partially supported by National Science Foundation Grant MCS74-13278-A01. The algorithms described in the last two sections were developed with the extremely competent assistance of T. J. Chou.

Computer Sciences Department
The University of Wisconsin
Madison, Wisconsin 53706

Representation and Approximation of Surfaces

Robert E. Barnhill

ABSTRACT

The modelling of free-form surfaces comes up in many applications. Examples are the design of airplanes, automobiles, ships, and bottles, and modelling the surface of the human heart and of scientific phenomena.

Effective interactive design usually requires the use of local interpolation schemes. We discuss "Coons patches", defined over squares and triangles, as well as generalizations of these methods. We also consider interpolation to arbitrarily spaced data and show how to combine these methods with the patch methods, in order to achieve more smoothness and fairer shapes.

This paper contains pictures from several editing sessions with our computer software system, SURFED. The interactive design capabilities of SURFED are illustrated in the movie which goes with this paper.

69

TABLE OF CONTENTS

1.   INTRODUCTION.

2.   INTERPOLATION METHODS DEFINED OVER RECTANGLES.

3.   INTERPOLATION METHODS DEFINED OVER TRIANGLES.

4.   INTERPOLATION METHODS FOR ARBITRARILY PLACED DATA.

5.   CONCLUSIONS.

1.   <u>INTRODUCTION</u>.

This paper is a survey of methods for representing surfaces. We consider "free-form" or "sculptured" surfaces, that
is, surfaces that are truly bivariate, rather than univariate
ones such as surfaces of revolution. We consider a variety
of data which, in particular, are not restricted to being
tensor product data.

There are many applications of surface approximation.
Some applications involve real-time interactive graphics, examples of which are shown in the movie that goes with this
paper. These applications include the design of the surfaces
of automobiles, airplanes, and ships. In these cases a designer makes changes to obtain a "fairer" surface, which must
be redisplayed quickly. For such real-time displays, "local"
methods are usually necessary. Other applications involve
modelling a surface, such as the human heart or brain or min-
eral deposits in the earth, from a set of spatial measurements. This kind of surface modelling may or may not be interactive. It does involve arbitrarily spaced data. Surfaces
that need not be displayed interactively can be based either
on global or local methods.

There are three geometric building blocks for surfaces:
squares, triangles, and points. Such surfaces can be written
parametrically, that is, a generic point (x,y,z) has the

equations

$$x = x(u,v), \quad y = y(u,v), \quad z = z(u,v) \, .$$

Section 2 deals with interpolation schemes defined over rectangles. These are the simplest bivariate interpolants and
hence preferable when they can be used, such as when the data
are given along "coordinate" lines. "Coons patches" are interpolants of this type defined over lines parallel to the
coordinate axes in the parametric uv-plane. These "transfinite" elements can be discretized to yield finite dimensional interpolants, which include the "serendipity elements"
of the (structural) engineers, as well as tensor product interpolants. Recently J. A. Gregory and L. E. Mansfield discovered that for Coons patches to be "smooth", i.e., C^1 or
better, requires that certain "compatibility conditions" hold.
The Coons patch and most standard transfinite interpolants,
as well as their discretizations, are not compatible. Ways to
fix this are given in Section 2.

Section 3 concerns interpolation over triangles. Triangles are essentially bivariate and hence are reasonable geometric units for truly bivariate problems. The first step in
forming such a surface is to obtain a triangulation of the
interpolation points. The triangulation is done as a two-
stage process: a first triangulation is obtained and it is
then "optimized". The next step is to use an appropriate interpolant. There is a wide choice, of which many are given
in Section 3. These include several triangular Coons patches
as well as finite dimensional interpolants.

Section 4 deals with interpolation to arbitrary point
data. Procedures for handling such data include the following:

(1) Use a global method such as Shepard's Formula.

(2) Mollify the global method into a local method.

(3) Triangulate and use the methods of Section 3.

Section 4 also contains combinations of methods. Barnhill
and Gregory (1975b) have shown that a Boolean sum $P \oplus Q$ has
at least the interpolation properties of P and the function
precision of Q . This Theorem has been used to construct

new, special purpose interpolants. Generalizations of
Shepard's Formula are also presented in this Section.

2.   INTERPOLATION METHODS DEFINED OVER RECTANGLES.

S. A. Coons' famous "little red book" (1964) introduced
interpolation schemes which are smooth and locally defined
over rectangles. The bilinearly blended Coons patch defined
on the unit square S: $0 \leqslant u,v \leqslant 1$, is given by

(2.1) $B(u,v) = \begin{bmatrix} 1-u & u \end{bmatrix} \begin{bmatrix} F(0,v) \\ F(1,v) \end{bmatrix} + \begin{bmatrix} F(u,0) & F(u,1) \end{bmatrix} \begin{bmatrix} 1-v \\ v \end{bmatrix}$

$- \begin{bmatrix} 1-u & u \end{bmatrix} \begin{bmatrix} F(0,0) & F(0,1) \\ F(1,0) & F(1,1) \end{bmatrix} \begin{bmatrix} 1-v \\ v \end{bmatrix}$

This scheme interpolates to positional data all around the
boundary of S, i.e., $B(u,0) = F(u,0)$, etc. Gordon calls
$B(u,v)$ a "transfinite" patch, to distinguish it from finite
dimensional interpolants. If $F(0,v)$ etc. are replaced by
their linear interpolants, e.g.,

(2.2) $F(0,v) \approx \tilde{F}(0,v) \equiv (1-v)F(0,0) + vF(0,1)$,

the result is the familiar bilinear interpolant, which is the
third term of (2.1). Picture 1 illustrates this bilinear interpolant. Our interactive graphics system, SURFED, contains
geometric handles with which to manipulate surfaces. Picture
1 is the resulting surface after a position has been moved,
starting with the identically zero function. SURFED has been
developed by F. F. Little, R. P. Dube, and G. J. Herron.

The C^1 bicubically blended Coons patch interpolates to
position and normal derivatives all around the boundary of
S . The bicubically blended Coons patch is the following:

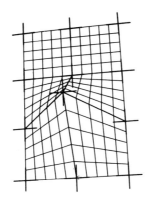

Picture 1.   Parametric Bilinear Interpolant

(2.3) $PF(u,v) = [h_0(u) \; h_1(u) \; \bar{h}_0(u) \; \bar{h}_1(u)] \begin{bmatrix} F(0,v) \\ F(1,v) \\ F_{1,0}(0,v) \\ F_{1,0}(1,v) \end{bmatrix}$

$+ \; [F(u,0) \; F(u,1) \; F_{0,1}(u,0) \; F_{0,1}(u,1)] \begin{bmatrix} h_0(v) \\ h_1(v) \\ \bar{h}_0(v) \\ \bar{h}_1(v) \end{bmatrix}$

$- \; [h_0(u) \; h_1(u) \; \bar{h}_0(u) \; \bar{h}_1(u)] \; B \begin{bmatrix} h_0(v) \\ h_1(v) \\ \bar{h}_0(v) \\ \bar{h}_1(v) \end{bmatrix} \qquad \text{where}$

$$(2.4)$$

$$B = \begin{bmatrix} F(0,0) & F(0,1) & F_{0,1}(0,0) & F_{0,1}(0,1) \\[2ex] F(1,0) & F(1,1) & F_{0,1}(1,0) & F_{0,1}(1,1) \\[4ex] F_{1,0}(0,0)\ F_{1,0}(0,1) & & \frac{\partial}{\partial u}F_{0,1}(0,0)\ \frac{\partial}{\partial u}F_{0,1}(0,1) \\[2ex] F_{1,0}(1,0)\ F_{1,0}(1,1) & & \frac{\partial}{\partial u}F_{0,1}(1,0)\ \frac{\partial}{\partial u}F_{0,1}(1,1) \end{bmatrix}.$$

The h_i and $\bar{h}_i$ are the univariate cubic Hermite basis functions

$$(2.5) \qquad h_0(t) = (1-t)^2(2t+1) \qquad \bar{h}_0(t) = t(1-t)^2$$

$$h_1(t) = t^2(-2t+3) \qquad \bar{h}_1(t) = t^2(t-1) .$$

The values $F(u,0)$, $F(u,1)$, $F(0,v)$, $F(1,v)$ represent positions around the boundary of the square S. The values $F_{0,1}(u,0)$, $F_{0,1}(u,1)$, $F_{1,0}(0,v)$, $F_{1,0}(1,v)$ represent derivatives in the directions normal to the sides of S. The parametric surface given by (2.3) is the sum of three terms. Let the first two terms be called P_1F and P_2F, respectively. That is,

$$(2.6) \qquad P_1F = h_0(u)F(0,v) \qquad + \quad h_1(u)F(1,v)$$

$$+ \ \bar{h}_0(u)F_{1,0}(0,v) \quad + \quad \bar{h}_1(u)F_{1,0}(1,v)$$

$$(2.7) \qquad P_2F = h_0(v)F(u,0) \qquad + \quad h_1(v)F(u,1)$$

$$+ \ \bar{h}_0(v)F_{0,1}(u,0) \quad + \quad \bar{h}_1(v)F_{0,1}(u,1) .$$

P_1F and P_2F are called "lofting" interpolants. The third term of (2.3) is the composition P_1P_2F, called the tensor product of P_1 and P_2. W. J. Gordon (1969,1971) has observed that $P = P_1 + P_2 - P_1P_2$ is the Boolean sum $P_1 \oplus P_2$. He has explored many of the algebraic properties of such interpolants. For example, the tensor product can be obtained by discretizing the lofting interpolants:

$$(2.8) \qquad F(u,0) \simeq \tilde{F}(u,0) \equiv h_0(u)F(0,0) + h_1(u)F(1,0)$$

$$+ \ \bar{h}_0(u)F_{1,0}(0,0) + \bar{h}_1(u)F_{1,0}(1,0) .$$

$$(2.9) \quad F_{0,1}(u,0) \simeq \tilde{F}_{0,1}(u,0) \equiv h_0(u)F_{0,1}(0,0) + h_1(u)F_{0,1}(1,0)$$

$$+ \bar{h}_0(u) \left. \frac{\partial F_{0,1}(u,0)}{\partial u} \right|_{u=0} + \bar{h}_1(u) \left. \frac{\partial F_{0,1}(u,0)}{\partial u} \right|_{u=1}$$

etc. The tensor product matrix B may be considered as a partitioned matrix of the form

$$(2.10) \quad \begin{bmatrix} \text{Positions} & \vdots & \text{v-Slopes} \\ \text{-----------} & \text{+} & \text{---------} \\ \text{u-Slopes} & \vdots & \text{Twists} \end{bmatrix}$$

The "twists" are the (1,1) derivatives. These are usually assumed to be independent of the order of differentiation, i.e., $\frac{\partial^2 F}{\partial u \partial v} = \frac{\partial^2 F}{\partial v \partial u}$, but this is false in cases of practical use, as we shall see. Since twists are difficult to envision, a standard procedure has been to set all the twists equal to zero. The geometric effect is to produce "pseudo-flats", i.e., flat spots, on the bicubic surface. An explanation of these flat spots is that this approximation is exact only for linear functions of u and v, which contrasts unfavorably with the bicubic precision of the original bicubic patch.

Barnhill, Brown, and Klucewicz (1977) have developed two c^1 schemes for computing twists as input data, based on preprocessing with c^0 schemes. Our paper also describes two other methods that do not require the calculation of twists as input data. These two methods are called "Gregory's square" and "Brown's square", respectively. Picture 2 is an editing session with 16-parameter bicubic patches. The geometric handles for bicubic patches are positions, tangents, and twists, i.e., the numbers in the partitions of the matrix B . The intersecting parabolas are the twist handles. At a given interpolation point, the two parabolas are the cross-sections of the local bilinear Taylor expansion at that point. The twist and tangent handles at an interpolation point form an eight-legged "spider". (Creator: F. F. Little)

Compatibility Conditions.

The original bicubically blended Coons patch given by (2.3) does not interpolate to all the given data. By direct calculation,

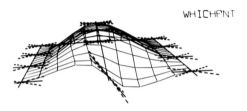

a. Original Function

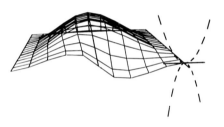

b. Twist Handle

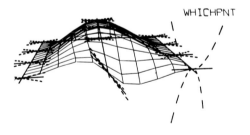

c. New Surface

Picture 2. Editing Session with Bicubic Patches

WHICHPNT

a. Zero Function

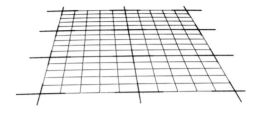

b. Position Handle

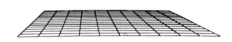

WHICHPNT

c. New Surface

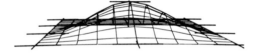

d. Tangent Handle

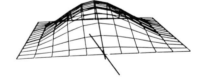

WHICHPNT

e. New Surface

Picture 3. Editing Session with Twelve Parameter Patch

(2.11) $\left.\dfrac{\partial PF}{\partial v}\right|_{v=0} =$

$F_{0,1}(u,0) + [\overline{h}_0(u)\overline{h}_1(u)]$ $\begin{bmatrix} \dfrac{\partial^2 F}{\partial v \partial u}(0,0) - \dfrac{\partial^2 F}{\partial u \partial v}(0,0) \\[2mm] \dfrac{\partial^2 F}{\partial v \partial u}(0,1) - \dfrac{\partial^2 F}{\partial u \partial v}(0,1) \end{bmatrix}$.

Compare equation (2.8) in Gregory (1974). The notation $\dfrac{\partial^2 F}{\partial u \partial v}(0,0)$ means $\left.\left.\dfrac{\partial}{\partial u}\left\{\dfrac{\partial F}{\partial v}\right|_{v=0}\right\}\right|_{u=0}$, etc. A result analogous to (2.11) also holds along $v=1$. The other interpolation conditions are all satisfied. Barnhill and Gregory (1975b) state a general theorem concerning such interpolation results. By (2.11), a necessary and sufficient condition for inter- polation to $\dfrac{\partial F}{\partial v}$ along $v=0$ and $v=1$ is that the twists be equal:

(2.12) $\dfrac{\partial^2 F}{\partial u \partial v} = \dfrac{\partial^2 F}{\partial v \partial u}$ at the four corners.

(2.12) is called a "compatibility condition". If the function F exists as a bivariate function, $F = F(u,v)$, then one can assume that $F \in C^{1,1}$ so that the compatibility conditions hold. However, in many practical applications, F is de- fined only for the values used in (2.3), which are called "wire frame data".

Gregory's Square.

This is a compatibly corrected bicubic Coons patch. (See equation (2.7) in Gregory (1974).) It can be written in the same form as (2.3) except that the twist partition in (2.3) is replaced by the following variable twist partition:

$$\begin{bmatrix} \dfrac{u\dfrac{\partial^2 F}{\partial v \partial u}(0,0) + v\dfrac{\partial^2 F}{\partial u \partial v}(0,0)}{u+v} & \dfrac{-u\dfrac{\partial^2 F}{\partial v \partial u}(0,1) + (v-1)\dfrac{\partial^2 F}{\partial u \partial v}(0,1)}{-u+v-1} \\[4mm] \dfrac{(1-u)\dfrac{\partial^2 F}{\partial v \partial u}(1,0) + v\dfrac{\partial^2 F}{\partial u \partial v}(1,0)}{1-u+v} & \dfrac{(u-1)\dfrac{\partial^2 F}{\partial v \partial u}(1,1) + (v-1)\dfrac{\partial^2 F}{\partial u \partial v}(1,1)}{u+v-2} \end{bmatrix}$$

(2.13)
(The (1,0) term in Gregory's article is incorrect and is cor- rected by (2.13).) If $\dfrac{\partial^2 F}{\partial v \partial u} = \dfrac{\partial^2 F}{\partial u \partial v}$ at the four corners,

then (2.13) reduces to the tensor product twist partition in (2.4). To obtain a finite dimensional interpolant, we can let the positions be cubic Hermite and the normal derivatives be either linear or cubic Hermite. These two possibilities lead to c^1 interpolants with 12 and 20 parameters, respectively. The twist partition for the 12 and 20 parameter interpolants has $\frac{\partial^2 F}{\partial u \partial v}$ and $\frac{\partial^2 F}{\partial v \partial u}$ interchanged from (2.13).

The 12-parameter case is illustrated in Picture 3. This editing session shows the effect of changing positions and slopes. The handles are manipulated with a cursor controlled by a stylus on a tablet. The interactive display terminal is an Evans and Sutherland Picture System I on a PDP 11/45 computer.

Little's Square.

F. F. Little has generalized these compatibility correction terms to take care of incompatibilities in F, $F_{1,0}$, and $F_{0,1}$, as well as $F_{1,1}$, at the corners. These incompatibilities arise in practice when independent measurements are taken along parallels to orthogonal axes. Little's interpolant LF is of the same form as (2.3) except that the matrix corresponding to $P_1 P_2$ is replaced by the following partitioned matrix:

$$(2.14) \quad \left[\begin{array}{c|c} F & F_{0,1} \\ \hline F_{1,0} & F_{1,1} \end{array} \right] \quad \text{where}$$

$$F = \left[\begin{array}{c|c} \dfrac{u^2 P_1 F(0,0) + v^2 P_2 F(0,0)}{u^2 + v^2} & \dfrac{u^2 P_1 F(0,1) + (1-v)^2 P_2 F(0,1)}{u^2 + (1-v)^2} \\ \hline \dfrac{(1-u)^2 P_1 F(1,0) + v^2 P_2 F(1,0)}{(1-u)^2 + v^2} & \dfrac{(1-u)^2 P_1 F(1,1) + (1-v)^2 P_2 F(1,1)}{(1-u)^2 + (1-v)^2} \end{array} \right]$$

where $P_1 F(0,0) \equiv \lim_{v \to 0} P_1 F(0,v) = \lim_{v \to 0} F(0,v)$, etc. and, dually,

$$P_2 F(0,0) \equiv \lim_{u \to 0} P_2 F(u,0) = \lim_{u \to 0} F(u,0),$$

$$F_{1,0}=\begin{bmatrix} \dfrac{u\dfrac{\partial P_1 F}{\partial u}(0,0)+v^2\dfrac{\partial P_2 F}{\partial u}(0,0)}{u + v^2} & \dfrac{u\dfrac{\partial P_1 F}{\partial u}(0,1)+(1-v)^2\dfrac{\partial P_2 F}{\partial u}(0,1)}{u + (1-v)^2} \\[4ex] \dfrac{(1-u)\dfrac{\partial P_1 F}{\partial u}(1,0)+v^2\dfrac{\partial P_2}{\partial u}(1,0)}{1-u + v^2} & \dfrac{(1-u)\dfrac{\partial P_1 F}{\partial u}(1,1)+(1-v)^2\dfrac{\partial P_2 F}{\partial u}(1,1)}{1-u + (1-v)^2} \end{bmatrix}$$

where $\dfrac{\partial P_1 F}{\partial u}(0,0)\equiv\lim\limits_{v\to 0}\dfrac{\partial P_1 F}{\partial u}(0,v)=\lim\limits_{v\to 0}\dfrac{\partial F(0,v)}{\partial u}$, etc. and, dually,

$\dfrac{\partial P_2 F}{\partial u}(0,0)\equiv\lim\limits_{u\to 0}\dfrac{\partial P_2 F}{\partial u}(u,0)=\lim\limits_{u\to 0}\dfrac{\partial F(u,0)}{\partial u}$, etc.

$$F_{0,1}=\begin{bmatrix} \dfrac{u^2\dfrac{\partial P_1 F}{\partial v}(0,0)+v\dfrac{\partial P_2 F}{\partial v}(0,0)}{u^2 + v} & \dfrac{u^2\dfrac{\partial P_1 F}{\partial v}(0,1)+(1-v)\dfrac{\partial P_2 F}{\partial v}(0,1)}{u^2 + 1-v} \\[4ex] \dfrac{(1-u)^2\dfrac{\partial P_1 F}{\partial v}(1,0)+v\dfrac{\partial P_2}{\partial v}(1,0)}{(1-u)^2 + v} & \dfrac{(1-u)^2\dfrac{\partial P_1 F}{\partial v}(1,1)+(1-v)\dfrac{\partial P_2}{\partial v}(1,1)}{(1-u)^2 + 1-v} \end{bmatrix}$$

where $\dfrac{\partial P_1 F}{\partial v}(0,0)\equiv\lim\limits_{v\to 0}\dfrac{\partial P_1 F}{\partial v}(0,v)=\lim\limits_{v\to 0}\dfrac{\partial F(0,v)}{\partial v}$, etc. and, dually,

$\dfrac{\partial P_2 F}{\partial v}(0,0)\equiv\lim\limits_{u\to 0}\dfrac{\partial P_2 F}{\partial v}(u,0)=\lim\limits_{u\to 0}\dfrac{\partial F(u,0)}{\partial v}$, etc.

$$F_{1,1}=\begin{bmatrix} \dfrac{u\dfrac{\partial^2 P_1 F}{\partial v\partial u}(0,0)+v\dfrac{\partial^2 P_2 F}{\partial u\partial v}(0,0)}{u + v} & \dfrac{-u\dfrac{\partial^2 P_1 F}{\partial v\partial u}(0,1)+(v-1)\dfrac{\partial^2 P_2 F}{\partial u\partial v}(0,1)}{-u + v-1} \\[4ex] \dfrac{(1-u)\dfrac{\partial^2 P_1 F}{\partial v\partial u}(1,0)+v\dfrac{\partial^2 P_2 F}{\partial u\partial v}(1,0)}{1-u + v} & \dfrac{(u-1)\dfrac{\partial^2 P_1 F}{\partial v\partial u}(1,1)+(v-1)\dfrac{\partial^2 P_2 F}{\partial u\partial v}(1,1)}{u + v-2} \end{bmatrix}$$

where $\dfrac{\partial^2 P_1 F}{\partial v\partial u}(0,0)\equiv\dfrac{\partial}{\partial v}\{\dfrac{\partial P_1 F}{\partial u}(0,v)\}\Big|_{v=0}=\dfrac{\partial}{\partial v}\{\dfrac{\partial F(0,v)}{\partial u}\}\Big|_{v=0}$ etc. and,

dually, $\dfrac{\partial^2 P_2 F}{\partial u\partial v}(0,0)\equiv\dfrac{\partial}{\partial u}\{\dfrac{\partial P_2 F}{\partial v}(u,0)\}\Big|_{u=0}=\dfrac{\partial}{\partial u}\{\dfrac{\partial F(u,0)}{\partial v}\}\Big|_{u=0}$ etc.

The reader may check that LF interpolates to F and F's
normal derivative all around the square, the most worthwhile
cases being $\left. \frac{\partial LF}{\partial u} \right|_{u=0,1}$. Notice the elegantly symmetric
roles played by P_1 and P_2 in these matrices.

   If the positions and normal derivatives are replaced by
their cubic Hermite interpolants, then P_1F and P_2F must
be interchanged in (2.14).

Brown's Square.

   Gregory observed that incompatibilities arise in Boolean
sums $P \oplus Q \equiv P+Q-PQ$ in the composition PQ . So he invented a "symmetric scheme" for the triangle which avoids com-
positions (See Section 3.). J. H. Brown invented a scheme
for the square that is somewhat similar in form to "Gregory's
triangle". Let

(2.15) $BF(u,v) = \alpha(u,v)P_1F(u,v) + \beta(u,v)P_2F(u,v)$

where $\alpha(u,v) = \dfrac{v^2(1-v)^2}{u^2(1-u)^2+v^2(1-v)^2}$, $\beta(u,v)=\dfrac{u^2(1-u)^2}{u^2(1-u)^2+v^2(1-v)^2}$.

BF is a convex combination of the two lofting interpolants
P_1F and P_2F . BF interpolates to F and its normal derivative all around the square and hence, over a network of
rectangles, is a C^1 interpolant. BF can be generalized to
being a C^n interpolant by replacing "2" by "n+1" in the
definitions of α and β, and P_1F and P_2F by their C^n
2-point Taylor interpolants. (The general 2-point Taylor
expansion is given in Davis (1963), p. 37.) BF is symmetric
in that $\beta(u,v)=\alpha(v,u)$ and P_1 and P_2 are both the univariate cubic Hermite interpolation operator. The monomial
precision of convex combinations is usually just the intersection of the components, P_1 and P_2 in (2.6) and (2.7).
The precision of B is, $\{u^iv^j, 0 \leq i,j \leq 3\}$, i.e., the
bicubic polynomials. BF can also be discretized, in the
same two ways as Gregory's square: Let the positions be
their cubic Hermite interpolants and the normal derivatives
be either linear or cubic Hermite. These choices lead to 20
and 12-parameter interpolants, respectively, formulas for
which are given in Barnhill, Brown, and Klucewicz (1977).

3.   INTERPOLATION SCHEMES DEFINED OVER TRIANGLES.

   a. Preprocessor: Triangulation

   Before coming to interpolation schemes defined over triangles, we need the triangles themselves. The triangles may
occasionally be user-specified, but usually not. Surprisingly, it's an open question as to how "best" triangulate a
given set of points $\{(x_i, y_i)\}_{i=1}^{n}$.

   (1) An Initial Triangulation

   The first step is to find a triangulation. This triangulation will then be improved by one of several optimizations. We mention two triangulations, the second being used
in the movie accompanying the verbal version of this paper.

   (i) Klucewicz' triangulation (1977).

   The key idea of this triangulation is: What points can
be seen from an edge?

   The algorithm is as follows: Form a first triangle
from the leftmost point and its two nearest neighbors. Given
the edge E_m as in Figure 3.1, consider those points that
can be "seen" from E_m. In Figure 3.1, (x_i, y_i) and (x_j, y_j)
can be seen from E_m and (x_n, y_n) cannot.

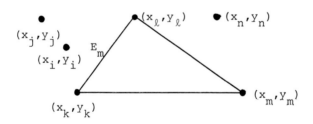

Figure 3.1 Klucewicz' Triangulation

   The point (x_i, y_i), nearest to the ends of E_m, is used to
form new triangles if possible. Checks are made to avoid
forming overlapping triangles or leaving "holes" in the triangulated region. A more precise statement of the algorithm,
as well as examples, is given in Klucewicz (1977). Pictures
7-10 were made with Klucewicz' method.

(ii) <u>Little's triangulation (1977)</u>.

The key idea of this triangulation is: What edges can be seen from a point?

Little's triangulation forms a convex region at each stage. The algorithm is as follows: Choose an origin. Then the points are sorted by increasing Euclidean distance from this origin. The first triangle is formed from the three points nearest the origin which are not collinear. As in Figure 3.2, let (x_i, y_i) be a point,i, not yet used. Point i can "see" edge E_{jk} if and only if i is on the opposite side of E_{jk} from the current triangulation T . The boundary of T is oriented counter-clockwise.

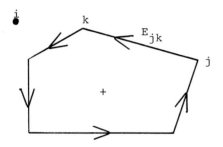

Figure 3.2 Little's Triangulation

Hence the determinant

(3.1) $D_{jk}(x,y) \equiv \begin{vmatrix} x_j & y_j & 1 \\ x_k & y_k & 1 \\ x & y & 1 \end{vmatrix}$ is positive

if and only if (x,y) lies to the left of E_{jk}. So the new triangle kij is added to T if and only if $D_{jk}(x_i, y_i) < 0$. For fixed i, one stage of this algorithm is to compare (x_i, y_i) with all of the boundary segments of T . The concluding step of one stage is to update the boundary of the new convex region T' by deleting the edges of T that are interior to T' . The menu for Little's algorithm is given in Picture 4.

(2) Optimizing a Triangulation

Little has developed several criteria for optimizing a triangulation. These are based on C. L. Lawson's idea (Lawson 1972) that there are two possible triangulations of a convex quadrilateral. Little's algorithm is as follows: Select one of the optimization criteria from the menu shown in Picture 4e. Form a first triangle. Each of its edges is shared with another triangle and so three quadrilaterals could be formed. (Boundary segments are bypassed.) Consider the neighboring triangle with lowest index and check to see if the corresponding quadrilateral is convex. If not, pass on; if so, then apply the optimization criterion selected.

Optimization Criterion.

Each optimization is an "optimal estimation in the sense of Golomb and Weinberger", which means to maximize a minimum. For example, the seventh criterion in the menu of Picture 4e is to   maximize   minimum   (area of inscribed circle/area of
          all T T

triangle). This criterion is rated as the best of the seven by Little. The above ratio is proportional to (area of the triangle/perimeter squared), which is what's actually computed.

If a change of triangles occurs, then a flag is set and one proceeds to the next triangle in the list. The algorithm terminates when the triangle list is gone through without a change.

The availability of this optimization technique makes the initial triangulation less important.

Both Klucewicz' and Little's triangulations produce the convex hull of the given points, a problem of frequent interest in its own right.

For these triangulations, the stopping criterion is simply that no more triangles can be formed. If the points are classified a priori as boundary and interior points, respectively, then

(3.2)   number of triangles = b + 2i - 2

where b is the number of boundary points and i is the num-

ber of interior points, respectively. This provides a precise stopping criterion if b and i are known. Formula
(3.2) was discovered by G. J. Herron. Subsequently, B. E.
Brown pointed out its occurrence in Ewing et al (1970).

Picture 4 a., b., and c. shows the initial points to be
triangulated, followed by Little's initial triangulation and
optimization. The menu options: ORIGIN permits the origin
to be chosen with the cursor. SORT causes the points to be
sorted into order from the origin. Sorting by Euclidean distance keeps the new points of interpolation from being in the
already formed convex triangulation. The DRW (drawing) options permit one to watch the formation of the triangles.
Long skinny triangles can certainly result from the initial
triangulation - compare the one that looks like a line segment in b . The optimization criterion is the one mentioned
earlier, as is indicated by the label in the upper left corner of c .

Picture 4 d., e., and f. shows an initial triangulation
followed by two different optimizations the first being:

$$\max_{\text{all } T} \quad \min_{\text{angles } \theta \text{ in } T} \quad \sin\theta$$

and the second as before.

Algorithm for Determining Which Triangle a Point Is in

Our surfaces are drawn along mesh lines and so, given a
point (x,y) , we must find which triangle (x,y) is in.
$D_{jk}(x,y)$ defined in (3.1) equals twice the area of the triangle with vertices $V_j=(x_j,y_j)$, $V_k=(x_k,y_k)$, and $V=(x,y)$.
For exposition, let's renumber V_j as V_1 and V_k as V_2 ,
respectively. Let V_3 be an interpolation point such that
the triangle 123 with vertices V_1,V_2,V_3 is in the triangulation T . The barycentric, or areal, coordinates of
$V=(x,y)$ are (b_1,b_2,b_3) where, e.g.,

(3.3) $b_1 = A_1/A$

where A_1 is the area of the subtriangle with vertices
V,V_2,V_3 and A is the area of triangle 123. b_2 and b_3
are analogously defined. See Figure 3.3.

ENOUGH

a. Spots

DRWOPT	DRWPNT	DRWTRG	DRWINT
1ST TRGL	EXTTRGLS	INTTRGLS	OPTIMIZE
QUIT	ORIGIN	POINTS	SORT

EXTTRGLS

b. Initial Triangulation

DRWOPT	DRWPNT	DRWTRG	DRWINT
1ST TRGL	EXTTRGLS	INTTRGLS	OPTIMIZE
QUIT	ORIGIN	POINTS	SORT

AREA/INS   CRITRION

c. Optimized Triangulation

DRWOPT	DRWPNT	DRWTRG	DRWINT
1ST TRGL	EXTTRGLS	INTTRGLS	OPTIMIZE
QUIT	ORIGIN	POINTS	SORT

Picture 4. Triangulation

d. Initial Triangulation

DRWOPT	DRWPNT	DRWTRG	DRWINT
1ST TRGL	EXTTRGLS	INTTRGLS	OPTIMIZE
QUIT	ORIGIN	POINTS	SORT

e. Optimized Triangulation

SINE XSML	LI/LJ-LK	SEC LARG	
AREA	SHORT/PR	RAD INS	AREA/INS

f. Optimized Triangulation

DRWOPT	DRWPNT	DRWTRG	DRWINT
1ST TRGL	EXTTRGLS	INTTRGLS	OPTIMIZE
QUIT	ORIGIN	POINTS	SORT

Picture 4. Triangulation

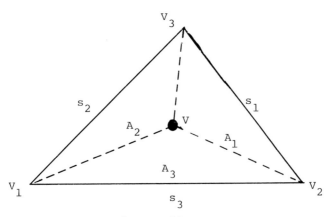

Figure 3.3 Barycentric Coordinates

The formula used to compute b_1 is

$$(3.3)' \quad \frac{A_1}{A} = \frac{\begin{vmatrix} V_2 & 1 \\ V_3 & 1 \\ V & 1 \end{vmatrix}}{\begin{vmatrix} V_1 & 1 \\ V_2 & 1 \\ V_3 & 1 \end{vmatrix}}$$

The numerator equals $(x-x_3)(y_2-y_3) - (x_2-x_3)(y-y_3)$ and the
denominator is similar. The point V is in triangle 123
if all three of its barycentric coordinates are non-negative,
i.e., if $D_{12}(x,y)$, $D_{23}(x,y)$, and $D_{31}(x,y)$ are all non-
negative.

b. Triangular Interpolants

History

Smooth, finite dimensional interpolants defined over
triangles have been known for about a decade now. Their
principle use has been as "finite elements" about which there
is a large literature (See Barnhill (1975).) There are two
widely known c^1 triangular finite elements, the 21 degree
of freedom quintic and the Clough-Tocher triangle. The former is a piecewise quintic interpolant to the data
$F, F_{1,0}, F_{0,1}, F_{2,0}, F_{1,1}$, and $F_{0,2}$ at each vertex and to the

normal derivative $\frac{\partial F}{\partial n}$ at the midpoints of the edges. These $\frac{\partial F}{\partial n}$ values can be eliminated to obtain an 18-parameter inter- polant. (See Gregory (1975).) The Clough-Tocher triangle is an interpolant that is piecewise cubic over *each* triangle, i.e., a given triangle is itself subdivided into three sub- triangles. The Clough-Tocher triangle interpolates to $F,F_{1,0}$, and $F_{0,1}$ at the vertices and to $\frac{\partial F}{\partial n}$ at the mid- points of the sides. The $\frac{\partial F}{\partial n}$ values can be eliminated to obtain a 9-parameter interpolant. These two interpolants are not suitable for our purposes for the following reasons:

(1) The quintic involves (C^2) data that we do not have and should not make up.

(2) The Clough-Tocher element has discontinuities in the second derivative inside the triangle.

Before listing some newer interpolants over triangles, we need to discuss the mapping of the standard triangle onto an arbitrary one.

Affine Transformation of the Standard Triangle to an Arbitrary Triangle.

The affine transformation A from the standard triangle in pq-space to the physical triangle in xy-space is the following (See Gregory (1975).):

(3.4) $x = x(p,q) = x_3 + (x_1 - x_3)p + (x_2 - x_3)q$

$y = y(p,q) = y_3 + (y_1 - y_3)p + (y_2 - y_3)q$

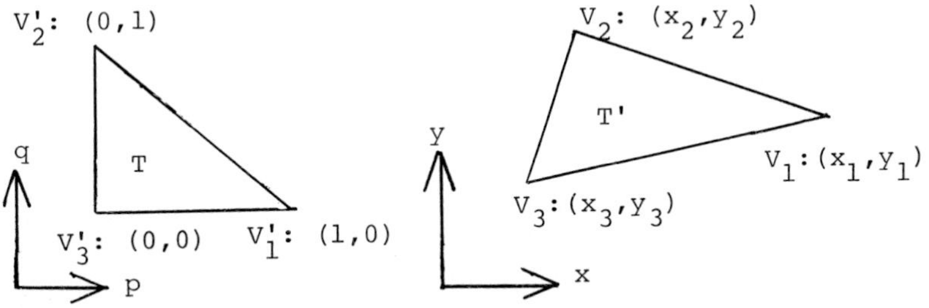

Figure 3.4   Affine Transformation of the Standard Triangle to an Arbitrary Triangle

The affine transformation (3.4) can be rewritten as

(3.5)
$$x = x_1 p + x_2 q + x_3 r$$

$$y = y_1 p + y_2 q + y_3 r$$

We recognize (p,q,r) as the barycentric coordinates for the image triangle 123. A fixed but arbitrary point (x,y) has the barycentric representation

(3.6)
$$(x,y) = pV_1 + qV_2 + rV_3 \ .$$

Parametric linear interpolation can be accomplished with barycentric coordinates by concatenating

(3.7)
$$z = z_1 p + z_2 q + z_3 r$$

with (3.5). (3.5) and (3.7) are an example of an "isoparametric mapping" of the engineers, which simply means that the geometric unit, the triangle, is mapped by an interpolation scheme,

(3.8)
$$F = pF_1 + qF_2 + rF_3$$

where
$$F_i = F(V_i), \quad i=1,2,3 \ .$$

Then $x(p,q) = px(1,0) + qx(0,1) + rx(0,0)$ and the identifications $x_1 = x(1,0)$, $x_2 = x(0,1)$, $x_3 = x(0,0)$ yield (3.5) and hence (3.4).

What is affine invariant and what is not? Affine invariant: parallels to sides of the triangle, relative positions along sides (e.g., midpoints), and the centroid, i.e., the point with barycentric coordinates $(1/3, 1/3, 1/3)$. Not affine invariant: perpendiculars to sides. So c^0 data are affine invariant and c^1 data are not. Or, put another way, positions and the directions of tangential derivatives are preserved under affine transformations, but the directions of normal derivatives are not preserved.

How to Handle C^1 Data over Triangles

Formulas are tabulated for the standard triangle T
whereas their use is for arbitrary triangles T' . Barnhill
and Brown (1975) and, consequently, Klucewicz (1977) show
what to do. We give only a sketch of the method here. The
key idea is that the normal derivatives for the triangle T'
in the physical xy-plane are what must match across the
boundaries of T' . If we wish to use C^1 interpolants tabulated on the triangle T in the parametric pq-plane, then
we must use directional derivatives in place of normal derivatives on T . That is, in Figure 3.5 our C^1 interpolants
must involve derivatives in the directions $\vec{\alpha}$, $\vec{\beta}$, and $\vec{\gamma}$,
respectively. Complete details are given in Klucewicz (1977).

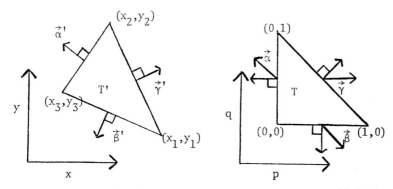

Figure 3.5 Transformation of the normal directions $\vec{\alpha}'$,$\vec{\beta}'$,$\vec{\gamma}'$ in
x-y space into non-normal directions $\vec{\alpha}$,$\vec{\beta}$,$\vec{\gamma}$ in
p-q space.

We list the interpolants which will be discussed in the
remainder of this Section:
1.   Barnhill, Birkhoff, Gordon (BBG) schemes
2.   Radial projectors
3.   Barnhill, Gregory - Nielson schemes
4.   Symmetric Gregory scheme
5.   Brown - Little triangle
6.   9 parameter C^1 triangle
7.   Little macro-triangle

Picture 5 shows three menus. The first menu is for choosing the basic geometric building block: squares, triangles, or arbitrarily spaced data. The second menu lists the triangular interpolants available in this particular package. These are the linear c^0 interpolant, which is illustrated in Picture 6, the 9-parameter Barnhill, Gregory discretization of BBG, the 9-parameter c^0 cubic and 9-parameter c^1 scheme of Little's and his macro-triangles. These last are items (1), (6), and (7) in the list of triangular interpolants. The third menu shows the interactive options available.

Picture 6 illustrates the effect of moving a position handle for piecewise linear interpolation.

(1)   <u>Barnhill, Birkhoff, and Gordon Schemes</u>

BBG (1973) initiated "triangular Coons patches", that is, interpolants to F and its normal derivatives all around the boundary of a triangle. These interpolants are built up from lofting interpolants to data on two sides of the triangle. For the standard triangle T with vertices (1,0), (0,1), and (0,0), the directions of the three projectors P_i are indicated in Figure 3.6.

 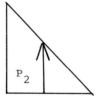

Figure 3.6   The BBG Lofting Projectors

Thus P_1F interpolates along parallels to y=0, etc.
c^0 Data

In order to see the structure of the BBG projectors, let us consider P_1F for the c^0 case of matching position values only. For fixed but arbitrary (p,q) in T , P_1F is

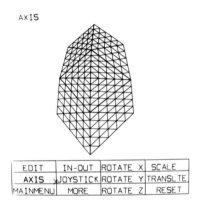

Picture 5.   Menus for Triangular Interpolants

a. Zero Function with Handles

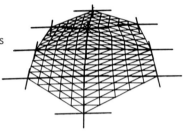

b. Position Handle

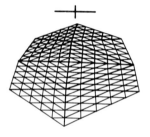

c. New Surface

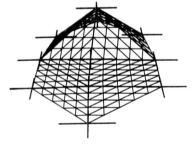

Picture 6. Linear Triangular Interpolants

defined as:

$$(3.9) \quad P_1F(p,q) = (\frac{1-p-q}{1-q})F(0,q) + (\frac{p}{1-q})F(1-q,q)$$

P_2 and P_3 are defined analogously.

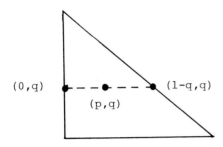

Figure 3.7   BBG P_1F

The Boolean sums $(P_i \oplus P_j)F \equiv P_iF+P_jF - P_iP_jF$, $i \neq j$, all interpolate to F around the boundary of T . These inter-polants have rational weighting, or blending, functions, such as $(1-p-q)/(1-q)$.

c^1 Data

The c^1 analogue of (3.9) is the following:

$$(3.10) \quad P_1F(p,q) = h_0(\frac{p}{1-q})F(0,q) + h_1(\frac{p}{1-q})F(1-q,q)$$

$$+ \bar{h}_0(\frac{p}{1-q})(1-q)F_{1,0}(0,q)+\bar{h}_1(\frac{p}{1-q})(1-q)F_{1,0}(1-q,q)$$

$$(3.11) \quad P_2F(p,q) = h_0(\frac{q}{1-p})F(p,0) + h_1(\frac{q}{1-p})F(p,1-p)$$

$$+ \bar{h}_0(\frac{q}{1-p})(1-p)F_{0,1}(p,0)+\bar{h}_1(\frac{q}{1-p})(1-p)F_{0,1}(p,1-p)$$

where the h_i and $\bar{h}_i$ are the cubic Hermite basis functions defined in (2.3). P_3F is analogously defined (Klucewicz, page 16). The Boolean sum of two of the P_i should inter-polate to F and its normal derivative all around the bound-ary of T . But, just as for rectangular Coons patches, this interpolation may fail. This time it depends on compatibility conditions of the form

$$(3.12) \quad \frac{\partial^2 F}{\partial s_i \partial s_j} (V_k) = \frac{\partial^2 F}{\partial s_j \partial s_i} (V_k)$$

where $\dfrac{\partial}{\partial s_i}$ means differentiation along parallels to side E_i and V_k is the vertex between the sides E_i and E_j. For P_1 and P_2 defined by (3.10) and (3.11) respectively, the Boolean sum $P_1 \oplus P_2$ can be corrected so that the modified interpolant satisfies compatibility conditions (3.12). Considerable theory has been developed about compatibly correcting such interpolants. One answer from Barnhill and Gregory (1975a, Section 3) is the following:

$$(3.13) \quad PF = (P_1 \oplus P_2)F + (P_2 \oplus P_3)R = (P_2 \oplus P_3 \oplus P_1 \oplus P_2)F$$

where $R \equiv F - (P_1 \oplus P_2)F$.

Formula (3.13) can be evaluated by the following:

$$(3.14) \quad (P_1 \oplus P_2)F = (P_1^2 + P_2 - P_1^2 P_2)F \quad \text{where}$$

$$(3.15) \quad P_1^2 G \equiv h_0(\frac{p}{1-q})G(0,q) + \bar{h}_0(\frac{p}{1-q})(1-q)G_{1,0}(0,q) \text{ and}$$

$$(3.16) \quad (P_2 \oplus P_3)R = -\frac{p^2 q(p+q-1)^2}{p+q}\left[\frac{\partial^2 F}{\partial q \partial p}(0,0) - \frac{\partial^2 F}{\partial p \partial q}(0,0)\right] .$$

Equation (3.16) is a rational correction term for $(P_1 \oplus P_2)F$ and it is similar in structure to those for rectangular interpolants.

As we saw for rectangular interpolants, transfinite C^1 schemes can be discretized in a variety of ways, but the most direct, perhaps, is to let the positions along sides be Hermite cubics and the normal derivatives be their linear interpolants. Klucewicz has implemented this form of the compatibly corrected BBG interpolant given by (3.13)-(3.16) and some of her results follow. Pictures 7-10 each follow the sequence: triangulate the given points; form a piecewise linear interpolant to the data; and then form the C^1 9 pa-

a. A Triangulation of the x-y Data

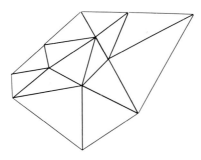

b. A C^0 Surface through the Points

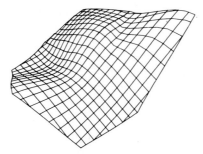

c. A C^1 Surface through the Points

Picture 7. Triangulation and Surfaces

a. A Triangulation of the x-y Data

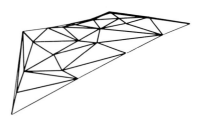

b. A C^0 Surface through the Points

c. A C^1 Surface through the Points

Picture 8. Triangulation and Surfaces

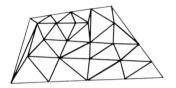

a.   A Triangulation of the x-y Data

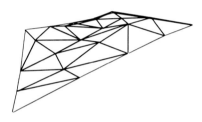

b.   A C^0 Surface through the Points

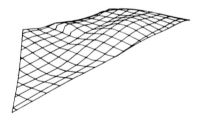

c.   A C^1 Surface through the Points

Picture 9.   Triangulation and Surface

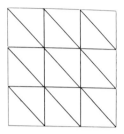

a. A "Standard" Triangulation of (0,2)x(0,2)

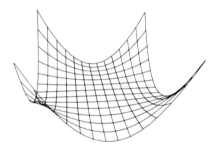

b. The Test Function F(x,y)

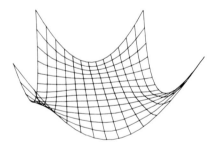

c. The Interpolant PF(x,y)

Picture 10. $F(x,y) = (1-x)^2(1-y)^2$ over (0,2)x(0,2)

rameter discretization of the Barnhill and Gregory BBG interpolant. Pictures 7, 8, and 9 are for given point data and
the data for Picture 10 comes from the function described
there.

(2) Radial Projectors

This type of triangular interpolant was first mentioned
to me by G. M. Nielson in a phone conversation in 1971. J.
A. Marshall (1975) has discussed them in his Ph.D. thesis,
where they are called "side vertex schemes". We shall only
describe the interpolant to C^0 data (Marshall). Let

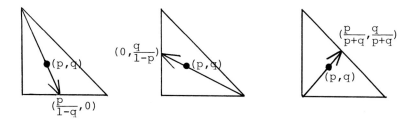

Figure 3.8   Radial projectors Q_1, Q_2, Q_3,   respectively

(3.17) $Q_1F = qF(0,1) + (1-q)F(\frac{p}{1-q},0)$

(3.18) $Q_2F = pF(1,0) + (1-p)F(0,\frac{q}{1-p})$

(3.19) $Q_3F = (1-p-q)F(0,0) + (p+q)F(\frac{p}{p+q},\frac{q}{p+q})$

The overall interpolant is

(3.20) $QF \equiv (Q_1 \oplus Q_2 \oplus Q_3)F$.

These radial projectors have the property that they commute,
i.e., $Q_iQ_j=Q_jQ_i$. Most triangular interpolants do not have
this property.

The above is a direct definition of radial projectors.
They can also be developed as mappings of the unit square.

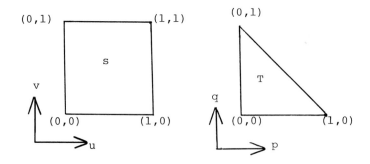

Figure 3.9   Mapping the square to the triangle

The mapping

(3.21) $p = (1-u)v$

                          $q = (1-u)(1-v)$

takes S onto T with the side u=0 going onto q=1-p and
the side u=1 going onto $(p,q)=(0,0)$.   Then

(3.22) $Q_1F(p,q) = P_1F(p(u,v),q(u,v))$

where Q_1 is defined by (3.17) and $G=G(u,v)$ implies that

(3.23) $P_1G(u,v) = (1-u)G(0,v) + uG(1,v)$.

(3)   Barnhill, Gregory - Nielson Interpolant

The two preceding interpolants are each rational: the
BBG is rational in its blending functions and the radial
schemes are rational in the function arguments.   Nielson
stated a C^0 interpolant involving only polynomials, as follows:

(3.24) $NF(p,q) = qF(p,1-p)+pF(1-q,q)+F(p,0)+F(0,q)-F(0,0)$

        $-q\{F(0,1-p)+F(p,0)-F(0,0)\}-p\{F(0,q)+F(1-q,0)-F(0,0)\}$

This interpolant treats one side of the triangle differently
from the others, which is undesirable for general triangles,

but is good when matching boundary values of a triangle with a curved side. See Barnhill (1975) and Ensign (1976). Barnhill and Gregory (1975b) determined a general Boolean sum structure of which this C^0 interpolant is a special case. This study led them to discover a constructive Theorem on the interpolation properties of $P \oplus Q$ from the interpolation properties of P and Q separately. (See Barnhill and Gregory (1975b), Theorems 2.1 and 2.2.) Barnhill and Gregory also found a kind of duality principle for Boolean sums. We recall that the precision set of an interpolant is the set of functions reproduced exactly by the interpolant. Then:

(3.25) P $\oplus$ Q has (at least) the interpolation properties of P
and (at least) the function precision of Q .

We use this Theorem to construct other new interpolants later.

(4)   Symmetric Gregory Scheme

Gregory observed that the composition PQ in the Boolean sum P $\oplus$ Q is what leads to incompatibilities. Therefore, he devised a transfinite C^N triangular interpolant of the form

$$(3.26) \quad GF = \alpha_{0,0}(p,q)P_1F + \beta_{0,0}(p,q)P_2F + \gamma_{0,0}(p,q)P_3F$$

where the P_i interpolate to data on two sides of T as in Figure 3.10.

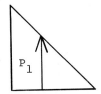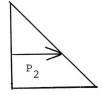

Figure 3.10   Symmetric Gregory Projectors

The functions $\alpha_{0,0}$, $\beta_{0,0}$, and $\gamma_{0,0}$ have the properties that

(3.27) $\alpha_{0,0} + \beta_{0,0} + \alpha_{0,0} \equiv 1$

(3.28) $(D^\nu \alpha_{0,0})(E_1) = (D^\nu \beta_{0,0})(E_2) = (D^\nu \gamma_{0,0})(E_3) \equiv 0, |\nu| \leqslant N$.

For N=1, these are the tricubic basis functions of Birkhoff, derived from a discretization of the C^1 BBG interpolants. For more details, consult Gregory (1973), (1974), (1975).

    (5) <u>Brown-Little Triangle</u>

    Gregory's symmetric scheme is of the form

$$\alpha P_1 F + \beta P_2 F + \gamma P_3 F$$

where α, β, and γ are polynomials and the P_i are the rational BBG projectors. Brown and Little (in some combination) have defined an interpolant of just this form, but with the P_i involving data only on one side of the triangle. For the standard triangle, the C^1 case is the following:

(3.29)   (BL) $F = \dfrac{q^2 r^2}{D} P_1 F + \dfrac{p^2 r^2}{D} P_2 F + \dfrac{p^2 q^2}{D} P_3 F$

    where $D = p^2 q^2 + p^2 r^2 + q^2 r^2$ and

(3.30) $P_1 F = F(0,q) + F_{1,0}(0,q) p$

        $P_2 F = F(p,0) + F_{0,1}(p,0) q$

        $P_3 F = F(\frac{1+p-q}{2}, \frac{1-p+q}{2}) - (1-p-q)(F_{1,0} + F_{0,1})(\frac{1+p-q}{2}, \frac{1-p+q}{2})$

The C^N case is obtained by changing the exponent "2" to "N+1" and using the Nth order Taylor expansions for the P_i. Little considers the arbitrary triangle with vertices V_i and opposite sides S_i , i=1,2,3 . Recall the barycentric coordinates (3.3) for the point (x,y) . Since p,q, and r are the barycentric coordinates in the standard triangle, the weighting functions α, β, and γ of BL for the arbitrary triangle are the following:

(3.31) $\alpha = \dfrac{b_2^2 b_3^2}{D}$, $\beta = \dfrac{b_1^2 b_3^2}{D}$, $\gamma = \dfrac{b_1^2 b_2^2}{D}$ where

(3.32) $D = b_1^2 b_2^2 + b_1^2 b_3^2 + b_2^2 b_3^2$.

P_1F must interpolate to F and to $\dfrac{\partial F}{\partial n_1}$ along s_1 , where n_1 is the direction normal to s_1 . Let P_1 be the Taylor projector

(3.33) $P_1 F(x,y) = F(p_1) + [(x,y)-p_1] \dfrac{\partial F}{\partial n_1}(p_1)$,

where

p_1 is the (geometric) projection of (x,y) onto s_1 . That is,

(3.34) $p_1 = \in(x,y)(x_3,y_3) + \delta(x,y)(x_2,y_2)$,

where
$$\in(x,y) = \frac{(x_3-x_2)(x-x_2) + (y_3-y_2)(y-y_2)}{(x_3-x_2)^2 + (y_3-y_2)^2}$$

and
$$\delta(x,y) = 1-\in(x,y) = \frac{(x_3-x_2)(x_3-x) + (y_3-y_2)(y_3-y)}{(x_3-x_2)^2 + (y_3-y_2)^2}$$

P_2 and P_3 are obtained by a cyclic permutation of the indices. P_1F can also be written as

(3.35) $P_1F = F(p_1) + \dfrac{\partial F}{\partial b_1}(p_1) \ b_1 = F(p_1) + \dfrac{\partial F}{\partial n_1}(p_1) \ b_1 \ \dfrac{2A}{||s_1||}$

where $||s_1||$ is the length of s_1 .

(6) Little 9-parameter C^1 Interpolant

This scheme is derived using an analogy from univariate interpolation. Consider the Boolean sum $P_1 \oplus P_2 = P_2 + P_1(I-P_2)$, I the identity operator. For $f = f(x)$, let

(3.36) $P_2f = (1-x)f(0) + xf(1)$ and

(3.37) $P_1 f = h_0(x) f(0) + h_1(x) f(1) + \bar{h}_0(x) f'(0) + \bar{h}_1(x) f'(1)$

where the h_i and $\bar{h}_i$ are the cubic Hermite basis functions (2.5). Then $P_1 = P_1 \oplus P_2 = P_2 + P_1(I-P_2)$. Let $R_2 = I - P_2$. Then

(3.38) $P_1 f = P_2 f + P_1 R_2 f$

$$= P_2 f + \bar{h}_0(x) \frac{dR_2 f(0)}{dx} + \bar{h}_1(x) \frac{dR_2 f(1)}{dx} \quad .$$

This procedure can be carried out for higher order interpolation. The basis functions corresponding to $f^{(n-1)}(0)$ and $f^{(n-1)}(1)$ are $(1-x)^n x^{n-1}/(n-1)!$ and $x^n(x-1)^{n-1}/(n-1)!$, respectively.

The bivariate analogue for the triangle is the following:

(3.39) $(BL \oplus C \oplus L)F = LF + C(I-L)F + BL[I-L-C(I-L)]F$

where

(3.40) $LF = \sum\limits_{i=1}^{3} b_i F_i$

(3.41) $CH = \sum\limits_{i=1}^{3} b_i^2 L_i H$

where $H = (I-L)F$ and L_i is the bivariate linear Taylor expansion about the ith vertex.

(3.42) $(BL)G = \alpha P_1 G + \beta P_2 G + \gamma P_3 G$

where $G = [I-L-C(I-L)]F$ and α, β, γ are defined by (3.31). Now consider F to be cubic in position and quadratic in normal derivative around the boundary of the triangle. Then

(3.43) $P_i G = 4 b_1 b_2 b_3 \dfrac{\partial G}{\partial b_i} \begin{vmatrix} b_i = 0 \\ b_j = 1/2 \\ b_k = 1/2 \end{vmatrix}$, i, j, k all different.

(3.44) $\dfrac{\partial G}{\partial b_i} = \dfrac{2A}{||s_i||} \dfrac{\partial G}{\partial n_i}$ as before.

The normal derivative $\frac{\partial G}{\partial n_i}$ is what one would have and so (3.44) is necessary for computation. Equations (3.39)-(3.44) define Little's 12-parameter C^1 interpolant. Equation (3.42) follows from the fact that, e.g.,

$$P_1 G = G(p_1) + b_1 \frac{\partial G}{\partial b_1}(p_1), \; G \equiv 0 \text{ along } s_1 \text{, and } \frac{\partial G}{\partial b_1}\bigg|_{s_1}$$

is a quadratic in b_2 and b_3 that is zero at both ends of s_1. Hence this interpolant is a discretization of the Brown-Little triangle. The 12 parameters can be reduced to 9 by letting the normal derivative at the midpoint of a side be the average of the normal derivative at the ends of that side. This is equivalent to considering the normal derivatives to be linear functions along the sides.

Picture 11 illustrates the C^0 9-parameter discretization of the transfinite interpolant

$$(3.45) \qquad (C \oplus L)F = LF + C(I-L)F \; .$$

Picture 11b. shows the effect of changing one tangent handle and 11c. shows the effect of changing six tangent handles. Picture 12 shows the C^1 9-parameter interpolant to the same data as are in 11c. These schemes are also shown in our movie.

(7) Little's Macro-Triangles

This is an approximation, but not an interpolation, scheme. Let

$$(3.46) \qquad MF = \frac{\sum w_i \, L_i F}{\sum w_i}$$

where L_i is linear interpolation on the ith triangle and $w_i = \prod_{j=1}^{3} (b_{ij} + 1)^3_+$ where $b_{ij} = A_j/A_i$ is the jth barycentric coordinate of the ith triangle. The exponent 3 makes this a C^2 approximant. MF does interpolate in the special case of data on a uniformly spaced rectangular grid. This scheme is illustrated in Picture 13 for the same data as in Picture 12 and it is also shown in our movie.

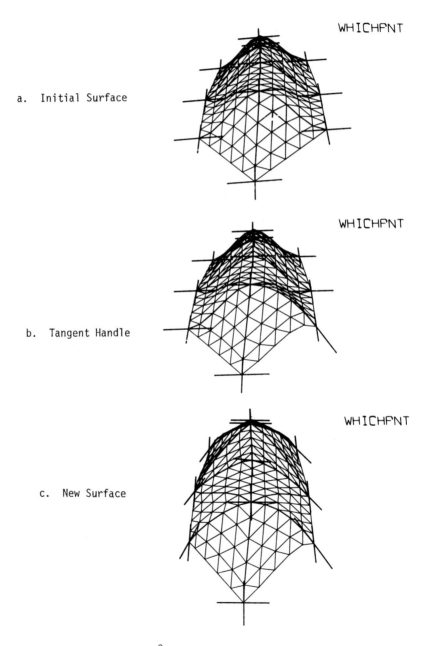

WHICHPNT

a.   Initial Surface

WHICHPNT

b.   Tangent Handle

WHICHPNT

c.   New Surface

Picture 11. C^0 Nine Parameter Interpolant

WHICHPNT

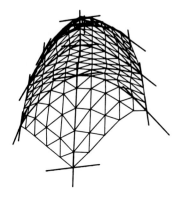

Picture 12. C^1 Nine Parameter Interpolant

WHICHPNT

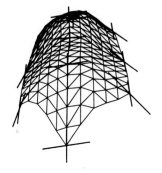

Picture 13. C^2 Approximation

4.   INTERPOLATION METHODS FOR ARBITRARILY PLACED DATA.
    The basic problem is: given $\{(x_i, y_i, F_i)\}_{i=1}^{n}$,

find a surface S that interpolates to these data,

(4.1) $S(x_i, y_i) = F_i$, $i=1,\ldots,n$.

This Section complements Schumaker's recent survey (1976).
We consider the following interpolation schemes:

    (1)   Shepard's Formula

    (2)   Boolean Sums and Shepard's Formula

    (3)   McLain's Least Squares

    (4)   Franke's Method

    (5)   Transfinite Shepard

    (1)   Shepard's Formula

    Shepard's Formula (1965) is the following:

(4.2) $SF \equiv \begin{cases} \dfrac{\sum\limits_{i=1}^{n} \dfrac{F_i}{d_i^{\mu}}}{\sum\limits_{i=1}^{n} \dfrac{1}{d_i^{\mu}}} & (x,y) \neq (x_i,y_i),\ i=1,\ldots,n \\ F_i & (x,y) = (x_i,y_i)\ \text{for some}\ i\ . \end{cases}$

where $\mu > 0$ and $d_i \equiv \{(x-x_i)^2 + (y-y_i)^2\}^{1/2}$. Shepard's
Formula is an "inverse distance" interpolation method.
Poeppelmeier (1975) and Gordon and Wixom (1976) contain pictures and discussions of Shepard's Formula. SF has the following properties:

    a.   Interpolation

    SF interpolates, i.e., $SF(x_i, y_i) = F_i$, $i=1,\ldots,n$.   A
useful form of Shepard's Formula is the following:

(4.3) $SF = \dfrac{\sum\limits_{i=1}^{n} w_i F_i}{\sum\limits_{i=1}^{n} w_i}$

where $w_i = \prod\limits_{\substack{j=1 \\ j \neq i}}^{n} d_j^{\mu}$. This form makes the interpolation clear
and also removes the singularities in (4.2).

b.   Continuity Class

The continuity class of Shepard's Formula depends upon μ and , for $\mu > 0$, is as follows:

(i)   If μ is an even integer, then $SF \in C^{\infty}$.

(ii)   If μ is an odd integer, then $SF \in C^{\mu-1}$.

(iii) If μ is not an integer, then $SF \in C^{[\mu]}$,

where $[\mu] \equiv$ the largest integer $< \mu$.

c.   Flat Spots

For $0 < \mu < 1$, Shepard's Formula has cusps at the interpolation points and, for $\mu = 1$, corners. This behavior is illustrated in Poeppelmeier's thesis (Figures 2.1 and 2.4) and in Gordon and Wixom's paper (Figure 1). $\mu = 2$ seems to be the best choice of μ, visually. However, $\mu > 1$ implies that

$$(4.4) \qquad \frac{\partial SF}{\partial x}(x_i,y_i) = 0 = \frac{\partial SF}{\partial y}(x_i,y_i) , \quad i=1,\ldots,n .$$

The visual effect is that flat spots occur at the (x_i,y_i) . This undesirable feature requires that Shepard's Formula be generalized and one solution is the following:

$$(4.5) \qquad S_1F \equiv \frac{\sum\limits_{i=1}^{n} \dfrac{L_iF}{d_i^2}}{\sum\limits_{i=1}^{n} \dfrac{1}{d_i^2}}$$

where $L_iF = F(x_i,y_i)+F_{1,0}(x_i,y_i)(x-x_i)+F_{0,1}(x_i,y_i)(y-y_i)$, the linear Taylor expansion of F about (x_i,y_i) . (Precisely speaking, S_1F is defined to be F_i when $(x,y)=(x_i,y_i)$ for some i , but we omit this in the rest of this paper.) S_1F interpolates to the C^1 data:

$$(4.6) \qquad S_1F(x_i,y_i) = F_i$$

$$\frac{\partial S_1F}{\partial x}(x_i,y_i) = F_{1,0}(x_i,y_i)$$

$$\frac{\partial S_1F}{\partial y}(x_i,y_i) = F_{0,1}(x_i,y_i) , \quad i=1,\ldots,n .$$

To use (4.5), we need the derivative data

$$F_{1,0}(x_i,y_i) , \quad F_{0,1}(x_i,y_i) , \quad i=1,\ldots,n .$$

Klucewicz (1977) used the average of the derivatives from the linear interpolants $L_j F$ of the surrounding triangles. Other solutions are given later in this Section.

   d.   Function Precision

      Representation (4.3) shows that SF is a convex combination of the F_i. In general, a convex combination of the form

(4.7)
$$\frac{\sum w_i \; G_i F}{\sum w_i}$$

is precise for those functions F for which *all* the G_i are precise. Hence S is precise for constant functions and S_1 is precise for linear functions. S is not exact for linear functions, as can be verified directly. An alternative verification: Recalling our discussion of zero twists in Section 2, we can say that S can be precise only for those functions whose first derivatives are zero. These are the constant functions. The analogous reasoning shows S_1 to be exact only for linear functions, since S_1 has the higher order

flat spots $\dfrac{\partial^2 S_1 F}{\partial x^2} = \dfrac{\partial^2 S_1 F}{\partial x \partial y} = \dfrac{\partial^2 S_1 F}{\partial y^2} = 0$ at the (x_i, y_i). At

least quadratic precision is necessary for "fair" shapes, so an improved S_1 will be presented shortly. S_1 can be generalized to n^{th} order derivative data by replacing $L_i F$ with the suitable n^{th} order Taylor expansion. This makes S_1 more precise. For $S_1 F$ to be in continuity class C^n, μ must be an even integer or else μ must be larger than n.

   e.   Local Support

      Shepard's Formula is a global interpolant, i.e., SF at (x,y) is affected by *all* the data. Shepard (p.519) shows a way to localize the support, i.e., to make SF at (x,y) depend only on data "near" (x,y). Franke and Little have proposed an even simpler scheme, which is to make the replacement

(4.8)
$$\frac{1}{d_i^2} \;\leftarrow\; \left[\frac{(R_i - d_i)_+}{R_i d_i} \right]^2$$

where R_i is the radius of the circle of support and

$$(R_i - d_i)_+ \equiv \begin{cases} R_i - d_i & \text{if } R_i - d_i \geq 0 \\ 0 & \text{if } R_i - d_i < 0. \end{cases}$$

(2) Boolean Sums and Shepard's Formula

Barnhill and Gregory (1975b) prove that the Boolean sum $P \oplus Q$ has at least the interpolation properties of P and the function precision of Q. Shepard's projector S_1 has the desired c^1 interpolation properties, so we make the replacement $P \leftarrow S_1$ in $P \oplus Q$. Q is to be replaced by something with at least quadratic precision. Another possibility is to use S instead of S_1. Since S has zero derivatives at the (x_i, y_i), then $S \oplus Q$ inherits the derivatives of Q at the (x_i, y_i). We consider the following possibilities for $S_1 \oplus Q$:

(i) QF is a piecewise triangular interpolant involving a proper subset of the (x_i, y_i).

(ii) QF is a least squares approximation.

(i): The formula for S_1 can be simplified in this case.

$$(4.9) \qquad S_1 F = \frac{\sum\limits_{i \in S} w_i \, L_i F}{\sum\limits_{i \in S} w_i}$$

where $S = \{1, 2, \ldots, n\}$ and $w_i = d_i^{-2}$. Let QF be an interpolant such that

$$(4.10) \qquad L_i Q = L_i F \quad \text{for all} \quad i \in \mathcal{Q}, \qquad \text{where } \mathcal{Q} \text{ is a proper}$$
$$\text{subset of } S. \quad \text{Then}$$

$$(4.11) \qquad (S_1 \oplus Q)F = QF + S_1(I - Q)F$$
$$= QF + \sum_{i \in S - \mathcal{Q}} \varphi_i L_i [(I - Q)F]$$

where $\varphi_i \equiv w_i / \sum\limits_{i \in S} w_i$. In Poeppelmeier's thesis, we let $Q = Q_1$ be the Barnhill, Gregory c^1 9-parameter BBG discretization. The results are a distinct improvement over $S_1 F$

itself. (See Figures 4.5 and 4.6 in Poeppelmeier.) We let
$\mu = 2$, so that $S_1F \in C^\infty$. Since $Q_1 \in C^1$ and Q_1 has
quadratic precision, $S_1 \oplus Q_1$ interpolates to the C^1 data;
is in continuity class C^1 ; and has quadratic precision.

(ii): $Q = Q_2$ is the quadratic least squares approxi-
mation to the C^1 data $F_i, F_{1,0}(x_i, y_i), F_{0,1}(x_i, y_i)$ i=1,...,n
in this case. Picture 14 illustrates an editing session with
this Boolean sum. The defining values are all zero (n=5) ,
making S_1F the zero function in Picture 14a. A position is
changed in b. and the resulting function is shown in c. A
tangent handle is changed in d. and the resulting surface is
shown in e.

(3) <u>McLain's Least Squares</u>

Schumaker has pointed out that Shepard's Formula is
weighted least squares approximation by a constant function,
that is, it solves the problem:

$$(4.12) \quad \min_{c} \sum_{i=1}^{n} w_i (F_i - c)^2 .$$

McLain (1976) has considered the least squares problem:

$$(4.13) \quad \min \sum w_i [F_i - \Gamma(x_i, y_i)]^2$$

where Γ is a polynomial of given degree or a quadric and
the weight function w is e^{-d^2}/d^2 , $1/d^2$, or $1/d^4$.
McLain's paper contains some good examples for testing
methods.

(4) <u>Franke's Method</u>

R. H. Franke (1975) has considered interpolants of the
form

$$(4.14) \quad S_2F \equiv \frac{\sum w_i G_i F}{\sum w_i} .$$

He has defined a family of methods based on the following:
Let $\varphi_i \equiv w_i / \sum w_i$. If $\varphi_i(x_j, y_j) \neq 0$ implies that
$G_iF(x_j, y_j) = F_j$, then S_2F interpolates at (x_j, y_j) . The
weight functions φ_i defined from the $w_i = d_i^{-2}$ of Shepard's

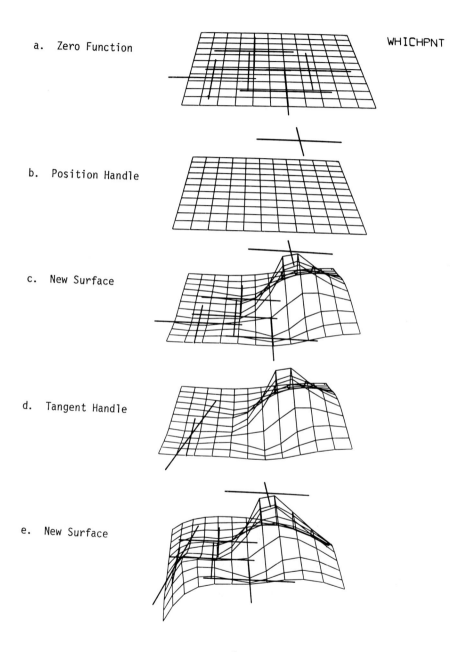

a. Zero Function

WHICHPNT

b. Position Handle

c. New Surface

d. Tangent Handle

e. New Surface

Picture 14. Editing Session with C^1 Interpolant to Arbitrary Data

Formula have the Kronecker delta property that

(4.15) $\varphi_i(x_j, y_j) = \delta_{ij}$.

Franke considers more general weight functions and various $G_i F$. Two examples are the following:

(i)   Maude's method: The w_i have local support, by being mollified cubic Hermite functions:

(4.16) $w_i(x,y) = \begin{cases} h_0(d_i/r_i) & \text{for} \quad d_i \leq r_i \\ 0 & \text{for} \quad d_i > r_i \end{cases}$,

where the radius r_i is chosen so that (x_i, y_i)'s five nearest neighbors are just in the corresponding circle centered at (x_i, y_i) . The $G_i F$ are the quadratic interpolants to the six points. Maude's method is not recommended, because of the instability of the $G_i F$.

(ii)   Optimal approximation: The w_i are as in (4.16). The $G_i F$ are the bivariate splines of L. E. Mansfield. These schemes give the best results.   (See Franke (1975).)

(5)   Transfinite Shepard

The Brown-Little triangle (3.31)-(3.33) is of the following form:

(4.17)   (BL) F = $\dfrac{b_2 b_3 P_1 F + b_1 b_3 P_2 F + b_1 b_2 P_3 F}{b_1 b_2 + b_1 b_3 + b_2 b_3}$

$= \dfrac{\dfrac{P_1 F}{b_1} + \dfrac{P_2 F}{b_2} + \dfrac{P_3 F}{b_3}}{\dfrac{1}{b_1} + \dfrac{1}{b_2} + \dfrac{1}{b_3}}$

which is a Shepard's Formula.   This suggests the generalization

(4.18) $S_3 F = \dfrac{\dfrac{P_1 F}{b_1} + \dfrac{P_2 F}{b_2} + \dfrac{P_3 F}{b_3} + \dfrac{F_4}{d_4} + \dfrac{F_5}{d_5}}{\dfrac{1}{b_1} + \dfrac{1}{b_2} + \dfrac{1}{b_3} + \dfrac{1}{d_4} + \dfrac{1}{d_5}}$

where $d_4 = \{(x-x_4)^2 + (y-y_4)^2\}^{1/2}$ etc.

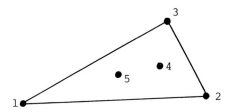

Figure 4.1   Transfinite Shepard

An analogous interpolant can be derived using Brown's square. This also suggests even more general Shepard's Formulas, e.g.,

(4.19) $S_4 F = \dfrac{\dfrac{F_1}{d_1} + \dfrac{F_2}{d_2}}{\dfrac{1}{d_1} + \dfrac{1}{d_2}}$ where F_1 is a Taylor expansion

at the projection of (x,y) onto line 1 and F_2 is data at spot 2 .

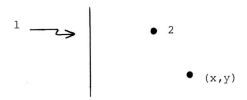

Figure 4.2   General Shepard's Formula

5.   CONCLUSIONS

There is a considerable and growing choice of bivariate interpolants, which makes this an exciting research area. The application determines which set of schemes should be considered, but a few general guidelines may be useful. Rectangular patches are the simplest to understand and hence preferred by users, so rectangular patches should be used when possible. The compatibility conditions must be taken into account, as indicated in Section 2. Irregularly spaced data is treated either by triangulating and then using triangular interpolants or else by the appropriate form of Shepard's Formula. Maintaining shape fidelity requires that the scheme have at least quadratic precision. Smoothness requirements are that the method be at least C^1, in most applications. Surfaces are too complicated to visualize via numerical values, so interactive graphics or actual three-dimensional models are necessary to "see" surfaces.

REFERENCES

1.   R. E. Barnhill (1974), Smooth Interpolation over Triangles, Computer Aided Geometric Design, edited by R. E. Barnhill and R. F. Riesenfeld, 45-70, Academic Press, New York.

2.   _____ (1975), Blending Function Interpolation: A Survey and Some New Results. Proceedings of the Conference on Numerical Methods in Approximation Theory, Oberwolfach, Germany, ISNM 30, pp. 43-90 and University of Dundee Numerical Analysis Report No. 9.

3.   _____, G. Birkhoff and W. J. Gordon (1973), Smooth Interpolation in Triangles, J. Approx. Theory 8, 114-128.

4.   _____ and J. H. Brown (1975), Curved Nonconforming Elements for Plate Problems, University of Dundee Numerical Analysis Report No. 8.

5.   _____, J. H. Brown and I. M. Klucewicz (1977), A New Twist for Computer Aided Geometric Design.

6.   _____ and J. A. Gregory (1975a), Compatible Smooth Interpolation in Triangles, J. Approx. Theory 15, 214-225.

7. _____ and J. A. Gregory (1975b), Polynomial
    Interpolation to Boundary Data on Triangles, Math-
    ematics of Computation 29, 726-735.

8. S. A. Coons (1964), Surfaces for Computer Aided Design,
    Design Division, Mech. Engin. Dept., MIT, revised,
    1967.

9. P. J. Davis (1963), Interpolation and Approximation,
    Blaisdell Publ., republished by Dover Publ., 1975.

10. M. G. Ensign (1976), A Polynomial Boolean Sum Interpolant
    for Computer Aided Geometric Design, M.S. thesis,
    Mathematics Department, University of Utah.

11. D. J. F. Ewing, A. J. Fawkes, and J. R. Griffiths (1970),
    Rules Governing the Numbers of Nodes and Elements
    in a Finite Element Mesh, International Journal for
    Numerical Methods in Engineering 2, 597-601.

12. R. H. Franke (1975), Locally Determined Smooth Interpo-
    lation at Irregularly Spaced Points in Several
    Variables, Naval Postgraduate School Technical Re-
    port. To appear in JIMA (1977).

13. W. J. Gordon (1969), Distributive Lattices and the Ap-
    proximation of Multivariate Functions, Proceedings
    of the Symposium on Approximation with Special Em-
    phasis on Splines, ed., I. J. Schoenberg, Univ. of
    Wisconsin Press, Madison, Wisconsin.

14. _____ (1971), "Blending-function" Methods of Bi-
    variate and Multivariate Interpolation and Approx-
    imation, SIAM J. Numer. Anal. 8, 158-177.

15. _____ and J. A. Wixom (1976), On Shepard's Method
    of "Metric Interpolation" to Bivariate and Multi-
    variate Data, General Motors Research Publ. GMR-
    2152, GMR Lab., Warren, Michigan.

16. J. A. Gregory (1973), Symmetric Smooth Interpolation on
    Triangles, TR/34, Brunel University.

17. _____ (1975), Piecewise Interpolation Theory for
    Functions of Two Variables, Ph.D. thesis, Brunel
    University.

18. _____ (1974), Smooth Interpolation Without Twist
    Constraints, Computer Aided Geometric Design, edited
    by R. E. Barnhill and R. F. Riesenfeld, Academic
    Press, 71-87.

19. I. M. Klucewicz (1977), A Piecewise C^1 Interpolant to
    Arbitrarily Spaced Data, M.S. thesis, Mathematics
    Department, University of Utah.

20. C. L. Lawson (1972), Generation of a Triangular Grid with Application to Contour Plotting, Jet Propulsion Laboratory Technical Memorandum No. 299.

21. _____ (1976), C^1-Compatible Interpolation Over a Triangle, Jet Propulsion Laboratory Computing Memorandum No. 407.

22. _____ (1977), Software for C^1 Surface Interpolation, this volume, pp. 159-192.

23. F. F. Little and J. L. Schwing (1977), Automatic Generation of Triangulations, in preparation.

24. L. Mansfield (1974), Higher Order Compatible Triangular Finite Elements, Numer. Math. 22, 89-97.

25. J. A. Marshall (1975), Application of Blending Function Methods in the Finite Element Method, Ph.D. thesis, University of Dundee.

26. D. H. McLain (1974), Drawing contours from arbitrary data points, The Computer Journal, 17, 318-324.

27. C. Poeppelmeier (1975), A Boolean Sum Interpolation Scheme to Random Data for Computer Aided Geometric Design, M.S. thesis, Computer Science Department, University of Utah.

28. L. L. Schumaker (1976), Fitting Surfaces to Scattered Data, Approximation Theory II, edited by G. G. Lorentz, C. K. Chui, L. L. Schumaker, Academic Press, 203-268.

29. D. Shepard (1965), A Two Dimensional Interpolation Function for Irregularly Spaced Data, Proc. 23rd Nat. Conf. ACM, 517-523.

ACKNOWLEDGEMENTS

The author is pleased to acknowledge the help of many colleagues. Particular thanks go to Frank Little, who helped make things work at the necessary times and with whom the author has had many useful discussions. Myke Klucewicz and Dick Franke helped by reading parts of this manuscript. The 12 minute movie that goes with this paper was produced by the following members of the Computer Aided Geometric Design Group at Utah: R. E. Barnhill, R. P. Dube, G. J. Herron, F. F. Little, and R. F. Riesenfeld. This research was supported in part by The National Science Foundation with Grant MCS 74-13017 A01.

Department of Mathematics
The University of Utah
Salt Lake City, Utah 84112

Simulation: Conflicts between
Real-Time and Software
C. W. Gear

ABSTRACT

When a dynamic system has to be simulated, we usually
find that there are two very important considerations. The
first is that such systems are non-linear and have some large
eigenvalues, both near the imaginary axis (due to natural
oscillations in the system) and near the negative real axis
(due to rapidly reacting, stable control systems). The
second is that the system is being changed frequently in a
design process, which implies that the software structure
must reflect the structure of the physical system, particularly with respect to its control flow, so that the model can
be changed and compared to the proposed design easily. It is
not, in general, possible to write down differential
equations describing the system; rather we must work with
sets of programs describing each component.

Real-time simulation is required when it is necessary to
simulate part of the system and use actual equipment or
people in other parts of the system. This introduces a
number of additional problems. Significant delays between
the input of a signal from people or equipment and response
to that signal cannot be tolerated, so a smallish integration
step is indicated. Real-time also implies that implicit
methods cannot be used in the usual sense. The length of the
program and the need to retain system structure in the
program imply that the basic steps cannot be very small, so

that integration methods are restricted to single function
evaluation explicit methods.

   This paper addresses these conflicting requirements and
discusses some of the quasi-implicit methods that have been
investigated.

1.   INTRODUCTION

   The design of many systems, such as aircraft and their
automatic control equipment, requires real-time simulation.
Simulation is used to test designs, both to check the way in
which individual pieces of equipment interact with other
pieces of equipment, and to check if the total system inter-
acts correctly with its environment. The environment
consists of another piece of equipment, a person, or both, as
shown in Figure 1. In this paper we will examine some of the
many difficulties and constraints imposed by real-time
operation. Additional constraints are imposed by the software because the software is changed frequently during
design iterations. Currently, a number of ad hoc methods are
used to try and overcome many of the problems caused by real-
time, but these are only partial solutions; as with most
computer applications, the applications expand to use all
available resources, so the ability to handle more complex
designs depends on the introduction of faster computers or
the derivation of faster methods. In real-time applications,
this is an absolute limit; once the computation time for a
simulated time period exceeds the simulated time period, the
program cannot be used. In this situation, it is not
possible to improve results by using more computer time--no
more accuracy is possible.

   This paper surveys some of the methods currently in use
and discusses other possible approaches. It is, unfortunately, an area with few results because most of the classical
theory deals with aspects of no interest. For example,
convergence or asymptotic error estimates for integration
methods are not meaningful because it is not possible to
reduce the time step below the real-time limit. The object
is to develop techniques to minimize the simulation error
subject to real-time and software constraints. Solution of
this problem awaits, first, a satisfactory definition of

error in this class of problems.

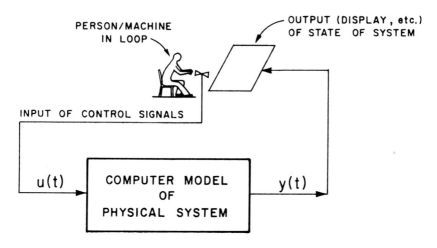

Figure 1.   Real-Time Simulation

2.   SIMULATION

It is important to distinguish between simulation and emuluation in real-time applications. In emulation, the objective is to develop a computer program that behaves "like" the physical system to be modeled in Figure 1. The definition of "like" is from the point of view of the person or machine in the environment. Consequently, it is only necessary to model enough of the system to achieve sufficiently accurate external behavior. There is no need for the computer model to reflect the design of the object being emulated. Emulation is used in training (of, for example, pilots), and testing of external devices. In simulation, on the otherhand, the objective is to test a proposed design. Therefore, it is necessary to model each component of the physical system accurately. From this point of view, emulation is a top-down process in which details of the physical system are added until the model is indistinguishable from the real world to the accuracy desired, whereas simulation is a bottom-up process in which the model is constructed from a collection of models of individual components as shown in Figure 2.

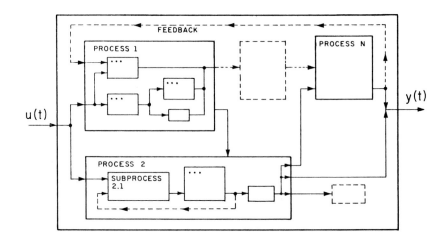

Figure 2.   Components of Computer Model

During the design process, the engineer specifies the
behavior of components of the system by mathematical models.
These may be approximate models because they represent a
process over which the engineer has little control (e.g., the
fundamental laws of aerodynamics) or they may be reasonably
accurate because they represent parts of the system which are
to be built to achieve a particular behavior (e.g., a part of
an automatic control system for a plane). These may be
converted to computational models by the engineer or, in a
more useful arrangement, converted to computational models
automatically. The models are then interconnected by the
engineer to obtain the complete system model for simulation.
As a result of the simulation, the system may be redesigned,
causing changes at any level. Consequently, it is very
important to reflect the structure of the model in its
software implementation. Each basic process in the model
must be reflected in a module in the software so that, when
the model is updated, the corresponding module can be changed.
(While it is conceivable that an automatic coding package
could modify the modular structure to improve efficiency, the
primary definition must reflect the original structure of the
model. At the moment there are no such packages nor any
conjectures as to what such a package could do.)

It is not normally practical to perform much mathematical analysis on the full system. This is true for a number
of reasons in addition to the overall size of the system,
including:

> (i) many parts of the model are specified by tabular
>   data (e.g., aerodynamic forces),
>
> (ii) frequent changes in the design of one or more
>   modules could invalidate any earlier analysis,
>
> (iii) such an analysis may not allow any alternate
>   solution techniques to be used because of
>   restrictions on software structure.

Usually, numerical techniques used must be directly applicable to the individual modules.

As an example, consider the simulation of a helicopter.
A part of this system is the helicopter rotor assembly. This
includes the rotating hub and a number of blades. The blade
is usually approximated as a series of segments such that the
flow can be assumed to be uniform over each segment. The
innermost model is a tabular function relating lift and drag
to velocity and angle of attack for a particular blade
profile. Each blade is modeled at the next higher level by
computing the velocities and angles at the center of each segment and summing the forces and moments of the lift, drag
and hub reactions, to relate them to the equations of motion
for the blade. Finally, at the next level, the reactions of
the hub on the blades are related to the equations of motion
of the hub. At any stage in the design process, it may be
necessary to modify the tabular data to reflect a change in
the basic blade design.

3. REAL-TIME OPERATION

To analyze real-time simulation, it is necessary to have
some idea about the behavior of the person or machine in the
loop. This behavior depends very much on the application,
but, in general, we can expect the input to the physical
system to be a delayed response to the output from the
physical system. For example, if a person is performing a
tracking task, the input, $u(t)$ in Figure 1, might be of the
form $u(t) = \mu(d(t) - y(t - \Delta_p)) + \nu d(t)$ where $d(t)$ is the
signal to be tracked and Δ_p is the delay in a person's

response. (The coefficients μ and ν usually change slowly as the person learns the "feel" of the system.)

When the physical system is simulated digitally, the input must be sampled at discrete times, so that the value of $u(t)$ is known only at a sequence of points $t = t_n$. This means that any action taken by the external person or machine after t_n will not be detected until $t_{n+1} = t_n + h$, creating an average of another $h/2$ delay. After the input $u(t)$ has been sampled, it takes a non-zero amount of computation time, Δ_c, before any approximation to the output y is available, so that the delay Δ_p caused by the external person or machine is increased to a minimun of $\Delta_p + \Delta_c + \Theta h$, where $0 \le \Theta < 1$. These additional delays have two implications. The first is that, even if there is no external delay Δ_p, an implicit procedure for solving the total system (the model plus environment) is not possible. The second is that a stable system may become unstable because of additional delays. In practice, if the external component is a person, an adjustment in the response to make the system stable is learnt if a stable response exists. However, the simulation is unrealistic if the adjustment necessary is very large. Accurate simulation implies that the additional delays must be small, even if the computational model is an exact model of the system.

4. NUMERICAL INTEGRATION IN REAL-TIME

Most mathematical models involve initial-value problems for differential equations. Real-time operation imposes a number of constraints on integration methods, and affects their stability. The requirement that simulated time must keep up with real-time, namely, that the computation time for a single step must no exceed the length of the simulated time, means that there is a maximum computational resource for each step. In practice this means a fixed resource because there is usually no reason to use less. (If the computer is timeshared, it can make sense, but many of these applications use 100% of a computer such as a CDC 6600 so timesharing is not possible. Even if timesharing is used, it is normally necessary to allocate fixed amounts of time to each task to guarantee minimum service.)

The fact that the computation resource per time step is fixed means that there is no point in using variable time steps, so no error control is possible. A method, or set of methods, that minimizes the error must be chosen subject to the real-time limitation of the time step. That is, we want to select from a class of methods such that we achieve

$$\min_{\{methods\}} \text{ERROR} | \text{step size} = \text{computation time for one step}$$

For most problems the dominant part of the computation time is the function evaluation, so that

$$\text{step size } h = K * \# \text{ function evaluations}$$

For many applications, $K \cong 30$ msecs (that is, the application has grown to fill whatever computer is available when the simplest method is used with the largest reasonable time step). This restricts the class of methods severely! Explicit multistep methods (PE--predict evaluate) and pre-dictor-corrector with one evaluation (PEC) are about the only type of methods that can be used in an obvious way. PECE and PECEC can be used if the time step is doubled. This increases the delay, probably to an unacceptable level. If the delay can be tolerated, the methods can be considered, but it is almost certainly necessary to generate output more frequently than every 60 msecs. This can be done by extrapolation from the last integration point. (Note that interpolation cannot be used because the output is needed before the next integration step can be computed.)

Delays decrease the region of absolute stability of common numerical integration schemes. If, for example, a Euler method is used but the information for the derivative is delayed by an additional time h, the method actually used in $y_{n+1} = y_n + hy'_{n-1}$. Figure 3 shows the regions of absolute stability of this method compared to that of the Euler method. Similarly, the region of absolute stability of the trapezoidal rule shrinks, but even more drastically, from the whole of the whole of the left-half plane to that shown in Figure 4 for the method $y_{n+1} = y_n + h(y'_n + y'_{n-1})/2$. (The order of the trapezoidal method also drops to one when a delay is intro-duced, as does the order of any multistep method when a delay of a multiple of h is introduced. However, the order is not a particularly useful characterization of the class of methods, all of whose step size is fixed.)

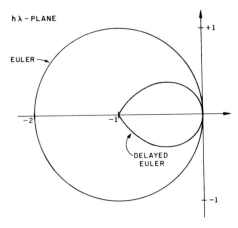

Figure 3.   Region of Absolute Stability of
Euler and Delayed Euler Methods

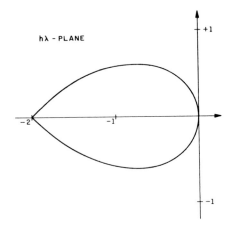

Figure 4.   Region of Absolute Stability of
Delayed Trapezoidal Rule

5. ERRORS IN NUMERICAL INTEGRATION

It is necessary to define the error of an integration scheme if a rational basis for choosing between schemes is to be developed. There are a number of fairly obvious definitions of error for classical integration problems; global error, local error and backward error are the most common. Those are measures of error for an integration scheme applied to a fixed, self-contained problem (that is, a differential equation with given initial values and no external environment).

Global error is a measure of the deviation of the computed solution from the true solution over the range of integration or at one or more fixed points. Local error is a measure of the deviation of the computed solution at t_{n+1} from the true solution of the differential equation matching the computed solution at t_n. (This is difficult to define precisely for multistep methods because, in general, no solution of the equation passes through the set of points used to advance from t_n to t_{n+1}. However, the concept is useful, even if loosely defined.) Backward error is the perturbation that must be made to the differential equation to make it pass through the computed points.

In real-time problems, global error does not seem to be a very useful concept. In the absence of an external feedback path (that is, u(t) independent of y), an integration of a model over any significant time range is likely to lead to ridiculous results--a plane flying without a pilot. The difference in the position of the plane when it crashes for different integrators is not usually of great interest. If the external feedback path is included in the test, it will usually reduce the global error, at least in some components-- for example, in a tracking task, the external feedback is used to force the solution to a desired value.

A small local error is certainly important, but factors other than its size may be as important. For example, an oscillating error is certainly undesirable in emulation as it makes the system "hard to handle"--the effect of badly unbalanced front wheels on a car at high speed. A "constant error" (a tendency to turn to one side in an automobile) is

much simpler for a person to handle. Therefore, one suspects
that an oscillating error is more likely to cause a
simulated system to be unstable (impossible for a person to
control stably) than a slowly changing error, even if much
larger. Since one of the purposes of simulation is to
determine if the system is "stable" in the sense that it can
be controlled by a person, it appears that an oscillating
error can lead to false conclusions.

Backward error may offer the best measure of real-time
simulation error for a number of reasons. The usual one is
that if the computed solution can be shown to be the solution
of a system perturbed by no more than the tolerances in
implementation (in the case of control systems, wing
construction, etc.) or in measurement (in the case of wind
tunnel data), there is as much reason to believe the computed
solution as the true solution of the model. The second is
that if a small change is needed in the behavior of the
external machine/person to achieve the same solution to the
computed model as would be obtained in the mathematical
model without the change, the computation is at least a good
emulation. However, there is a catch here; the change
needed in the external reaction must be a feasible change,
that is, one which does not require a change in the external
reaction to account for a future error. With this restriction, there is, in most cases, no change in the external
reaction that will offset the computed error because by the
time it has happened and been observed, it is already too
late to correct it. (That is, in the tracking example, it
is reasonable to ask if the driving function can be changed
from $u(t) = \mu[d(t) - y(t - \Delta_p)] + \nu d(t)$ to $u(t) =$
$\mu_1[d(t) - y(t - \Delta_p)] + \nu_1 d(t) + f$ where μ_1, ν_1 and f are
functions of values of y and d for earlier times, but they
cannot be functions of time or determined by future values
of y and d.)

Usually, the major questions that the designer wants to
answer are related to stability. If the numerical system
behaves unstably, does it mean that the physical system is
also unstable? Conversely, if the numerical system is stable,
can we be reasonably certain that the physical system is

stable? Secondarily, the designer is interested in other
statistics such as fuel consumption to execute a particular
flight pattern. Accuracy in the latter statistics is
related to global errors, so these should not be totally
neglected, but the important criteria seem to be

   a.   minimizing delay--because of its effect on stability
   b.   accurately representing the important eigenvalues of
        the system--probably those near the imaginary axis
   c.   not introducing spurious components--no high
        frequency oscillations which look like additional
        eigenvalues near the imaginary axis.
   d.   small local or backward errors.

6.   METHODS FOR REDUCING DELAY AND IMPROVING STABILITY

   Many simulations involve second order differential
equations representing the equations of motion. These
equations usually have little, if any, damping, so have
eigenvalues close to the imaginary axis. In some cases, the
eigenvalues will actually be in the right-half plane when a
block of equations is isolated from the total system, and it
is only feedback through other processes in the system which
stabilize them. Other processes in typical models are highly
damped first order equations or systems of equations
representing control systems, etc.

   As Figure 2 indicates, there are a number of internal
feedback paths within the model which could be made implicit
were it not for real-time constraints. A number of methods
are in current use and have been proposed to try and achieve
the effects of implicitness with a single function evaluation,
thus reducing delay and enlarging the region of absolute
stability. Figure 5 shows a system of three first order
equations fed on the left by a driving function $u(t)$ and
generating an output $y(t)$ on the right. A direct explicit
process applied to this results in a delay of $3h$ between a
change in u and any effect of that change appearing in y.
Instead, the equations can be treated from left to right,
starting with all values known at t_n. First, u_n and y_n can
be used to compute w_{n+1}. Then, x_{n+1} can be computed using
w_{n+1}, so the integration formula for x can be partially
implicit. Finally, y_{n+1} can be computed with a partially

implicit integration formula using the value x_{n+1} just computed. It is as if the loop has been broken between y and w. Clearly, the choice of places to break implicit loops can affect the results.

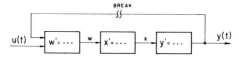

Figure 5.   Three Coupled First Order Equations

The effect of breaking loops can be reduced if an approximation to the appropriate Jacobian is known. (These must be known a priori as there is no time available for their calculation.) Such methods amount to using an implicit integration method of the form

$$y_{n+1} = h\beta_0 f(y_{n+1}) + \ldots$$

where $f(y_{n+1})$ is replaced by

$$f(y_n) + J(y_{n+1} - y_n)$$

Unless J is exact, the order of the method drops to one (but we don't care particularly). However, even a relatively inaccurate J can give much better stability than an explicit method. For example, if we start with the trapezoidal method and replace $f(y_{n+1})$ with $\mu(y_{n+1} - y_n) + f(y_n)$ and study the test equation $y' = \lambda y$, we find that the region of absolute stability is a circle, center $- (1 + h\mu/2)$ and radius $1 + h\mu/2$. If $\mu = 0$, it is, of course, Euler's method. For negative approximations, μ, to the Jacobian, the region expands.

Some special equations can be integrated directly. Many of the first order equations are linear over most of their range. The nonlinearities are usually limiters which simply prevent a value from exceeding a design range. These equations, of the form

$$y' = \lambda y + f(t)$$

are handled by integrating them to get

$$y_{n+1} = \int_{t_n}^{t_{n+1}} e^{\lambda(t-\tau)} f(\tau)d\tau + e^{\lambda h}y_n$$

and then approximating the integrand numerically. If the
solution exceeds its limits, it is simply set to the
prescribed value. This method is particularly useful for
low order systems with large negative λ as happens in control
systems.

In some cases, systems can be handled conveniently in
this form. Such a case is described in [1] in which the
system

$$y' = Ay + u(t)$$

has an approximately constant A with the property that
$A^2 = -\omega^2 I$. The terms e^{Ah} can be calculated conveniently
from the relation

$$e^{Ah} = I \cos \omega h + Ah \sin \omega h$$

which is obtained from a power series expansion. However, in
general, it is not convenient to evaluate e^{Ah} for large
systems with other than small eigenvalues.

Delay can be reduced by ordering the calculations
appropriately. Although we normally think of a single
function predictor-corrector method as a PEC method, in real-
time applications it should be used as an ECP method as shown
in Figure 6.

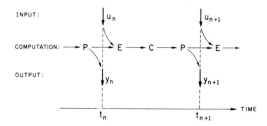

Figure 6. Evaluate, Correct, Predict Method

Immediately an input is received, the function is
evaluated. Then a correction can be made to the last value--
even thought it has already been output--and a prediction of
the next value made. The key point is that the predicted
value is output because it is more "up-to-date" than the
corrected value at the previous point. This is really a
special case of the "EXCP" methods shown in Figure 7,

where X stands for <u>extrapolation</u>. The value to be output is
an extrapolation from available information; the extrapolation formula should be chosen to optimize the important
properties such as delay, overshoot, oscillation, etc. Low
order formulas appear to be more appropriate than high order
formulas because they exhibit less "ringing" to step inputs.
However, the characteristics desired for the output value are
not necessarily the characteristics wanted in the integration
formula, so separate formulas should be used to correct and
predict. Tests on simple problems subject to step inputs
indicated that a corrector-predictor pair of third order
gave a good compromise between accuracy and oscillation,
while a first or second order extrapolation formula could be
used to keep the output ringing small.

   While use of the computation shown in Figure 7 reduces
the computation delay to a minimum, evaluation is the largest
part of the computation time; the computation time for the C
and P steps are relatively small so Δ_c will not be appreciably
less than h.

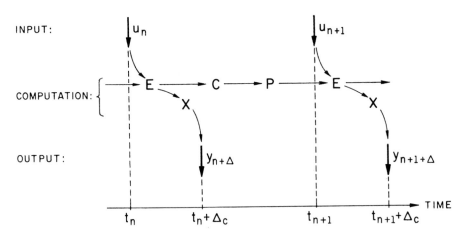

Figure 7. EXCP Method

   Exponential fitting can be used to improve both
accuracy and stability of numerical methods. If coefficients
are chosen to make a method exact for $y(t) = e^{\lambda_0 t}$, the method
will be reasonably accurate for solutions $e^{\lambda t}$ when λ is in
the neighborhood of λ_0. If λ_0 is on the imaginary axis, the

boundary of the region of absolute stability will pass
through λ_0 as shown in Figure 8. Consequently, the method
will probably be unstable for slightly larger or small
imaginary λ. This can be overcome by adding a small amount
of damping. We have found that forcing $e^{\lambda_0 t + \Theta}$ to be the
exact solution of the numerical method when $y' = \lambda_0 y$ will
move the stability boundary. If $\Theta = -10^{-3}$, it will move to
the right enough to put a large part of the imaginary axis
near X_0 within the region of absolute stability. It is
probably important not to push the stability boundary too far
to the right, both because it will reduce the size of the
region elsewhere and because it is probably important to
conserve energy approximately in oscillating components
corresponding to imaginary eigenvalues. (It is interesting
to ask if there are any methods that conserve energy.
Unfortunately, all such methods are implicit, corresponding
to generalizations of the trapezoidal rule.)

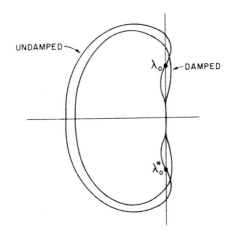

Figure 8.   Damped Exponential Fitting

If a system of the type shown in Figure 5 is handled by
a sequence of integrators, one for each process, and these
integrators are tuned for each process, oscillations can
occur because of the feedback path(s) that are neglected.
These oscillations often have a period equal to twice the
time step, that is, they are a ringing due to overshoot
followed by subsequent over-corrections. This ringing can be

reduced by using multistep methods as filters. If the
multistep method

$$\rho(E)y_n + \sigma(E)hy_n' = 0$$

is used, an oscillating input can be damped by choosing
coefficients such that $\sigma(-1) = 0$ (that is, $\beta_0 - \beta_1 + \beta_2 - \ldots$
$= 0$). This is the reason that the delayed trapezoidal rule
$y_{n+1} = y_n + h(y_n' + y_{n-1}')/2$ may have better overall behavior
than the more accurate Euler method.

Multirate methods are often proposed as a way of
reducing computation time. If a system can be partitioned
into two or more subsystems, say

$$y' = f(y, z, t)$$
$$z' = g(y, z, t)$$

such that z is slowly varying while y changes more rapidly,
a smaller time step can be used for y than z, possibly
saving a number of computations of g. There is no problem
with the classical theory--such methods converge as the two
step sizes go to zero provided that obvious stability
conditions are satisfied. (It should be realized that
evaluation of f requires "correct" values of z, so that z
must be extrapolated from the last integration point to an
appropriate order--actually at least one less than the
order of the method--to achieve the expected order, namely,
the minimum of the two orders. If z is not extrapolated, the
order will drop to one. However, this may not matter in
real-time systems where order is not an important
characteristic.)

If multirate methods are used, the calculation of the
slower components--the evaluation of g in the example above--
must be spread uniformly over several time steps, requiring
either incredibly careful coding or a multi-level operating
system which will allow one task to preempt another on the
basis of real-time interrupts.

Because some of the equations are second order, it is
natural to consider the direct integration of second order
systems. Multistep methods have the form

$$\rho_1(E)y_n + \sigma_1(E)hy_n' + \tau_1(E)h^2y_n'' = 0$$

$$\sigma_2(E)hy_n' + \tau_2(E)h^2y_n'' = 0$$

for the differential equation $y'' = f(y, y', t)$. Again, standard convergence theory applies, but, of more interest, the usual analysis for absolute stability breaks down, as shown in [2]. In methods for first order systems, we consider the test equation $y' = Ay$. The method leads to a difference system involving polynomials or rationals in A, so the method can be diagonalized by the same similarity transformation that diagonalizes A. Hence, the stability of the method can be determined from the eigenvalues of A, so a region of absolute stability can be defined such that the method is absolutely stable if the eigenvalues of A are inside this region. Unfortunately, the only reasonable second order test equation is $y'' = Ay' + B$, leading to a generalized eigenvalue problem $(\lambda^2 I - A\lambda - B)\underline{x} = 0$. The transformation of this problem to "diagonal" form is not the transformation that takes the numerical method to a similar form, so it is not possible to define regions of absolute stability in the same way. In fact, there exist methods which are stable if both eigenvalues of a single equation are in a given region, but which are unstable even if all eigenvalues of two coupled second order equations are in that region. This is unfortunate because an eigenvalue characterization of problems is very natural for engineers.

7. CONCLUSIONS

The problem of real-time integration is still very much insolved. There exist a number of promising techniques but it appears to be difficult to develop general purpose methods. We finish these remarks with some very discouraging experimental evidence; the simulation of a helicopter subsystem referred to previously. In this problem, a five bladed rotor advanced about 40° in each time step due to the real-time constraints. The model is quite nonlinear, but from a linear point of view, there is a lot of energy at the rotor frequency (which also is approximately an eigenvalue of the system) and a fair amount in the fifth harmonic (due to coupling between each blade and the body). The method in use, known as the Sikorsky method, selects the coefficients b, c, d and e in

$$y_{n+1} = y_n + by_n' + cy_n''$$

$$y_{n+1}' = dy_n' + ey_n''$$

to match the first harmonic. In non-real-time tests, this method outperforms a fourth order Runge-Kutta method until the Runge-Kutta method is used at a quarter of the step size-- or about 16 times as much work. This indicates the importance of tuning the methods to the problem and the difficulty of developing general purpose software.

REFERENCES

[1] L. E. Barker, Jr., et al. (1973), Development and Application of a Local Linearization Algorithm for the Integration of Quaternion Rate Equations in Real-Time Flight Simulation Problems, NASA TN D-7347, National Aeronautics and Space Administration, Washington, DC.

[2] C. W. Gear (1977), The stability of numerical methods for second order ordinary differential equations, SIAM Journal on Numerical Analysis (to appear).

Many of the ideas discussed arose from work performed jointly with L. Brown of the University of Virginia, and J. Rosenbaum of the Virginia Commonwealth University. This was supported in part by the US Energy Research and Development Administration and by NASA while author was in residence at ICASE, NASA Langley Research Center, Hampton, Virginia.

Department of Computer Science
University of Illinois
Urbana, Illinois 61801

Mathematical Software
and Exploratory Data Analysis
David C. Hoaglin

ABSTRACT

Developments in data analysis in recent years
have placed increasing emphasis on flexible exploration, and data on the behavior of algorithms and
their implementations often responds favorably to
such an approach. Many new data-analytic techniques
make a wide range of demands on available numerical
algorithms, and software components must be
packaged in a way which provides flexible control
over the data-analysis process. This paper
examines a few of the ways in which mathematical
software and exploratory data analysis should
interact to satisfy their respective needs.

1. INTRODUCTION.

As a computing statistician, I have two broad reasons
for being concerned with mathematical software. First, it is
indispensable for most calculations in modern data analysis
and statistical theory; and as I develop new techniques, I
naturally want to implement them and gain further insight by
trying them on real data. Second, those who develop software
frequently test it in various ways to learn about its performance, and these experiments produce data. In many cases
available statistical techniques can readily reveal the
essential behavior and determine how much is signal and how
much is noise. But sometimes the situation is new and
provides a challenge for the statistician to meet by developing a new technique or model. And so the cycle continues,
with both statistics and mathematical software drawing on
each other.

In studying an algorithm empirically or comparing its
performance to that of other algorithms, the initial need is
less for the inferences of classical statistics and more for
flexible tools which promote fruitful contact with the data by
uncovering, displaying, and summarizing behavior, both expected and unexpected. Exploratory data analysis, as
embodied in a collection of techniques developed by
John W. Tukey [21], is well suited to such needs. In this
account I will examine both sides of the connection between
mathematical software and exploratory data analysis. After a
brief description of the attitudes and major principles of
exploratory data analysis, I will apply a number of them in
analyzing a set of data from a comparative timing experiment.
Then I will turn to the sorts of demands which the exploratory
mode of data analysis is likely to make on mathematical
software.

2.   OVERVIEW OF EXPLORATORY DATA ANALYSIS.

Modern data analysis can broadly be divided into two
phases: exploratory and confirmatory. It is often helpful
to subdivide the confirmatory phase [20], but that need not
concern us here. Exploratory data analysis probes a body of
data to see what behavior, what appearances, are present. At
this stage we naturally ask such questions as "How should we
look at the data?" "How do we summarize the appearances?" and
"What further layers or components of behavior are there?"
The emphasis is on flexibility, on letting the data contribute to guiding the analysis from one step to the next.

Confirmatory data analysis then focuses on assessing the
strength of the evidence, asking whether we should believe
the appearances we have found, what other patterns we might
have found, and whether there is really a signal in the noise.
It is at this stage that probability and the techniques of
statistical inference begin to enter in.

In giving an overview of exploratory data analysis, I
would like to identify four major themes which motivate many
of the techniques: displays, residuals, transformations, and
resistance. The example in the next section will show all of
these in action.

In any serious data analysis it is hard to overemphasize the need to see behavior. Thus a variety of graphical and semi-graphical displays have been invented to reveal features of both the raw data and the summaries fitted to it. Substantial gains in analysis often come from being brought face to face with the unexpected.

Usually we uncover a systematic pattern (such as a straight-line shape in a scatterplot) which can be summarized in a model for the structure of the data. We must then look beneath this summarized or fitted behavior by calculating and examining residuals. The simple equation

$$(2.1) \qquad\qquad \text{data} \;=\; \text{fit} \;+\; \text{residual} \quad ,$$

trivial though it may seem, is one of the most important in data analysis. It should always remind us to look at both parts, the fit and the residuals; and it explains why good data analysis generally produces more output than it has input -- the constants required to specify the fit, as well as one residual for each raw data value, to say nothing of other diagnostic information. In any complex body of data we can expect several layers of behavior; we summarize each in turn and lift it away so that we can focus on the next.

As an intermediate step in summarizing behavior, we may need to subject the data to a transformation such as square root, logarithm, or reciprocal. At the very least, a good choice of transformation can simplify the pattern, as in changing a curved relationship between two variables into a straight line. This change of viewpoint may make the situation easier to understand, and it can have other benefits such as stabilizing variability.

The processes of display, fitting, and transformation are often more effective when they can take advantage of resistance. The basic notion of a resistant summary or fit is that, if a small part of the data is perturbed a lot, the summary should be affected only slightly. For example, a gross error in one data point should produce a large residual

and call attention to itself instead of distorting the fit.
Unfortunately the popular least-squares procedures are not
resistant; we shall return to this in Section 4.

Highly skilled data analysts have used techniques in an
exploratory spirit for some time. The thrust of exploratory
data analysis has been to sharpen available tools, develop
new ones, and unify the whole approach. We turn now to an
example to show how some of these techniques work.

3. AN EXAMPLE: TIMING DATA

Recently Barwell and George [2] compared algorithms for
solving symmetric indefinite n × n systems of linear
equations, Ax = b . For n = 25(25)200 they generated a
random test matrix A and a suitable right-hand side b ,
and they studied timings for eight methods or implementations
on two machines. The structure of this experiment provides a
number of handles for the data analyst, and I will now use it
to illustrate several of the techniques of exploratory data
analysis.

Table 1 reproduces (from Table III of [2]) the timings,
using a Honeywell 6050, for the five methods most directly of
interest:

Aasen's method [1],

The Bunch-Kaufman method [4],

Parlett and Reid's tridiagonal method [17],

Bunch's block-diagonal pivoting method [3], and

Householder tridiagonalization.

To label these in tables and plots, I will use the tags A,
K, P, B, and H, respectively. In approaching this two-way
table of data we know that the algorithms require $O(n^3)$
multiplications and divisions, but it is useful to ask whether
we can summarize it in a way which separates the contributions
of the method and of the size of the problem to the timing
figures. That is, we should try a model of the form

(3.1) $T_{ij} = \mu + \alpha_i + \beta_j + \varepsilon_{ij}$,

where T_{ij} is the time required by method j to solve
problem i , μ is an overall constant, α_i is the effect
(or additional contribution) for problem i , β_j is the

			method		
$\underline{n}$	$\underline{A}$	$\underline{K}$	$\underline{P}$	$\underline{B}$	$\underline{H}$
25	18	11	19	24	33
50	87	69	123	144	218
75	238	191	388	440	690
100	495	408	886	996	1584
125	896	822	1697	1891	3032
150	1464	1377	2891	3204	5169
175	2229	2121	4548	5021	8131
200	3218	3121	6734	7416	12050

Table 1. Timings for the Honeywell 6050 (unit = .01 sec.)

effect for method j , and ε_{ij} is a random disturbance or
fluctuation (reflecting primarily timing imprecision --
Barwell and George point out that their timings are accurate
only to about .1 sec.). From the operation counts for the
various methods it is clear that the model (3.1) oversim-
plifies matters, but by beginning with it we can learn a good
deal about what models might be more appropriate. Besides,
knowing something about the "answer" will later give us a way
of judging how well the exploration has done.

For two-way tables the basic resistant exploratory
technique is "median polish" [21], which iteratively removes
row and column medians from the table $\{T_{ij}\}$ and arrives at
the fit

(3.2) $\hat{T}_{ij} = m + a_i + b_j$

with the side conditions median$\{a_i\} = 0$ and median$\{b_j\} = 0$.
Median polish can be regarded as a relaxation technique for
fitting the model (3.1) in the L_1 norm, but it generally is
carried only through two full cycles (e.g., first rows, then
columns, then rows, then columns). Table 2 shows the result
of applying median polish to the data in Table 1 (in this
case one full cycle suffices). We immediately see that the
timings for the Parlett-Reid method fell consistently in the
middle, so that the other methods are summarized relative to
it, and that the residuals, $r_{ij} = T_{ij} - \hat{T}_{ij}$, in the body of
this table are very systematic. The upper left and lower

			method			
n	A	K	P	B	H	effect
25	595	668	0	-147	-1002	-1273
50	560	622	0	-131	- 921	-1169
75	446	479	0	-100	- 714	- 904
100	205	198	0	- 42	- 318	- 406
125	- 205	- 199	0	42	319	405
150	- 831	- 838	0	161	1262	1599
175	-1723	-1751	0	321	2567	3256
200	-2920	-2937	0	530	4300	5422
effect	- 596	- 676	0	152	1016	1292

Table 2. Analysis of Timings by Median Polish (unit=.01 sec.)

right corners are all positive, while the other two corners
are all negative, and the sizes of the residuals increase
toward the corners. This tendency of the data to warp away
from the fit is a strong indication that it should be transformed before trying to use equation (3.1) as a model, and we
can readily find out from the data what transformations may
be appropriate.

To probe for a simple transformation in a two-way table,
we use a "diagnostic plot," which plots the residual r_{ij}
against its corresponding "comparison value," cv_{ij}, defined
by

$$(3.3) \qquad cv_{ij} = a_i \times b_j / m \qquad .$$

The pattern to look for is a rough straight line; and it is
straightforward to show that when the data should be transformed by the p th power, the slope will be approximately
1-p (for purposes of data analysis, the logarithm plays the
role of the zeroth power). Figure 1 shows the diagnostic plot
for the residuals in Table 2. Since there is very strong
evidence that the slope is 1 , we take logs (to the base 10)
of the data in Table 1. The result is Table 3, and performing
median polish on this table yields Table 4. There are still
systematic appearances in four columns of this table, but they
are not so directly related to the effects that we should look

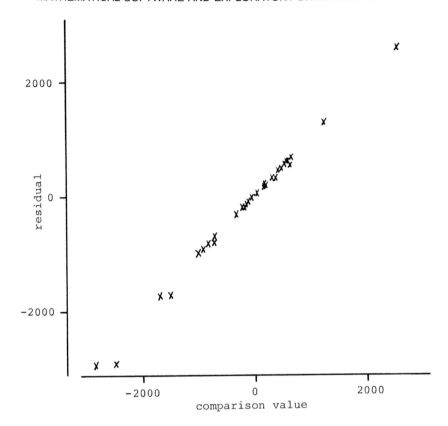

Figure 1. Diagnostic Plot for Timing Data (unit = .01, one point off scale)

	method				
n	A	K	P	B	H
25	-745	-959	-721	-620	-481
50	- 60	-161	90	158	338
75	377	281	589	643	839
100	695	611	947	998	1200
125	952	915	1230	1277	1482
150	1166	1139	1461	1506	1713
175	1348	1327	1658	1701	1910
200	1508	1494	1828	1870	2081

Table 3. The Timings in a Logarithmic Scale (unit = .001)

			method			
n	A	K	P	B	H	effect
25	189	26	-52	0	-64	-1758
50	96	46	-19	0	-23	- 980
75	48	3	- 5	0	- 7	- 495
100	12	- 21	- 1	1	0	- 141
125	- 13	1	0	-2	0	141
150	- 26	- 2	4	0	4	368
175	- 39	- 9	6	0	6	563
200	- 48	- 11	7	0	8	732
effect	-265	-316	0	49	252	1089

Table 4. Analysis of Log Timings by Median Polish (unit=.001)

for another transformation. Besides, we can probably agree
that the logarithmic scale is a very convenient one for this
set of data -- comparisons by ratios in the raw data (as in
Tables IV, V, and VI of [2]) become differences here, and the
sizes of fluctuations are more likely to be the same over the
whole table. We will return to the residuals shortly, but
first we should examine the parts of the fit.

The common constant, 1.089 , tells as much as one
number can about the behavior of the data in the log scale.
We could transform it back into the raw scale, but that seems
unnecessary at the moment. The row effects (one for each
value of n) can be interpreted as summarizing the relative
difficulty of the eight test problems for this set of five
methods. Since each test problem represents a different value
of n , we naturally ask how these effects are related to n .
Their spacing suggests plotting them against $\log_{10}n$; and the
result (Figure 2) looks quite straight, except for n=25 and
perhaps n=50. Ignoring these two points (which may have been
affected by timer resolution) and fitting a line by eye to the
rest, we find a slope of about 2.88 , not quite up to the
asymptotic value, 3 , predicted by the operation counts.

The column effects (one for each method) reflect
considerable differences between some of the methods over this
set of test problems:

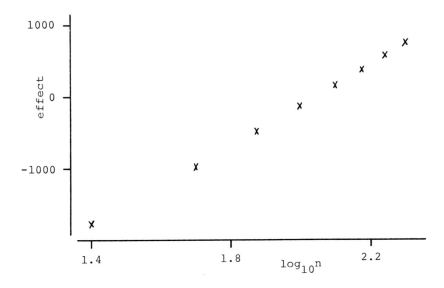

Figure 2. Relation of Effects for Size of Problem to $\log_{10}n$
(timings in log scale, unit = .001)

tag:	K	A	P	B	H
effect:	-.316	-.265	0	.049	.252

The customary centering leads most directly to ratios based on
the Parlett-Reid method, but it is simple to find any other
difference and its corresponding ratio of typical timings.
For example, the Householder tridiagonalization typically
takes 3.7 (=$10^{.568}$) times as long as the Bunch-Kaufman
method, and the ratio of Aasen to Bunch-Kaufman is 1.125 .
       Now a close look at the residuals in Table 4 suggests
that we plot those for each method against $\log_{10}n$ in order
to bring out the trends which remain. Figure 3 does this for
A, K, P, and H ; P coincides with K for n=125 , and H
coincides with P for n $\geq$ 75 . Most of these are close
enough to linear trends that we may fit straight lines to them,
but we will need to do this resistantly if we are to guard
against stray points. Thus we need to use another exploratory
technique, the "resistant line."

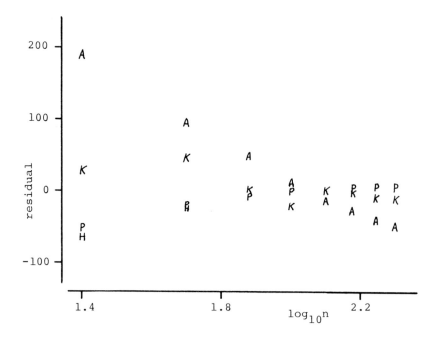

<u>Figure 3</u>.   Relation of Residuals (Table 4) to $\log_{10} n$
              (timings in log scale, unit = .001)

For a set of (x,y)   data points, the basic idea of the
resistant line is to determine the slope from two summary
points, one for low values of x and the other for high
values of x . Specifically we sort the points into order on
the basis of increasing x , split them into portions
(according to their x-values) so that roughly one-third of
them fall into each portion, and then take the median of the
x-coordinates and (separately) the median of the y-coordinates
in each portion. These give the coordinates of the summary
points, and the low and high summary points determine the
slope. (As in other resistant analyses, some iteration may
be required.) Table 5 illustrates this technique for the
residuals from column K of Table 4. Removing the trial
slope, -64 , still leaves some slope, so we simply treat
these adjusted y-values as a new set of data (with

x	y	y+64x	y+40x	new residual
1.398	26	115	81	0
1.699	46	155	114	33
1.875	3	123	78	- 3
2.000	-21	107	59	-22
2.097	1	135	85	4
2.176	- 2	137	85	4
2.243	- 9	135	81	0
2.300	-11	136	81	0

median = 81

summary points

	x	y	y+64x	y+40x
low	1.699	26	123	81
mid	2.048	-10	121	72
high	2.243	- 9	136	81

$$\text{trial slope} = \frac{-9 - 26}{2.243-1.699} = -64 \quad ; \quad \text{adjustment} = \frac{136-123}{.544} = 24$$

final slope = -40 , intercept = 81

Table 5. Fitting a Resistant Line ($x = \log_{10}n$, y = residual
          from column K of Table 4)

x-coordinates unchanged) and obtain the slope adjustment, 24.
Subtracting this yields a net slope of -40 and no need for
further adjustment. The median of these adjusted values, 81 ,
serves as an intercept, and removing it brings us to a new
set of residuals.

Fitting resistant lines to the other columns of
residuals in Table 4 gives the following result:

tag:	A	K	P	B	H
slope:	-248	-40	46	0	53
intercept:	516	81	-96	0	-112 .

To get a composite picture of how the methods compare, we
need to combine the intercept with the effect found earlier
and recenter these new effects. Table 6 has the completed
analysis, including the residuals. It is much easier to
integrate our comparison of the five methods if we plot the
fitted line,

	method					
n	A	K	P	B	H	effect
25	20	0	- 20	0	-26	-1758
50	1	33	- 1	0	- 1	- 980
75	- 3	- 3	5	0	6	- 495
100	- 9	-23	2	0	5	- 140
125	- 9	4	0	-2	1	141
150	- 2	4	0	0	1	368
175	1	0	- 1	0	- 1	563
200	6	0	- 3	0	- 2	732
effect	202	-284	-145	0	91	1138
$\log_{10}n$	-248	- 40	46	0	53	

Table 6.   Analysis after Fitting a Line to Each Column of
Table 4   (unit = .001)

$$(\text{combined intercept}) \; + \; (\text{slope}) \; \log_{10}n$$

for each of them. When we do this in Figure 4, we see
considerable variety in behavior. (Of course, we need to
remember that we have removed the effect of the size of the
test problem, something Figure 2 told us is close to a
straight line in $\log_{10}n$. That is, we have subtracted a
common straight line from all five methods. Part of the
reason for looking at residuals is to see such departures more
clearly.) Bunch's method now provides a horizontal reference
line, while Householder and Parlett-Reid are close to parallel,
indicating that their timings differ by a constant factor
(namely 1.7). The most striking appearance in Figure 4 is
the narrowing gap between Aasen and Bunch-Kaufman; the crossover point (on the Honeywell 6050) should lie just beyond
n=200 (say about n=220). We also notice, of course, that
the fitted lines for these two methods have negative slopes,
emphasizing that they execute faster than the rest.
    Examining the residuals in Table 4 led us to take a
further step and fit a line in $\log_{10}n$ to each column. We
owe ourselves a look at the residuals which remain after
removing those lines. Returning to Table 6, we find the
residuals generally much smaller than in Table 4. Only five,

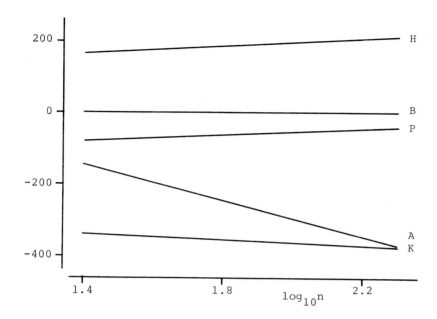

Figure 4.   Relative Trends for the Five Methods (timings in
            log scale, unit = .001)

with magnitudes greater than 20 , demand attention. Three
of these are for n=25 , where the times were short enough to
reflect discreteness or imprecision in the timer. The other
two involve the Bunch-Kaufman method but do not seem to be
part of any systematic pattern. In such a situation one
might seek an explanation in the circumstances under which
these timings were made, but I have gone as far as I can.
     We have learned quite a lot about the performance of the
five methods on the Honeywell 6050, but we have so far ignored
completely the other machine for which Barwell and George
reported timings, the IBM 360/75. In analyzing the corresponding data for this machine we should expect tc find both
similarities and differences, and we can now skip such steps
as the diagnostic plot. Transforming the timings (from
Table II of [2]) into the log scale immediately, we apply
median polish and then resistantly fit a linear trend in
$\log_{10}n$ for each method. The result is Table 7, which can

readily be compared to Table 6. Most notable is the
excellent agreement between the two sets of row effects.
Thus the test problems have the same effect on timings for
both machines. (This may, of course, be primarily the effect
of n : Barwell and George do not say whether the same
random-number generator was used on both machines.)

n	A	K	P	B	H	effect
			method			
25	9	40	- 39	- 7	0	-1728
50	14	- 8	- 3	0	14	- 974
75	0	- 8	5	1	0	- 492
100	-11	13	4	0	- 2	- 139
125	- 8	12	1	0	- 7	138
150	- 8	- 5	1	0	1	370
175	1	- 6	0	0	2	563
200	4	5	- 3	0	- 1	733
effect	362	-224	-156	0	114	551
$\log_{10} n$	-298	- 26	51	-27	75	

Table 7. Analysis of Timings for the IBM 360/75 (log scale,
          unit = .001)

Qualitatively the straight lines for methods are similar
on the two machines, but there are noticeable differences in
both slopes and intercepts. As a consequence the crossover
point for Aasen and Bunch-Kaufman falls around n=150. Given
this consistent comparison between Aasen and Bunch-Kaufman, I
am not quite so ready to regard the difference in execution
times between them as insignificant [2, p.247].

The difference between the common constants (1.138 for
the Honeywell 6050 and 0.551 the IBM 360/75) summarizes
their difference in speed, roughly a factor of 4 .

The one remaining part of the two analyses is the
residuals, and it is evident that those for the IBM 360/75
tend to be somewhat larger. We would generally not expect
the smaller times to be more variable, and this may have to
remain a loose end in the present analysis. We can again see,
however, that the two very large residuals belong to n=25 .

We have now examined this timing example in considerable detail, both to illustrate several techniques of exploratory data analysis and to give a fairly clear picture of how times for solving symmetric indefinite systems respond to the size of the problem, the method, and the machine. (We should now be able to apply what we have learned to the timing data given by Bunch, Kaufman, and Parlett [5].) This analysis is not the same as the direct approach of fitting a cubic polynomial in n to the times for each method, but it has certain advantages. The column effects in Table 4 summarize how the methods behave over the given range of n and permit comparisons of typical performance. This is not the whole story (as we have seen in Figure 4), but such overall statements are often useful. Further, by bringing all the data together and fitting an additive model (in the log scale) we have been able to get a better picture of the sizes of fluctuations which occur. If the size of a fluctuation in the original data is related to the size of the data value, a transformation which promotes additivity will also tend to equalize sizes of fluctuations. Finally, the resistant analysis is far less sensitive to wild values than fitting cubics. If we still wanted to fit the polynomials and study the cubic and quadratic coefficients, we could deal with the large residuals in Table 6 by using only the "smoothed" data, that is, the fit -- we would discard all the residuals, calculate the table of fitted values according to fit = data - residual , undo the logarithmic transformation, and fit the cubic polynomials in n to the resulting values.

In presenting this analysis there are still more opportunities to use displays. We could have made a two-way plot of the additive fit (3.2), and we could have used a stem-and-leaf display to show each set of residuals as an unstructured batch, but for now we leave these for the reader to pursue [21].

It should be easy to imagine many other kinds of data which could profitably be explored. A few examples are counts of function evaluations in adaptive quadrature or nonlinear optimization, relative errors in approximation, and perhaps storage requirements for debugging options. An

analyzed example [12] concerns loop optimization scores in a
study of Fortran programs. Another class of opportunities
for data analysis is in developing direct approximations [13],
of limited accuracy, to serve as quick and dirty substitutes
for more complicated tables and functions.

4.   SOFTWARE NEEDS OF EXPLORATORY DATA ANALYSIS.

Having given a detailed example of what data analysis
can reasonably do for mathematical software, I now want to
sketch several areas in which data analysts would hope to
benefit from further developments in mathematical software.
It would, however, be wrong to begin this discussion without
an expression of gratitude for the continuing and valuable
help which a number of computer scientists have provided so
far. Numerical linear algebra [9, 11, 16] is the best
example, and nonlinear least-squares problems [10, 7] have
also received considerable attention. Computer graphics and
programming languages and systems are areas where we should
expect some impact in the not-too-distant future.

The previous section gave us a glimpse of the role of
polishing in resistant analyses: Not only are several
iterations often necessary in making the basic resistant fits
such as the two-way model (3.2) and the resistant line, but
further iterations also arise when we must combine the simpler
components into a more complicated fit. This is not unbear-
able, and it is part of the price we must pay (and are now
able to pay) for resistant analyses. As such techniques are
more widely implemented and used, we will want to do what we
can to see that the likely combinations go together smoothly
and that the algorithm for a particular simple analysis uses
intermediate results from an earlier iteration when later
polishing is required. Careful attention to how algorithms
are modularized may be a major element here, and guiding the
overall flow of polishing when a user builds a complicated
model interactively will require special features in the
programming or data-analysis system.

Whether one uses resistant techniques or the more
standard least squares, an exploratory spirit puts considerable emphasis on diagnosing stray data points and points of
unusual sensitivity. A good example is the "hat matrix" in

fitting the usual linear regression model

(4.1) $y = X\beta + \varepsilon$

by least squares. Here, in the statistician's customary
notation, y is $n \times 1$, X is $n \times p$ (with $n > p$ and rank p),
β ($p \times 1$) is the vector of regression coefficients to be
estimated, and ε ($n \times 1$) is the random error or disturbance
term. The fitted y-values, $\hat{y}_i$, are related to the data
values y_j through

(4.2) $\hat{y} = Hy$

where $H = X(X^T X)^{-1} X^T$ is the hat matrix. In general H is
quite dense, and this emphasizes the lack of resistance of
ordinary least squares -- each data value y_j has non-zero
leverage on every fitted value $\hat{y}_i$. Since H depends only
on X , we can examine the leverage situation in the design
or factor space without regard to y . The diagonal elements
h_{ii} are the easiest to interpret: they tell us how much
impact the data value y_i will have on the corresponding
fitted value $\hat{y}_i$, entirely as a function of X. If h_{ii} is
too large, we must pay careful attention to y_i to guard
against its being a stray value and distorting the analysis.
Since H is a projection (onto the p-dimensional subspace
spanned by the columns of X), we must have $0 \le h_{ii} \le 1$,
but it is not quite as easy to say when h_{ii} is too large.
One rough rule of thumb [14] regards any row of X with
$h_{ii} > 2p/n$ as a high-leverage point, but we generally want
to look at all the diagonal elements of H as a batch of
numbers to see whether any stand out as large. When we are
concerned about a possible stray y-value, we will set it
aside and calculate its fitted value from the other n-1 data
points. This can be done without starting over, but it is
another thing to plan for in implementing least-squares
regression. Similarly, we would want the diagonal elements
of H as a by-product of decomposing X , and this may
influence the choice of algorithm, especially if n can be
quite large. Indeed, the growing need to deal with large data

sets may force us to find a cheaper substitute for the
diagonal of H , guided in part by what can be extracted from
various decompositions.

If we turn now to nonlinear least-squares problems, it
seems clear that such diagnostic information will be at least
as important as in linear problems. We could base a hat
matrix on a local linearization of the nonlinear problem, but
now the choice of neighborhood matters, and the initial
parameter estimate may not be a good choice for this purpose.
There is a great deal to be learned about these situations.

Since least squares lacks resistance, a number of
statisticians have recently been studying alternatives for
the model (4.1). Many of these come under the heading
"iteratively reweighted least squares"; that is, they start
at an initial estimate for β , re-estimate β by weighted
least squares with weights which depend on the residuals, and
iterate. One popular weight function [15] is

$$
(4.3) \qquad \begin{aligned}
w_h(t) &= 1 & \text{for } |t| &\leq h \\
&= h/|t| & \text{for } |t| &> h \qquad .
\end{aligned}
$$

The need for diagnosis remains, and now it is natural also to
study the sensitivity of the solution to the "trimming
parameter" h . Denby and Mallows [6] have proposed two
displays which trace the estimated coefficients $\hat{\beta}_j$ and the
residuals $r_i = y_i - \hat{y}_i$ as functions of h . They present
an algorithm which constructs these traces by successively
trimming one point at a time, but (as they point out) this is
not adequate for all cases, and it may be possible to overcome all the drawbacks without greatly increasing the cost.
These and similar displays are a desirable adjunct to
resistant regression analysis, and they will become much more
convenient as implementations which support them become
generally available.

Finally, when we are able to make substantial use of
interactive graphics hardware and software [8, 18, 19], we
can broaden our thinking about displays. We can have ready
access to various representations of data, fit, and
residuals; and, as we become accustomed to looking at these,

we will doubtless invent new special-purpose displays. These
may occasionally strain the capabilities of the available
mathematical software, but it would be good if, as far as
possible, that software meshed smoothly with the displays.
This may be primarily a matter of modularization, and the
important thing is to provide flexibility.

5.   SUMMARY.

    In discussing some of the connections between exploratory
data analysis and mathematical software, I have given a brief
sketch of attitudes and techniques in exploratory data
analysis. The analysis of the timing data showed how some of
these work, both individually and together. From this and
other examples it is clear that exploratory data analysis can
contribute to understanding many bodies of data on mathematical software and, equally, that it can be more effective
when aided by the right software. There is much interesting
cooperative work that we can do, and I am happy to have been
able to present a statistician's viewpoint on some of it.

REFERENCES

1.   J. O. Aasen (1973), On the reduction of a symmetric
        matrix to tridiagonal form. BIT, 11, pp. 233-242.

2.   V. Barwell and A. George (1976), A comparison of
        algorithms for solving symmetric indefinite systems
        of linear equations. ACM Trans. Math. Software,
        2, pp. 242-251.

3.   J. R. Bunch (1971), Analysis of the diagonal pivoting
        method. SIAM J. Numer. Anal., 8, pp. 656-680.

4.   J. R. Bunch and L. Kaufman (1975), Some stable methods
        for calculating inertia and solving symmetric
        linear systems. Report CU-CS-063-75, Department of
        Computer Science, University of Colorado.

5.   J. R. Bunch, L. Kaufman, and B. N. Parlett (1976),
        Decomposition of a symmetric matrix. Numer. Math.,
        27, pp. 95-109.

6. L. Denby and C. L. Mallows (1977), Two diagnostic
    displays for robust regression analysis.
    Technometrics, 19, pp. 1-13.

7. J. E. Dennis, Jr. and R. E. Welsch (1976), Techniques
    for nonlinear least squares and robust regression.
    Proc. Statist. Comput. Sect. Amer. Statist. Assoc.,
    2, pp. 83-87.

8. M. A. Fisherkeller, J. H. Friedman, and J. W. Tukey
    (1974), PRIM-9, An interactive multidimensional
    data display and analysis system. AEC Scientific
    Computer Information Exchange Meeting, 2-3 May 1974.

9. G. H. Golub (1969), Matrix decompositions and statistical
    calculations. Statistical Computation (R.C. Milton
    and J.A. Nelder, eds.), Academic Press, pp. 365-397.

10. G. H. Golub and V. Pereyra (1973), The differentiation
    of pseudo-inverses and nonlinear least squares
    problems whose variables separate. SIAM J. Numer.
    Anal., 10, pp. 413-432.

11. G. H. Golub and G. P. H. Styan (1973), Numerical
    computations for univariate linear models. J.
    Statist. Comput. Simul., 2, pp. 253-274.

12. D. C. Hoaglin (1973), An analysis of the loop
    optimization scores in Knuth's "Empirical study of
    FORTRAN programs." Software -- Practice and
    Experience, 3, pp. 161-169.

13. D. C. Hoaglin (1977), Direct approximations for χ^2
    percentage points. J. Amer. Statist. Assoc., 72,
    (to appear).

14. D. C. Hoaglin and R. E. Welsch (1976), The hat matrix
    in regression and ANOVA. Memorandum NS-341,
    Department of Statistics, Harvard University.

15. P. J. Huber (1972), Robust statistics: A review. Ann.
    Math. Statist., 43, pp. 1041-1067.

16. C. L. Lawson and R. J. Hanson (1974), Solving Least
    Squares Problems, Prentice-Hall.

17. B. N. Parlett and J. K. Reid (1970), On the solution
    of a system of linear equations whose matrix is
    symmetric by not definite. BIT, 10, pp. 386-397.

18. S. Steppel, ed. (1973), PRIM-9. Film produced by Bin 88
    Productions, Stanford Linear Accelerator Center,
    Stanford, California.

19. M. E. Tarter and R. A. Kronmal (1976), An introduction
       to the implementation and theory of nonparametric
       density estimation. Amer. Statist., 30, pp. 105-112.

20. J. W. Tukey (1972), Data analysis, computation and
       mathematics. Quart. Appl. Math., 30, pp. 51-65.

21. J. W. Tukey (1977), Exploratory Data Analysis,
       Addison-Wesley.

Supported in part by NSF Grant SOC75-15702.

Department of Statistics
Harvard University
Cambridge, Massachusetts 02138

Software for C^1
Surface Interpolation
C. L. Lawson

1. <u>INTRODUCTION</u>.

This paper is a result of our fourth effort in software for surface representation. We developed subroutines for rectangular grid contour plotting in 1965 with N. Block and R. Garrett, least squares bicubic spline surface fitting in 1970 with R. Hanson, and contour plotting via triangular grid construction and linear interpolation in 1972.

The latter two subroutines deal with irregularly located data. However, applications continue to arise in which one would like the interpolatory capability of the triangular grid program but with at least C^1 continuity. Such an algorithm with underlying theory and implementing software are the topics of this paper.

In Secs. 2, 3, and 4 we introduce the problem and give a brief survey of the pertinent literature. Sections 5 through 10 describe our algorithm and conclude with examples of surfaces produced by our new subroutines. We express appreciation to Bob Barnhill and Frank Little for valuable discussions that particularly influenced our triangulation algorithm of Sec. 6.

There has been practically no theory to guide the development of algorithms for triangulation and no practical static global criterion to characterize a preferred triangulation. We are indebted to Michael Powell and Robin Sibson for conversations and correspondence in 1976 that introduced us to

Thiessen proximity regions and the fact that this concept can be used to define a triangulation as is related in Sec. 12.2.

In our initial effort to determine the relationship of the Thiessen criterion to the max-min angle criterion we had used in 1972, we discovered the circle criterion, which served as a convenient mathematical link between the other two. The outcome is the material of Sec. 11, showing the equivalence of these three criteria when used for local optimization of a triangular grid.

The local equivalence results opened the way to certain global equivalences reported in Sec. 12 and new algorithmic insights reported in Secs. 13 and 14.

Our conclusions regarding the state of the art for this problem appear in Sec. 15.

2.   PROBLEM STATEMENT.

The following surface interpolation problem will be treated: Given a set of triples of data (x_i, y_i, z_i), i=1, ..., n, construct a conveniently computable C^1 function $f(x,y)$ satisfying the interpolation conditions

$$z_i = f(x_i, y_i), \quad i=1,\ldots,n$$

The data (x_i, y_i) are not assumed to lie in any special pattern such as at the nodes of a rectangular grid. It is assumed, however, that all (x_i, y_i) pairs are distinct; i.e., $(x_i, y_i) = (x_j, y_j)$ only if i=j.

3.   EXPECTED APPLICATIONS.

The usual situation in which the author has seen a need for this type of computation is that in which a scientist or engineer has in hand a set of (x_i, y_i, z_i) data representing measured or computed values of some phenomenon and desires to obtain a visual impression of a smooth surface of the form z = f(x, y) interpolating the data. In such a case, an interpolation algorithm, such as is treated in this paper, must be interfaced with algorithms for contour plotting or surface perspective plotting. If, as is the case at JPL, subroutines are available for doing contour or surface perspective plotting for data given on a rectangular grid, then the surface interpolation algorithm can be used to produce the values needed at the lattice points of a rectangular grid.

Other applications have arisen which can be regarded as the inverse of contour plotting. Certain handbook data is available in the form of contour plots. To use the data in a computer program it is necessary to produce a computable representation of the function depicted by the contour plots. A convenient way to do this is to develop a list of (x_i, y_i, z_i) values from appropriately spaced points along the contour lines and then use a surface interpolation algorithm such as is discussed in this paper.

We have also seen applications which can be regarded as implicit function problems. One may have a rectangular table or a contour plot giving z as a function of x and y, but then need to be able to determine x as a function of y and z in some computational procedure. If the data has appropriate monotonicity for this to make sense, then the interpolation algorithm of this paper can be used for such problems.

4. <u>PUBLISHED WORK ON SURFACE INTERPOLATION TO IRREGULARLY</u>
    <u>LOCATED DATA</u>

A variety of algorithmic ideas have been developed for this problem or closely related problems.

Two of the most recent papers giving methods for C^1 surface interpolation to irregularly located data are Akima (1975) and McLain (1976). Akima's report contains listings of a set of Fortran subroutines to handle this problem. This code and a second version of it using a more economical triangulation subroutine due to Lawson (1972) have been made available to requestors by Akima.

Both Akima (1975) and McLain (1976) contain introductory sections giving useful brief characterizations of other approaches, particularly those of Bengtsson and Nordbeck (1964), Shepard (1968), Maude (1973), and McLain (1974). Franke (1975) reports on computer tests of eleven methods constructed using a combination of ideas from Sard (1963), Mansfield (1972), Maude (1973), McLain (1974), Nielson (1974), and Barnhill and Nielson (1974).

Powell (1976) and Schumaker (1976) give surveys of methods for surface fitting and related problems of bivariate function representation.

The computerized representation of surfaces is a central issue in the field of computer-aided geometric design (CAGD) and plays an important role in the field of finite element methods (FEM). For discussions of surface representation from the point of view of CAGD see Forrest (1972) and Barnhill (1977). For descriptions of surface elements used in FEM see Birkhoff and Mansfield (1974) as well as any of the current books on FEM.

Some methods of building a triangular grid with a given set of nodes start by locating the boundary points of the convex hull of the point set. Algorithms for locating these boundary points are treated in Graham (1972), Jarvis (1973), Preparata and Hong (1977), and Eddy (1976).

Some interesting new triangular grid elements providing C^1 continuity through the use of piecewise quadratics are described in Powell and Sabin (1976).

5.   OUTLINE OF THE ALGORITHMIC APPROACH SELECTED.

Our approach to the C^1 surface interpolation problem consists of the following four steps.

1.   Construct a triangular grid covering the convex hull of the given set of (x_i, y_i) data using the (x_i, y_i) data points as vertices of the triangular cells.

2.   Estimate first partial derivatives of z with respect to x and y at each of the (x_i, y_i) data points.

3.   For an arbitrary (x, y) point, perform a lookup in the triangular grid to identify which triangle, if any, contains the point.

4.   For an arbitrary (x, y) point in a triangle, compute an interpolated value of z and optionally of $\partial z/\partial x$ and $\partial z/\partial y$ also. Make use of the nine items of data associated with the triangle, i.e., the values of z_i and its two first partial derivatives at each of the three vertices.

This same top level description of the approach also characterizes the methods of Akima (1975) and McLain (1976), with the exception that their methods estimate different quantities at Step 2 for use in the interpolation at Step 4.

At the more detailed level of devising algorithms for each
of the four steps, there are substantial differences between
our approach and that of Akima and that of McLain.

The four steps will be discussed in the following four
sections.

6.   CONSTRUCTING A TRIANGULAR GRID.

Given the set S of distinct points, (x_i, y_i), i=1,$\cdots$, n,
the triangular grid T to be constructed is to cover the convex hull of this set of points. Each triangular cell in the
grid is to have three of the given points as its vertices and
is to contain no other points of S as interior or boundary
points.

Conceptually there is no difficulty in manually constructing such a triangular grid. For example, one can just
start drawing edges connecting pairs of points and continue
as long as edges can be drawn that do not intersect any previously drawn edges. An edge must not contain any points of
S other than its own two endpoints.

In general, there exist many different triangulations of
a set S. It is noteworthy, however, that all possible triangulations of S have the same number of triangles and the
same number of edges. Let n_b denote the number of points of S
on the boundary of the convex hull of S and let n_i denote the
number in the interior so that $n = n_b + n_i$. Then the number
of triangles is

$$n_t = n_b + 2(n_i - 1) \le 2n$$

and the number of edges is

$$n_e = 2n_b + 3(n_i - 1) \le 3n$$

Taking these relationships into account we selected the
data structure illustrated by Figs. 1 and 2 to represent a
triangular grid. Column 1 of Fig. 1 is not stored so each
triangle is represented in storage by six integers. Since
$n_t \le 2n$, a total of 12n integer storage locations suffices
to represent the triangular grid for n points. This of
course is in addition to storage for the (x_i, y_i) data.

Three subroutines for storing and fetching in this
structure are used throughout the package so that the actual
mode of storing these pointers can be "hidden" from the main

TRIANGLE INDEX	INDICES OF ADJACENT TRIANGLES IN COUNTERCLOCKWISE ORDER. A ZERO INDICATES THE REGION EXTERIOR TO THE TRIANGULAR GRID			INDICES OF VERTEX POINTS IN COUNTERCLOCKWISE ORDER. THE FIRST VERTEX IS AT THE POINT OF CONTACT OF THE THIRD AND FIRST NEIGHBORING TRIANGLE		
1	2	0	4	5	8	7
2	5	3	1	5	3	8
3	6	0	2	3	1	8
.	.	.	.	.	.	.
.	.	.	.	.	.	.
.	.	.	.	.	.	.

Fig. 1.   Data Structure Representing a Triangular Grid.

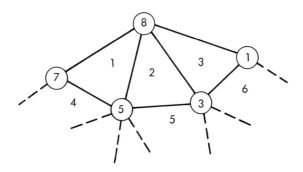

Fig. 2.   The Portion of a Triangular
Grid Described by the Data
Structure of Fig. 1.

subroutines. On many computers one could easily pack two or
three of these pointers per computer word. Our triangulation
algorithm has the property that it makes additions and
changes to the list of triangles but no deletions. Thus
there is no garbage collection problem.

In some reasonable triangulation algorithms the number
of boundary points of the convex hulls of a sequence of subsets of S has an effect on the operation count. Thus it is
desirable to have some notion of the expected value of n_b as
a function of n. Clearly, any value of n_b from 3 to n is
possible.

Consider the case in which S is a random sample of n points from a uniform distribution on a disc. Let v_n denote the expected value of n_b in this case. Renyi and Sulanki (1963, 1964) and also Raynaud (1970) show that v_n is asymtotically proportional to $n^{1/3}$ as $n \to \infty$. Efron (1965) derives the following formula for v_n:

$$v_n = \frac{n (n - 1) \pi^2}{3} \int_{-1}^{1} F^{n-2} f^3 \, dp$$

where

$$f(p) = \frac{2}{\pi} (1 - p^2)^{1/2}$$

and

$$F(p) = \int_{-1}^{p} f(t) \, dt = \frac{1}{2} + \frac{1}{\pi} \left[p (1 - p^2)^{1/2} + \arcsin (p) \right]$$

We have evaluated this formula by numerical integration and corroborated the results by a computer program that counted the number of boundary points of the convex hulls of a large number of point sets generated as pseudorandom samples from a uniform distribution on the unit disc. Selected values are shown in Table 1.

Since a given point set S generally admits many different triangulations, how is one to characterize and produce a preferred triangulation? So far there does not appear to be any fundamentally compelling best answer to this question.

A very satisfactory candidate, however, emerges from the theoretical results presented in Secs. 11 - 14. There it is shown that three differently stated criteria for choosing the preferred triangulation of a quadrilateral are in fact equivalent in that they produce the same decisions in all cases. It is also shown that if all quadrilaterals consisting of pairs of adjacent triangles in a triangulation satisfy one of these optimality criteria, then the triangulation as a whole has some pleasant properties, and in fact is unique to within some arbitrariness associated with subsets of four or more neighboring points lying on a common circle.

n	v_n	$c_n = v_n/n^{1/3}$
4	3.7	2.3
10	6.1	2.8
100	15.2	3.3
1000	33.6	3.4
10000	72.8	3.4

Table 1. v_n Is the Expected Number of Boundary Points in the Convex Hull of an n-point Sample from the Uniform Distribution on a Disc.

It is further shown that these local criteria have favorable properties for use in triangulation algorithms. In particular it is shown that the final triangulation is reached in a finite number of steps and that the operation of changing an optimized triangulation to include a new data point has some properties that can be exploited to simplify an algorithm.

Our triangulation subroutine TRIGRD presently uses the max-min angle criterion as its local optimization procedure. This is one of the three equivalent local criteria defined in Sec. 11.

The TRIGRD algorithm starts by finding the point of S having the smallest x coordinate. Any ties are broken by minimizing on y. The point p^* found in this way is an extreme point of the convex hull of S. Finding p^* requires $O(n)$ operations.

The points of S are next sorted on increasing (squared) Euclidean distance from p^*. Denote the points with this ordering by q_1, q_2, $\cdots$, q_n with $q_1 = p^*$. We estimate the operation count for the sort to be $O(n \log n)$.

The first edge is drawn connecting q_1 and q_2. The next point in the q_i sequence not colinear with q_1 and q_2 is connected to q_1 and q_2 to form the first triangle. If this third vertex is not q_3 but rather q_k with $k > 3$, relabel the points q_3 through q_k so that q_k is called q_3 and the indices of the intervening points are each increased by one. These steps assure that q_j is strictly outside the convex hull of $\{q_1, \cdots, q_{j-1}\}$ for all $j = 4, 5, \cdots, n$.

Let c denote the centroid of $\Delta q_1 q_2 q_3$. Let r be the half ray from c through q_1. When an angular coordinate is needed for a point, the angle will be measured counterclockwise around c from r. Note that the angular coordinate of q_1 is zero, and all other points q_i for i > 1 have angular coordinates strictly between 0 and 2π. The program does not actually compute angles but rather computes a less expensive function monotonically related to the angle.

Build an initial boundary list consisting of q_1, q_2, q_3, and q_1 (again) along with their angles, assigning the angle 2π to the second occurrence of q_1.

This finishes the preliminaries. The algorithm proceeds to loop through the points q_k, k=4, $\cdots$,n, doing the following for each one:

Determine the angular coordinate of q_k and use that coordinate as a key to search for a pair of boundary points whose angles bracket that angle. This is a linear search requiring an average of $n_b^{(k)}/2$ scalar comparisons, where $n_b^{(k)}$ is the number of points on the boundary of the convex hull of $\{q_1, \cdots, q_{k-1}\}$. If we estimate $n_b^{(k)}$ to be about $3k^{1/3}$ (recall Table 1), then the total cost of this lookup as k runs from 4 to n is $O(k^{4/3})$. This appears to be the highest-order operation count in the triangulation algorithm.

Having found two boundary points to which q_k can be connected, attach q_k to these points and record the edge opposite q_k in the new triangle in a stack, identifying edges to be tested for possible swapping.

If the stack is nonempty, unstack one edge and apply the the local optimization procedure to it. If the decision is to swap the edge, do so, and stack the two edges that are opposite q_k in the two new triangles. Continue processing the stack until it is empty.

When the stack is empty try to connect q_k to another neighboring boundary point. If this is possible, then run through the stacking and testing again, starting with the edge opposite q_k in the new triangle. When q_k cannot be connected to any more boundary points, the processing of q_k is completed.

We estimate the average operation count to process q_k is a constant, independent of k. Thus the total cost to process all the points q_k, k=4, $\cdots$, n is $O(n)$.

The total operation count for TRIGRD is thus estimated to be $O(n^{4/3}) + O(n \log n) + O(n)$. Actual timing on the Univac 1108 for cases having four different values of n are shown in Table 2.

The data of Table 2 suggests that in the range $25 \leq n \leq 500$, either $O(n^{4/3})$ or $O(n \log n)$ may be used as a model of the execution time of this triangulation algorithm.

7.   ESTIMATING PARTIAL DERIVATIVES AT THE GRID NODES.

To estimate $\partial z/\partial x$ and $\partial z/\partial y$ at a nodal point $p = (x_k, y_k)$ of the triangular grid, the subroutine ESTPD sets up and solves a local least squares problem. All of the immediate grid neighbors of point p are used up to a maximum of 16 immediate neighbors. If the number of immediate neighbors is less than six, then additional nodes beyond the immediate neighbors are used to bring the total number of points in addition to p up to six.

A six-parameter quadratic polynominal in x and y is fit to the z data values at this set of points. The quadratic is forced to interpolate the z value at p, and it fits the remaining points in a weighted least squares sense. The weighting is used to diminish the effect of the more distant points.

n	t	$t/(n^{4/3})$	$t/(n \log n)$
25	0.061	0.00084	0.00175
100	0.346	0.00075	0.00173
200	0.951	0.00081	0.00207
500	2.211	0.00056	0.00164

Table 2.   t Denotes the Time in Seconds for Execution of TRIGRD for a Case Having n points

The values at p of the first partial derivatives of this quadratic are stored as estimates of $\partial z/\partial x$ and $\partial z/\partial y$ at p. Execution time on the Univac 1108 averages 8 milliseconds per point at which partials are estimated.

This method of estimating derivatives is the most ad hoc part of our entire surface interpolation method. We intend to investigate the effect of various parametric and algorithmic changes in this procedure.

8. LOOKUP IN THE TRIANGULAR GRID.

Given an arbitrary point q = (x, y) and an index k in the range $1 \leq k \leq n_t$, where n_t is the total number of triangles, the subroutine TRFIND tests to see if q is in the triangle whose index is k.

If so, the index k is returned. If not, q must be outside one of the edges of the triangle. In this case, TRFIND resets k to be the index of the neighboring triangle on the other side of that edge and loops back to test q in this new triangle k. If there is no neighboring triangle, the fact that q is outside the triangular grid is reported.

This approach is particularly efficient for the case of interpolating to points of a rectangular grid, since the search can always be started at the triangle in which the previous point was found. When a new row of the rectangular grid is started, the search can be started in the triangle in which the first point of the previous row was found.

9. INTERPOLATION IN A TRIANGLE.

The interpolation subroutine TVAL makes use of the piecewise cubic macroelement of Clough and Tocher (1965). A tutorial derivation of this element and a discussion of some alternative ways to organize its computation are given in Lawson (1976a). Quadrature properties of the element are derived in Lawson (1976b).

Definition of this element involves partitioning the triangle into three subtriangles by drawing internal boundaries from the centroid to each vertex. In each of these three subtriangles the element is a cubic polynomial in x and y

$$z = \sum_{i=0}^{3} \sum_{j=0}^{3-i} a_{ij} \, x^i \, y^j$$

The element matches nine items of data, the function value and first partials with respect to x and y at the three vertices. It has C^1 continuity across the internal and external boundaries of the triangle. It is exact for quadratic data.

Since it is a piecewise cubic, it is straightforward to obtain expressions for computing its first partial derivatives. The subroutine TVAL includes an option to compute $\partial z/\partial x$ and $\partial z/\partial y$ as well as z.

Starting with the information x, y, z, $\partial z/\partial x$, and $\partial z/\partial y$ at the vertices of a triangle, this method requires 55 multiplies, 65 adds, and 4 divides to compute one interpolated value. There are various possibilities for saving computed quantities that depend only on the triangle's data in order to cut down the time to interpolate for a number of points in the same triangle.

Execution time on the Univac 1108 averages 750 microseconds per interpolated point. This is about 10 times the cost of EXP or SIN.

10. EXAMPLES.

Figure 3 shows a set S consisting of 26 points in the plane. Figure 4 is the triangular grid constructed for the set S by TRIGRD. In view of the results of Sec. 12, this is a Thiessen triangulation for S.

10.1. QUADRATIC TEST CASE.

Values are assigned at the points of Fig. 1 by computing $z = (-1 + 2x - 3y + 4x^2 - xy + 9y^2)/8$. Using ESTPD to estimate first partial derivatives and TRFIND and TVAL to interpolate to points of a 51 x 51 point rectangular grid, we then obtained the contour plot of Fig. 5 and the perspective plot of Fig. 6. This illustrates the exactness of the method for quadratic data.

This case required 1.9 sec of Univac 1108 CPU time to build the triangular grid and interpolate to the rectangular grid. It then used 15.3 sec in the plotting subroutines.

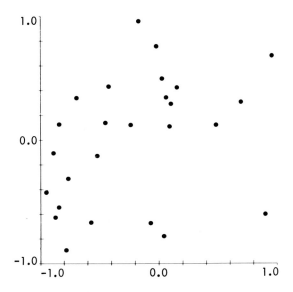

Fig. 3.   Set of 26 (x_i, y_i) Points for Examples 1 and 2.

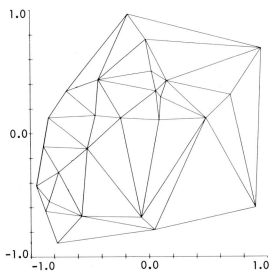

Fig. 4.   Thiessen Triangular Grid for Examples 1 and 2.

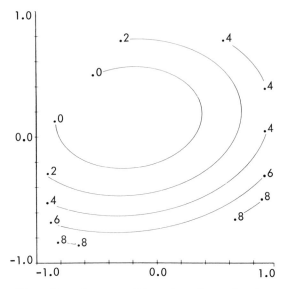

Fig. 5.   Contour Plot for Example 1.

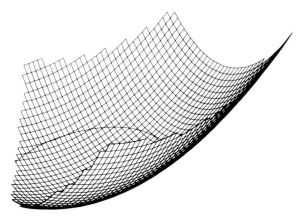

Fig. 6.   Perspective Plot for Example 1.

10.2.   <u>EXPONENTIAL TEST CASE</u>.

For this case the z data is computed as

$$z = e^{-2(x^2+y^2)}$$

Again estimating partial derivatives at the 26 data points and then interpolating to a 51 x 51 rectangular grid, Figs. 7 and 8 are obtained. The most noticeable defect in the surface produced is the kink in the contour plot near $(x,y) = (0.2,-0.4)$. This also appears as a groove in the perspective plot. From Fig. 3, however, it is seen that this corresponds to a region in which there is a lack of data. Computer time was similar to the first test case.

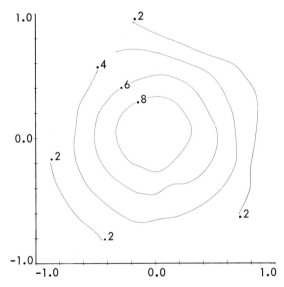

Fig. 7.   Contour Plot for Example 2.

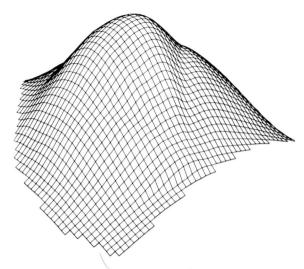

Fig. 8. Perspective Plot for Example 2.

10.3. A CASE WITH MORE POINTS.

The third test case is the same exponential function on a set of 500 points. The grid produced for this case has 985 triangles.

This data was interpolated to a 21 x 21 point rectangular grid for plotting (see Figs. 9, 10, and 11). This case used 6.25 sec of CPU time to triangulate and interpolate. It used 4.01 sec in the plotting subroutines. The plotting was faster because of the much coarser rectangular grid.

11. THREE CRITERIA FOR TRIANGULATION OF A STRICTLY CONVEX QUADRILATERAL.

We will call a quadrilateral Q strictly convex if each of its four interior angles measures less than 180°. Such a quadrilateral can be partitioned into two triangles in two possible ways. Three criteria will be described for choosing a preferred triangulation of a strictly convex quadrilateral.

11.1. THE MAX-MIN ANGLE CRITERION.

Choose the triangulation of Q that maximizes the minimum interior angle of the two resulting triangles. Either choice can be made in the case of a tie. For example, in Fig. 12 $\angle$cab is the smallest angle in triangles f_1 and g_1, $\angle$cdb is the

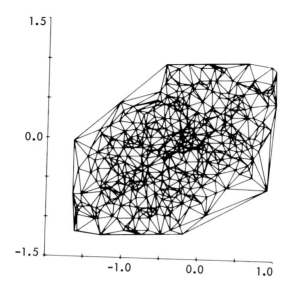

Fig. 9.   Thiessen Triangular Grid for Example 3:
           500 Points and 985 Triangles.

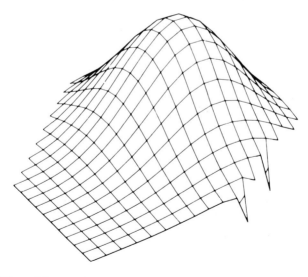

Fig. 10.   Perspective Plot for Example 3.

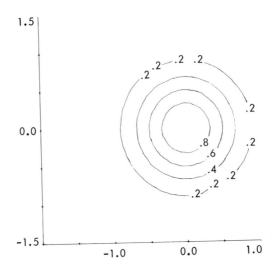

Fig. 11. Contour Plot for Example 3.

smallest angle in triangles f_2 and g_2, and $\angle cdb$ is larger than $\angle cab$. Thus, the triangulation (b) is preferred over (a).

11.2. THE CIRCLE CRITERION.

Let K denote a circle passing through three of the vertices of a strictly convex quadrilateral Q. If the fourth vertex
is interior to K, insert the diagonal from this fourth vertex
to the opposite vertex. If the fourth vertex is exterior to K,
insert the other diagonal. If the fourth vertex is on K,
insert either diagonal (see Fig. 13 for an example). Note that
when all four vertices are not on a common circle, the same
triangulation will be selected regardless of which set of three
vertices is used to construct the circle.

11.3. THE THIESSEN REGION CRITERION.

Let R_a denote the closure of the region of the plane consisting of all points that are closer to point a than to points
b, c, or d. Similarly define regions R_b, R_c, and R_d surrounding points b, c, and d, respectively. These regions are
called Thiessen regions following Powell (1976) and
Rhynsburger (1973). These proximity regions are also identified by other names in the mathematical literature.

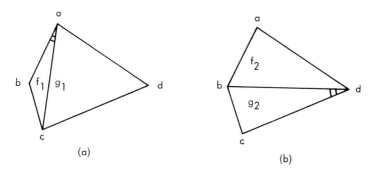

Fig. 12.   The Max-Min Angle Criterion.

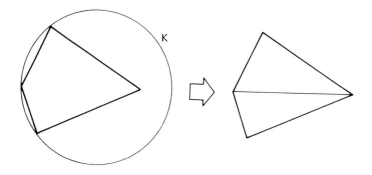

Fig. 13.   The Circle Criterion.

Two of the points a,b,c, or d will be called <u>Thiessen</u>
<u>neighbors</u> if their Thiessen regions are in contact. They are
<u>strong Thiessen neighbors</u> if the contact is along a line seg-
ment of nonzero length. They are <u>weak Thiessen neighbors</u> if
the contact is at one point only.

To triangulate a strictly convex quadrilateral Q, insert
the diagonal that connects a pair of strong Thiessen neighbors. A strictly convex quadrilateral can have at most one
pair of opposite vertices that are strong Thiessen neighbors.
If neither pair of opposite vertices are strong Thiessen
neighbors, then both pairs will be weak neighbors and either
diagonal can be inserted (see Fig. 14 for an example).

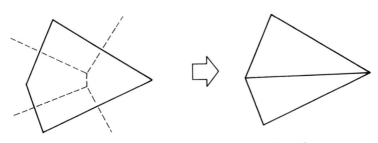

Fig. 14.   The Thiessen Region Criterion.

11.4. EQUIVALENCE OF THESE THREE CRITERIA FOR STRICTLY CONVEX QUADRILATERALS.

The first observation to be made about these three criteria is that they give identical results for strictly convex quadrilaterals. This can be verified by noting that all three criteria have the same neutral case and then studying perturbations from the neutral case.

The neutral case for all three criteria is the case in which all four vertices of the quadrilateral lie on a common circle.

To verify this last statement consider a quadrilateral Q whose vertices a,b,c, and d all lie on a common circle K. See Fig. 15. Suppose arc $\widehat{bc}$ is shorter than arcs $\widehat{cd}$, $\widehat{da}$, or $\widehat{ab}$. If the angular measure of arc $\widehat{bc}$ is 2θ, then angles cab and cdb are each of measure θ, and these two angles are each the minimum angle for one of the possible triangulations. Thus, this is a tie case for the max-min angle criterion.

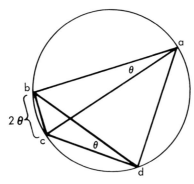

Fig. 15.   The Neutral Case for the Max-Min Angle Criterion.

For points in general position, the grid will in fact con-
sist of triangles. Any polygon of the grid that is not a
triangle will have all of its vertices on a circle and all
nonadjacent pairs of vertices will be weak Thiessen neighbors.
Any such k-point polygon can be triangulated by connecting any
k-3 pairs of its vertices as long as no crossing lines are
drawn. A triangulation in which all strong Thiessen neighbors
are connected will be called a Thiessen triangulation.

12.2.1. LEMMA.

Let S be a set of n points in the plane and let $\tilde{S}$ be a
subset of S. Two points of $\tilde{S}$ that are Thiessen neighbors in
S remain so in $\tilde{S}$ and if they are strong Thiessen neighbors
in S they remain strong Thiessen neighbors in $\tilde{S}$.

Proof. Consider the effect of removing one point, say p,
from S, leaving a subset S'. The only change that takes place
in transforming the Thiessen regions for S to form the Thiessen
regions for S' is a redistribution of the part of the plane
that was the Thiessen region for p. This region will be
partitioned, with various portions being absorbed into the
neighboring Thiessen regions. In this process no boundaries
between pairs of remaining Thiessen regions are shortened.
Thus neighbors remain neighbors and strong neighbors remain
strong neighbors. Clearly the same is true for the removal
of any number of points from a finite set, as the removals can
be done one at a time. ∎

12.2.2. THEOREM.

All internal edges of a triangulation T of a finite point
set S are locally optimal if and only if T is a Thiessen
triangulation of S.

Proof of "if". Assume T is a Thiessen triangulation of S.
Let e be an internal edge of T connecting vertices a and c and
belonging to triangles △abc and △cda. If the quadrilateral
Q = abcd is not strictly convex, then e cannot be swapped and
is thus locally optimal.

Consider then the case of Q being strictly convex. By
hypothesis, a and c are Thiessen neighbors in S. By
Lemma 12.2.1 they are also Thiessen neighbors relative to the
point set {a, b, c, d}. With the quadrilateral Q = abcd
being strictly convex, this implies e is locally optimal.

Proof of "only if". Assume all internal edges of T are locally optimal. Suppose the theorem is false. Then there is some pair of strong Thiessen neighbors in S, say points p and q, that are not connected by an edge in the triangulation T.

Define B to be the polygonal curve whose constituent line segments are the segments that occur as edges opposite vertex q in those triangles that have q as a vertex. If q is not a boundary point of T, then B is a closed polygon with q in its interior and p lying exterior to it. Clearly a line segment from p to q would intersect B.

If q is a boundary point of T, then B is an open polygonal curve with end points on the boundary of T at the two points immediately adjacent to q on each side of q along the boundary. Although in this case B does not surround q, it still follows that $\overline{pq}$ must intersect B owing to the convexity of the region covered by T.

Since p and q are strong Thiessen neighbors in S, there can be no other points of S on the line segment $\overline{pq}$. Thus the intersection of $\overline{pq}$ with B is not at a point of S on B but must be strictly between a pair of points of S on B, say points r and s.

Thus the triangle $\triangle qrs$ is a triangle of T having the property that r and s are on strictly opposite sides of $\overline{pq}$ and p and q are on strictly opposite sides of $\overline{rs}$, as is illustrated in Fig. 19.

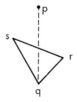

Fig. 19.   Theorem 12.2.2.

By hypothesis, all internal edges of T are locally optimal. By Theorem 12.1.2 this implies that point p is not in the interior of the circumcircle K of $\triangle qrs$. From the equivalence

of the circle test and the Thiessen criterion for strictly
convex quadrilaterals, this would imply that p is not a strong
Thiessen neighbor of q relative to the point set $\{p, s, q, r\}$.

By Lemma 12.2.1, however, p and q are strong Thiessen
neighbors relative to $\{p,s,q,r\}$ since they are strong Thiessen
neighbors in S. Thus a contradiction has been reached.∎

13. McLAIN'S TRIANGULATION METHOD.

The triangulation method described in McLain (1976) builds
a grid one triangle at a time in such a way that each triangle
constructed is a triangle of the final grid. This is in contrast to methods that involve triangle modification steps such
as are used in Sec. 6, in Lawson (1972), and by Frank Little of
the University of Utah CAGD group.

The paper, McLain (1976), with the subsequent errata,
leaves open the question of the characterization of the grid
the algorithm produces. We find that the results of the
preceding sections can be used to show that the grid produced
by McLain's method is in fact a Thiessen grid.

Let S be a set of n points. Define T_0 to be a single edge
belonging to some Thiessen triangulation for S. For example,
T_0 could be a boundary edge of the convex hull of S. For
$k \geq 1$ define T_k to be a configuration of k triangles that is
a subset of some Thiessen triangulation of S and contains
T_{k-1} as a subset. In general, the configurations T_k are not
necessarily convex.

Given some T_k, how can one more triangle of a Thiessen
triangulation of S be found to advance to T_{k+1}?

Let $\overline{ab}$ be an edge belonging to just one triangle, say
$\triangle abc$, in T_k. Let S_k be the subset of S consisting of the
points lying on the opposite side of $\overline{ab}$ from c. (If there are
none, then try another edge as $\overline{ab}$ or terminate.)

From our inductive assumption that T_k is a subset of a
Thiessen triangulation of S, there must be a point p in S_k
such that adjoining $\triangle abp$ to T_k gives a configuration T_{k+1}
that is also a subset of a Thiessen triangulation of S.

By Theorems 12.1.2 and 12.2.2 we know that the triangle
$\triangle abp$ must not contain any points of S_k in its interior. Such
a triangle is just what is selected by McLain's method, since

he selects p such that the signed distance from $\overline{ab}$ of the center of the circumcircle of $\triangle abp$ is the algebraically smallest possible among all choices of p in S_k. The signed distance from $\overline{ab}$ is positive on the side of $\overline{ab}$ opposite to c.

14.   LIMITS ON GRID CHANGES WHEN ADDING A NEW POINT.

This section presents results that limit the amount of edge testing needed in algorithms such as ours in Sec. 6 that transform from the Thiessen triangulation of one point set to that for the set augmented by one new point.

Let S_{n-1} be a set of n-1 points in the plane. Let p be a point not in S_{n-1} and define $S_n = S_{n-1} \cup \{p\}$. Let T^*_{n-1} be a Thiessen triangulation for S_{n-1}.

Given T^*_{n-1}, an initial triangulation $T_n^{(1)}$ for S_n can be constructed by inserting all edges that connect the new point p to points of S_{n-1} without crossing edges already present in T^*_{n-1}. A special case arises if p falls on an edge, say $\overline{ac}$, already present in T^*_{n-1}. Then the edge $\overline{ac}$ must be replaced by the two edges $\overline{ap}$ and $\overline{pc}$. For our theoretical discussion it will be easier to assume p does not fall on an edge of T^*_{n-1}. The case of p arbitrarily close to an edge of T^*_{n-1} is of course permitted, and analysis of this case can be used to justify the replacement of $\overline{ac}$ by $\overline{ap}$ and $\overline{pc}$.

An edge e in a triangulation will be called converged if it is locally optimal in the present triangulation and if in addition it can be proved that no sequence of applications of the local optimization procedure to the various edges could lead to a decision to swap e.

Assuming p does not lie on any edge of T^*_{n-1}, it will be shown that all of the initial edges inserted connecting p to points of S_{n-1} are converged. Any edge opposite to p in a triangle must be tested once using the local optimization procedure. If it remains unchanged after testing, then it is converged. If it is swapped by the procedure, then the new edge introduced is converged and the two edges opposite p in the two new triangles must each be tested.

14.1.   THEOREM.

Assume p is strictly outside the convex hull of S_{n-1} and $T_n^{(1)}$ is formed by connecting p to all boundary points of T^*_{n-1}

that can be reached without crossing any edges of T^*_{n-1}. Then all of the new edges are converged.

Proof. Let $\overline{pq}$ be a new edge connecting p to a point q on the boundary of T^*_{n-1}. If in the course of triangulating S_n it is ever to be decided to swap $\overline{pq}$ for some other edge $\overline{ab}$, then a and b must (at least) be points of S_{n-1} such that a and b are on strictly opposite sides of $\overline{pq}$ and p and q are on strictly opposite sides of $\overline{ab}$.

This is impossible since the line segment $\overline{ab}$ can not pass outside the convex hull of S_{n-1} and thus could not intersect $\overline{pq}$ strictly between the boundary point q and the point p which is exterior to the convex hull of S_{n-1}.∎

14.2.   THEOREM.

Assume p is interior to the convex hull of S_{n-1} and in fact interior to some triangle $\triangle abc$ of T^*_{n-1}. Assume $T_n^{(1)}$ is formed by connecting p to a, b, and c. These three new edges are converged.

Proof. Since T^*_{n-1} is a Thiessen triangulation of S_{n-1}, the circumcircle K of $\triangle abc$ contains no points of S_{n-1} in its interior. If in the course of triangulating S_n it is ever decided to swap $\overline{pa}$, for instance, for some other edge, $\overline{rs}$, then r and s must not be interior to K, r and s must be on strictly opposite sides of $\overline{pa}$, p and a must be on strictly opposite sides of $\overline{rs}$, and a must be strictly outside the circle K' through r, p, and s (see Fig. 20).

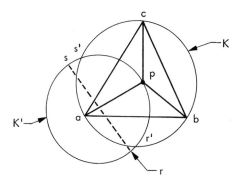

Fig. 20.   Theorem 14.2.

Partition circle K' into the three arcs $\overparen{rp}$, $\overparen{ps}$, and $\overparen{sr}$.
Note that arc $\overparen{rp}$ intersects circle K since p is inside K and
r is on or outside K. Call this intersection point r'.
Similarly, arc $\overparen{ps}$ intersects circle K, say at a point s'.
Then arc $\overparen{r'ps'}$ of K' is inside K because p is inside K and
r' and s' are intersection points of K' with K. It follows
that arc $\overparen{s'srr'}$ of K' is outside K. The arc of K between s'
and r' that lies inside K' contains the point a. Thus it is
impossible for a to be outside K' as it must be for $\overline{pa}$ to be
swapped. ∎

14.3. <u>THEOREM</u>.
    Let $T_n^{(i)}$ <u>be a triangulation of</u> $S_n = S_{n-1} \cup \{P\}$. <u>Let</u>
△cbp <u>and</u> △abc <u>be adjacent triangles of</u> $T_n^{(i)}$ <u>and assume</u>
△abc <u>was also a triangle of</u> T_{n-1}^*. <u>Suppose application of the</u>
<u>local optimization procedure to edge</u> $\overline{bc}$ <u>leads to a swap</u>,
<u>replacing</u> $\overline{bc}$ <u>by</u> $\overline{pa}$. <u>Then edge</u> $\overline{pa}$ <u>is converged</u>.

    <u>Proof</u>. Note that the symbols a, b, and c do not neces-
sarily denote the first vertices to which p was connected as
was the case in Theorem 14.2. The notation for this theorem
was selected, however, to permit the proof to be identical to
that of Theorem 14.2 (see Fig. 21). ∎

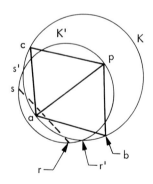

Fig. 21.   Theorem 14.3.

15.   <u>CONCLUSIONS</u>.
    Triangular grid construction is certainly not as well
understood as sorting of scalars, but at least a general
notion of what to expect in running time, storage usage, and
properties of the final triangulation is now available. Thus
an algorithm with an $O(n^2)$ time estimate must be regarded as

inefficient except possibly for small n. There remain a wide
variety of possible triangulation algorithms with time estimates in the neighborhood of $O(n^{4/3})$. It will require more
time, experience and direct comparative testing to sort these
out.

C^1 interpolation on triangles is still very ad hoc. Three
different methods are used by Akima (1975), McLain (1976), and
the present paper. It appears that our method requires the
least amount of auxiliary stored information per node (two
first partial derivatives per node) and the fewest number of
operations per interpolated value once the auxiliary nodal
information has been computed and stored. Direct comparative
tests would be needed, however, to assess accuracy and actual
execution times.

There is much scope for additional work on this problem,
including generalizations such as smoothing instead of interpolation, the introductions of constraints, and permitting the
domain of the independent variables to be the surface of a
sphere or three-dimensional space instead of the plane.

REFERENCES

1. Hiroshi Akima, (1975), A method of bivariate inter-
    polation and smooth surface fitting for values given at
    irregularly distributed points, U.S. Depart. of Commerce
    OT Report 75-70. An improved version of this algorithm
    will appear in ACM TOMS.
2. Robert E. Barnhill, (1977), Representation and approxi-
    mation of surfaces, this volume, pp. 68-119.
3. Robert E. Barnhill and Gregory M. Nelson, (1974), Repro-
    ducing kernel functions for Sard spaces of type B*,
    SIAM J. Numer. Anal., pp. 37-44.
4. Bengt-Erik Bengtsson and Stig Nordbeck, (1964), Con-
    struction of isarithms and isarithmic maps by computers,
    BIT, 4, pp. 87-105.
5. Garret Birkhoff and L. E. Mansfield, (1974), Compatible
    triangular finite elements, Jour. Math. Anal. Appl. 47,
    pp. 531-553.

6. R. W. Clough and J. L. Tocher, (1965), Finite element stiffness matrices for analysis of plates in bending, <u>Proc. Conf. Matrix Methods in Struct. Mech.</u>, Air Force Inst. of Tech., Wright-Patterson A.F.B., Ohio.

7. W. F. Eddy, (1976), A new convex hull algorithm for planar sets, Carnegie-Mellon Univ., to appear in ACM TOMS.

8. Bradley Efron, (1965), The convex hull of a random set of points, <u>Biometrika</u>, <u>52</u>, <u>3</u> and <u>4</u>, p. 331.

9. Richard Franke, (1975), Locally determined smooth interpolation at irregularly spaced points in several variables, Naval Postgraduate School, AD-A010 814, Monterey, Calif

10. A. R. Forrest, (1972), On Coons and other methods for representation of curved surfaces, <u>Comput. Graphics Inform. Process.</u>, <u>1</u>, pp. 341-359.

11. R. L. Graham, (1972), An efficient algorithm for determining the convex hull of a finite planar set, Information Processing Letters <u>1</u>, pp. 132-133.

12. R. A. Jarvis, (1973), On the identification of the convex hull of a finite set of points in the plane, Information Processing Letters <u>2</u>, pp. 18-21.

13. C. L. Lawson, (1972), Generation of a triangular grid with application to contour plotting, Jet Propulsion Laboratory Section 914 Tech. Memo. No. 299 (an internal report).

14. C. L. Lawson, (1976a), C^1-Compatible interpolation over a triangle, Jet Propulsion Laboratory TM 33-770.

15. C. L. Lawson, (1976b), Integrals of a C^1-compatible triangular surface element, Jet Propulsion Laboratory TM 33-808.

16. L. E. Mansfield, (1972), Optimal approximation and error bounds in spaces of bivariate functions, <u>J. Approx. Th.</u>, <u>5</u>, pp. 77-96.

17. A. D. Maude, (1973), Interpolation - mainly for graph plotters, <u>Comput. J.</u>, <u>16</u>, pp. 64-65.

18. D. H. McLain, (1974), Drawing contours from arbitrary data points, <u>Computer J.</u>, <u>17</u>, pp. 318-324.

19. D. H. McLain, (1976), Two dimensional interpolation from random data, Comput. J., 19, No. 2, pp. 178-181. (See also Errata for this paper in Comput. J., 19, No. 4, Nov. 1976, p. 384.)

20. G. M. Nielson, (1974), Multivariate smoothing and inter-polating splines, SIAM J. Numer. Anal., pp. 435-446.

21. M. J. D. Powell, (1976), Numerical methods for fitting functions of two variables, A.E.R.E. Harwell, Computer Science and Systems Division Report 30, presented at the IMA Conference on the State-of-the-Art in Numerical Analysis, University of York, April, 1976.

22. M. J. D. Powell and M. A. Sabin, (1976), Piecewise quad-ratic approximations on triangles, Univ. of Cambridge, to appear in ACM TOMS.

23. F. P. Preparata and S. J. Hong, (1977), Convex hulls of finite sets of points in two and three dimensions, Commun. ACM., 20, No. 2, pp. 87-93.

24. H. Raynaud, (1970), Sur l'enveloppe convex des nuages de points aleatoires dans R^n. I, J. Appl. Prob., 7, pp. 35-48.

25. A. Renyi and R. Sulanke, (1963-1964), Uber die convexe hulle von is zufallig gewahlten punkten, I and II, Z. Wahr. 2, pp. 75-84, 3, 138-148.

26. D. Rhynsburger, (1973), Analytic delineation of Thiessen polygons, Geograph. Anal., 5, pp. 133-144.

27. Arthur Sard, (1963), Linear approximation, Mathematical Surveys, No. 9, American Mathematical Society, Providence, R.I.

28. L. L. Schumaker, (1976), Fitting surfaces to scattered data, Approximation Theory II, edited by G. G. Lorentz, C. K. Chui, and L. L. Schumaker, Academic Press, pp. 203-268.

29.   Donald Shepard, (1968), A two-dimensional interpolation
      function for irregularly-spaced data, <u>Proc. 23rd Nat.</u>
      <u>Conf. ACM</u>, pp. 517-524.

The author was supported by the National Aeronautics
and Space Administration under Contract No. NAS 7-100.

                              Information Systems Division
                              Jet Propulsion Laboratory
                              California Institute of Technology
                              Pasadena, California 91103

Mathematical Software Production

W. R. Crowell

L. D. Fosdick

ABSTRACT

Locally constructed collections of mathematical routines are gradually being replaced by mathematical software that has been produced for broad dissemination and use. The process of producing such software begins with algorithmic analysis, and proceeds through software construction and documentation, to extensive testing, and finally to distribution and support of the software products. These are demanding and costly activities which require such a range of skills that they are carried out in collaborative projects. The costs and effort are justified by the utility of high quality software, the efficiency of producing it for general distribution, and the benefits of providing a conduit from research to applications.

In this paper we first review certain of the early developments in the field of mathematical software. Then we examine the technical problems that distinguish software production as an intellectual activity, problems whose descriptions also serve to characterize ideal mathematical software. Next we sketch three mathematical software projects with attention to their emphasis, accomplishments, organization, and costs. Finally, we comment on possible future directions for mathematical software production, as extrapolations of the present involvement of universities, government laboratories, and private industry.

I.   Introduction

The term "mathematical software" refers to computer
programs which perform the basic mathematical computations
of science and engineering. As with most broad concepts,
an understanding of what mathematical software is may be
best inferred from reading the subject matter, for instance
the proceedings of the Purdue Mathematical Software Symposia
[1, 2] and the contents of the ACM Transactions on Mathematical Software (TOMS). It will be apparent that programs
to approximate functions, solve equations, analyze experimental data, etc., are included while compilers, assemblers,
and operating systems are not, although many of the practical problems of producing and using mathematical software
stem directly from such "systems" software.

Before about 1970, most mathematical software was
written by users or individuals closely associated with
users and was available to workers in a particular group or
at a particular installation. Early efforts to develop
mathematical software for a wider audience (e.g., [3, 4, 5])
led to increased interest in the production process and
stimulated several major projects which have matured during
the past half-dozen years. Consequently, mathematical
software intended for general distribution has begun to
replace "home-made" routines while libraries of mathematical
routines are being accepted as software products in the
same sense as compilers and operating systems. In Section V
we shall comment on the stability of this trend.

Mathematical software production is not a simple
extension of do-it-yourself programming. Programs intended
for public distribution must perform as advertised across
a broad range of input data, compilers, operating systems,
and hardware characteristics. The nature of their usage
must be clearly specified in functional terms and they must
detect and recover from (or at least report) anomalous
situations. Production of software of such quality requires
detailed analysis and planning, extensive testing, and
comprehensive documenting. These, together with distribution and maintenance of the software products, are demanding and costly activities.

From an accounting standpoint, the costs of mathematical software production are justified in terms of wide
distribution which results in a saving of expensive effort.
However, there are more profound questions of science
resource management that help provide meaningful justification of the costs. As computer power has increased, so
have both the complexity of the computing environment and
the scope of problems undertaken by users. Now expert
knowledge is required for effective utilization of present
computing power. We can no longer expect that chemists,
mechanical engineers, and physicists will have enough
special knowledge about computing to develop the best
algorithms for their own use. Roughly fashioned software
will sometimes do the job but in many other cases (e.g., (1)
the success of singular value decomposition for dealing
with difficult problems in data analysis; (2) the development of ordinary differential equations algorithms for stiff
systems), expertly crafted algorithms were the difference
between solving a problem or not solving it. There is no
obvious end to the growth of computing power and hence to
the need for expert attention to the expanding problem set.
This demand for expertise has inspired advances in algorithm
construction and analysis whose embodiment in widely-
distributed software is one of the fruits of mathematical
software production.

We must also view the production of mathematical
software from the standpoint of the mathematicians and
computer scientists who construct algorithms in the course
of their research. Software provides the means whereby
algorithms are utilized and thus deserves the attention that
a responsible scientist gives to the use of his creations
and discoveries. In the case of the proof of a mathematical
theorem or the discovery of an elementary particle, the
simple reporting of the information is generally a fulfill-
ment of this responsibility. But new ideas in algorithms
are intimately associated with machines and the relationship
is so complex that software is one of the means of communi-

cating ideas. From this standpoint, mathematical software production bridges the gap between algorithmic research and effective machine implementations.

We hope that readers will recognize how many of these problems of mathematical software production are intellectually challenging and worthy of the best efforts of talented individuals. To cultivate such interest we shall first review selected early developments in mathematical software, then examine current activities, and finally offer a few predictions about the future.

II. The Evolution of Mathematical Software Production

Criteria for good software have changed with experience and technology. Broadly speaking, we have always insisted that good software be accurate and efficient, but over the years the meanings of these terms have changed and a more explicit standard for good software is still evolving. Looking back several machine generations to the late 1940's and early 1950's, the computers were much slower and had very small memories. High level languages could not be supported on such machines, so programming was done at a very low level, not far from machine language. The small memories forced programmers to employ various tricks permitting multiple use of memory cells.

Good programs generally employed such tricks since they allowed more powerful programs to fit in the limited memory. Indeed it was amazing how much computing power could be packed into a small amount of memory. For example, the assembly program written for the ILLIAC by David Wheeler occupied just 25 words of memory. It was primitive by current standards but it did permit such things as decimal addresses, decimal constants, relative and absolute addressing, and block loading of memory.

The tricks employed to cope with the small memories resulted in code which was difficult to understand and which sometimes imposed strange constraints on the user. For example, in the description of a Runge-Kutta subroutine, G1, for the EDSAC library [6], the following comment is found:

"...G1 should be placed in the upper half of the
store to obtain maximum accuracy (the ideal position is 386 onwards). This is because one of the
orders forms part of a constant which thus depends
slightly on the location of the routine. In normal
use the effect is quite negligible..."

Another example from the same source is this comment:

"...The conversion of decimal fractions is slightly
simpler if the least significant digit is read
first and subroutines R5 and R7 are designed in
this way. The number tape can, however, be
punched in the ordinary way with the most significant digit first and reversed during the process
of copying onto the final tape..."

With our present notions of good programs we would exclude programs with these properties. However, at the time,
these programs were among the best and they exerted a strong
influence on program library development because of the way
they were injected into the bloodstream of scientific computing. First, the principal contributors to the EDSAC library, Wilkes, Wheeler, and Gill, wrote the unique book [6],
quoted above, the first in which a subroutine library was
published. It was widely read and the authors visited the
small number of computing laboratories of that time and contributed their ideas. In visiting the University of Illinois for extended periods, David Wheeler and Stanley Gill
wrote a good portion of the ILLIAC library. The order code
of the ILLIAC was copied on other machines: SILLIAC (University of Sidney), CYCLONE (Iowa State University), MISTIC
(Michigan State University), ORDVAC* (Aberdeen Proving
Ground), MUSASINO I (Nippon Telegraph and Telephone Public
Corp.). Through this process, the ILLIAC library was transported to these other machines and became the basis for
their program libraries. Here we see the first instance of
the distribution of software as a consequence of the existence of several copies of a machine.

---

*This machine was completed slightly earlier than the
ILLIAC.

The days of the one thousand word memory soon disap-
peared but a residue of tricky programming remained. It is
finally becoming widely recognized [7] that clarity of
programming style is a criterion for good software.
Programming languages, made practical by larger memories
and faster machines, permitted programs to be written in a
fashion more clearly understood by humans. Also, these
languages appeared for a time to make machine independent
programming possible, whetting appetites for the wide distribution of programs. In this atmosphere, style and portability emerged as criteria for good software.

Another important factor influencing our notions about
software was the enormous growth in the number of computers
and the size of the user community. User groups were
formed in response to the need for exchange of software
and other forms of information, the first and largest being
SHARE for IBM computers. For some years a group within
SHARE was responsible for a program "library" which was
essentially a repository and exchange point for programs
whose quality varied so widely that all the programs in the
library became suspect. Attempts were made to impose
standards and to critique the programs without much success.
One fact emerging from this experience is that a collection
of high quality software cannot be produced through such a
process.

As attitudes toward programming evolved, the publication
of algorithms in professional journals reflected the state
of the art. The early articles emphasized programming
techniques rather than algorithms as illustrated by a 1949
program for solving a Laplace boundary value problem on a
rectangle [8]. As indicated by the following excerpt the
intent of this article was to introduce UNIVAC programming,
rather than to communicate a program to potential users:

> "It is believed that there is wide
> interest in the question of instructing
> high-speed electronic computers now
> under design to perform the sequences
> of operations pertinent to selected

problems. This article, submitted
by members of the staff of a company
engaged in the development and construction of electronic digital
computers, is considered to be a
useful introduction to the use of
the instruction code for the computer
therein discussed."

Around this period there were a number of articles
dealing with the solution of particular problems on computers, especially problems in the area of linear algebra.
(The inversion of a matrix of order 38 on the Aiken relay
calculator was reported in 1948 [9]; the computing time
was 59½ hours.) In January 1953, Joe Wegstein initiated
the publication of a bibliography of coding procedures
in MTAC [10]. Later, in February, 1960, through his
efforts, the regular publication of algorithms in the
Communications of the ACM began. As with the example cited
earlier, it seems that the main purpose of this was to
illustrate and promulgate the use of a new tool: in this
case, the programming language Algol. However, by 1966,
it was recognized that the algorithms appearing in *CACM*
were a valuable resource and they were collected and
published separately in *Collected Algorithms of the ACM*.
The Algorithms Department of *CACM* was transferred to the
new *ACM Transactions on Mathematical Software* in 1975.
Other journals, too, *(BIT, Computer Journal, Numerische
Mathematik)* began the publication of algorithms.

The programs available from the published literature
have been of mixed quality. While the refereeing process
these journals have used represents more control on the
programs submitted for publication than in the case of
SHARE, it has not been sufficient to assure a collection
of high quality software. Refereeing is a voluntary
activity and it is extremely difficult to find good people
willing to devote the time and energy required to thoroughly
check the programs submitted. Also, authors have rights
and opinions that must be respected; therefore, there are
limits to the rules on style that one can impose in this

environment. Certainly, the publication of programs has been an important mechanism for the exchange of algorithmic ideas and programming techniques but, unfortunately, it has been less successful as a mechanism for communicating executable programs. To support this assertion, we remark that from June, 1975 when the algorithm distribution service started in the *Transactions on Mathematical Software*, making published programs available in machine readable form (tape or cards), to December, 1976, only 44 orders have been received for the 18 algorithms published; i.e., less than three requests per algorithm.

Users' expectations have significantly changed over a quarter-century, including attitudes toward the ease of use. A program which is the fastest and most accurate will be ignored if there are even a small number of impediments to its use. The commercial developers of software understand this, but many researchers do not and they will expend great effort to produce a program embodying the very best algorithm only to see the fruit of their labor ignored. For example, consider the matter of consistency among the subroutines in a library. It is common for several subroutines from a library to be used within a program. If the global variables for these subroutines are not defined in a consistent way, then passing information from one program to another becomes error prone and awkward, and users are repelled.

Reliability has always been a criterion for good software but now it is a far more significant issue. Programs are larger and much more complex than they were in the early years, so the problem of determining whether or not they are error free is a problem of major proportions. At the same time computers are being used in very sensitive situations where an error is extremely costly. In the early years, it was sufficient to employ a few debugging tools and run some test cases. Under the present circumstances, the production of reliable software requires a disciplined approach to the design and creation of the software itself, as well as very sophisticated tools to assure the reliability of the product.

Efficiency too has always been a criterion for judging software, but the notion of what constitutes efficiency has changed. In the early years, efficient use of memory was a matter of primary concern as we have already mentioned. Memory is now so large and cheap that its efficient use is of less concern. Naturally, speed of computation is important, but machines have become very fast and so this component of efficiency is less important, relatively speaking, than it once was. The big change in our notion of efficiency is the importance we assign to the human time involved in using a program. If large amounts of human effort are required to use a program, even though it executes twice as fast, say, as any other program for the same task, then that program is inefficient in a very real sense. Similar remarks apply to the maintenance of a program. Thus the early preoccupation with raw speed and minimal use of memory has been replaced with a growing concern for the interrelationship between man and machine.

III. Intellectual Challenges

By about 1970 there was enough experience with software to enable those who had acquired a taste for quality to articulate their requirements. The check list would look something like the following:

(1) Algorithmic foundations. The algorithm employed should be the best available for the intended purpose, as demonstrated by careful analysis.

(2) Style. The program must be written so as to clearly exhibit the logical organization of the computation. System dependencies should be minimal, localized, and well-identified.

(3) Documentation. The documentation must be clear and thorough. It must be organized in a way that permits an occasional user to obtain necessary information easily.

(4)   Reliability. The operation of the program must
be consistent with its documentation; there must
be no surprises in its use. Provision must be
made to verify that all conditions on input
data are met. Extensive testing must show
evidence of satisfactory numerical performance.

In addition, if the software is part of a distributed
collection, the requirements include:

(5)   Consistency. Documentation and conventions
for use of programs in the collection must
be consistent.

(6)   Maintenance. Responsibility for maintenance
must be assumed. This includes responding
to users' queries, making modifications and
extensions, and correcting errors.

Attitudes in the early 1950's tended to discriminate
between the "intellectual" task of algorithm formulation
and the "clerical" task of coding. The challenges implied
by the above requirements for high quality software makes
such a division of labor and difference of status an
anachronism. The computer science community has come to
realize that the brainpower needed to create such software
is as great, if somewhat differently oriented, as that
which provides the algorithmic foundations. Moreover,
there are significant research questions associated with
software creation. We suggest several in the remainder
of this section.

Consider the issue of good documentation. How does
one guarantee the consistency of documentation with the
software it purports to describe, given the complexities
of a typical program and the fact that it will change
from time to time? It seems reasonable to consider some
automatic way of assuring this consistency. One avenue
of approach might be to use the ideas of stepwise refinement [11]. In particular, let the initial description
of the program be the documentation or some part of it;
then, by a well-defined process, refine this initial

description into the code itself. Another approach might
be to use ideas from the work on proving programs correct.
In this approach one might let relevant parts of the
documentation play the role of assertions, or conversely,
and attempt to prove automatically from the code that these
assertions are correct. Another aspect of the documentation
problem is the automatic preparation of documentation for
different versions of a program corresponding to different
computing environments.

Programming style is a matter of considerable interest
to programmers these days. As we have already observed,
our notions of good style have changed. In the early
years, that style was good which used the least amount of
memory. (Now we seem to wish to use the smallest number
of go to's!) The ultimate objective of the style formalized
as "structured programming" is to produce programs which
are less likely to contain errors. The guidelines for
structured programming are heuristics which people believe
programmers should follow to meet this objective. One way
this approach could be put on a firmer foundation would be
to tie it to the relative ease of automatic error detection.
For example, one technique for automatic detection of errors
in a program uses data flow analysis [12]. Certain programming practices greatly complicate data flow analysis (e.g.,
the use of EQUIVALENCE), reducing the error detection
capability. It would seem reasonable to recommend that
programmers avoid the use of such constructs. Redundancy
is another aid to error detection. Languages which permit
greater redundancy would, in this sense, encourage a better
programming style.

The new machine architectures and microprogrammable
machines pose new and challenging problems for the algorithm
designer. It is becoming possible to mould a machine to a
class of problems through micro-programming. Perhaps it
would be fruitful to think of designing algorithms with
this additional degree of freedom in mind. Here we see
the need for an important, but all too rare, combination of
talents in numerical analysis, algorithm design, and computer architecture.

Articles in the area of software reliability have appeared with increasing frequency in recent years and there have been several conferences and a recent book devoted to this subject [13, 14, 15, 16]. We are still a long way from being able to prove the correctness of a sizeable numerical routine in a formal sense. However, it does seem that good progress can be made in the area of informal proofs and, if we are ever to achieve truly reliable software, more serious attention should be given to this subject (e.g., see [17]).

There is a very interesting connection between optimization techniques and error detection in programs that is worth mentioning here. In data flow analysis the flow graph of a program is examined and certain patterns of data flow are recognized [12]. Some patterns are symptomatic of errors; however, if these patterns arise on a path which is not executable then they are of no interest. Thus it becomes important to distinguish the executable paths. One attack on this problem has been described by Clarke [18] where it is shown that the problem reduces to a non-linear programming problem, and frequently to a linear programming problem.

The exploration of such problems may appropriately be labeled computer science research. It has become fashionable to call the application of the knowledge thus acquired "software engineering." We shall see in the remainder of the paper how software engineering links to numerical analysis and to a delivery system to form integrated production projects that are carried out in the real world where economics and politics leave their mark.

IV.   Projects to Produce Mathematical Software

Because the people who can contribute the required skills are dispersed geographically and have various primary sources of financial support, mathematical software projects are organized as collaborative endeavors involving individuals in universities, government laboratories, and private enterprises.

The accomplishments of a mathematical software project can be listed under the following three headings:

1.   Utility:
      Software provided by the project is readily available to and usable by the scientific and engineering public.

2.   Research Exploitation:
      The project is a conduit for the flow of research results in numerical analysis and algorithmics into applications.

3.   Software Production Improvement:
      Production tools and techniques have been developed and knowledge about the production process has been acquired by the project.

Every successful mathematical software project we have observed could claim accomplishments under all three headings although each project is characterized by a particular distribution of emphasis. Opinion will vary among individuals on a particular project as to the relative importance of these categories. We believe that all three orientations are necessary to mathematical software production and that the success of a project (assuming adequate funding and physical resources) is largely measured by the extent to which differently moti-vated individuals have merged their efforts to everyone's satisfaction. These differing perspectives will emerge as we describe three representative mathematical software projects, namely NATS (National Activity to Test Software), NAG (Numerical Algorithms Group), and IMSL (International Mathematical and Statistical Libraries), Inc.

NATS

NATS [19] commenced in early 1971 when grants from the National Science Foundation were awarded to Argonne National Laboratory, The University of Texas at Austin, and Stanford University. The objectives of the project were (1) to assemble, test, certify, disseminate, and support packages of mathematical software for eigensystem computation and function approximation; (2) to explore the methodology,

costs, and resources required to do (1). The second objective was primary and was approached by carrying out the
first as a prototypical effort. Therefore, NATS was a
study of the means of mathematical software production,
more explicitly so than any other project we know. By
focusing on two computational areas with such intensity
that great care could be taken in code construction, testing, and documentation, NATS attempted to establish bench-
marks and guidelines for mathematical software production.
By organizing the project as a university-government laboratory collaboration, NATS explored the interfaces and
division of responsibilities among several collaborating
institutions.

The software products of NATS were called "systematized
collections" [20]. There were two, EISPACK [21, 22] and
FUNPACK [23] in the areas of eigensystem computation and
function approximation respectively. Two releases of each
collection have been distributed, the second release, in
each case, extending the capabilities of the first. EISPACK
is available in six machine versions (IBM 360-370, CDC 6000-
7000, Univac 1108-1110, Honeywell 6070, DEC PDP-10,
Burroughs 6700) and has been distributed to approximately
450 installations. FUNPACK exists in three machine versions
(IBM 360-370, CDC 6000-7000, Univac 1108-1110) and has been
distributed to about 165 installations. Thus, a significant computational resource has been produced. It is
limited in the number of computational areas it covers but
is of very high quality within its scope.

The algorithms realized by the NATS software were the
culmination of years of work. The eigensystem algorithms
published in Algol [24], are generally acknowledged as
representing state-of-the-art methods, supported by
penetrating error analysis. Release 2 of EISPACK also
contains the algorithm discussed in [25]. In the function
approximation area, the algorithms were expressed as
running Fortran codes that had been developed for use at
Argonne National Laboratory. However, such codes are
highly machine-dependent and a significant amount of work

was required to prepare different machine versions, assemble a modularized package for each machine, test and fine-tune the software, and write the documentation required for widely distributed software. As the work progressed, NSF grants to the University of Kentucky and Jet Propulsion Laboratory brought collaboration with those institutions in the function approximation area. By producing EISPACK and FUNPACK the NATS project made analytic and algorithmic research results in these areas of computation readily accessible to scientific users for application in many fields.

An important form of collaboration was field-testing in which some two dozen computer installations at universities and research laboratories, representing the machines for which the package was being developed, cooperated by running tests supplied by the software developers and by making the software locally available for application to "real" problems.

Satisfactory performance at the test sites leads to "certification" of the codes; i.e., issuance of a warranty that the codes have performed satisfactorily in extensive testing and assurance of the continued interest of the developers. Certified NATS software is distributed by the Argonne Code Center.

The importance of coordination from some central point becomes very real when one considers the information flow among the various collaborators: numerical analysts supplying algorithms expressed as code developed on different machines in different locations, field test representatives attempting to implement code on a different machine than used by the developers, numerical analysts and software specialists writing documentation, the enormous clerical task of accurately processing many hundreds of requests for a package, and finally a continuing responsive point of contact for questions about the codes and their performance. These are the operational issues after the project has been organized and commitments made. They are preceded by an exploratory effort to determine the feasibility of a particular package development, involve those who could contribute, and seek funds to support the activity. Indeed a significant investment is required before a major mathematical software project can begin. Argonne National Laboratory played the central coordinating role for these pre-NATS organizational and operational activities.

The clerical burden on the project stimulated the development of computer based techniques for managing the large volume of source code and documentation for several computers. From this beginning there evolved a system, now called TAMPR [26, 27], which analyzes Fortran source programs, constructs an abstract form of the code which can be manipulated to produce alternate versions (e.g., for different computers, with various subroutine options, in greater or less precision, using real or complex arithmetic) which are reconstituted as running Fortran. This innovative work on the production process was intimately associated with the mathematical software development activities of NATS. It has long range research goals but is applicable in a very practical sense. It is an example of the delicate balance between short-term and long-term needs. If NATS had been under greater pressure to meet production deadlines, TAMPR necessarily would have focused on helping to meet those deadlines, probably to the detriment of the system's generality and its larger computer science implications. On the other hand, an attack on program transformation problems without relevance to real production needs could have led to more abstract formulations of less help in the production process.

The NATS project, having lived out its prototypical life, is now deceased. Its products, EISPACK and FUNPACK, have been well-received and its descendents are alive and well. These include the LINPACK project [28, 29], a collaborative effort among Argonne, the University of Maryland, the University of New Mexico, the University of California at San Diego, and the test sites to produce a systematized collection of linear systems routines; the

MINPACK project [30] aimed, in the long term, at producing a systematized collection of codes to solve non-linear optimization problems and systems of non-linear equations; and the research in program transformation exemplified by TAMPR.

NATS was supported by funds from the National Science Foundation and the Energy Research and Development Administration. We offer the following information (see [31]) to convey a sense of the resources required for such a project.

    EISPACK, Release 1

      Duration - 34 months.

      Total Personnel Effort - Senior Professional Staff (Ph.D. or equivalent): 96 months; Professional Staff (M.S. or equivalent): 16 months; Clerical Staff: 14 months.

      Cost - $528,000

      Size - 34 routines totalling about 6000 source cards for each machine version; The IBM version includes a control program of about 2500 cards.

    EISPACK, Release 2

      Duration - 41 months (About 16 months overlap with work on Release 1).

      Total Personnel Effort - Senior Professional Staff: 60 months; Professional Staff: 32 months; Clerical Staff: 17 months.

      Cost - $371,000

      Size - 70 routines plus certified drivers totalling about 12,000 source cards for each machine version; The IBM version includes a control program of about 3500 cards; Machine-readable documentation requires about 12,000 cards.

NAG

In 1970 a group of British universities, all users of the ICL 1906A, initiated joint action to produce a numerical software library for that machine. Now run from a central office in Oxford, the NAG (Numerical Algorithms Group) project [32] has considerably enlarged its original scope. It aims at the creation of a comprehensive numerical software library that can readily be implemented in virtually any scientific computing environment. The current library is available in Fortran and Algol 60 (an Algol 68 version is under construction) for a number of machines manufactured by Burroughs, CDC, DEC, Honeywell, IBM, ICL, Prime, Siemens, Telefunken, Univac, and Varian. There is widespread use of the library, especially in British universities. NAG maintains more than 100 copies in 8 countries [33].

The NAG library project remains a collaborative endeavor among British universities and government research laboratories, notably the National Physical Laboratory and the Atomic Energy Research Establishment at Harwell. Its activities have been subsidized in part by the government; however, it has become a non-profit corporation which will attempt to achieve financial self-sufficiency by renting its library products and services.

The NAG project emphasizes utility. It was created in response to the need for a product and it retains that orientation. The current release (Mark 5) contains over 300 routines (in each of Fortran and Algol 60). A new Mark of the library is issued approximately once a year.

Software for the NAG library originates with contributors who decide upon the coverage of some area of computation, select the methods, and write, test, and document the software. The contributors are experts in the computational area under development and are usually from one of the cooperating universities or research laboratories. Their software and documents are subject to validation by other experts who review the material for algorithmic merit and usability. It is thus largely the judgment of the

contributors and validators which determines the way NAG
functions as a conduit for algorithmic research.

Validated routines are examined by the NAG central
office, using various software aids, for adherence to
language standards, formatting, and general software
performance. The product of these contribution-validation-
examination activities is known as the "contributed
library." It is not distributed as certified software in
the NATS sense but passes through an implementation phase
for each machine range, an activity overseen by a
coordinator for that machine.

Accepted implementations are returned to the central
office for inclusion in a master library file system
which retains a complete history of each piece of software
in its various incarnations. Information in these files
has proved very valuable in determining programming standards to promote portability [34]. This type of case study
and the development of the master library file system [35]
are among the specific contributions of NAG to software
production tools and techniques.

Perhaps the greatest methodological contribution of
NAG has been its organization as a collaborative enterprise.
It has become a national effort that brings a great deal
of the best analytic and programming talent in Britain to
focus. The project now has 22 full time staff in the
central office and associated universities. Some 120
people work in part-time and voluntary capacities. During
the period June 1, 1970 to May 31, 1976, the total economic
cost of the NAG project is estimated to have been
£ 1,025,000 [36]. (£ 1 ≈ $1.70) The effort during the
same period is estimated to have been 152 man-years which,
in the United States, would have cost approximately
$6,000,000, about three and a half times as much.

Considering its success, is NAG a good model for
government-sponsored mathematical software production in
North America? We think not, at least it was not in 1970,
because the emulation of NAG would have brought North
Americans into conflict with the way government funds for
mathematical software development had been dispensed on this

side of the Atlantic. Under the rubric of "mathematics research" or "computing support," such funds were dispersed among many groups serving the interests of various agencies and sub-agencies. By 1970 when "mathematical software" assumed an identity, nearly every major computing establishment in North America had a mathematical subroutine library. Effort was duplicated, quality variable, and attempts to transport codes were rarely completely successful; nevertheless, the local codes had the virtue of familiarity and most users would not abandon their local software for anything less than codes of the quality of EISPACK.

Meanwhile, in Europe, first class algorithmic research offered a superb foundation for software development but less work had been done toward developing software libraries for a variety of computers. Both NAG and NATS entered this picture, NAG dedicated to satisfying immediate needs for mathematical software through collaborative action and NATS determined to show the benefits of collaboration in producing very high quality packages. NATS was limited in breadth of coverage; NAG software varied in quality though it was, in general, highly competitive with other software then available. (Later Marks of the NAG library show a steady improvement in quality while NATS-like projects, e.g., LINPACK and MINPACK, have entered other computational areas.)

A government-sponsored NAG-like project in North America would, therefore, have been in conflict with the decentralized way mathematical software had been produced on this continent. To gain acceptability, its product library would have needed to be EISPACK-like in each computational area. Even if algorithmic research were sufficiently mature to permit this, the effort would have been very expensive because (1) it costs more to do this work in North America than it does in Britain, and (2) the cost curve rises very sharply as one approaches EISPACK-like quality. The concentration of funds required to produce such a library would not have been politically

acceptable. The same discussion shows, incidentally, why
a NATS-like project would have been unacceptably extrava-
gant in Britain in 1970.

IMSL

IMSL (International Mathematical and Statistical
Libraries), Inc. is a for-profit corporation in Houston,
Texas which offers to lease a proprietary mathematical
software library containing about 400 subroutines to users
of Burroughs, CDC, DEC, Honeywell, IBM, Univac, and Xerox
computers [37]. The corporate intent is to provide software
that realizes the state-of-the science in methods and
algorithms. The emphasis at IMSL is on utility: satisfying the needs of customers.

The company was established in 1970 by scientist-
managers who had earlier helped develop program libraries
for IBM. The founders were aware of the local library
syndrome discussed above. Since they were using private
capital they were not bound by the decentralized approach
of government agencies. However, they were faced with the
problem of marketing their product in the climate created
by that approach. Moreover, they were not possessed of
the capital to produce EISPACK-like codes across a broad
spectrum. Their response in this tightly-constrained
situation was to produce a library that was comprehensive
in mathematics and statistics (thereby covering a broader
base than most local libraries), to keep its quality as
high as possible by involving expert advisers, to under-
score their responsiveness to customer problems, and to
encourage trial of the library by keeping the subscription
price fairly low.

We believe that IMSL assumed substantial risk and that
the success of the venture from a business standpoint is
still not assured. At its lowest point, the company
showed a net loss of about $350,000 in 1972. It broke
into the black in the third quarter of 1976. Techniques
that are being developed to moderate problems of portability
will significantly enhance the ability of IMSL and other
producers of mathematical software to disseminate that

software widely; indeed IMSL has, with support from NSF, carried out a portability study that resulted in a system called the Converter [38] used by the company and available to the public. This improvement of software production techniques is of central interest to the company in breaking down barriers to acceptance of its product. We note that both NATS and NAG have also regarded portability as a crucial issue.

IMSL is far more centralized than NATS or NAG. We underscored the collaborative nature of the latter projects which are coordinated, rather than directed, from a central place. IMSL certainly draws on the expertise of the numerical analysis community through its board of advisers but this partnership is limited to a flow of technical advice on request. The structure of the library, and the tactics and overall strategy of the company are, naturally, the responsibility of the corporate officers who answer to the investors.

We believe that the company has demonstrated its ability to act as a conduit for research results. IMSL's source for methods, algorithms, and software is primarily published material in leading journals as well as doctoral theses and contributions from advisers. The President of IMSL has declared that the company's role is "to quickly move research results on algorithms and software development into programs which operate ... in a scientific environment." [39]

Cost and income figures quoted by IMSL [39] add to our information about the expenses involved in mathematical software development. The company spends approximately $2000 for each code for the first implementation while the cost of moving that software to a new environment is about one-sixth of the original cost. The gross revenue derived per code per year per customer is $3.75. It is expected that this figure will decrease as the library grows while the cost of production will decrease as more sophisticated portability techniques are employed. A gross comparison of these costs with the EISPACK development

costs quoted earlier indicates that the NATS costs were
about three times as great as IMSL costs for a given
volume of code, further evidence that exceptionally high
quality software is exceptionally expensive.

V.   Trends in Mathematical Software Production

In this section we shall confine our attention to the
North American scene in an attempt to predict future
patterns of mathematical software production.   The
following trends are already apparent and will combine
to exert a strong influence:

  (1)   The demand for good general-purpose mathematical
         software is increasing among the user public;

  (2)   Relationships between the quality and cost of
         mathematical software are becoming better
         understood by producers and users;

  (3)   Computer-based production techniques, now
         under development, show promise of improving
         quality and decreasing cost.

Users have become more receptive to mathematical software produced for dissemination.   EISPACK and FUNPACK are
acceptable because they are of very high quality while
IMSL and other libraries offer good quality and broad
coverage.   The responsiveness of the developers of these
packages to user problems has helped overcome the
resistence to non-local software.   This acceptance is
still very fragile.   Users are uncertain about the highest
price they are willing to pay, either in terms of subscription fees or the toleration of imperfections.   These
are closely related since, as we have already remarked,
the cost of production rises sharply as one approaches
NATS-like quality.   If users do not become disillusioned
because of some particularly disappointing software that
appears, then there is a good chance that mathematical
software production for a mass audience will remain viable
long enough for improved production techniques to strengthen
the whole enterprise.   We believe that users and producers
are becoming sharp enough in their evaluation of cost-
quality relationships to sustain the present momentum.

Three areas of production technique research show particular promise of providing the tools needed to start an escalation of good mathematical software, cost reduction, and user confidence. These are (a) computer-aided analysis and transformation of source programs, (b) testing methods, and (c) networks.

Example of program analysis systems are DAVE [40], PFORT [41], FACES [42], PET [43]. Examples of program transformation systems are TAMPR [26, 27] and the Program Generator [44]. Analysis systems permit a probe of the structural details of complex programs with identification of anomalous and erroneous constructions. The transformation systems also analyze the structure of a program but for the purpose of transforming it in various ways. For example, programs from various sources may be brought into conformance with a set of formatting standards. Such systems may use a master program or set of instructions to automatically generate software tailored to a particular machine or with variations in program structure. By storing and maintaining only the master programs, developers and distributors have far fewer data to manage in error-prone information processing operations.

Testing methods are being developed that take into account a fundamental distinction between two classes of software [45]. The first class (called "precision-bound" software; for example, numerical eigenanalysis, linear systems, and function approximation) suffers primarily from round-off error due to the finiteness of machine number representations. This type of error is rather well understood theoretically (see [46]) and the testing techniques used in the NATS project appear adequate in principle. The second class ("heuristic-bound" software; for example, the numerical treatment of quadrature, ordinary differential equations, and non-linear optimization) is a victim of errors derived from the manner of simulating analytic constructs, in particular convergence. These errors dominate round-off so that such software requires an approach to testing which permits careful statements to be made about the cost of obtaining reliability at some specified confidence level. A testing

methodology along these lines has been developed for
quadrature routines [47]. Further work will be essential
to the production of high quality heuristic-bound software,
accompanied by meaningful statements about performance.

Computer networks will facilitate interaction among
geographically dispersed collaborators [48]. Such
networks will also enable users to obtain both information
about software applicable to their needs and the software
itself. Experimentation along these lines is under way
at several ERDA laboratories.

We are optimistic that tools based on this research
will facilitate the passage of algorithmic ideas into
useful software. However, we do not believe that future
mathematical software projects will simply be streamlined
versions of earlier efforts. Rather we foresee certain
basic changes in institutional roles, the principal one
being a shift of government support away from NATS-like
efforts in which a government laboratory acts as a mediator
between university research and end-users. The effectiveness of such programs has been demonstrated and we have
argued for their expansion [31]. However, the required
concentration of resources remains politically unacceptable.
Our hope now is that present trends will lead to commer-
cially viable production activities which draw heavily
on expertise in the research community. We predict that
the government will encourage these trends by supporting
state-of-the-science studies and algorithmic and systems
research, buying the mathematical software products,
and developing the use of these products in government
programs. In this view of the future, the actual production will be carried out through commercial enterprises
which maintain a working partnership with universities
and research laboratories, often taking the form of
interaction with individual scientists.

We must, however, admit a second possible future for,
as we have already suggested, the commercialization of
mathematical software production is in a somewhat precarious
situation and its growth is not assured. After all, the
same improved techniques that make the production of

commercial libraries more feasible also make it easier for small groups in universities and research laboratories to do what they have always done - produce mathematical software for their own use and for limited distribution within a specialized community. We rate such a "cottage industry" approach as inferior to "mass production" that strives to be a conduit for the best research results. The real future will probably be a mixture of commercialization and local developments in a proportion impossible to foresee. In any case, the mathematical software production events of the last half-dozen years have raised standards and influenced tastes so that the state of scientific computing is the better for it.

REFERENCES

1. Rice, John R. (Ed.) *Mathematical Software*, Academic Press (1971), 515 pp.

2. *Mathematical Software II - Informal Proceedings of a Conference.* Purdue University, May 29-31, 1974. 324 pp.

3. Battiste, E. L. The production of mathematical software for a mass audience. In *Mathematical Software*, John R. Rice, ed., Academic Press (1971), 121-130.

4. Traub, J. F. High quality portable numerical mathematics software. In *Mathematical Software*, John R. Rice, ed., Academic Press (1971) 131-139.

5. Newbery, A. C. R. The Boeing library and handbook of mathematical routines. In *Mathematical software*, John R. Rice, ed., Academic Press (1971) 153-169.

6. Wilkes, Maurice V.; Wheeler, David J.; and Gill, Stanley. *The Preparation of Programs for an Electric Digital Computer*, Addison-Wesley (1951), 167 pp.

7. Kernighan, Brian W. and Plauger, P. J. *The Elements of Programming Style*, McGraw-Hill (1974), 147 pp.

8. Snyder, Francis E. and Livingston, Hubert M. Coding of a Laplace boundary value problem for the UNIVAC. *Math. Tables and Other Aids to Computation* (now Mathematics of Computation) 3, 25 (Jan. 1949), 341-350.

9. Mitchell, Herbert F., Jr. Inversion of a matrix
    of order 38. *Math. Tables and Other Aids to*
    Computation (now Mathematics of Computation)
    3, 23 (July 1948), 161-166.

10. Todd, John. Bibliography of coding procedures.
    Math. Tables and Other Aids to Computation (now
    Mathematics of Computation) 7, 41 (Jan. 1953),
    47-48.

11. Wirth, Niklaus. Program development by stepwise
    refinement. *Comm. ACM* 14, 4 (1971), 221-227.

12. Fosdick, Lloyd D. and Osterweil, Leon J. Data
    flow analysis in software reliability. *ACM Comp.*
    Surv. 8, 3 (September 1976), 305-330.

13. *Proceedings IEEE Symposium on Computer Software*
    Reliability, New York City, April 30-May 2, 1973.

14. *Proceedings International Conference on Reliable*
    Software, Los Angeles, Ca., April 21-23, 1975.
    567 pp. IEEE Cat. No. 75CHO940-7CSR.

15. Hetzel, William C. (Ed.) *Program Test Methods,*
    Prentice-Hall (1973), 311 pp.

16. Myers, Glenford J. *Software Reliability: Principles*
    & Practices, Wiley (1976), 360 pp.

17. Hull T. E.; Enright, W. H.; Sedgwick, A. E. The
    correctness of numerical algorithms. *Proc. ACM*
    Conference on Proving Assertions About Programs,
    New Mexico State University, Las Cruces, N. M.,
    January 1972, pp. 66-73.

18. Clarke, Lori. A system to generate test data and
    symbolically execute programs. *IEEE Trans. on*
    Software Engineering SE-2, 3 (Sept. 1976),
    215-222.

19. Boyle, J. M.; Cody, W. J.; Cowell, W. R.; Garbow,
    B. S.; Ikebe, Y.; Moler, C. B.; and Smith, B. T.
    NATS, A collaborative effort to certify and
    disseminate mathematical software, *Proceedings 1972*
    National ACM Conference, 630-635.

20. Smith, B. T.; Boyle, J. M.; Cody, W. J. The NATS
    approach to quality software. In *Software for*
    Numerical Mathematics, D. J. Evans, ed., Academic
    Press (1974), 393-405.

21. Garbow, B. S. EISPACK - A package of matrix
    eigensystem routines. *Computer Physics Communications*
    7, 4 (April 1974), 179-184.

22. Smith, B. T.; Boyle, J. M.; Dongarra, J. J.; Garbow, B. S.; Ikebe, Y.; Klema, V. C.; Moler, C. B. *Matrix Eigensystem Routines - EISPACK Guide*, Lecture Notes in Computer Science, 6, 2nd Edition. Springer-Verlag (1976).

23. Cody, W. J. The FUNPACK package of special function subroutines. *ACM Trans. on Math. Soft.* 1, 1 (March, 1975), 13-25.

24. Wilkinson, J. H. and Reinsch, C. *Handbook for Automatic Computation, Volume II, Linear Algebra*, Part 2. Springer-Verlag (1971).

25. Moler, C. B., and Stewart, G. W. An algorithm for generalized matrix eigenvalue problems. *SIAM Journ. of Numer. Anal.* 10, 2 (April, 1973) 241-256.

26. Boyle, J. M. and Dritz, K. W. An automated programming system to facilitate the development of quality software. In *Information Processing 74*, North Holland Pub. Co. (1974), pp. 542-546.

27. Dritz, Kenneth W. Multiple program realizations using the TAMPR system. In *Proceedings of the Workshop on Portability of Numerical Software*, To appear.

28. The LINPACK Prospectus and Working Notes, Applied Mathematics Division, Argonne National Laboratory, Argonne, Ill. 60439.

29. Stewart, G. W. Research, development, and LINPACK. These Proceedings.

30. Brown, K.; Minkoff, M.; Hillstrom, K.; Nazareth, L.; Pool, J.; and Smith, B. Progress in the development of a modularized package of algorithms for optimization problems. In *Optimization in Action*, L. C. W. Dixon, ed., Academic Press (1976), pp. 185-211.

31. Cowell, Wayne R. and Fosdick, Lloyd D. A program for development of high quality mathematical software, Report #CU-CS-079-75 (Sept. 1975), Department of Computer Science, University of Colorado, Boulder, Colorado, 80302.

32. Ford, B. and Sayers, D. K. Developing a single numerical algorithms library for different machine ranges. *ACM Trans. on Math. Soft.* 2, 2 (June, 1976) 115-131.

33. Annual Report of the Numerical Algorithms Group:
    1 June, 1975 to 31 May, 1976, NAG Central Office,
    13 Banbury Road, Oxford OX2 6NN.

34. Bentley, J. and Ford B. On the enhancement of
    portability within the NAG project. In *Proceedings
    of the Workshop on Portability of Numerical Software*,
    To Appear.

35. DuCroz, J. J.; Hague, S. J.; Siemieniuch, J. L.
    Aids to portability within the NAG project.
    In *Proceedings of the Workshop on Portability
    of Numerical Software*, To Appear.

36. Ford, B. Private Communication (1977).

37. *IMSL Numerical Computation Newsletter*, issue no. 1
    (January, 1972), International Mathematical and
    Statistical Libraries, Inc., Sixth Floor, GNB Bldg.,
    7500 Bellaire Blvd., Houston, Texas 77036.

38. Aird, T. J. The IMSL Fortran Converter: An
    approach to solving portability problems. In
    *Proceedings of the Workshop on Portability of
    Numerical Software*, To Appear.

39. Battiste, E. L. Mathematical software and the
    private sector, Talk at ACM Annual Conference
    (1976).

40. Osterweil, Leon J. and Fosdick, Lloyd D. DAVE -
    a validation, error detection and documentation
    system for FORTRAN programs. *Software-Practice
    and Experience* 6 (1976), 473-486.

41. Ryder, Barbra G. The PFORT verifier, *Software-
    Practice and Experience* 4 (1974), 359-378.

42. Ramamoorthy, C. V. and Ho, Siu-Bun F. Testing
    large software with automated software evaluation
    systems. *IEEE Trans. on Software Engineering*
    1, 1 (March 1975), 46-58.

43. Stucki, Leon G. and Foshee, Gary L. New assertion
    concepts for self-metric software validation.
    pp. 59-65 in reference 14.

44. Voevodin, V.; Gaisaryan, S. ; Kabanov, M. Automated
    program generation. In *Numerical Analysis in Fortran*,
    Vol. 1. Moscow State University Press (1973) (In
    Russian).

45. Cowell, Wayne. The validation of mathematical
     software. In *Proceedings of INFOPOL-76, International
     Conference on Data Processing,* To Appear.

46. Wilkinson, J. H. Modern error analysis. *SIAM
     Review* 13, 4 (October, 1971) 548-568.

47. Lyness, J. N. and Kaganove, J. J. A technique for
     comparing automatic quadrature routines. *Computer
     Journal,* To Appear.

48. Greenberger, M.; Aronofsky, J.; McKenney, J. L.;
     Massy, W. F., eds. *Networks for Research and
     Education.* M.I.T. Press (1974).

Work supported in part by the U.S. Energy Research
and Development Administration and the National
Science Foundation.

Applied Mathematics Div.   Dept. of Computer Science
Argonne National Lab.   Univ. of Colorado
Argonne, Illinois 60439   Boulder, Colorado 80302

Computational Aspects
of the Finite Element Method
I. Babuška
W. Rheinboldt

1. INTRODUCTION

In the past two decades computational structural analysis and
design have developed into very broad and deep subject areas. A major
contributing factor certainly is the evolution of the finite element
method into a powerful tool for the solution of a broad range of applications (see, e.g., the bibliographies [27], [19]). As part of this
world-wide use of the method, numerous, often large, general- and
special-purpose programs for practical finite element computations have
been written and are extensively applied to increasingly complex problems (see, e.g., [22], [21]).

Not unexpectedly there is cause for praising as well as criticizing
the existing finite element software. At the same time any assessments
of the present situation and future trends in the area must recognize
the method as a major practical tool in engineering, science, etc., and
not just as an object of academic study. It is important to take into
account the opinions and broad experience of the users' communities of
the existing software. These have been expressed in various papers and
conference proceedings (see, e.g., [22], [15]) and there appears to be
no need to give another summary here.

Instead, on the basis of this accumulated experience, we attempt to
present the rationale for a set of, albeit idealized, design criteria
for the next generation of finite element programs. These criteria
correspond well with the trends that are now beginning to emerge in the
area (see, e.g., [24], [15]). Moreover, our own experience has shown
that they are realistic and implementable (see, e.g., [5], [6], [2], and

Section 5 below).

Rather broadly speaking the principal aspects of these criteria may be characterized as follows:

(1) The programs should no longer be designed for specific classes of applications, but instead should constitute more flexible "finite element solvers" based on a general (weak) mathematical formulation in terms of bivariate forms. This will provide for a much needed broader applicability and flexibility.

(2) It should be easy to learn the use of the software for common practical problems. Hence as much as possible the user should not have to understand the internal operation or to make difficult a-priori decisions about the desired computations. For this the user interfaces should be strictly separated, say, into flexible pre- and post-processors, and the main programs should incorporate extensive application of adaptive techniques.

(3) The solution process should provide optimal accuracy within a prescribed range of computational cost. The accuracy should reflect the error of the results in relation to the solution of a "higher" mathematical formulation. It should also be possible to assess the practical reliability of the results, that is the effect of the choice of mathematical formulation and numerical method. Hence the design should include well thought-out provisions for the estimation of all errors and for the corresponding adaptive modification of the course of the computation.

(4) In line with recent results provisions for a-posteriori computations should be available to improve the accuracy of the results whenever possible.

(5) In the implementation modern advances in the design of software systems, programming languages, data structures, numerical subroutines, user-systems interfaces, etc. should be taken into account.

Clearly, these design criteria are still ideals and extensive research will be needed before they can be fully realized. Such research is in the interface between mathematics, numerical analysis, computer science, software engineering, and the applications disciplines, and will require a much closer cooperation between contributors from these fields than has been existent so far.

In order to provide a rationale and further explanation of the above criteria we begin in Section 2 with a formulation of some of the broad

goals of the finite element computation as seen from the viewpoint of
the practical user. They show that it is not sufficient to consider
only the numerical procedure itself and its implementation but that it
is essential to look at the complete solution process. At the same
time it is important to realize that the computational analysis from
the specification of the characteristics of an original practical problem to the final numerical results of the finite element computation
is extremely rich in its potential flexibility. In order to illustrate
this, we exemplify in Section 3 the principal stages of the overall
analysis. In conjunction with the computational goals, this will provide reasons for our choice of the above criteria. Then in Section 4
we give some further details about the criteria and our views of the
next generation of finite element software. Finally Section 5 presents
some results obtained with an experimental program that meets, at least
in part, several of the above design criteria.

By necessity the discussion cannot enter into much mathematical
or computational detail. Moreover, for simplicity we restricted ourselves to a class of linear, stationary problems although the observations also apply to nonlinear and nonstationary problems. Finally, it
should be stressed that we consider here only aspects of general-
purpose finite element software for practical applications. These
terms are used in a pragmatic sense based more or less on present
terminology in the area (see, e,g., [22]).

2. GOALS OF THE COMPUTATIONAL ANALYSIS

In the development of much of the mathematical software included,
for instance, in present subroutine libraries a principal aim is to
achieve--whenever possible--a prescribed and typically high accuracy.
Usually here the term "accuracy" refers only to the size of the errors
introduced by the particular numerical method. Moreover, reliability
considerations mainly center on a reduction of the failure rate of the
program.

In the case of general-purpose, finite element software for practical applications the requirements are rather different. Here the fore-
most aim of the computations is the analysis of a given practical
problem, say, in structural engineering. Thus the user wishes to obtain
results which predict, with an acceptable degree of reliability and
accuracy, the actual behavior of the mechanical structure at hand.

In other words the terms "accuracy" and "reliability" are used here
in a much broader context than before. It is clearly inadequate to

assess the results solely on the basis of the errors introduced by the numerical method. Often these errors are much smaller than those caused by earlier decisions about the mathematical formulations used for modelling the given problem. Therefore, the accuracy of the numerical results should be a measure of their deviation from the solution of a "higher" mathematical model. Moreover these results can only be considered reliable if changes in the reference model and, more generally, in the overall sequence of steps from the problem formulation to the final outcome have relatively small effects.

This reliability concept is of central importance. In comparison the accuracy of the results plays only a secondary role. In fact considerations of computational cost are even more important. This is due to the fact that the computations involved are generally very extensive and highly demanding on the available computer resources[1]. Hence in most cases the user is forced to set a maximum allowable cost for any one computational analysis. Ideally then the goal is to achieve optimal, acceptable accuracy within the prescribed cost range. Here it is essential that often relatively low accuracies are already acceptable. In fact in the analysis of many technical problems relative errors of several, say, five to ten percent tend to be entirely satisfactory. Without doubt the design criterion of optimal results within some cost range represents a serious challenge and is not realized in today's finite element software.

Clearly the general goals outlined so far require a closer look at the overall computational finite element analysis. Broadly speaking we may distinguish at least six major stages of this analysis, each of which allows for a surprisingly wide range of decisions:

(0) Specification of the characteristics of the practical problem.

(1) Formulation of a basic mathematical model.

(2) Reformulation of the basic model to further the theoretical and numerical analysis.

(3) Definition of a corresponding (weak) mathematical formulation in terms of a bivariate form on appropriate function spaces.

(4) Design of the overall--necessarily adaptive--numerical process including the error estimates for the control of the computation.

(5) Selection of a-posteriori analyses applicable to the results.

---

[1] In addition the demands on personnel resources tend to be equally formidable.

The first stage was numbered zero since it transcends the mathematical analysis. The next section illustrates some of the principal aspects of the remaining five stages and of the many choices available at each one of them. Generally it appears to be essential that future general-purpose, finite element software incorporates more of the flexibility reflected in the richness of choice of these five stages.

3. THE PRINCIPAL STAGES OF THE COMPUTATIONAL ANALYSIS

The following five subsections correspond to the five analysis stages (1) to (5) introduced in the previous section. By necessity the discussion can be by example only.

3.1 THE BASIC MATHEMATICAL MODEL

In general the formulation of the basic mathematical model is considered outside of any software design. However in defining this formulation we are already faced with a range of difficult decisions as, for example, whether a plate or shell may be considered thin or whether nonlinear behavior may be disregarded. The assumptions made here often have a more critical influence upon the final results than any of the subsequent ones. In the software design it is desirable to allow for some of the possibilities for estimating the effect of these decisions during later phases of the computation.

As a simple example, consider the analysis of a piece of building foundation in the form of a partly supported, square plate subject to a uniform load (see Figure 1). For simplicity the material is assumed to be homogeneous and isotropic with Poisson ratio $\sigma = 0$ and modulus of elasticity E.

Two different mathematical models are readily available here, namely, a pure plate formulation based on the Kirchhoff hypotheses, or the full three-dimensional elasticity formulation. The equations for either case are well known (see, e.g., [25]) and are certainly not mathematically equivalent. In deciding between them the crucial question will be whether the thickness d is sufficiently small for the plate formulation to represent an acceptable approximation.

Neither one of the formulations is solvable explicitly and hence suitable discretizations have to be used. Figure 3 shows some comparative computational results for the case $d = 1/6$. More specifically the stresses σ_{11}, σ_{22} are given along the cross-sections I and II of Figure 2. For the plate model nonconforming square plate elements[1] with

---

[1]These are elements using incomplete fourth-order and complete third-order polynomials (see [28], p. 178).

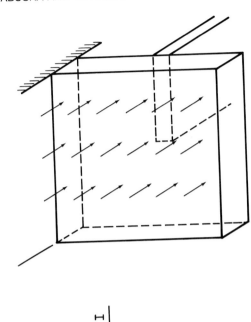

Figure 1

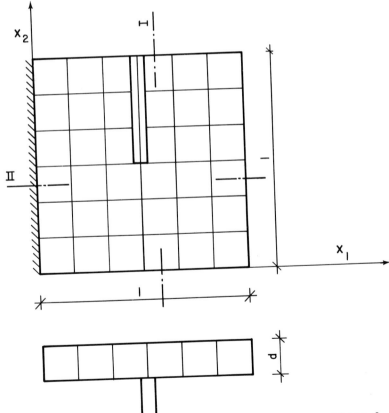

Figure 2

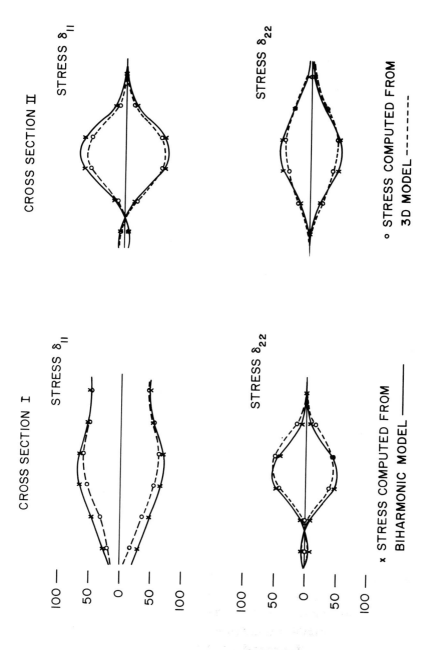

Figure 3

side length 1/6 were used while the full model was based on three-dimensional, trilinear, cube-elements again with side length 1/6. The mesh in the x_1, x_2-plane was the same in both cases and is shown in Figure 2 but, of course, in the three-dimensional case each element extends through the entire thickness of the plate.

The differences in the calculated stresses are of the order of 20%. Moreover the plate theory leads to stress components which are either symmetric or antisymmetric with respect to the midplane. On the other hand the three-dimensional formulation shows mildly nonsymmetric stresses through the thickness, and it also allows for better incorporation of the boundary conditions such as, for instance, the support conditions on the lower side of the plate. We note that for the stresses the asymptotic orders in terms of element size are the same in both cases although, of course, for the case of our coarse mesh this does not imply much. Generally it is well known that for thin plates, where deflection is mainly due to bending, the three-dimensional model with linear, tensor-product elements overemphasizes the shear stresses and hence gives smaller deflections than the pure plate model.

For the practical application the question remains how to decide upon either model. This decision certainly becomes difficult when the thickness is not particularly small as in our case with $d = 1/6$--, or when there are areas--as in our example near the tip of the support-- where the stresses are large and shear stresses play an important role, a situation that is only approximately reflected in the plate model (see [6]).

At present no generally satisfactory answers are available here. However certain possibilities are opened up by the observation that two-dimensional plate formulations are in fact instances of dimensional reduction which can be interpreted as the use of special elements for the three-dimensional formulation (see [6]). Some of the error estimation procedures discussed in later sections then allow for an analysis of the relative reliability of the results of both formulations.

The example discussed here is typical for many problems. In particular, a variety of shell models are given in the literature which often turn out to lead to substantially different results (see again [16]). There can be little doubt that the choice of the basic model for the analysis is of critical importance for the entire work. Hence the software should be flexible enough to allow for a wide variety of basic formulations and the output should include information for some comparative evaluation of the results.

3.2 EQUIVALENT MATHEMATICAL FORMULATIONS

Suppose that a basic mathematical model has been decided upon. For example, consider the deflection of a nonisotropic, nonhomogeneous membrane which may be formulated in terms of the equation

$$(3.1) \qquad \frac{\partial}{\partial x_1} a \frac{\partial u}{\partial x_1} + \frac{\partial}{\partial x_2} b \frac{\partial u}{\partial x_2} = \frac{\partial F}{\partial x_1} + \frac{\partial G}{\partial x_2} , \ \forall \ (x_1, x_2) \in \Omega \subset R^2$$

with the boundary conditions

$$(3.2) \qquad u = g, \ \forall \ (x_1, x_2) \in \partial\Omega$$

with given functions a, b, F, G, and g.

This is a well-posed classical mathematical problem. In particular, for smooth boundaries and appropriately given input functions, its theoretical aspects are fully understood (see, e.g., [23]). A survey of the more delicate case of nonsmooth boundaries may be found in [17].

The equation (3.1) may also be formulated as a Petrowski system of the first order

$$(3.3) \qquad \begin{aligned} a \frac{\partial u}{\partial x_1} + \frac{\partial v}{\partial x_2} &= F \\[2mm] b \frac{\partial u}{\partial x_2} - \frac{\partial v}{\partial x_1} &= G \ . \end{aligned}$$

Alternately (3.1) may be rewritten as an elliptic system of Douglis-Nirenberg (non-Petrowski) type:

$$(3.4) \qquad \begin{aligned} a \frac{\partial u}{\partial x_1} - \sigma_1 &= 0 \\[2mm] b \frac{\partial u}{\partial x_2} - \sigma_2 &= 0 \\[2mm] \frac{\partial \sigma_1}{\partial x_1} + \frac{\partial \sigma_2}{\partial x_2} &= \frac{\partial F}{\partial x_1} + \frac{\partial G}{\partial x_2} \end{aligned}$$

The three problems (3.1-2), (3.3-2), (3.4-2) are mathematically equivalent in the sense that their solution is unique (in appropriate spaces) and that the resulting functions u are the same in all cases. Many other such equivalent reformulations of the original problems may be given. But from a numerical point of view they are, in general, far from equivalent. Certainly for easy, extremely smooth problems the computational results for different formulations may be relatively close to each other, but the differences soon become significant for more complex problems.

As a simple example we consider the one-dimensional, periodic, and self-adjoint eigenvalue problem

(3.5) $$-(\frac{1}{\tau(x)} u')' + \rho(x)u = \lambda\rho(x)u, \quad 0 < x < 2\pi$$

with the boundary conditions

(3.6) $$u(0) = u(2\pi), \quad (\frac{1}{\tau} u')(0) = (\frac{1}{\tau} u')(2\pi)$$

where $0 < \alpha \leq \tau(x), \rho(x) \leq \beta < \infty$. As before this problem can be refor-
mulated as the system

(3.7) $$-\sigma' + \rho u = \lambda\rho u, \quad u' = \tau\sigma$$

with the boundary conditions

(3.8) $$u(0) = u(2\pi), \quad \sigma(0) = \sigma(2\pi) .$$

For the application of the finite element method we associate with
(3.5-6) and (3.7-8) the bilinear forms

(3.9) $$\int_0^{2\pi} (\frac{1}{\tau} u'\bar{v} + \rho u\bar{v})dx = \lambda \int_0^{2\pi} \rho u(x)\bar{v}dx$$

and

(3.10) $$\int_0^{2\pi} (u'\bar{s} - \tau\sigma\bar{s} - \sigma'\bar{v} + \rho u\bar{v})dx = \lambda \int_0^{2\pi} \rho u\bar{v}dx ,$$

respectively. Here $\bar{v}$ etc. denotes the conjugate complex function.
For the desired eigenvalue λ, (3.9) or (3.10) have to hold for all v,
or v and s, respectively, in appropriate function spaces.

The finite element method now requires the selection of suitable
finite-dimensional subspaces of functions and the solution of the resulting generalized matrix eigenvalue problems (see, e.g., [4]). In our
case we choose subspaces of trigonometric polynomials of degree N, that
is, we set

$$u = \sum_{k=-N}^{N} a_k e^{ikx}, \quad \sigma = \sum_{k=-N}^{N} b_k e^{ikx} .$$

Then we wish to determine λ_j^N so that (3.9) holds for all $v = e^{ikx}$,
$k = -N,\ldots,N$, and (3.10) for all $v = e^{ikx}$, $s = e^{ijx}$, $i,j = -N,\ldots,N$.
Clearly finite elements could have been used here as well.

We consider the specific case when $\tau(x) = g(x)^{-1}$, $\rho(x) \equiv 1$ and g
is defined by

$$g(x) = \begin{cases} 2 + \sqrt{3}, & x \in I_j, \; j \in J_1 \\ 2 - \sqrt{3}, & x \in I_j, \; j \in J_2 \end{cases}$$

with

$$I_j = \left[\frac{\pi j}{64}, \frac{\pi(j+1)}{64} \right), \quad j = 0,1,\ldots,63 .$$

For the specification of the index set J_1, J_2 consider the base four representation

$$j = \sum_{k=0}^{2} d_k^{(j)} 4^k, \quad 0 \le d_k^{(j)} \le 3 ;$$

then we set $j \in J_1$ if at least one digit $d_k^{(j)}$ equals 1 or 3, and $j \in J_2$ otherwise.

The following Tables 1 and 2 show some computational results for this particular problem (except for the obvious eigenvalue $\lambda = 1$). The differences are self-evident. We note also that in this case all λ_j^N represent upper bounds for the exact eigenvalues, and $\lambda_j^N \to \lambda_j$ for $N \to \infty$.

The example clearly shows that equivalent mathematical formulations may lead to very different numerical results, and, as before, the question arises which formulation should be used in a particular case. Once again we see that the software should allow for the use of various different formulations and should provide, as much as possible, estimates of the relevant errors.

N	λ_1^N	λ_2^N	λ_3^N	λ_4^N	λ_5^N
5	4.2011938	4.2448674	13.588305	14.566439	30.520416
10	4.1821456	4.2398342	13.395898	14.376096	29.502732
20	4.0084361	4.0810097	12.864945	14.017717	28.496707
30	3.9859419	4.0679036	12.780292	13.934870	28.239821
40	3.9193785	4.0647326	12.609956	13.917917	27.605097
50	3.5789367	3.9391686	11.732314	13.519697	25.829411
60	3.3674973	3.8203314	11.138698	12.951891	23.04808

Table 1. Results based on (3.9)

N	λ_1^N	λ_2^N	λ_3^N	λ_4^N	λ_5^N
5	2.3864699	2.3868424	7.3740194	8.4411605	16.502603
10	2.3853182	2.3856739	7.2522002	8.2398985	14.972700
20	2.3808835	2.3808985	7.1959693	8.2091849	14.861027
30	2.3807822	2.3807881	7.1920789	8.2043920	14.844143
40	2.3807646	2.3807773	7.1917303	8.2039635	14.839562

Table 2. Results based on (3.10)

3.3 THE WEAK MATHEMATICAL FORMULATION

At this point in the analysis we have chosen a specific formulation involving a differential equation. Its solution has to be understood in a weak sense. In other words, we associate with this problem a bilinear[1] form $B(u,v)$ defined on a pair of Hilbert (or Banach) spaces $H_1 \times H_2$. The form B is called <u>proper</u> on $H_1 \times H_2$ if

(3.11)

(a) $|B(u,v)| \le c_1 \|u\|_{H_1} \|v\|_{H_2}$, $\forall u \in H_1$, $v \in H_2$, $c_1 < \infty$

(b) $\displaystyle \sup_{v \in H_2, v \ne 0} \frac{|B(u,v)|}{\|v\|_{H_2}} \ge c_2 \|u\|_{H_1}$, $\forall u \in H_1$, $c_2 > 0$,

(c) $\displaystyle \sup_{u \in H_1} |B(u,v)| > 0$, $\forall v \in H_2$, $v \ne 0$.

The (weak) solution of the differential equation is now the (unique) $u_0 \in H_1$ such that

$$(3.12) \qquad B(u_0,v) = f(v), \quad \forall v \in H_2 ,$$

where $f \in H_2'$ is a given functional. It is important to note that B has to be considered together with the spaces H_1, H_2. A selection of different spaces changes the problem and the error estimates. At the same time if the error estimates are not incorporated, then the numerical procedure itself is not affected by the change.

With any of the problems obtained in the previous stages, we may associate a variety of different forms B. In order to illustrate this, consider the problem

$$(3.13) \qquad -\Delta u + u = F(x) \quad \text{on } \Omega \subset R^2$$

$$(3.14) \qquad \frac{\partial u}{\partial n} + \alpha(s) \frac{\partial u}{\partial s} + \beta(s)u = G(s) \text{ on } \partial\Omega ,$$

where n is the outward normal of $\partial\Omega$. Such problems involving oblique directional derivatives on the boundary arise, for instance, in connection with rotating fluids.

With this problem we may associate the form

$$(3.15) \quad B(u,v) = \int_\Omega (\frac{\partial u}{\partial x_1} \frac{\partial v}{\partial x_1} + \frac{\partial u}{\partial x_2} \frac{\partial v}{\partial x_2} + uv)dx + \oint_{\partial\Omega} (\alpha \frac{\partial u}{\partial s} + \beta u)vds$$

and the functional

$$(3.16) \qquad f(v) = \int_\Omega Fvdx + \oint_{\partial\Omega} Gvds .$$

---

[1] In the nonlinear case B depends nonlinearly on u.

Under suitable conditions on (3.13-14) B is a proper form on the spaces $H_1 = H_2 = H^1(\Omega)$ where $H^1(\Omega)$ is the usual Sobolev space of functions with first square-integrable derivatives on Ω.

Any proper form B on $H_1 \times H_2$ introduces an isomorphism $u \in H_1 \longmapsto B(u,.) \in H_2'$ between H_1 and the adjoint space H_2' of H_2. Now note that when F is a Dirac function (concentrated load) then f is not in $H^{-1}(\Omega)$ and hence the Green's function of (3.13-14) is not in $H^1(\Omega)$. Since a Dirac function belongs to $H^{-1-\varepsilon}(\Omega)$, we may ask the question whether B is a proper form on $H^0(\Omega) \times H^2(\Omega)$. The answer is affirmative (see, e.g., [3]) and hence we have two different weak formulations involving the same form (3.15) but two distinct pairs of spaces.

The boundary condition (3.14) is complementary to (3.13) as well as normal (see [3]). If we replace (3.14) by

$$(3.17) \qquad \alpha(s) \frac{\partial u}{\partial n} + \frac{\partial u}{\partial s} + \beta(s)u = G(s)$$

we obtain a nonnormal condition whenever $\alpha(s) = 0$ for some s. With (3.12)/(3.17) we may associate the form and functional

$$B((u,\xi),(v,\eta)) = \int_\Omega [\; \frac{\partial u}{\partial x_1} \frac{\partial v}{\partial x_1} + \frac{\partial u}{\partial x_2} \frac{\partial v}{\partial x_2} + uv]dx$$

$$+ \oint_{\partial\Omega} [(\alpha\xi + \frac{\partial u}{\partial s} + \beta u)\eta - v\xi]ds, \quad (u,\xi) \in H_1, (v,\eta) \in H_2$$

$$f(v,\eta) = \int_\Omega Fvdx + \oint_{\partial\Omega} G\eta ds$$

and B is proper on the spaces

$$H_1 = H^1(\Omega) \times H^{-1/2}(\Omega), \; H_2 = H^1(\Omega) \times H^{1/2}(\Omega) \;.$$

The solution consists here of u as well as of ξ which will be the normal derivative $\frac{\partial u}{\partial n}$ on $\partial\Omega$.

We return to the original problem (3.13/14) and introduce the form

$$(3.18) \qquad B(u,v) = \int_\Omega (-\Delta u + u)(-\Delta v + v)dx$$

$$+ \oint_{\partial\Omega} (\; \frac{\partial u}{\partial n} + \alpha \frac{\partial u}{\partial s} + \beta u)(\; \frac{\partial v}{\partial n} + \alpha \frac{\partial v}{\partial s} + \beta v)ds \;.$$

Now it turns out that for neither one of the choices

$$(3.19) \qquad H_1 = H_2 = H^1(\Omega), \quad H_1 = H_2 = H^2(\Omega)$$

B is a proper form (see [3]). However, if $H(\Omega)$ denotes the completion of the space of smooth functions on Ω under the norm

$$\|u\|^2_{H(\Omega)} = \|-\Delta u + u\|^2_{H^0(\Omega)} + \|u\|^2_{H^{3/2}(\partial\Omega)} ,$$

then (3.18) is a proper form on $H_1 = H_2 = H(\Omega)$.

In our discussions here the differential equation was the original model and the bilinear form was associated with it. Frequently, in practice the bilinear form corresponds to a physically meaningful variational principle. In that case the form represents the primary formulation and the differential equation is obtained from it as the corresponding Euler equation. There are various variational principles in mechanics and physics and many of them provide a sound basis for good finite element procedures (see, e.g., [26]).

The choice of the bilinear form is a major step in the finite element analysis. It has a crucial influence upon the numerical procedure, and the selection of the spaces H_1, H_2 directly affects the error analysis and hence the adaptive control of the process and the reliability analysis. It appears to be of central importance to incorporate in future finite element software a maximum degree of flexibility in the definition of the form B.

3.4 THE FINITE ELEMENT SOLUTION

Once the problem has been cast in the weak form (3.12) involving a particular choice of the bilinear form B and the spaces H_1, H_2, the next major step is the choice of suitable subspaces $M_1 \subset H_1$, $M_2 \subset H_2$ and the numerical determination of the solution $\hat{u}_0 \in M_1$ such that

(3.20) $B(\hat{u}_0, v) = f(v), \forall v \in M_2 .$

The form B is assumed to remain proper on M_1, M_2; this ensures the existence and uniqueness of $\hat{u}_0$. More generally entire classes of such pairs of subspaces are considered and then certain uniformity conditions must be satisfied as well.

In practice the spaces M_1, M_2 derive from the choice of the specific finite elements; that is, their definition is equivalent with the construction of a suitable finite element mesh on the domain Ω. Details of the element formulation and hence of the specification of the approximating spaces have been discussed in numerous texts (see, e.g., [28], [20]) and there is no need to enter into this here.

For today's software the construction of the mesh represents a separate activity from the numerical process; that is, the mesh data are specified at input time and never modified thereafter. In order to simplify the generally tedious task of the mesh input, various mesh generators have been developed (see, e.g., [13]). But all of them represent preprocessors and hence are independent of the solution process itself.

Theoretical results show that the accuracy of the finite element solution is strongly influenced by the existence of singularities in the solution. Such singularities are usually present when the boundary or an interface is not smooth or the coefficients change rapidly (see, e.g., [8], [1]). Clearly we expect the mesh to reflect such singularities as far as they are known; this depends, of course, on the particular error norms. Such a mesh design is rarely possible during the input phase, especially since experience shows that the influence of different types of singularities also depends on the desired accuracy.

For efficient computations the finite element mesh should correspond to the desired accuracy of the needed data. In any a-priori construction of the mesh it is difficult, if not impossible, to avoid over- or under-refinements in some parts of the domain resulting in decreased efficiency or accuracy or both. The use of adaptive techniques appears to be the only realistic way of resolving these problems.

Thus except for the construction and input of a (coarse) basic mesh, the refinement and hence the definition of the mesh corresponding to the final solution becomes an integral part of the numerical process. This is the reason why we departed from today's practice in combining mesh construction and numerical computation in the list of analysis steps of Section 2.

Any adaptive approach is predicated on the availability of good error tolerance measures for the control of the course of the computation. Moreover if the control is aimed at achieving at each stage a mesh design which is optimal in some sense, then it will also become possible to meet our goal of Section 2 to obtain a solution which is optimal for a given cost range.

Disregarding round-off errors, we find that the error $e = u_0 - \hat{u}_0$ between the exact solution u_0 of (3.11) and the approximation $\hat{u}_0$ obtained from (3.20) may be estimated by

(3.21) $$\varepsilon = \|e\|_{H_1} \leq \frac{1}{c_2}\, \varepsilon^*$$

with

(3.22) $$\varepsilon^* = \sup_{\substack{v \in H_2 \\ v \neq 0}} \frac{1}{\|v\|_{H_2}}\, |B(e,v)|\ .$$

Here c_2 is the constant of (3.11b) and hence depends only on B and the spaces H_1, H_2 but not on the approximation. Evidently

$$B(e,v) = B(\hat{u}_0, v) - f(v)$$

may be evaluated for any $v \in H_2$.

In [7] it is shown that under suitable conditions a close estimate of $\|e\|_{H_1}$ and ε^* may be obtained. The approach is rather generally applicable, but for simplicity we illustrate it here on a simple one-dimensional example.

Consider the problem

(3.23) $-u'' + u = F(x), \; 0 < x < 1, \; F(x) = -x^\beta + \hat{\beta} x^{\beta+2}, \; \hat{\beta} = 1/(\beta+2)(\beta+1)$

with the nonzero boundary conditions

(3.24) $$u(0) = 0, \quad u(1) = \hat{\beta} \; .$$

Obviously for $\beta > -2$ the exact solution is

(3.25) $$u_0(x) = \hat{\beta} x^{\beta+2} \; .$$

The associated form

(3.26) $$B(u,v) = \int_0^1 (u'v' + uv) dx$$

is proper on $H_0^1 \times H_0^1$ where, as usual, $H_0^1 \subset H^1 = H^1(0,1)$ is the closure of all functions $v \in H^1$ with compact support in $(0,1)$.

For $\beta > -1.5$ we have $u_0 \in H^1$. Hence if $\varphi \in H^1$ is any function that satisfies (3.24) then $w_0 = u_0 - \varphi \in H_0^1$ is the unique solution of

(3.27) $$B(w_0, v) = f(v), \; \forall v \in H_0^1, \; f(v) = \int_0^1 Fvdx - B(\varphi, v) \; .$$

Consider any partition $0 = x_0 < x_1 < \ldots < x_{n-1} < x_n = 1$ of $[0,1]$ and let ψ_i $(i = 0,1,\ldots,n)$ be the piecewise linear function which is zero outside (x_{i-1}, x_{i+1}), linear in $[x_{i-1}, x_i]$ and $[x_i, x_{i+1}]$, and satisfies $\psi_i(x_i) = 1$. These functions represent a partition of unity

(3.28) $$\sum_{i=0}^n \psi_i(x) = 1, \; \forall x \in [0,1] \; .$$

Let $M \subset H_0^1$ be the linear subspace spanned by $\psi_1, \ldots, \psi_{n-1}$ and $M^* \subset H^1$ the hyperplane $\varphi + M$ with $\varphi = \hat{\beta} \psi_n$. Then the finite element solution $\hat{u}_0 = \varphi + \hat{w}_0 \in M^*$ is uniquely determined by the condition

$$B(\hat{w}_0, v) = f(v), \; \forall v \in M \; .$$

Of course, in practice the term $B(\varphi, v)$ in f is combined with that on the left and we compute directly $\hat{u}_0 \in M^*$.

The error function $e = u_0 - \hat{u}_0$ belongs to H_0^1 and, in place of (3.22), we consider the expressions

$$(3.29) \qquad \varepsilon_i^* = \sup_{\substack{v \in H_0^1 \\ v \neq 0}} \frac{|B(e,\forall_i)|}{\|\forall_i\|_{H_0^1}} \qquad , \qquad i = 0,1,\ldots,n$$

which are well defined since $\forall_i \in H_0^1$ for $v \in H_0^1$. As before $B(e,\forall_i)$ can be evaluated for any given $v \in H_0^1$.

It can be shown (see [7]) that

$$(3.30) \qquad d_2 \left(\sum_{i=0}^{n} \varepsilon_i^{*2} \right)^{1/2} \le \|e\|_{H^1} \le d_1 \left(\sum_{i=0}^{n} \varepsilon_i^{*2} \right)^{1/2}$$

where d_1 and d_2 depend on the type of element and the problem but not on the specific mesh. In our case we have $d_1 = 1$, $d_2 \ge 1/2$.

From the definition of the norm on H^1 it follows that for $i = 0,1,\ldots,n$

$$(3.31) \qquad \varepsilon_i^{*2} = {}_0\varepsilon_i^{*2} + {}_1\varepsilon_i^{*2}, \quad {}_j\varepsilon_i^{*2} = \int_{x_{i-1+j}}^{x_{i+j}} [(z_i' - \hat{u}_0')^2 + (z_i - \hat{u}_0)^2]dx, \quad j=0,1$$

where z_i is the exact solution of (3.23) on (x_{i-1}, x_{i+1}) such that

$$z_i(x_{i-1+2j}) = \hat{u}_0(x_{i-1+2j}), j = 0,1 \ .$$

These functions z_i may be computed approximately as finite element solutions on the mesh

$$x_{i-1}, \tfrac{1}{2}(x_{i-1}+x_i), x_i, \tfrac{1}{2}(x_i+x_{i-1}), x_{i+1}$$

with the same type of elements. By replacing the z_i in (3.31) with these results we obtain a typically very satisfactory approximation ${}_j\eta_i$ of ${}_j\varepsilon_i$, $j = 0,1$, $i = 0,1,\ldots,n$.

In line with the computational goals of Section 2, we wish to compute the finite element solution for which $\|e\|_{H^1}$ is minimal for a given number of elements. It can be shown (see again [7]) that in some asymptotic sense this optimal solution is obtained when all ε_i^* are equal.

As mentioned before, this procedure applies also in more general cases. We begin with a partition of unity (3.28) of the domain consisting of functions ψ_i which have supports of the size of the elements. These ψ_i need not be the element shape functions as in our example.

They are only required to meet certain growth restrictions; for instance, the first derivative should not exceed the reciprocal of the element size, etc.

With the ψ_i we may define the quantities (3.29) (of course with the appropriate norm). Then again (3.30) holds with constants that are rarely large and that do not depend on the specific mesh. However, we have to assume that--in a certain sense--the local variations of the mesh are not too rapid. For instance, the ratio of the size of all neighboring elements must be uniformly bounded. As before, it turns out that, asymptotically, the optimal solution for a fixed number of elements is characterized by the equality of the ε_i^*.

There are various ways of computing approximations $_j\eta_i$ of the $_j\varepsilon_i^*$. In particular, the approach of our example may be extended. Then the aim of our mesh refinement procedure is to equalize as much as possible the η-values at the next step. An algorithm for this is discussed in [7]. Basically, a simple prediction scheme is used to assess the effect of the possible subdivision of an element upon the distribution of the η-values. The element is divided only when this contributes to a more equal distribution. In addition, we estimate the cost of executing the next mesh refinement step, that is, the probable time needed for it, the added storage requirements, etc. This allows us to terminate the process within a prescribed cost range. At the same time our control on the η-values ensures that the solution is approximately optimal for this cost limit.

In practice the refinement in a part of the mesh does not influence the η-values in the other part, and there is indeed theoretical justification for this. Therefore it is unnecessary to recompute at each step the entire system of equations. Only at the final step a complete solution and accuracy analysis is used to determine whether a (highly unlikely) further readjustment of the mesh is needed.

The resulting mesh design applies, of course, only to the particular problem. However, frequently a problem (3.12) is to be solved for several different right sides f. Then it is usually sufficient to use the same mesh for all cases as long as this is justified by the accuracy analysis.

We present here some numerical results with this procedure for our one-dimensional example (3.23). More specifically let $\beta = -0.9$ and define the initial mesh by $x_i = i/4$, $i = 0,1,\ldots,4$. As expected, we find that $_1\eta_i \stackrel{\triangle}{=} _0\eta_{i+1}$ so that any interval contributes to (3.30) about twice the same amount. Hence it was natural to associate with $[x_i, x_{i+1}]$ the average $\bar{\eta}_i = (1/2)(_1\eta_i + _0\eta_{i+1})$. At any nonterminal step all those intervals are halved that result in a more equal distribution of the $\bar{\eta}_i$. Figure 4 shows the partition points x_i at successive steps as well as the distribution of the interval lengths $h_i = x_{i+1} - x_i$. These lengths are drawn as stepfunctions with the value in the center of each interval and with the corresponding $\bar{\eta}_i$-value underneath. Asymptotically the distribution of the h_i-values with best H^1-accuracy for a minimal number of elements turns out to be given by

$$h_i = Hx(\frac{x_i + x_{i+1}}{2}) \text{ as } H \to 0, \quad x(t) = t^{-2\beta/3} .$$

The last graph includes this asymptotically optimal distribution of interval lengths.

3.5 A-POSTERIORI ANALYSIS

The finite element computation leads to a function $\hat{u}_0$ over the given domain which approximates the exact solution u_0 of (3.12) in a certain sense. In many problems there is also a need for some related information about u_0, say, for the values of certain derivatives of u_0 at a number of points. This occurs, for instance, when stress data are required in structural analysis. In other words, we wish to determine an approximation of the value $\zeta(u_0)$ of some given functional ζ over H_1.

In the example of the stress data the exact location of the stress evaluation points is rarely important as long as the density of this point set is maintained. The problem then arises how to make best use of the earlier obtained results in locating these points and in calculating the desired quantities, such as the derivatives. It has been shown (see, e.g., [6], [29], [9]) that--by means of special averaging techniques--it is possible to calculate values which have higher accuracy than those obtained by a straightforward use of $\hat{u}_0$. Along the same lines we may analyze the best choice of certain functionals for the approximation of specific quantities computed from the original results.

This represents a very important approach for the improvement of the desired output for practical applications. It would lead too far to enter into details here. But there should be little doubt that features of this type need to be incorporated into future finite element software wherever possible.

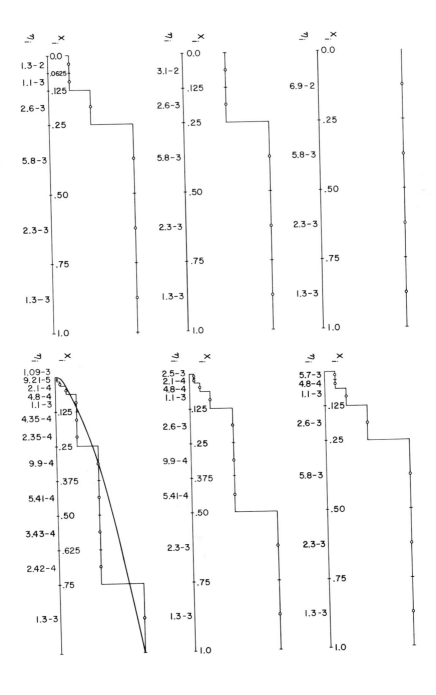

Figure 4

4. SOME SOFTWARE ASPECTS

As mentioned earlier, considerable research is still required
before it will be possible to implement reasonably general, efficient,
and practically useful finite element software that meets our design
criteria and computational goals and incorporates the various features
discussed in the previous section. In this section we sketch some of
the general aspects of such software and detail some of the open questions.

It was stressed several times that the mathematical foundation of
the programs should be the bilinear form B (see Section 3.3 above).
More specifically we must select a reasonably general class of such
forms to cover a range of practical problems and finite element methods.

For example, for two-dimensional problems involving m unknown
functions on some domain $\Omega \subset R^2$ we may consider the second order form

$$
\begin{aligned}
B(u,v) = &\int_\Omega \sum_{i,j=1}^{m} \left[\sum_{k,\ell=1}^{2} a_{k,\ell}^{i,j}(x) \frac{\partial u_i}{\partial x_k} \frac{\partial v_j}{\partial x_\ell} \right. \\
&+ \sum_{k=1}^{2} \left(b_k^{i,j}(x) \frac{\partial u_i}{\partial x_k} v_j + b_k^{i,j}(x) u_i \frac{\partial v_j}{\partial x_k} \right) \\
&\left. + c^{i,j}(x) u_i v_j \right] dx \\
&+ \oint_{\partial\Omega} \sum_{i,j=1}^{m+n} \left[\alpha^{i,j}(s) \frac{\partial u_i}{\partial s} \frac{\partial v_j}{\partial s} + \beta^{i,j}(s) \frac{\partial u_i}{\partial s} v_j \right. \\
&\left. + \hat{\beta}^{i,j}(s) u_i \frac{\partial v_j}{\partial s} + \gamma^{i,j}(s) u_i v_j \right] ds \quad .
\end{aligned}
$$

(4.1)

Here we have

$$u = (u_1, \dots, u_m, u_{m+1}, \dots, u_{m+n})$$
$$v = (v_1, \dots, v_m, v_{m+1}, \dots, v_{m+n})$$

with the functions $u_1, \dots, u_m, v_1, \dots, v_m$ being defined on Ω and the remaining ones on $\partial\Omega$.

In general the right side of the equation

$$B(u,v) = f(v) \quad ,$$

has the same form as (4.1) after u is fixed; but, of course, the coefficients may be different. It should be evident how more general classes
of forms may be defined.

The formulation (4.1) is already fairly general. It includes not only most classical problems and finite element methods but also the elliptic problems of Douglis-Nirenberg type, the forms arising in the use of the least squares method for first-order systems, various versions of the Lagrange multiplier methods, and many others.

In general the coefficient functions can be defined on some fixed domain, say, R^2, etc. This makes them independent of the specific domain under consideration. For storage of some class of forms it then appears to be best to break each form into components and to establish a library of all practically important components in the class. In addition appropriate generator programs are needed to ease the definition of new entries in the library. It will be an interesting task to choose a good library of forms. Equally challenging should be the design of preprocessors which allow a user to define a problem in an accustomed terminology without reference to specific bilinear forms.

Together with the form B we should consider, of course, specific spaces H_1, H_2. It will have to be assumed that B is proper on H_1, H_2 even though this cannot be proved today in the desired generality we wish to consider here. The spaces H_1, H_2 only affect the norm used in the error estimates for mesh refinement. Hence a library of programs must be provided to compute function norms on the most important spaces.

A central part of the input is now the characterization of the geometrical shape of the domain Ω and its boundary $\partial\Omega$ as well as of the basic mesh on it. Here the data specification techniques of today's software are readily applicable and the same type of preprocessors may be used to simplify and ease the input task.

However, the internal organization of the mesh data and various related information has to be considerably more flexible than is now standard in order to accommodate an efficient mesh refinement procedure. The design of good data structures for this purpose is as yet an open question (see, e.g., [5]).

The representation of the equations to be solved involves primarily the storage of large, sparse matrices. Once again in the adaptive environment most of the available general-purpose, sparse matrix packages appear to be inefficient. Instead it will be necessary to design and analyze approaches and data structures that are more closely tied to the mesh refinement and the corresponding stages of the solution process. In particular it is generally unnecessary to reassemble the full equations but only the portions that were refined. This has also a direct implication upon the solution procedures, especially in the case of (block) elimination methods where unchanged and earlier decomposed blocks may be employed to good advantage.

In the case of iterative methods considerable gains in efficiency may be achieved by using information obtained on different meshes. This was suggested in [14],[9], later analyzed in [18], and used in [12] primarily for finite difference grids. Again the extension of this work to the finite element case quickly leads to data structure problems.

The adaptive approach requires an efficient implementation of the procedures for error estimation. The approach mentioned in Section 3.4 is computationally very attractive. For details we refer to [7]. As indicated in 3.4, it is important to avoid large local variations in the mesh. But this requirement is also advantageous from the viewpoint of program design.

The design of software of the type discussed here involves numerous computer science questions. We mentioned already the data structures problems. In addition, there are questions relating to programming systems design and to the construction and use of suitable programming languages.

From the viewpoint of the programming systems designer, the adaptive finite-element solver appears to fall halfway between the traditional domains of applications programs and operating systems. As with most large applications programs, it consists of a number of parts whose interactions have known, specific purposes and patterns; it is usually expected to run under some general-purpose operating system. On the other hand any adaptive system of the type under consideration needs to be highly flexible and--from the user's viewpoint--highly interactive. In this it has strong similarities to operating systems since it involves massive input/output operations, interactive use, logical concurrency, resource management, and flexible interfaces between its various parts. This suggests that a concurrent process structure, in which each module has its own locus of control, would prove as successful here as it has in the design of operating systems. Certainly this would provide for a richer, more flexible communication between modules than the traditional subroutine structure--without which the interactive, adaptive aspects of the system may be curtailed.

Many of the problems raised here lead quickly to questions in the programming language area. Recent advantages in this field suggest that hierarchies of high-level languages and compilers may ultimately be the best approach for complex problems of this type (see, e.g., [10]).

As mentioned in the introduction, we have restricted our discussions to the problem related to large, general-purpose finite element programs for use on large computers. There are considerable differences in program design philosophy when it comes to special-purpose programs especially those that are to run on smaller machines. Such programs are very important in practice, and it should be interesting to see how some of the approaches discussed here may be applied to them as well.

It has been widely observed that we are now seeing the development of a second generation of finite element software. The design criteria presented here differ considerably from those used today and hence may well be considered a call for a new third generation of programs. Experience has shown that it takes at least ten to fifteen years to conceive, design, and produce a new program of this type and to see it accepted and widely applied by the community of users. It appears to be desirable to consider more actively the various proposals that have been made to shorten this time.

5. SOME COMPUTATIONAL RESULTS

We conclude the discussion with some results computed by a still simple version of a finite element solver which incorporates several of the ideas presented above. More specifically the program is based on the bilinear form (4.1) with m = 2 and piecewise constant coefficient functions on R^2. At present it allows only for square bilinear elements and for domains that can be expressed as a finite union of such elements. The error estimation, mesh refinement, and cost control procedures of Section 3.4 and [7] are used. Moreover, provisions are included to permit at any stage the solution of a linear subsystem corresponding to some subdomain with boundary values set equal to earlier computed results.

As sample problem we consider the Cauchy-Riemann equations

$$(5.1) \qquad \frac{\partial u_1}{\partial x_1} = \frac{\partial u_2}{\partial x_2} , \frac{\partial u_1}{\partial x_2} = - \frac{\partial u_2}{\partial x_1} , \forall (x_1,x_2) \in \Omega$$

on the L-shaped domain Ω shown in Figure 5a together with the boundary condition

$$(5.2) \qquad u_1 = g, \forall (x_1,x_2) \in \partial\Omega .$$

Evidently (5.1) is an elliptic system in the sense of Petrowski and (5.2) is a complementary boundary condition. We associate with (5.1-2) the bilinear form

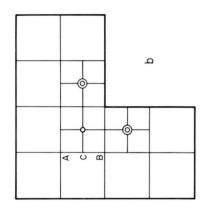

b

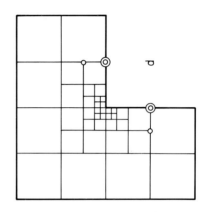

d

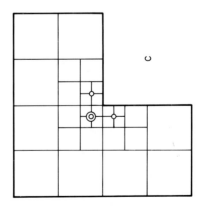

c

a

Figure 5

$$B(u_1,u_2;v_1,v_2) = \int_{\Omega} \left[\left(\frac{\partial u_1}{\partial x_1} - \frac{\partial u_2}{\partial x_2} \right)v_1 + \left(\frac{\partial u_1}{\partial x_2} + \frac{\partial u_1}{\partial x_1} \right)v_2 \right] dx_1 dx_2$$

which is proper on

(5.3) $H_1 \equiv H_0^1(\Omega) \times \hat{H}^1(\Omega), \quad H_2 \equiv H^0(\Omega) \times H^0(\Omega)$

where $\hat{H}^1(\Omega)$ is the quotient space of $H^1(\Omega)$ modulo the constant functions.

As mentioned before, only square bilinear elements are used. This defines the class of subspaces $M_1 \subset H_1$. When refinement causes some elements of different size to border on each other as, for instance, in the case of Figure 5b between nodes A and B, then the nodal value at C is defined by continuity. Hence in our case this value at C is simply the arithmetic average of those at A and B. For given M_1 we then set

$$M_2 = \left\{ (v_1,v_2) \in H_2 \,\middle|\, v_1 = \frac{\partial u_1}{\partial x_1} - \frac{\partial u_2}{\partial x_2} \,,\; v_2 = \frac{\partial u_1}{\partial x_2} + \frac{\partial u_2}{\partial x_1} \,,\; \forall\, (u_1,u_2) \in M_1 \right\}$$

It may be shown that this class of subspaces M_1,M_2 satisfies all the required conditions. Moreover, the particular choice of H_2 allows for a simple computation of ε^* as well as the ε_i^*.

For the computational example the function g of (5.2) has been chosen such that the exact solution has the form

(5.4)
$$u_1 = \alpha r^{2/3} \sin \frac{2}{3}\varphi + \gamma e^{\beta x_1} \cos \beta x_2$$
$$u_2 = -\alpha r^{2/3} \cos \frac{2}{3}\varphi + \gamma e^{\beta x_1} \sin \beta x_2$$

where (r,φ) are polar coordinates. It is easy to verify that these boundary conditions are "smooth". The resulting singularity at the origin is typical for many applications.

The errors are, of course, controlled by the norms of H_1 and H_2. However, in this case the L_∞-norm is also accessible. In Table 3 and Figure 5 we present results for the case $\alpha = 1$, $\beta = \gamma = 0$. The figures show the successive meshes as obtained by the program; the nodes with the largest and second largest errors are indicated by a circle and double circle, respectively. Clearly further stages lead also to some refinement of the elements away from the singularity.

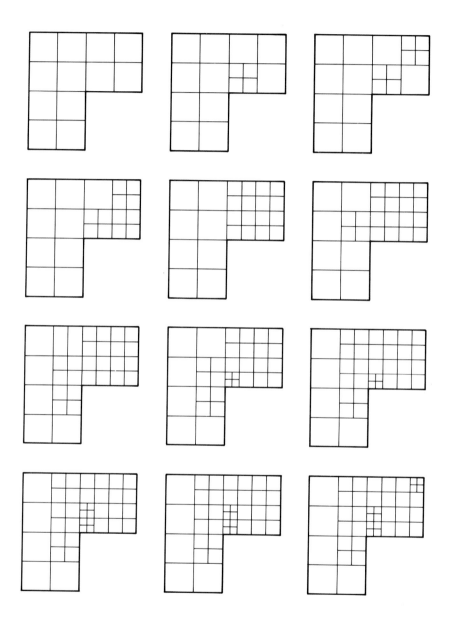

Figure 6a

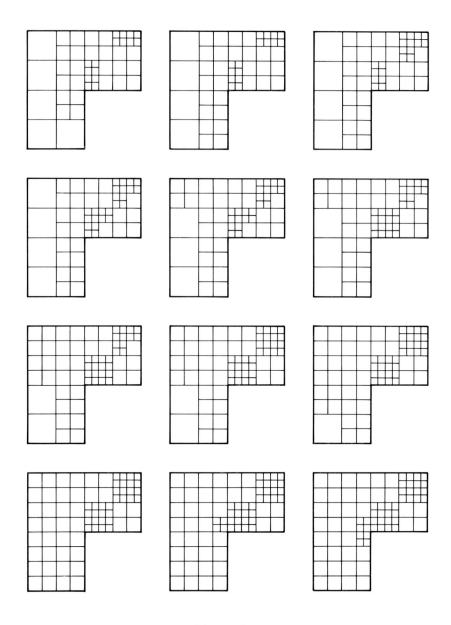

Figure 6b

Case	No. of elements	Absolute nodal errors Largest	Next largest	Norm error
Fig. 5a	12	3.45(-2)	2.51(-2)	2.09(-1)
Fig. 5b	21	1.53(-2)	1.45(-2)	1.46(-1)
Fig. 5c	30	8.13(-3)	6.11(-3)	1.11(-1)
Fig. 5d	39	9.50(-3)	9.21(-3)	9.33(-2)
Uniform	48	1.90(-2)	1.69(-2)	1.35(-1)
mesh	192			8.50(-2)

Table 3, Results for $\alpha = 1$, $\beta = \gamma = 0$

The table includes the results for uniform meshes of 48 and 192 elements, that is, with mesh sizes $h = 1/8$ and $h = 1/16$, respectively.

It is interesting to note that the maximal (L_∞)-error may increase while the error norm based on the choice of spaces (5.3) decreases. This possibility is frequently overlooked. In the above computation the cost was defined as a monotonically increasing function of the number of elements. But already these numbers themselves show the extreme ineffectiveness of the uniform meshes.

Figure 6 shows the successive meshes obtained for the case $\alpha = \beta = \gamma = 1$. Here the solution not only has a singularity at the origin but becomes less "smooth" for increasing x_1 and x_2. It is interesting to see the interplay between the two effects.

REFERENCES

1. I. Babuška (1974), Solution of problems with interfaces and singularities, in "Mathematical Aspects of Finite Elements in Partial Differential Equations", (ed.) C. de Boor, Academic Press, New York, pp. 213-278.

2. _____ (1976), The self-adaptive approach in the finite element method, in "The Mathematics of Finite Elements and Applications", (ed.) J. R. Whiteman, Academic Press, London, pp. 125-143.

3. _____, A. K. Aziz (1972), Survey lectures on the mathematical foundations of the finite element method, in "The Mathematical Foundations of the Finite Element Method", (ed.) A. K. Aziz, Academic Press, New York, pp. 3-363.

4. _____, J. Osborn (1977), Numerical treatment of eigenvalue problems for differential equations with discontinuous coefficients, University of Maryland, Institute for Physical Science and Technology Technical Note BN-853.

5. _____, W. Rheinboldt, C. Mesztenyi (1975), Self-adaptive refinements in the finite element method, University of Maryland, Computer Science Technical Report TR-375.

6. _____, W. Rheinboldt (1975), Mathematical problems of computational decisions in the finite element method, in "Proc. Conf. Mathematical Aspects of the Finite Element Method, Ist. Appl. del Calcolo Rome 1975", Lecture Notes in Mathematics, Springer Verlag, to appear.

7. _____, W. Rheinboldt (1977), Error estimates for adaptive finite element computations, University of Maryland, Institute for Physical Science and Technology Technical Note BN-854.

8. _____, M. B. Rosenzweig (1972), A finite element scheme for domains with corners, Num. Math. 20, pp. 1-21.

9. N. S. Bakhvalov (1966), On the convergence of a relaxation method with natural constraints on the elliptic operator, Ž. Vyčisl. Mat. i Mat. Fiz. 6, pp. 861-885.

10. V. Basili (1976), The SIMPL family of programming languages and compilers, in "Graphensprachen und Algorithmen auf Graphen", Appl. Comp. Sci. 1, Carl Hauser Verlag, Munich, pp. 49-85.

11. J. H. Bramble, A. H. Schatz (1977), Higher order local accuracy by averaging in the finite element method, Math. Comp. 31, pp. 94-111.

12. A. Brandt (1976), Multi-level adaptive techniques (MLAT), I. The multi-grid method, IBM Research Division, Yorktown Heights, NY, Research Report RC 6026 (#26087).

13. W. R. Buell, B. A. Bush (1973), Mesh generation--a survey, Trans. ASME J. Eng. 95, pp. 332-338.

14. R. Federenko (1961), A relaxation method for the solution of elliptic difference equations, Ž. Vyčisl. Mat. i Mat. Fiz. 1, pp. 922-927.

15. R. H. Gallagher (1976), Computerized structural analysis and design --the next twenty years, Keynote Lecture, 2nd Nat. Symp. Computerized Structural Analysis, George Washington University, Washington, D.C.

16. A. Goldenveizer (1961), Theory of Elastic Thin Shells, Pergamon Press, New York.

17. P. Grisvard (1976), Behavior of the solution of an elliptic boundary value problem in a polygonal or polyhedral domain, in "Numerical Solution of Partial Differential Equations III, SYNSPADE 1975", (ed.) B. Hubbard, Academic Press, New York, pp. 207-275.

18. D. A. Nicolaides (1977), On the ℓ^2-convergence of an algorithm for solving finite element equations, Math. Comp., to appear.

19. D. H. Norrie, G. de Vries (1976), A Finite Element Bibliography, Plenum Press, New York.

20. J. T. Oden, J. N. Reddy (1976), An Introduction to the Mathematical Theory of Finite Elements, Wiley-Interscience, New York.

21. W. B. Pilkey (1975), Shock and vibration computer programs, U.S. Dept. of Defense, Shock and Vibration Information Center.

22. W. Pilkey, K. Sacralski, H. Schaeffer (1974), Structural Mechanics Computer Programs, University of Virginia Press, Charlottes-ville.

23. J. A. Rojtberg (1975), Theorems about the complete isomorphisms for elliptic systems in the sense of Douglis-Nirenberg, Ukrain. mat. Ž. 8, pp. 544-548.

24. E. Schrem (1975), Finite element software in the next decade, Proc. World Congress on the Finite Element Method, Bourne-mouth.

25. S. Timoshenko, J. N. Goodier (1970), Theory of Elasticity, McGraw-Hill, New York.

26. K. Washizu (1968), Variational Methods in Elasticity and Plasti-city, Pergamon Press, New York.

27. J. R. Whiteman (1975), A Bibliography for Finite Elements, Academic Press, London.

28. O. Zienkiewicz (1971), The Finite Element Method in Engineering Science, McGraw-Hill, New York.

29. M. Zlamal (1975), Some superconvergence results in the finite element method, in "Proc. Conf. Mathematical Aspects of the Finite Element Method, Ist. Appl. del Calcolo Rome 1975", Lecture Notes in Mathematics, Springer Verlag, to appear.

This work was in part supported by ERDA grant E-(40-1)3443 and NSF grant MCS 72-03721 A06 (formerly GJ-35568X).

Institute for Physical Science
and Technology
University of Maryland, College Park

Computer Science Center
University of Maryland, College Park

The Art of Writing
a Runge-Kutta Code, Part I
L. F. Shampine
H. A. Watts

1. INTRODUCTION

For years we have been studying methods and codes to
solve initial value problems for ordinary differential
equations with the goal of developing software of the highest
quality. In this paper we examine Runge-Kutta methods of
moderate order and their implementation as a computer code.
Any code worthy of general use must be easy to use, robust,
transportable, reliable, and efficient. How to achieve these
goals is the object of our study and its product is the code
RKF45.

The investigation splits naturally into two parts. The
first part, presented here, deals with the selection of a
basic formula. This involves considerations of quality such
as the number of stages, accuracy, the estimation of errors,
stability, and various aspects of efficiency. Although these
considerations are relevant to the general task of selecting
a Runge-Kutta formula, we are mainly interested in formulas
of order four which have adequate error estimators associated
with them. The second part, which will appear elsewhere,
deals with the algorithmic and software engineering matters.
There is a widely held belief that writing a Runge-Kutta code
is not much more than a transcription of the basic formula
into a high level computer language. The fact that the
second part is much more involved than the first contradicts
this belief. Furthermore we describe the workings of a good

many specific codes; the great diversity of implementations
clearly shows that the proper way to proceed is not obvious.
Lastly we point out that performance tests [1] show there are
great differences among even carefully written codes as a
consequence of algorithmic and software design decisions.

This paper, especially the first part, relies on computational results accumulated over a long period of investigation. Naturally we cannot display here even a fraction of
this important material and we shall have to refer the reader
to other papers and reports. A large part of this support
is found in the lengthy report [2] we published some time ago.
If we do not cite a specific source in the text, the reader
should consult this document for more details. Because we
describe the "art" of writing Runge-Kutta codes, we attempt to
communicate lore hard-won by the solution of real problems
over many years and by the experiences of our associates and
other workers in the field. Our objectives and computing
environment influence our interpretation of our observations
so that the reader should weigh our arguments in his own
context and consider this study as advice on the subject
illustrated by an actual production-grade code.

2. RUNGE-KUTTA METHODS

2.1 Explicit s-stage formulas

We are interested in the numerical integration of
the system of ordinary differential equations

$$\underline{u}' = \underline{f}(x, \underline{u})$$

where the vector $\underline{u}(x)$ represents the unknowns. Usually
we have no need to distinguish the case of a single
unknown from that of a system so we shall suppress the
additional notation indicating vectors. The initial
value problem specifies a particular solution of the
differential equation by giving its value at a single
point: $u(x_n) = y_n$.

An explicit s-stage Runge-Kutta method is defined by

$$(1) \qquad y_{n+1} = y_n + h_n \sum_{i=1}^{s} c_i f_i \qquad \text{where}$$

(2)
$$f_i = f(x_n + a_i h_n, y_n + h_n \sum_{j=1}^{i-1} b_{ij} f_j)$$

for $i = 1, \ldots, s$.

Here y_{n+1} is to approximate the solution $u(x_{n+1})$ at $x_{n+1} = x_n + h_n$. The number of stages s refers to the number of times f has to be evaluated, or as we shall say, the number of derivative or function evaluations. By Taylor's series expansions one finds that the local error, that is, the error introduced in stepping from x_n to x_{n+1}, has the form

$$le = y_{n+1} - u(x_{n+1}) = h_n \sum_i \tau_{1i} D_{1i} + h_n^2 \sum_i \tau_{2i} D_{2i} + \ldots$$

In this expansion several factors have been separated. The step size h_n is chosen by the user of the formula. The scalars τ_{ki} depend only on the choice of formula. The D_{ki}, vector elementary differentials, are the various partial derivatives of f evaluated at (x_n, y_n) which depend only on the problem and the approximate solution. A formula is said to be of order p if the local error is of order h_n^{p+1} for all sufficiently smooth functions; for sufficiently smooth f one can establish uniform convergence of the numerical solution to the true solution of order p.

2.2   Error estimation and local extrapolation

Most procedures for estimating the local error amount to comparing the numerical result of a formula of order p to one of order $p+1$. For if the higher order formula yields the approximation $\hat{y}_{n+1}$ we have

$$est = y_{n+1} - \hat{y}_{n+1} = \left[y_{n+1} - u(x_{n+1}) \right] + \left[u(x_{n+1}) - \hat{y}_{n+1} \right]$$

$$= le + O\left(h_n^{p+2} \right).$$

We shall consider only formulas for which such an estimator is available. This excludes some possibilities involving memory and by virtue of being asymptotically

correct excludes others. Here we say an estimator
producing the value 'est' is asymptotically correct if

$$\lim_{h_n \to 0} \frac{est}{le} = 1 .$$

Later we shall discuss a widely used formula which has an
incorrect estimator.

With an asymptotically correct estimator it is
tempting to "improve" the numerical solution at each step
by subtracting out the estimated error. Because
y_{n+1} - est = $\hat{y}_{n+1}$, we see the net effect is to raise the
effective order of the numerical scheme. This procedure
is termed local extrapolation and represents an important
choice as regards the use of the formula.

2.3 Methods to be considered

We shall restrict our attention to methods which are
of order four, but because of local extrapolation this
may also involve formulas of orders three and five. Of
the great many possibilities we have examined, we shall
report here only those of particular merit or fame.

A four-stage fourth order formula of Kutta [3] is
known as the "classical" scheme and has been extremely
popular because of its simple coefficients. Another four-
stage fourth order scheme was derived by Gill [4] with
the objectives of minimizing storage and propagated round-
off error. Neither of these formulas has a natural error
estimator. Usually their errors are estimated by the
general principle of doubling. This principle involves
taking two half steps with the basic formula and combining the result with that from one whole step of the basic
formula so as to estimate the error of the more accurate
result. Such an estimator is easily seen to lie within
the class we consider and we shall suppose that it is
used with each of these formulas. We note that if the
step is not acceptable and if one chooses to reduce the
step size by half for a second try, he can save several
function evaluations because of the form of the error
estimate.

The other formulas we study here all have error

estimators which were derived along with the formulas.
Two valuable fourth order formulas were given by Fehlberg
[5] and we follow him in calling them Fehlberg #1 and
Fehlberg #2. England [6] derived a scheme which can be
viewed as taking two half steps with a basic fourth order
formula and then doing an extra function evaluation to
form an estimate of the local error incurred in the two
half steps. Because this extra evaluation is done before
the second half step is completed, one can decide whether
to accept the step before doing a final evaluation and so
save an evaluation in the event it is rejected. Zonneveld
[7] presents a similar scheme which is a bit cheaper and
allows the same saving. (Zonneveld intended that local
extrapolation be done with his fourth order formula so he
describes it as fifth order.) Shintani [8] has also given
a scheme which may be viewed similarly but which does not
permit this saving.

Lastly we mention a very popular scheme of Merson [9]
which requires some discussion. The Merson scheme uses a
four-stage fourth order formula to compute y_{n+1} for which
he attempted to provide an error estimate via an additional function evaluation. This estimate is not
asymptotically correct because, except for equations of
the form $f(x,y) = \alpha x + \beta y + \gamma$ with constants α, β, γ, the
estimate is of order h^4 instead of the correct order h^5.
However, the formula has proved rather satisfactory in
simulation work and considerable effort has been expended
to find out why. If 'est' is the error estimate given by
the Merson scheme, it turns out that $y^*_{n+1} = y_{n+1} + c \cdot est$
is a third order formula for any constant $c \neq 0$. If we
take $c = 1$, we can use the result of the Merson scheme,
y_{n+1}, and its "estimated error," est, by interpreting
them as arising from the use of the third order result
y^*_{n+1} with an asymptotically correct error estimate
followed by local extrapolation. An alternative given in
the literature is to note that there is already a third
order result $\bar{y}_{n+1}$ imbedded in the Merson scheme and it
turns out that $\bar{y}_{n+1} - y_{n+1} = 5 \cdot est$. Some prefer that the
basic formula and its error estimating companion not share

all the function evaluations because of a feeling that distinct function evaluations enhance the reliability of the pair. The first scheme, which we shall call Merson #1, does not have this property but the second, Merson #2, does. Of course with the second scheme we use a multiple of Merson's original estimator. In either case we shall suppose that local extrapolation is always done so as to yield a fourth order formula (the usual Merson result).

The scheme Merson #1 is the closer to Merson's original scheme but even it does not fully rehabilitate the original scheme because it must be regarded as third order, whereas the original scheme was to be regarded as fourth order. The accepted result at each step is, of course, the same, as is the estimated error, but the difference in justification (or lack of it) requires one to take different action in adjusting the step size. The crude step acceptance and adjustment strategies typical of differential equation solvers in simulation packages and the crude tolerances at which they typically operate mask almost completely this distinction and the method finds ardent partisans in the simulation field. One must be very careful in reading the literature on encountering references to "Merson's method" to be sure he knows exactly what scheme and even what order is being employed.

3. MEASURES OF QUALITY

Having defined some candidates for a "best" Runge-Kutta process of order four, we shall now look at some of their properties to help rank the formulas. We shall compare the methods with respect to the number of stages, accuracy, quality of error estimate, stability, and general efficiency.

3.1 Number of stages

It has been an intellectual challenge to derive Runge-Kutta formulas with as few stages as possible because the number of times the differential equation is evaluated is a significant measure of work. Actually this justification is spurious because it is the total number of stages in both the step and the error estimate which is relevant to practical computation. Some of the methods we consider make the distinction clear. The

classical fourth order formula uses only four stages,
which is the fewest possible, but when its error is
estimated by doubling, it costs 11 evaluations per step.
On the other hand, the Fehlberg formulas each represent
a pair of formulas, one of order four and the other of
order five. Since any fifth order formula by itself
requires six stages, it is clear we cannot hope for a
fourth order formula with error estimate of the kind we
consider which uses fewer than six evaluations. Fehlberg
has achieved this minimum.

A little reflection causes one to realize that it is
not really evident that a small number of stages is
desirable per se. After all, if formula A has 12 stages
and formula B has 6, formula A will still be the more
efficient if it can use step sizes more than twice the
size of those used by formula B. It is clear that a small
number of stages is advantageous in the event of step
rejection, but this is not a common event in a well-
written code. In reference [10] we emphasize that the
practical reason for preferring a small number of stages
is that one can change the step size more often. The
fact that formula B can change its step size twice as
often is never a serious disadvantage relative to formula
A and can substantially increase the efficiency as well
as avoid step rejections for many problems. Illuminating
examples can be found in [10]. Because we are concerned
with formulas involving a small number of stages, this
measure of quality is significant. At rather higher
orders the cost of all the formulas by this measure is
high and the relative distinction is not so important.
In Table 1 we display this measure of quality.

3.2 Accuracy and order

The most important single aspect of a formula is its
accuracy for it is the main factor affecting efficiency.
We have considered this aspect in a number of related
ways. In one we recall that the local error has the form

$$le = h^{p+1} \sum_i \tau_{p+1,i} D_{p+1,i} + \cdots .$$

	successful	unsuccessful
Gill	11	10,7 if halve
Classical	11	10,7 if halve
England	9	7
Shintani	7	6
Zonneveld	7	5
Fehlberg	6	5
Merson	5	4

Table 1. The number of stages per step

Considering the $\mathbf{T}_{p+1,i}$ as a vector we have computed its norm in the measures $\|\cdot\|_1$, $\|\cdot\|_2$, and $\|\cdot\|_\infty$, and we have also considered similarly higher order terms in the error expansion. To make meaningful comparisons of formulas with different numbers of stages, it seems necessary to scale the step sizes to account for equal amounts of work. Thus we consider $h^* = sh$ so that for an s-stage method the error coefficients of order h^{p+1} are multiplied by s^{p+1}. In this way we can compare the methods on the basis of accuracy when allowed an "equal amount of work." While relative comparisons vary somewhat when using the different norms, the overall ranking from most accurate to least remains the same. In Table 2 we summarize this ranking, proceeding from the least accurate at the top to the most accurate at the bottom. We display the average value of the three norms after normalizing with respect to the most accurate formula.

Fourth Order Formulas		Fifth Order Formulas	
Zonneveld	200.	England	5.2
Classical	21.	Zonneveld	3.7
Gill	20.	Fehlberg #2	2.5
England	7.2	Shintani	2.2
Fehlberg #1	3.4	Fehlberg #1	1.0
Merson	3.3		
Fehlberg #2	2.0		
Shintani	1.0		

Table 2. Relative accuracy of the formulas.

In this comparison we, in effect, set the problem dependent partial derivatives $D_{p+1,i}$ to a constant value. We have also done a statistical study of a randomly generated set of nonlinear problems as in [11] to find the expected value μ in

$$le = \mu h^{p+1} + \ldots$$

(and similarly higher order terms). In general the accuracy rankings made in this way agree well with those just displayed. The biggest change is that the Merson formula is rather worse, being then comparable to the England formula.

As we have already stated, the reason that accuracy is important is because of its effect on efficiency. The crudest measure is the order of the formula. If one asks for enough accuracy, a given formula will always be more efficient than a lower order one except in pathological instances. By restricting our attention to variants of fourth order formulas we have implicitly restricted our attention to low or moderate accuracy. Monitoring of the usage of our computer library as described in [12] reveals that the favorite accuracy request is 10^{-6} in both the relative and absolute error parameters of a mixed test on our CDC 6600s and is a bit less stringent on our PDP-10. Our environment predisposes us to the higher end of the 3-5 order range considered in this paper because our experience is that the higher orders really pay off for the tolerances mentioned, with little penalty at crude tolerances and great benefits for the costly runs at stringent tolerances. In an environment such as simulation we would be (and have been) much more interested in lower order formulas [13]. These qualitative remarks based on experience in a particular environment are very significant to our selection because we see no reasonable quantitative way to compare formulas of different orders. We shall return to this point in discussing our choice.

To show more clearly the effect of the accuracy we shall compare the methods in a crude, but illuminating, way. Suppose we integrate a problem for which

$$\left\| \sum \tau_{p+1, i} D_{p+1, i} \right\|$$

is a multiple of $\left\| \tau_{p+1, i} \right\|$ (which we have tabulated in the report [2]). The constant of proportionality will not matter in what follows and may change slowly from step to step. Further, we shall ignore all but leading terms in error expansions for our rough comparison. For brevity we shall write $\epsilon_A = \left\| \tau_{p+1, i} \right\|$ for method A, etc. If method A uses a step size h_A and is of order q, it has a local error a multiple of $\epsilon_A h_A^{q+1}$. If method B, of the same order, is to produce the same error, it must use a step size h_B where

$$h_B = h_A \left(\frac{\epsilon_A}{\epsilon_B} \right)^{\frac{1}{q+1}} .$$

For the sake of efficiency the method is to be used with as large a step size as possible and the error criterion is to be error/step, i.e. the formula is to have an error no larger than a specified quantity at each step. To cover a given interval, method A of s_A stages must do $s_A N_A$ derivative evaluations where N_A is the number of steps taken by method A. Method B must do $s_B N_B$ derivative evaluations where, using the equation relating h_B to h_A,

$$N_B = \left(\frac{\epsilon_B}{\epsilon_A} \right)^{\frac{1}{q+1}} N_A .$$

Comparing the costs of the methods in this way, relative to the most efficient method, we find the results displayed in Table 3.

3.3 Overhead and storage

One of the measures of efficiency is the overhead in the computational algorithm -- the cost of the method after excluding the cost due to evaluating the derivatives. Of importance here are the number of stages and the density of the non-zero values of the Runge-Kutta

Fourth Order Formulas		Fifth Order Formulas	
Zonneveld	2.9	Zonneveld	1.23
Gill	1.9	England	1.24
Classical	1.9	Fehlberg #2	1.14
England	1.5	Shintani	1.10
Fehlberg #1	1.3	Fehlberg #1	1.00
Merson	1.3		
Fehlberg #2	1.1		
Shintani	1.0		

Table 3. Relative evaluation costs.

parameters. We present here a very simple and rough
comparison of overhead by counting the number of non-zero
values of the parameters relative to the number of stages.
The measure is somewhat crude because how one actually
programs the evaluation may be important in comparisons
of this kind. In fact it is rather common to find codes
which do not take advantage of zero coefficients. The
coefficients (as well as the intermediate derivatives)
are stored in two-dimensional arrays. Although the basic
formula can then be conveniently programmed within a
simple DO loop construct, one pays a significant penalty
through higher overhead. (See [1] for some specific
examples.) Furthermore one may have to, or choose to,
trade some overhead for reduced storage requirements and
similar practical reasons.

    We also consider the storage required. It is easy
to see that the basic algorithm for any s-stage method can
be written with s + 2 arrays of storage for the vectors
$y_n, f_1, \ldots, f_s$, and perhaps a temporary work array. For
the methods we have examined, it is possible to write the
algorithms using the storage indicated in Table 4 without
needing to re-evaluate derivatives after either successful
or unsuccessful steps.

    We do not consider the differences exhibited in
Table 4 to be very significant.

Operation Count/Stages		Storage
Classical	2.8	7
Gill	3.4	8
Merson	3.8	6
England	3.9	9
Zonneveld	4.7	8
Fehlberg	5.0	7
Shintani	5.3	8

Table 4.   Measures of overhead and storage.

3.4   Error estimation

In [11] we proposed a way of comparing error estimators and applied it to several estimators when used with the basic Runge-Kutta method of the England process. Here we shall use the approach to compare the estimators for all the methods given. We make both asymptotic and non-asymptotic comparisons, and we consider the effect of extrapolation as well. Our study of this question is somewhat complex so that we must refer the reader to the report [2] for details and content ourselves here with indicating the general nature of the comparisons.

We introduce the notation for the local error of the method and its estimator

$$le = ah^{p+1} + bh^{p+2} + 0\left(h^{p+3}\right) ,$$

$$est = \alpha h^{q+1} + \beta h^{q+2} + 0\left(h^{q+3}\right) .$$

If the estimator is asymptotically correct, we must have $q = p$ and $\alpha = a$. For our asymptotic comparison we compute approximations to

$$D(f) = \lim_{h \to 0} \frac{le - est}{h^{p+2}} = b - \beta .$$

Computationally we proceed as follows: Given a problem $y' = f(x,y)$ we compute the local error and estimate it for one step of length h with a sequence of h values tending to zero. This is done for each method until

successive approximations to D(f) differ by less than a
prescribed amount. Finally we compute the average and
maximum values of the approximations to $|D(f)|$ over an
ensemble of 500 randomly chosen problems for each method.
The class of problems we treat are single equations of the
form $y' = \sum a_{ij} x^i y^j$ (which have a power series solution
$y' = \sum c_k x^k$). The a_{ij} are generated randomly and uniformly distributed in the interval $[-1,1]$.

Once again we need to scale the measured quantities
to account for the work allowed each method. One should
also consider the size of β relative to α because the
significance of having a very accurate estimate of the
second term in the expansion of the local error depends
on the size of the leading term. As it turns out, the
ratios of averaged values of $|\beta|$ to those of $|\alpha|$ are about
the same for the methods considered and this ensemble of
problems. ($|\beta|/|\alpha|$ was approximately two.)

To see the effect of local extrapolation we also
compared the estimated error with the true error of the
more accurate solution. Naturally, in this situation the
usual limit comparisons are meaningless so we computed
the magnitude of the ratio of est to le when multiplied
by h. Asymptotically we have

$$h \ est/le \doteq h(\alpha h^p)/(ah^{p+1}) \doteq \alpha/a \ .$$

Again we scale for equal work. The Shintani and Fehlberg
#2 formulas show up very well in this mode of error
estimation. The Merson and Fehlberg #1 schemes appear
reasonable but Zonneveld's scheme is relatively bad.

Another type of comparison we make is based on
"large" step size behavior. Here we merely compare the
relative accuracy of the estimated error to the actual
local error for the different step sizes. We measure the
effectiveness of local extrapolation in this way, too.

We summarize these comparisons by the rather
subjective ranking given in Table 5. No clear choice
exists between some of the procedures. In the unextrapolated case, all the error estimators are quite adequate.

In the extrapolated case, the Shintani and Fehlberg #2 formulas are considerably better than the rest and perform quite satisfactorily.

Unextrapolated	Extrapolated
Shintani, Fehlberg #2	Zonneveld
Merson #1, Fehlberg #1	Fehlberg # 1
England, Classical, Gill	Merson
Merson #2	Shintani
Zonneveld	Fehlberg # 2

Table 5.   Ranking of error estimators, from least effective at the top to best at the bottom.

3.5 Stability

Another measure of the quality of a method is its behavior when encountering mildly stiff differential equations. The concept of stiffness is explained informally in [14] and the behavior of Runge-Kutta methods in the presence of stiffness is studied in [15]. One should not try to solve truly stiff problems with explicit Runge-Kutta formulas, but some stiffness is not unusual. The essence of the matter is that the step size is limited for reasons of stability in the presence of stiffness rather than for reasons of accuracy as is more commonly the case. The amount of this limitation is easy to measure. When the formulas are applied to the equation $y' = \lambda y$ with step size h, one finds that $y_{n+1} = P(h\lambda)y_n$ for a polynomial $P(z)$ characteristic of the method. The region of absolute stability is that region in the left half of the complex plane enclosed by the locus of points z such that $|P(z)| = 1$. When solving this test equation, h must be restricted so that $h\lambda$ is within the region of absolute stability.

This same situation applies to more general equations after identifying λ as an eigenvalue of the Jacobian of the differential equation evaluated on the approximate solution. Because of the restriction we would like a

large stability region. As usual we must scale according
to the number of stages so as to allow methods an equal
amount of work.

All the stability regions for the methods, both
unextrapolated and extrapolated, can be seen in [16].
Here we shall just report in Table 6 the average radius
to the boundary of the stability region.

	Unextrapolated	Extrapolated
Merson #1	.697	.671
Merson #2	.725	.671
Classical	.507	.450
Gill	.507	.450
Zonneveld	.372	.538
England	.620	.449
Shintani	.552	.525
Fehlberg #1	.459	.623
Fehlberg #2	.485	.576

Table 6. Average radius to the scaled stability boundary.

3.6 Choice of basic formula

It is clear from examination of the various measures
of quality presented that no one method ranks best in all
categories. In choosing a "best" formula we therefore
must weight the various measures according to our expected
use of the formula. As we have already noted in the
section on accuracy, our computing environment has caused
us to favor the extrapolated fourth order formulas,
resulting in fifth order. If one were interested in less
accurate results, the Merson scheme would be much more
attractive. (We have considered elsewhere such problems
[13] and believe we have found superior formulas for such
computation.) Because of the difficulty of comparing
formulas of different orders we actually implemented the
various procedures in research oriented computer codes
and extensively tested them on a large variety of
problems. We collected local statistics in the spirit
of [17] and global statistics in the spirit of [1] and this

form of performance testing led to conclusions entirely
consistent with those derived from the results here along
with the anticipated effect of order. Out of the
formulas tested we believe that the two Fehlberg and the
Shintani schemes with extrapolation offer the best
formulas for a code to serve in a scientific computing
library. The code which we have developed and which we
shall discuss in detail in the succeeding part of this
paper uses the second Fehlberg formula.

There is not a great deal of difference between the
two Fehlberg and Shintani formulas. We eliminated the
Shintani scheme for two main reasons -- the number of
stages is largest and the scaled stability region is
smallest. Because we use extrapolation we have been
especially concerned about the effectiveness of the error
estimate, particularly at large step sizes. Fehlberg's
second formula is considerably better than the first in
this respect and this is more important to us than the
fact that the latter is somewhat more accurate. Although
the average radius of the stability region for the first
formula is larger than that of the second, one should
actually examine the plotted regions. We prefer the
stability region of the second formula because it is
superior near the imaginary axis whereas the advantage of
the first formula elsewhere is not too large. It is
worth comment that there is a noticeable difference in
the way these two formulas perform in a typical computation because of the relative sizes of the estimated
and true errors. When solving a problem at a given
tolerance the first formula will take 15-20% more steps
than the second formula, but will yield more accurate
results. Since both will provide the requested accuracy,
the first formula is less efficient at delivering what
the user wants. However, as we have noted, it is somewhat more efficient in terms of cost for a given accuracy
attained. Because this difference originates in the
local extrapolation we do not see how to eliminate it by
tuning.

If one should prefer to make a different selection of "best" formula, he will find it easy to alter the code we present so as to incorporate his choice, with one exception. In [15] we derived a way of detecting stiffness which has been incorporated in the code and which was tailored to the Fehlberg #2 formula. It is clear how to do this for other formulas, but it would necessitate some developmental work by the reader if he wished to use a different formula and still provide this protection to the user.

4. SUMMARY

In this first part of a two part paper describing the development of a high quality Runge-Kutta code, we have discussed the choice of a Runge-Kutta formula based on various measures of quality such as the number of stages, accuracy, error estimator, stability, general efficiency, and reliability. We stress the fact that a Runge-Kutta method is composed of a basic formula for advancing the solution together with an adequate scheme for estimating the error of the process because it is the pair which is relevant to practical computing. The code RKF45 is the product of our study and will be discussed in detail in the second part of this paper.

REFERENCES

1. L. F. Shampine, H. A. Watts, and S. M. Davenport (1976), Solving non-stiff differential equations -- the state of the art, SIAM Review, 18, pp. 376-411.

2. L. F. Shampine and H. A. Watts (1976), Practical solution of ordinary differential equations by Runge-Kutta methods, Sandia Laboratories Report SAND 76-0585, Albuquerque, New Mexico.

3. W. Kutta (1901), Beitrag zur naherungsweisen integration totaler Differentialgleichunge, Zeit. Math. Physik, 46, pp. 435-453.

4. S. Gill (1951), A process for the step-by-step integration of differential equations in an automatic digital computing machine, Proc. Cambridge Philos. Soc., 47, pp. 96-108.

5. E. Fehlberg (1969), Low-order classical Runge-Kutta
    formulas with stepsize control and their application
    to some heat transfer problems, NASA Technical Report
    NASA TR R-315.

6. R. England (1969), Error estimates for Runge-Kutta type
    solutions to systems of ordinary differential
    equations, The Computer Journal, 12, pp. 166-170.

7. J. A. Zonneveld (1964), Automatic Numerical Integration,
    Mathematical Centre Tracts 8, Amsterdam.

8. H. Shintani (1966), Two-step processes by one-step
    methods of order 3 and of order 4, J. Sci. Hiroshima
    Univ. Ser. A-I, 30, pp. 183-195.

9. R. H. Merson (1957), An operational method for the study
    of integration processes, Proceedings of conference
    on data processing and automatic computing machines
    at Weapons Research Establishment, Salisbury, South
    Australia.

10. L. F. Shampine (1976), The quality of Runge-Kutta
    formulas, Sandia Laboratories Report SAND 76-0370,
    Albuquerque, New Mexico.

11. L. F. Shampine and H. A. Watts (1971), Comparing error
    estimators for Runge-Kutta methods, Math. Comp., 25,
    pp. 445-455.

12. C. B. Bailey and R. E. Jones (1975), Usage and argument
    monitoring of mathematical library routines, ACM
    Trans. on Math. Software, 1, pp. 196-209.

13. L. F. Shampine (1976), Solving ordinary differential
    equations for simulation, Sandia Laboratories Report
    SAND 76-5866, Albuquerque, New Mexico.

14. L. F. Shampine and C. W. Gear (1976), A user's view of
    solving stiff ordinary differential equations, Univ.
    of Illinois Dept. of Comp. Sci. Rept. UIUCDCS-R-76-
    829.

15. L. F. Shampine and K. L. Hiebert, Detecting stiffness
    with the Fehlberg (4,5) formulas, Computers and
    Mathematics with Applications, (to appear).

16. H. A. Watts (1976), Runge-Kutta-Fehlberg methods:
    scaled stability regions, Sandia Laboratories Report
    SAND 76-323, Albuquerque, New Mexico.

17. T. E. Hull, W. H. Enright, B. M. Fellen, and
    A. E. Sedgwick (1972), Comparing numerical methods for
    ordinary differential equations, SIAM J. Numer. Anal.,
    9, pp. 603-637.

This work was supported by the U.S. Energy Research and Development Administration (ERDA), Contract No. AT(29-1)-789. By acceptance of this article, the publisher and/or recipient acknowledges the U.S. Government's right to retain a nonexclusive, royalty-free license in and to any copyright covering this paper.

Numerical Mathematics Division 5122
Applied Mathematics Division 2642
Sandia Laboratories
Albuquerque, New Mexico   87115

Multi-Level Adaptive Techniques (MLAT) for Partial Differential Equations: Ideas and Software

Achi Brandt

ABSTRACT

A survey is given of solution techniques which simultaneously use a sequence of increasingly finer discretizations
(finite-difference or finite-element equations) for the same
continuous problem. The solution process acts, on one hand,
as a fast solver, and provides, on the other hand, for very
efficient, nearly optimal discretizations. A flexible and
economic multi-grid data structure is presented, together with
the software developed to support grid manipulations in
general, and MLAT programming in particular.

INTRODUCTION

The multi-level adaptive technique (MLAT) is a general
numerical strategy for solving continuous problems such as
differential and integral equations and functional minimization
problems. It will be surveyed here mainly in terms of the
numerical solution of partial differential boundary-value
problems.

The usual approach to such problems is first to discretize
them in some preassigned manner (e.g., finite-element or
finite-difference equations on a fixed grid), and then to
submit the resulting discrete system to some numerical solution
process. In MLAT, however, discretization and solution
processes are intermixed with, and benefit from, each other.
The problem is not discretized on just one given grid, but

conceptually, on a sequence of uniform grids (or "levels")
$G^0, G^1, \ldots, G^M$. G^0 is a very coarse grid, and each subsequent G^k typically has the mesh-size $h_k = \frac{1}{2} h_{k-1}$. The
cooperative solution process on these levels involves
relaxation sweeps over each of them, coarse-grid-to-fine-grid
interpolations of corrections, and fine-to-coarse transfers
of residuals.

This process has several advantages. First, it can be
regarded as a fast solver for the finest (G^M) system of
equations. The cyclic interaction with coarser grids solves
this system, to the desired accuracy, in $O(n)$ computer
operations, where n is the size of the system (i.e., the
number of grid-points in G^M) . For example, in the case of
the 5-point Poisson equation, a solution with errors smaller
than the truncation errors is obtained in $42n$ operations
(most of them additions), and further error reduction costs
$27n$ operations per order-of-magnitude (i.e., per error
reduction by a factor 1/10). This efficiency does not depend
on the shape of the domain, the form of the boundary conditions
or the smoothness of the solution, nor does it involve any
problem-dependent parameters. Moreover, similar efficiency is
obtained for general nonlinear boundary-value problems, whether
elliptic, hyperbolic or of mixed type, including problems with
shocks and other discontinuities. The storage required for
the multi-grid process in its full efficiency is $\frac{5}{3} n$
locations (in 2-dimensional problems. Another, slightly less
efficient version of the process, called segmental refinement,
requires only a small fraction of this storage, with no need
for external memory).

Secondly, the above solution process can be adaptive.
The finer grids may be introduced only when and where needed.
They may be confined to increasingly smaller subdomains (each
G^k may cover only part of the domain covered by G^{k-1}), so as
to provide higher resolution only where desired. Moreover, we
may attach to each of these localized finer grids, its own
local system of coordinates, to fit curved boundaries, interfaces or discontinuities. This structure, in which non-
uniform discretization can be produced through a sequence of
uniform grids, is highly flexible. Discretization parameters,

such as mesh-sizes and approximation orders, can be locally
adjusted in any desired pattern, expending negligible amounts
of book-keeping work and storage. The discretization can thus
be progressively refined and adapted.

The adaptive solution process is governed by certain
criteria, derived from optimization considerations, which
automatically decide where and how to change the local discretization parameters. The resulting discretization will be
of high-order wherever the evolving solution is found to be
suitably smooth. Singularities of all kinds will automatically
be detected and treated, usually by introducing increasingly
finer levels toward the singularity. Boundary layers will
either be resolved or skipped, depending on the purpose of the
computations as expressed in advance by a certain control
function. All in all, we get a process in which the global
error (in solving the differential equation) decreases
exponentially as a function of the overall computational work,
even for problems containing singularities or singular perturbations.

A detailed account of these multi-level adaptive techniques is given in Brandt [1976], [1977]. In this paper, a
simplified survey will be given (Sections 1, 2 and 3). Note
the new remarks concerning Neumann boundary conditions
appearing in Subsection 1.4, the new numerical tests briefly
described in Subsection 1.5, and the new details on local
coordinate transformations in Subsection 2.3. The rest of
this article presents the QUAD data structure and the software
which were developed for grid manipulation in general, and for
MLAT programming in particular.

The QUAD structure is designed for full flexibility.
Each grid is organized in column-strings, and each column in
point-strings, with pointers connecting neighboring column-
strings in the same grid or neighboring point-strings in the
same column. With this structure, grids are easily extended
or contracted, and can be efficiently scanned. All grids are
collected in one general (real-type) vector, and all their
pointers in another general (integer-type) vector. This
enables us to write Fortran routines (e.g., a relaxation sweep
over a grid) in which the grid number is a programmable para-

meter.

The Fortran package which has been developed includes routines for constructing a grid (by specifying its domain, origin and mesh-sizes) and for performing unions, intersections and transpositions of grids; routines for defining function-values on grids, or transferring and interpolating values from one grid to another; routines for displaying grids or grid functions, and for exposing grids to the user's program; and various other, more technical routines. With this package, the programming of a fast multi-grid solver is essentially reduced to the programming of a usual relaxation routine. Furthermore, a Fortran preprocessor is planned which will much simplify the programming of grid scanning, with no essential loss in execution efficiency.

Table of contents.

1. Survey of multi-grid processes on uniform grids
    1.1   Relaxation sweeps
    1.2   Coarse-grid corrections
    1.3   Multi-grid algorithms
    1.4   Predictability and optimization
    1.5   Numerical tests

2. Non-uniform grids: organization and multi-grid processing
    2.1   Composite grids
    2.2   Difference equations and multi-grid processing
    2.3   Local coordinate transformations
    2.4   Segmental refinement

3. Survey of adaptation techniques
    3.1   The optimization equations
    3.2   Practice of discretization control
    3.3   Results

4. Data structure and software
    4.1   Definitions
    4.2   The QUAD structure
    4.3   GRIDPACK routines
    4.4   Fortran preprocessor

1.   SURVEY OF MULTI-GRID PROCESSES ON UNIFORM GRIDS

To understand the basic numerical processes of MLAT, consider first the usual situation where a partial differential problem

(1.1a) $LU(x) = F(x)$, for $x = (x_1, \ldots, x_d)$ in a domain $\Omega \subseteq \mathbb{R}^d$,

(1.1b) $\Lambda U(x) = \Phi(x)$, for x on the boundary $\partial\Omega$,

is discretized in a preassigned manner on a given uniform grid G^m , yielding the finite-difference equations

(1.2) $L^m U^m(x) = F^m(x)$ $(x \in G^m)$.

Here U and its discrete approximation U^m are q-dimensional vectors of unknown functions, L and Λ are linear or non-linear differential operators and $L^m U^m(x)$ is, correspondingly, a linear or nonlinear expression involving values of U^m at x and at neighboring grid points. At various instances of the solution process, we have on G^m an approximation to U^m , which we will generally denote by u^m .

1.1   Relaxation Sweeps.

One basic MLAT process is the relaxation sweep - for example, the Gauss-Seidel relaxation sweep. This is a process in which all the points x of G^m are scanned one by one in some prescribed order. At each point the old value $u^m(x)$ is replaced by a new value, which is computed so that (1.2) is satisfied at that particular point x , (or nearly satisfied, in case (1.2) is nonlinear). Having completed such a sweep, the system (1.2) is not yet solved, because its equations are coupled to each other, but the new approximation u^m is hope-fully "better" than the old one.

A well-known, and extensively used, method for solving the system (1.2) is by a long sequence of relaxation sweeps (see, e.g., Young [1972]). For linear systems, convergence to the solution U^m is obtained if and only if the system is definite. But the rate of convergence is very slow. Typically, if ℓ is the order of L and N_j is the number of grid intervals in the x_j direction, then the number of sweeps required for convergence increases as $(\min[N_1, \ldots, N_d])^\ell$.

A closer examination, e.g., by Fourier analysis of the error $V^m = U^m - u^m$, shows that the components slow to converge

are those whose wavelength is large compared with h , the
mesh-size of G^m . The high-frequency components converge
very fast, they practically disappear after a few sweeps. For
example, in the Gauss-Seidel relaxation for the 5-point
Poisson operator

(1.3) $L^m U^m(x,y) \equiv \Delta_h U^m(x,y) \equiv$

$\equiv \frac{1}{h^2}\{U^m(x+h,y)+U^m(x-h,y)+U^m(x,y+h)+U^m(x,y-h)-4U^m(x,y)\}$,

the convergence factor of the Fourier component
$\exp[i(\theta_1 x+\theta_2 y)/h]$ (i.e., the factor by which the magnitude of
its amplitude in the error expansion is reduced in one sweep)
is

(1.4) $\mu(\theta_1,\theta_2) = \left| \frac{e^{i\theta_1}+e^{i\theta_2}}{4-e^{-i\theta_1}-e^{-i\theta_2}} \right|$.

For the longest components $\theta_j = O(N_j^{-1})$,   and hence
$\mu = 1-O(N_1^{-2}+N_2^{-2})$. But for high-frequency components, say
with $\max|\theta_j| \geq \frac{\pi}{2}$, we have $\mu \leq .5$, so that in three
relaxation sweeps these components are reduced by almost an
order of magnitude.

      This means that relaxation sweeps, inefficient as they
are in solving problems, are <u>very efficient in smoothing out
the error V^m</u> . This property, which will be extensively used
below, is very general. It holds for Gauss-Seidel relaxation
of any uniformly elliptic scalar (q=1) difference operator,
whether linear or nonlinear. For elliptic systems (q > 1) ,
efficient smoothing is obtained by a suitable variant of the
Gauss-Seidel relaxation. Even degenerate and singularly-
perturbed elliptic operators are smoothed out with similar
efficiency, provided more sophisticated variants (line
relaxation in suitable directions) are used. Moreover, these
later variants are very efficient even for non-elliptic systems,
provided they are used "selectively", i.e., G^m is swept
successively in several directions, and new values are not
introduced at points where a local test shows the equation to
be non-elliptic, with its local time-like direction conflicting
with the current sweeping direction. It is also important to
note that fortunately the smoothing efficiency does not depend

on some sensitive relaxation parameters. Such parameters are sometimes needed (e.g., a relaxation factor is required in simultaneous-displacement relaxation schemes, which are of some advantage in some cases of parallel processing); but since smoothing is a local process, their optimal values depend on the local operator only, and can easily be calculated by local Fourier analysis. Large deviations from the optimal values have only mild effect.

1.2 Coarse-Grid Correction.

As soon as the sought correction v^m has been smoothed out by relaxation, a good approximation to it can be inexpensively computed on a coarser grid. This idea was used by Southwell [1935] and by others (cf. the historical notes in Brandt [1977]), and it has a central role in MLAT.

Let G^k be a grid coarser than G^m, covering the same domain Ω, on which a function v^k approximating v^m is to be computed. On G^m the equation satisfied by v^m is the "residual equation"

$$(1.5a) \qquad \hat{L}^m v^m(x) = r^m(x) , \qquad (x \in G^m)$$

where

$$(1.5b) \qquad \hat{L}^m v^m \equiv L^m(u^m+v^m) - L^m u^m , \quad r^m \equiv F^m - L^m u^m .$$

In the linear case $\hat{L}^m = L^m$, and on first reading it may be easier to keep this case in mind. (1.5) is of course fully equivalent to (1.2), but we are interested in this form because v^m, and not u^m, is the smooth function which we like to approximate on G^k. r^m is the "residual function", which is smoothed out along with v^m. Denoting by I_m^k an operation of interpolating from G^m to G^k (most often G^k is a subset of G^m and I_m^k is the straightforward "injection"), the approximation to (1.5) on G^k is

$$(1.6) \qquad L^k(I_m^k u^m + v^k) - L^k(I_m^k u^m) = I_m^k r^m ,$$

where L^k is the G^k approximation to L. In the linear case, one can write (1.6) directly in terms of v^k; this is called the Correction Scheme (CS). Generally, to avoid complicated linearizations, the function $u^k = I_m^k u^m + v^k$ is introduced, in terms of which (1.6) becomes

(1.7a) $L^k u^k(x) = F^k_m(x)$ $(x \in G^k)$,

where

(1.7b) $F^k_m = L^k(I^k_m u^m) + I^k_m r^m$.

This mode, in which the full approximation u^k , rather than
the correction v^k , is computed on G^k , is called the Full-
Approximation Scheme (FAS). Note that, by (1.7b), (1.5c) and
(1.2, k replacing m) ,

(1.8) $\tau^k_m \equiv F^k_m - F^k = L^k(I^k_m u^m) - I^k_m(L^m u^m)$,

so that τ^k_m thus defined, expresses the "truncation error on
G^k relative to G^m". In other words, (1.7) can be viewed as
the original G^k difference equations, with the forcing
function F^k corrected so as to obtain on G^k a solution
with the accuracy of the finer grid G^m . This point of view
will play an important role later (see Sections 2.2, 2.4,
and 3.2), explaining why FAS is preferable to CS even in many
linear problems.

Note that residuals r^m are defined, and are transferred
to the coarser grid, not only with respect to the interior
equations, but also with respect to the boundary conditions.
Similarly the relative truncation error τ^k_m is defined with
respect to both the interior difference equations and the
boundary conditions.

Let u^k denote an approximate solution to (1.7), obtained
by a method to be specified below (Section 1.3). Then
$v^k = u^k - I^k_m u^m$ is the desired approximation to the correction
v^m , and we can therefore correct our basic approximation u^m
by the replacement

(1.9) $u^m \leftarrow u^m + I^m_k(u^k - I^k_m u^m)$,

where I^m_k denotes interpolation from G^k to G^m . This
correction (1.9) is called the G^k correction to u^m. The
smooth part of the error v^m practically disappears by such a
correction. High-frequency error components are introduced by
the I^m_k interpolation, but they are easily liquidated by subsequent relaxation sweeps.

1.3 Multi-Grid Algorithms.

By combining relaxation sweeps that smooth out the error in u^k with coarse-grid corrections, all error components are efficiently reduced. There remains the question of how to solve the coarse-grid problem (1.7). This we do by a similar process of relaxation sweeps (over G^k) combined with still-coarser-grid corrections.

Thus, in multi-grid solution processes, a sequence of grids $G^0, G^1, \ldots, G^M$ is used, starting with a very coarse grid G^0, and ending with the fine grid G^M on which we like to get the solution U^M. Typically, the mesh size of G^k is $h_k = 2h_{k+1}$, and in most applications a grid-line of G^k is every other line of G^{k+1}. The coarser grid G^k is used not only for coarse-grid corrections to the next finer grid G^{k+1}, but also for obtaining the very first approximation on G^{k+1} by interpolation from G^k. A typical multi-grid algorithm flows as follows:

A. <u>Solving on the coarsest grid.</u> Compute an approximate solution u^0 to the coarsest system (1.2, $m=0$), either by relaxation or by some direct method (used iteratively, if the problem is nonlinear. In case of non-definite problems, direct methods must be used. Whatever the method, u^0 should be easy to obtain, since G^0 is very coarse). Set $m=0$. Generally, m will denote the currently finest grid, i.e., the finest grid so far for which some approximate solution has already been computed.

B. <u>Setting new finest grid.</u> If $m = M$ the algorithm is terminated. If not, interpolate u^m to serve as the first u^{m+1} approximation

(1.10)
$$u^{m+1} \leftarrow I_m^{m+1} u^m \quad ,$$

and then increase m by 1. Introduce the given right-hand F^m to f^m, to serve as the right-hand side of this new level. Also define ε_m, the desired tolerance (see below) for solving the new problem $L^m U^m = f^m$. Then set $k \leftarrow m$. Generally, k will denote the current operation level.

C. <u>Relaxation sweep.</u> Improve u^k by one relaxation sweep for the equation $L^k u^k = f^k$. Concurrently with the sweep

compute some norm e_k of the residuals (usually most convenient are the "dynamic" residuals, i.e., those computed
anyhow in calculating the relaxation corrections). It is
important that the norms used for the different grids are
comparable. That is, they must all be discrete approximations
to the same continuous norm, e.g., continuous L_2 or L_∞
norms, or, better still, the more relevant continuous norm
(see Section 3.1)

(1.10a) $$\|r\| = \int G(x) \; |r(x)| \; dx \quad .$$

D. **Testing the convergence and its rate.** If convergence
was obtained ($e_k \le \varepsilon_k$) , go to Step F. If not, and if the
relaxation convergence rate is still satisfactory ($e_k \le \eta \bar{e}_k$,
where $\bar{e}_k$ is the e_k from the previous relaxation sweep and
η is a prescribed factor; cf. Section 1.4), go back to Step
C. If the convergence rate is slow ($e_k > \eta \bar{e}_k$)[†] , go to
Step E (coarse-grid correction).

E. **Transfer to coarse grid.** Decrease k by 1. Introduce as the first approximation for the new (the coarser)
level k the function

(1.11) $$u^k \leftarrow I_{k+1}^k u^{k+1} \quad .$$

Define the problem on G^k by setting its right-hand side to
be (cf. (1.7))

(1.12) $$f^k \leftarrow L^k u^k + I_{k+1}^k (f^{k+1} - L^{k+1} u^{k+1}) \quad .$$

As the tolerance for this new problem set $\varepsilon_k = \delta e_{k+1}$, where
δ is a prescribed factor (see Section 1.4). If $k = 0$, solve
the problem $L^0 u^0 = f^0$ by relaxation or directly (see Step A
above) and go to Step F. If $k > 0$, go to Step C.

[†]Sometimes "slow convergence" should be further characterized.
For instance, in transonic flow problems, it is essential to
regard convergence as slow only when, in addition to $e_k > \eta \bar{e}_k$
we also have in the last sweep small change in the number of
supersonic points.

F. __Employing converged solution to correct a finer level.__
If $k = m$, go to Step B. If $k < m$ make the correction (cf.
(1.9))

(1.13) $$u^{k+1} \leftarrow u^{k+1} + I_k^{k+1}(u^k - I_{k+1}^k u^{k+1}) \quad ,$$

then increase k by 1 and go to Step C. It is essential
that the interpolations I_{k+1}^k in (1.13) and in (1.11) are
identical (usually they are simple injections).

The storage required for this algorithm is only a
fraction more than the, say, $2n$ locations, required to store
U^M and F^M on the finest grid, since all coarser grids
combined contain far less points. Moreover, with segmental
refinement (Section 2.4), the required storage can be reduced
far below n, even to $O(\log n)$.

1.4 __Predictability and Optimization.__
The multi-grid algorithm can be analyzed by local mode
analysis. This is a simple analysis that can be applied to
general nonlinear problems in the following way:
The difference-equations are linearized around the
(current) solution, and the coefficients of the linearized
difference equations are frozen at their local value. The
resulting constant-coefficient problem is then assumed to hold
in a grid covering the entire space, and its convergence
properties can be calculated in terms of the Fourier components
of the error. This local analysis fails to approximate the
behavior of the long Fourier components, which interact at long
distances and are therefore influenced by boundaries and by
variations in the coefficients. But these long components may
be ignored in the multi-grid work estimates, since their convergence is obtained on coarser grids, where the computational
work is negligible. The expensive process is that of smoothing
the error on the finer grids, and this is essentially a local
process which is very well approximated by the local mode
analysis. Indeed, the predictions of this analysis turn out
to be very realistic.
Since the behavior of any prescribed multi-grid algorithm
can be predicted to a good approximation, we can in fact predict which of several possible alternatives will give better

performance. Thus we can optimize our algorithm with respect
to several parameters, such as its relaxation mode (point-wise
or line-wise, marching directions, relaxation factors, etc.),
the degree of interpolations, stopping criteria (η or δ
above), mesh-size ratio (h_k/h_{k+1}) etc. For linear problems,
optimal parameters can be calculated once for all, since they
are essentially independent of the boundary shape, the boundary
conditions and the right-hand side F . For nonlinear problems,
some adjustment of parameters may be needed in the solution
process, but experience shows that the overall efficiency is
not sensitive to their precise optimization. In fact, by
computerized mode analysis of many problems, combined with
numerical tests of selected cases, some simple robust rules
emerged. The important rules are the following:

The mesh-size ratio $h_k/h_{k+1} = 2$ is close enough to
optimum to warrant its use in all cases. This offers a very
desirable standardization and is exploited in structuring the
data.

For relaxation, the most important quantity is the
"smoothing factor" $\bar{\mu}$, defined as the largest convergence
factor (cf. Section 1.1) among high-frequency components,
i.e.,

$$(1.14) \qquad \bar{\mu} = \max_{\frac{\pi}{2} \leqslant |\theta| \leqslant \pi} \mu(\theta) \quad ,$$

where, in d-dimensional problems, $\theta = (\theta_1, \ldots, \theta_d)$,
$|\theta| = \max|\theta_j|$, and $\mu(\theta)$ is the convergence factor of the
Fourier component $\exp(i\theta \cdot x/h)$, h being the mesh size and
$\theta \cdot x = \theta_1 x_1 + \ldots + \theta_d x_d$. The components with $\frac{\pi}{2} \leqslant |\theta|$ are those
which are missing on the coarser grid, and they are the ones
that should be reduced by relaxation. Optimizing relaxation
can therefore be made in terms of minimizing $\bar{\mu}$, which is
easily calculated. More precisely, the relaxation mode should
be decided so as to minimize the smoothing-rate per operation
$\frac{1}{w}\left|\log \bar{\mu}\right|$, where w is the number of operations per grid-point
per relaxation sweep.

For example, the best relaxation sweep found for 5-point
Poisson problems is the above-mentioned Gauss-Seidel relaxation,
for which $\bar{\mu} = 0.5$, $w = 5$. Methods with better smoothing
rates require too many more operations per grid point.

Interpolations. For full efficiency of the algorithm, the order I of the coarse-to-fine interpolation (I_k^{k+1} in (1.13)) should be no less than the order ℓ of the differential equations. Higher interpolation order ($I > \ell$) are of no advantage, except in the initial stages. The order of the initial interpolation (I_m^{m+1} in (1.10) above) should be $I \geqslant \ell+q$, where q is the order of smoothness of F. The i-th interpolation (1.13) should be of order

$$(1.15) \qquad I \geqslant \ell + \max[q - ip, 0]$$

where p is the order of approximation. As long as $I > \ell+p$, these interpolations should not be followed by relaxation sweeps (instead of Step C, go to Step E), since the interpolant is already smooth enough. The fine-to-coarse I_{k+1}^k interpolation (1.11) in case G^k is not a subset of G^{k+1}, should be of the same order as the subsequent I_k^{k+1} interpolation (1.13).

The fine-to-coarse <u>weighting of residuals</u> (I_{k+1}^k in (1.12)) has the form

$$(1.16) \qquad I_{k+1}^k r^{k+1}(x) = \sum_\nu \rho_\nu \, r^{k+1}(x+h\nu) , \qquad (\sum \rho_\nu = 1) ,$$

where $\nu = (\nu_1, \ldots, \nu_d)$, ν_j are integers and the summation is over a small set. Injection ($\rho_0 = 1$, other $\rho_\nu = 0$) is best in solving second-order differential equations with smooth coefficients. If the coefficients vary wildly over the grid, or generally, if low frequencies are strongly coupled with high frequencies (e.g., because of the relaxation scheme), then the suitable weighting is

$$(1.17) \qquad \begin{array}{ll} \rho_\nu = 2^{-d-|\nu|} & \text{for } |\nu| = \max|\nu_i| \leqslant 1 , \\ \rho_\nu = 0 & \text{for } \max|\nu_i| > 1 . \end{array}$$

For high-order equations, an optimal weighting is that which minimizes the "coarse-grid amplification factor" $\bar{\sigma}$,

$$(1.18) \qquad \bar{\sigma} = \max\{1 , \max_{|\theta| \leqslant \frac{\pi}{2}} |\sigma_0(\theta)|\}$$

where $\sigma_0(\theta)$ is the (local) amplification of the error component $\exp(i\theta \cdot x/h)$ due to a coarse-grid correction; but (1.17) can be generally used.

For the switching parameters δ, ε_m and η (see
Section 1.3), quite general good values are

(1.19) $\delta = 0.2$,

(1.20) $\varepsilon_m = 2^{-2p-1} \left\| \tau \begin{array}{c} m-2 \\ m-1 \end{array} \right\|$ (cf. (1.8)) ,

(1.21) $\eta = \max\limits_{x} \bar{\mu}(x)$ (cf. (1.14)) ,

where p is the approximation order, the norm $\| \cdot \|$ is the
same as in calculating e_k (see Step C), and $\bar{\mu}$ is written
as a function of the location x because it may vary over the
domain if the problem coefficients are not constant. More
sophisticated formulae for δ and η are given in Brandt
[1976]. Actually their precise values are not critical. Much
(sometimes even orders of magnitude) smaller values of δ or
ε_m can be used without significantly changing the overall
efficiency. If coarse-grid corrections are not efficient
enough, η may always be increased a little, a safe value
being for example $\eta = \bar{\mu}^{\frac{1}{2}}$. If the smoothing rate $\bar{\mu}$ (and
hence also η) has large variations over the domain, the
stopping test $(e_k \leqslant \eta \bar{e}_k)$ can be made separately in subdomains, possibly resulting in partial relaxation sweeps, i.e.,
sweeps which skip some subdomains. (Partial sweeps may be
important only in multi-grid processes, and not in pure
relaxation processes, because it is only with regard to high-
frequency components that errors on different subdomains are
practically decoupled from each other so that their different
convergence rates can be used independently).

Neumann and other "relational" boundary conditions (i.e.,
conditions which do not specify values of u^k at some boundary
points, but rather relate them to values at other points; non-
Dirichlet conditions) should be treated differently in the
multi-grid relaxation sweeps than in pure relaxation solutions.
The role of the multi-grid sweeps is to smooth out the error,
including the error in the boundary conditions. Forcing the
precise Neumann condition at a boundary point introduces large
residuals to the neighboring interior difference-equation(s).
This slows down the smoothing process and the overall convergence. Instead we should, at each relaxation sweep, only

smooth out the boundary conditions. A good procedure, for example, is to sweep over the boundary points (or the fictitious points introduced beyond the boundary to symmetrically express the Neumann condition) and replace the value at each point by a new value, such that the error in the Neumann condition at that point is an average of the errors at the two neighboring boundary points. Two such boundary sweeps per each interior relaxation sweep would normally ensure that smoothing at the boundary is not slower than in the interior.

The smoothing of the boundary error is especially important near regions with hyperbolic equations, where non-smoothness may be carried from the boundary to the interior.

Incidentally, for a full Neumann problem (Neumann conditions on all boundaries) the above procedure also ensures that the boundary conditions are compatible with the right-hand side of the equation. If the given problem is (slightly) incompatible, the procedure will still converge, but to a solution in which a (small) constant is added to the Neumann boundary values.

Never settle for any convergence rate slower than predicted by the interior local mode analysis! The predictability of multi-grid convergence rates can be used in debugging the programs. Because of the iterative character of the method, programming (or conceptual) errors often do not manifest themselves in catastrophic results, but rather in considerably slower convergence rates.

For 5-point Poisson problems, for example, we have $\ell = 2$, $p = 2$ and usually $q \leqslant 2$ (otherwise the 5-point formula is not the best approximation to use). Hence the first interpolation (1.10) should be of order 4 (cubic interpolation), while for the other coarse-to-fine interpolations (1.13) order 2 (linear interpolation) is enough. Injection can be used for the residual, and $\eta = \bar{\mu} = .5$. In fact, instead of using the stopping criteria in Step D, a fixed number of sweeps and coarse-grid corrections can be made (saving the work of computing e_k in Step C): 2 sweeps are made before switching to the coarser grid, and one additional sweep is made on coming back from the coarse grid before switching to the finer grid. If n is the number of points in G^M , this algorithm gives in 42n computer operations (most of them additions) solutions with residuals below 50% of the truncation errors. In 27n more operations another multi-grid correction cycle can be made, reducing the residuals to less than 5% of the truncation errors; etc.

1.5 Numerical Tests.

This 42n operations algorithm for 5-point Poisson problems was tested, and the above upper bound for the resulting residual norm was confirmed. On the CDC Cyber 175 computer at ICASE this algorithm required about 26n micro-seconds for solving a problem with n grid points.

Experiments with this and many other problems, Brandt [1972], Shiftan [1972], Brandt [1977] showed that the multi-grid efficiency (solution time per grid point) is essentially independent of the shape of the domain Ω , the right-hand side F and the finest mesh-size h_M . It is roughly proportional to $w|\log \bar{\mu}|^{-1}$, the inverse of the smoothing-rate per operation, which is easily calculated in advance by local analysis. This was found to be the case even for nonlinear, mixed-type (elliptic-hyperbolic) problems containing discontinuities, such as transonic flow problems.

Recent experiments showed considerably slower convergence for problems with non-Dirichlet boundary conditions, if these conditions were fully enforced at relaxation (cf. Section 1.4). For example, 40% loss was typically found in the asymptotic convergence rate of the Neumann problem for the 5-point Poisson equation (compared with the corresponding Dirichlet problem). When, however, the Neumann boundary conditions were treated in the manner explained above (Section 1.4), the convergence rate was fully restored to its value for Dirichlet problems. These experiments were conducted by Fred G. Gustavson, at IBM Thomas J. Watson Research Center.

Recent tests were also made with relaxation schemes which couple low frequencies with high ones. As in the case of highly-oscillating difference-equations (reported in Section A.4 of Brandt [1977]), it was found necessary to use the residual weighting (1.17). For example, the standard 5-point Poisson problem was tried with Gauss-Seidel relaxation with red-black (checkerboard) ordering. It is easy to see that such a relaxation scheme would introduce high-frequency error components to an approximation initially containing only low ones. High-frequency components of the residuals cannot be reduced below their low-frequency counterparts, and hence coarse-grid corrections with straightforward residual injection cannot be effective. Indeed, such a multi-grid scheme did not converge at all. With the residual weighting (1.17), however, the multi-grid algorithm with red-black relaxation proved as efficient as Gauss-Seidel relaxation with normal (e.g., lexicographic) ordering.

Other recent tests were made with the <u>Helmholtz equation</u> (cf. 1.3))

$$(1.22) \qquad L^m U^m (x_1, x_2) \equiv \Delta_h U^m (x_1, x_2) + CU^m (x_1, x_2) = F \ .$$

For $C < 0$ this equation has better smoothing rates than for the Poisson (C=0) equation, and indeed, its multi-grid con-vergence rates were at least as good, no matter how large $|C|$ was or what relaxation scheme was chosen. The difficult case is that of large positive C , for which (1.22) is non-definite. The equations for the coarsest grid should then be solved directly, and the coarse grid should be "fine enough" (see Section 4.1 in Brandt [1977]). Indeed, for moderate C (larger than the first few eigenvalues of $-\Delta_h$, but nicely bounded away from any of them), such a multi-grid algorithm was found to be almost as efficient as for the Poisson equation. In other cases the efficiency deteriorates, since G^0 is required to be too fine, and other techniques should be incorporated.

2. <u>NON-UNIFORM GRIDS: ORGANIZATION AND MULTI-GRID PROCESSING</u>

In principle, the multi-grid solution process described in Section 1 could work equally well when the finest grid G^M is non-uniform and even non-rectangular, with grid points at arbitrary locations. A relaxation with good smoothing rates on a general grid is obtained by employing all line and marching directions. The main difficulty with general grid, however, is practical: Merely to formulate and use the difference equations, let alone solve them, is complicated. It requires lengthy calculations and large memories for storing geometrical information, such as the location of each grid point, its neighbors, the coefficients of its difference equation, etc. The multi-grid processing of such arbitrary grids generates additional practical difficulties since it requires the introduction of coarser grids and the grouping of grid points in grid lines (for line relaxation).

These arbitrary general grids, however, are not really needed. We will show below (Section 2.1) a method or organization which is less general but in which any desired refinement pattern can still be obtained, and easily changed, with negligible book-keeping and with difference equations always defined on equi-distant points. This flexible organization will naturally lend itself to multi-grid processing (Section 2.2) and to local transformations (Section 2.3), and will lay the groundwork for efficient adaptation. It may also be used for a multi-grid procedure which can work with computer storage much smaller than the size of the finest grid (Section 2.4).

2.1 Composite grids.

It is proposed to organize non-uniform grids as "composite grids". A composite grid is a union of uniform subgrids $G^0, G^1, \ldots, G^M$, with decreasing mesh-sizes $h_0, h_1, \ldots, h_M$. Usually $h_k : h_{k+1} = 2:1$ and every other grid-line of G^{k+1} is a grid line of G^k. Unlike the description in Section 1, however, the subgrids are not necessarily extended over the entire domain Ω: The domain of G^{k+1} may be only a part of (but must be included in) the domain of G^k, so that different degrees of refinement can be created at different subdomains. Each G^k is extended, as a rule, over those subdomains where the desired mesh-size is roughly $1.5h_k$ or less. G^k may be thus disconnected. The effective mesh-size at each neighborhood will be that of the finest grid covering that neighborhood. Clearly, any desired mesh-size h can be approximated by some effective mesh-size h', where $0.75h \leqslant h' \leqslant 1.5h$. Mesh-sizes never require better approximation.

The composite grid is very flexible, since local grid refinement (or coarsening) is done in terms of extending (or contracting) uniform subgrids, which is relatively easy and inexpensive to implement, as we shall see below (Section 4).

Moreover, this composite structure will at the same time provide a very efficient solution process to its difference equations, by letting $G^0, G^1, \ldots, G^M$ also serve as the multi-grid sequence (as in Section 1). Each G^m will automatically play the role of the correcting coarse-grid whenever the finer subgrid G^{m+1} is present (see Section 2.2).

In adaptive procedures, the sequence of subgrids will be kept open-ended, so that we can add increasingly finer $(G^{M+1}, G^{M+2}, \ldots)$ or coarser $(G^{-1}, G^{-2}, \ldots)$ levels, as needed. (Increasingly coarser levels may be needed if the problem's domain Ω is unbounded and the bounded computational domain is chosen adaptively).

The coarsest subgrid G^0 should of course be kept coarse enough to have its system of difference equations relatively inexpensive to solve. Hence, there will usually be several subgrids $G^0, G^1, \ldots$ extending over the entire domain Ω. That is, they will not serve to produce different levels of refinement, but they are kept in the system for serving in its multi-grid processing.

There seems to be certain waste in the proposed system, because one function value may be stored several times when its geometrical point belongs to several subgrids G^k. This is not really the case: The extra values are exactly those needed for the multi-grid processing. In the process, the different subgrids may have different values at the same geometrical point. Moreover, it is only a small fraction (2^{-d}) of the points that are actually being repeated.

2.2 Difference Equations and Multi-Grid Processing

If the grid G^m covers the entire domain Ω, its difference equations (1.2), approximating both the differential equation (1.1a) and the boundary conditions (1.1b), are defined all over G^m, with as many equations as unknowns. If, however, G^m only covers a proper part of Ω, then at a grid point on or near the interior boundary of G^m the difference equation is not well defined, since some neighboring points employed in the equation are missing in G^m (see Figure 1). We call such a point an outer point of G^m. The collection of inner points (i.e., points where (1.2) does apply) in G^m is

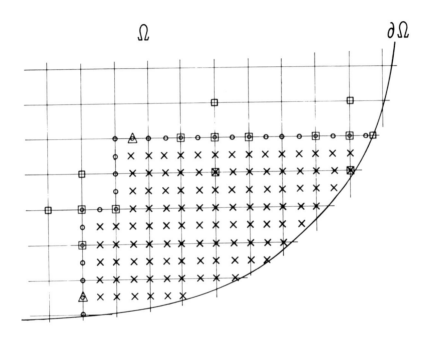

FIGURE 1.   Example of Non-Uniform Grid.
A section of the domain Ω and its boundary $\partial\Omega$ is shown, covered with a coarser grid G^k (line intersections) and a finer grid G^{k+1} (crosses and circles). For the case of 5-point difference equations, G^{k+1} inner points are marked with crosses, its outer points with circles. At outer points belonging to G^k, the solution should satisfy the G^k difference equations, such as the 5-point relations indicated by squares. At other outer points, such as those shown with triangles, the solution is always an interpolation from values at adjacent G^k points.

denoted by G_m^m. We assumed above that the subdomain covered by G^m is included in the domain of the coarser subgrid G^k. More precisely the assumption is that any point in G_m^m which lies in a position of the G^k level is also a point of G_k^k. The collection of such points (i.e., the intersection of G_k^k and G_m^m) is denoted[†] G_m^k. G_m^k is of course empty if G^m is empty, (e.g., if $m > M$). With this notation, our system of difference equations over $G^0 \cup G^1 \cup \ldots \cup G^M$ is

(2.1a) $U^k = I_{k-1}^k U^{k-1}$ in $G^k - G_k^k$

(2.1b) $U^k = I_{k+1}^k U_{k+1}^k$ in G_{k+1}^k

(2.1c) $L^k U^k = F^k$ in $G_k^k - G_{k+1}^k$ (cf. (1.2)) ,

where I_m^k is an interpolation from G^m to G^k (I_{k+1}^k in (2.1b) is usually an injection). Thus, at each grid point belonging to $G_k^k \cap G_{k+1}^{k+1} \cap \ldots \cap G_m^m$, the G^m difference equation is satisfied.

In the multi-grid solution process these equations are modified. Denoting by u^m the current approximation to U^m, we replace (2.1) by the multi-grid difference equations

(2.2a) $U^k = I_{k-1}^k U^{k-1}$ in $G^k - G_k^k$,

(2.2b) $L^k U^k = f^k$ in G_k^k ,

where

(2.3a) $f^k = F^k$ in $G_k^k - G_{k+1}^k$, $f^k = F_{k+1}^k$ in G_{k+1}^k ,

(2.3b) $F_m^k = \bar{I}_m^k (f^m - L^m u^m) + L^k (I_m^k u^m)$.

$\bar{I}_m^k$ is another interpolation from G^m to G^k ("residual weighting", having generally the form (1.16), with either the trivial weighting $\rho_0 = 1$ (injection), or the more costly weighting (1.17) in cases of wildly varying coefficients).

[†] When G^k and G^m do not use the same coordinate system (see Section 2.3), G_m^k can be defined as the intersection of G_k^k and the convex hull of G_m^m .

Clearly, at convergence (2.2) coincides with (2.1). In the process, however, (2.2) in G_{k+1}^k coincides with the coarse-grid correction equation (1.7). This enables G^k to act as the correcting coarse-grid on one hand, while on the other hand, it has the role of the finest grid when and where G^{k+1} is not present. These two roles are fully compatible and simultaneous, owing to the FAS approach (see Section 1.2), which thus turns out to be more than a device for treating nonlinear problems.

The multi-grid algorithm for solving (2.2) is the same as in Section 1.3, except for natural changes in the switching parameters. In particular, the prescription for ε_k in Step E should be generalized, e.g., to $\varepsilon_k = e_{k+1} A_k / A_{k+1}$, where A_k is the area (or volume) covered by the subgrid G^k.

An important advantage of this procedure is that difference equations are defined on uniform grids only (patched together by the usual multi-grid interpolations). Such difference equations on equidistant points are simple and can be read from small standard tables, while on general grids their weights would have to be recomputed (or stored) separately for each point, entailing very lengthy calculations especially for high-order approximations. Our system facilitates the use of high and variable (adaptive) order of approximation.

Another advantage is that relaxation sweeps, too, are done on uniform grids only. This simplifies the sweeping and is particularly essential where symmetric and/or alternating-direction line relaxations are required for obtaining high smoothing rates.

Numerical experiments have been conducted with this algorithm for the case of the 5-point Poisson problem in an L-shaped domain, where increasingly finer subgrids were introduced on increasingly smaller L-shaped subdomains near the singular corner. The efficiency of the solution process (e.g., the reduction in residual norm per Work-Unit of relaxation) turns out to be the same as in the uniform-grid case (roughly .55), except that the Work-Unit is suitably modified: Here it is defined as the computational work in one relaxation sweep not only over G^M (which may make up only a small part of the composite grid), but over all subgrids $G^0, G^1, \ldots, G^M$, counting only once each repeated geometrical point.

2.3 Local Coordinate Transformations.

Another dimension of flexibility and versatility can be added to the above system by allowing each subgrid to be defined in terms of its own set of coordinates.

Near a boundary or an interface, for example, the most effective local discretizations are made in terms of local coordinates in which the boundary (or interface) is a coordinate line. In such coordinates it is easy to formulate high-order approximations near the boundary; or to introduce mesh-sizes which are much smaller across than along the boundary layer; etc. Usually it is easy to define suitable local coordinates (see below), and uniformly discretize them, but it is more difficult to patch together all these local transformations, especially in an adaptable way.

A multi-grid method for patching together a collection of local subgrids $G^1, G^2, \ldots, G^M$ (each being uniform, but in its own local coordinates) is to relate them to one another and finally to a basic coarse grid G^0, which is uniform in the global coordinates and covers the entire domain. The relation is essentially as above (Section 2.2). Namely, each subgrid G^k is connected to a "father" subgrid $G^{k'}$, the next coarser grid. Previously, we had $k' = k-1$, but here we should allow some "fathers" to have more than a single "son" (more than one local refinement), so that instead of linear ordering the collection, $G^0, G^1, \ldots, G^M$ forms a tree. The domain covered by G^k is always included in the domain of $G^{k'}$. Finite-difference equations are separately defined in the inner points of each subgrid, and the FAS multi-grid process automatically combines them together through its usual interpolation periods. The algorithm is the same, switching to the "father" subgrid being of course made only when slow convergence is detected on every one of its "sons".

Each set of coordinates will generally have more than one subgrid defined on it, so that (i) local refinement can be made within each set of coordinates, and (ii) the multi-grid processing retains its full efficiency by keeping the mesh-size ratio $h_{k'}/h_k$ properly bounded.

Since local refinement can be made within each set of
coordinates, the only purpose of the coordinate transformation
is to provide a certain grid direction, i.e., to have a given
manifold (e.g., a piece of boundary) coincide with a grid
hyperplane. We can therefore limit ourselves to simple forms
of transformations. For example, in 2-dimensional problems,
let a curve (a boundary, an interface, etc.) be given in the
general parametric form

$$(2.4) \qquad x = x_0(s) \quad , \quad y = y_0(s) \qquad (0 \leqslant s \leqslant s_1) \quad ,$$

where s is the arclength, i.e.,

$$(2.5) \qquad x_0'(s)^2 + y_0'(s)^2 = 1 \quad .$$

To get a coordinate system (r,s) in which such a curve will
be a grid line, we can always use the transformation

$$(2.6) \qquad x(r,s) = x_0(s) - ry_0'(s) \quad , \quad y(r,s) = y_0(s) + rx_0'(s) \quad .$$

This transformation (a special case of transformations discussed in Starius [1974]) is orthogonal, owing to (2.5), and
transforms any small $h \times h$ square to another $h \times h$ square.
The main advantage of this transformation is that it is fully
characterized by the single variable functions $x_0(s)$, $y_0(s)$.
These functions (together with $x_0'(s)$, $y_0'(s)$ and
$q(s) = x_0''/y_0' = -y_0''/x_0'$) can be stored as one-dimensional
arrays, in terms of which efficient interpolation routines
from (x,y) grids to (r,s) grids, and vice versa, can be
programmed once for all. The difference equations in (r,s)
coordinates are also simple enough in terms of these arrays.
For example, by (2.5-6),

$$(2.7) \qquad \frac{\partial}{\partial x} = -y_0' \frac{\partial}{\partial r} + \frac{x_0'}{1+rq} \frac{\partial}{\partial s} \quad , \quad \frac{\partial}{\partial y} = x_0' \frac{\partial}{\partial r} + \frac{y_0'}{1+rq} \frac{\partial}{\partial s} \quad .$$

Hence we can easily approximate the (x,y) derivatives by
(r,s) finite-differences, with numerical values of $x_0'(s)$,
$y_0'(s)$ and $q(s)$ directly read from their stored tables. (No
interpolation is needed if the tables contain values for s
points which correspond to grid lines and half-way between
grid lines.)

Such a system offers much flexibility. Precise treatment
of boundaries and interfaces by the global coordinates is not
required, since along boundaries the global grids are only

correction grids to the local ones. The local coordinates
are easily changeable (changing only the one-dimensional
tables of x_0, y_0, x_0', y_0', q) and can therefore be adapted to a
moving interface.

2.4   Segmental Refinement.

The composite grid structure and its multi-grid algorithm
(Sections 2.1, 2.2) can be used not only for affecting
different refinement levels, but also for problems where the
finer grids are too large to be stored in the computer memory.

Consider for example a uniform problem, where the finest
grid G^M covers the entire domain. In the FAS multi-grid
algorithm (Sections 1.2 - 3) the fine-grid solution u^M is
also obtained on all coarser grids. On a coarser grid G^k,
$I_M^k u^M$ is fully determined by the "corrected" difference
equations, with F_M^k replacing F^k. It is therefore not
necessary to keep the fine-grid, once F_M^k has been computed.

F_M^k can be computed by "segmental refinement" as follows:
Taking only a segment of the fine-grid G^M, use the composite
multi-grid algorithm (Section 2.2) to obtain a multi-grid
solution, including the values of F_M^k in that segment. Then
discard this segment and take another, and so on, through a
sequence of segments, thus computing F_M^k throughout. The
values of F_M^k replace F^k as soon as they are computed, so
that corrected forcing terms are in effect in the subdomain
covered by the previous segments.

This segmental refinement approach assumes that the
corrections $\tau_M^k = F_M^k - F^k$ in different segments are decoupled
from each other. In elliptic problems this is approximately
true: A correction of small relative magnitude in the forcing
function outside a given segment will have small relative
influence on the values $\tau_M^k(x)$ inside that segment, except
for points x near (upto few mesh-widths away from) the
segment's boundary. Thus, if the segments are chosen so that
neighboring segments overlap (several mesh intervals into each
other), then τ_M^k is automatically recomputed wherever it
could change much. If extra accuracy is desired, another
cycle of segmental refinement can be performed. When the
problem contains hyperbolic regions, one should have, for each

local time-like direction, at least one cycle of segmental refinements consistent with it.

Another way of viewing this technique is to observe that the roll of the finer levels, relative to the coarser ones, is mainly to liquidate high-frequency error components which cannot be "seen" on the coarser grids. These components have a short (just a few mesh-widths) coupling range, and can therefore be computed at any point by refining only few neighboring meshes.

For similar reasons, whenever we operate with a certain G^M segment, we can actually also restrict ourselves to just segments of $G^{M-1}, G^{M-2}, \ldots, G^{k+1}$, each G^m segment covering a domain only few mesh intervals wider than the G^{m+1} domain. With this technique one can operate the multi-grid algorithm almost in its full efficiency, using a storage area which is only a small fraction of the size of the finest grid, without using any external memory. In principle, the required storage area can be reduced to only a constant cube of J^d locations on each level (where even $J = 10$ probably offer enough overlap), so that the total storage is less than $2J^d(1+\log_2 n)$. For this extreme case, however, the computational work multiplies by an $O(\log n)$ factor.

3.   SURVEY OF ADAPTATION TECHNIQUES

The flexible organization and solution process, described above, facilitate the implementation of variable mesh-size $h(x)$ and the employment of high and variable approximation order $p(x)$. How, then, are mesh-sizes and approximation-orders to be chosen? Should boundary layers, for example, be resolved by the grid? What is their proper resolution? Should high-order approximation be used at such layers? How does one detect such layers automatically? In this section we survey a general framework for automatic selection of $h(x)$, $p(x)$ and other discretization parameters in a (nearly) optimal way. This system automatically resolves or avoids from resolving thin layers, depending on the goal of the computations, which can be stated through a simple function.

3.1 The Optimization Equations.

As our directive for sensible discretization we consider
the problem of minimizing a certain error estimator E
subject to a given amount of solution work W (or minimizing
W for a given E . Actually, the control quantity will be
neither E nor W , but their rate of exchange). This optimization problem should of course be taken quite loosely,
since full optimization would require too much control work
and would thus defeat its own purpose.

The error estimator E has generally the form[+]

$$(3.1) \qquad E = \int\limits_{\Omega} G(x)\tau(x)\,dx \quad ,$$

where $\tau(x)$ is the truncation error at x . $G(x) \geqslant 0$ is the
error-weighting function. It should in principle be imposed
by the user, thus defining his goal in solving the problem.
In practice $G(x)$ serves as a convenient control. It is only
the relative orders of magnitude of $G(x)$ at different points
x that really matter, and therefore it can be chosen by some
simple rules (see Brandt [1977] , and the example in Section
3.3 below). The work functional W is roughly given by[+]

$$(3.2) \qquad W = \int\limits_{\Omega} \frac{w(p(x))}{h(x)^d}\,dx \quad ,$$

where d is the dimension and h^{-d} is therefore the number
of grid points per unit volume. w is the solution work per
grid point. In multi-grid solution processes with difference
equations defined on equidistant points, we have $w \approx w_0 p$,
where w_0 is a constant independent of $h(x)$ and $p(x)$ and
thus immaterial to our optimization problem. More generally,
$w = w(p)$.

Treating $h(x)$ and $p(x)$ as continuous variables, the
Euler equations of minimizing (3.1) given (3.2) can be written
as

[+]In principle there should be added to E and W similar
integrals along the boundary of Ω , expressing contribution
of truncation errors and work, correspondingly, in approximating (non-Dirichlet) boundary conditions. This would later
give us criteria for adapting the boundary approximations.

(3.3a) $G \dfrac{\partial \tau}{\partial h} - \dfrac{\lambda\, dw(p)}{h^{d+1}} = 0$,

(3.3b) $G \dfrac{\partial \tau}{\partial p} + \dfrac{\lambda\, w'(p)}{h^{d}} = 0$,

where λ is a constant (the Lagrange multiplier), representing the marginal rate of exchanging optimal accuracy for work: $\lambda = dE/dW$. The = sign in (3.3b) should be replaced by $\geqslant$ at points x where p attains its minimal allowable value (usually 1 or 2).

In principle, once λ is specified, equations (3.3) determine, for each $x \in \Omega$, the local optimal values of $h(x)$ and $p(x)$, provided the truncation function $\tau(x,h(x),p(x))$ is fully known. In practice we never actually solve (3.3), but use these relations to decide upon changes in h and p , so that we need to estimate τ only for h and p close to their current local values.

In fact, whenever adaptive procedures are desired, the discrete problem is essentially nonlinear, even if the original differential problem was linear, since h and p are themselves unknown. The solution process will therefore usually include a <u>continuation (or embedding) process</u>: The problem, its discretization, and its approximate solution are driven from an easily solvable (e.g., linear and regular) problem toward the desired problem, in steps small enough to ensure that the solutions are kept near physical solutions. This process is inexpensive, since it can be done with crude accuracy (coarse grids) and little work, by selecting a large value for our control parameter λ . When the desired problem is finally reached, we decrease λ and thus refine the solution.

3.2   <u>Practice of Discretization Control.</u>

In the multi-grid solution process (possibly incorporating a continuation process), incidentally to the stage of computing f^k (Step E in Section 1.3), we can get an estimate of the decrease in the error estimator E introduced by the present discretization parameters. For example, the quantity

(3.4) $-\Delta E(x) = G(x) \left| f^k(x) - F^k(x) \right|$

may serve as a local estimate for the decrease in E per unit volume owing to the refinement from h_k to h_{k+1} (cf. (1.8), (3.1)). Each such decrease in E is related to some additional work ΔW (per unit volume). For example, that refinement from h_k to h_{k+1} required the additional work (per unit volume)

(3.5) $$\Delta W = \frac{w(p)}{h_{k+1}^d} - \frac{w(p)}{h_k^d} \ .$$

We say that the present parameter (h_{k+1} in the example) is highly profitable, if the local rate of exchanging accuracy for work $Q = -\Delta E / \Delta W$ is much larger than the control parameter λ .

More sophisticated tests may be based on assuming τ to have some form of dependence on h and p . Instead of calculating Q for the previous change (from h_k to h_{k+1} in the example) we can then extrapolate and estimate the rate $\bar{Q}$ for the next change (from h_{k+1} to h_{k+2}), which is the more appropriate rate in testing whether to make that next change. The "extrapolated test" is not, however, much different in practice, and may actually be equivalent to testing the former Q against another constant λ .

In deciding whether and where to change the discretization, we adopt rules which stabilize the adaptive process. For example, a change (e.g, refinement) is introduced only if there is a point where the change is "overdue" (e.g., a point where $\bar{Q} > 10\lambda$). But, together with each point where the change is introduced, it is also introduced at all neighboring points where the change is "due" (e.g., where $\bar{Q} > 3\lambda$) .

We can use the Q vs λ test to decide on all kinds of possible changes, such as: Changing the mesh-size h to $\frac{h}{2}$ in only one of the space directions, or changing the order p to $p+1$ (or $p-1$), or changing the computational boundaries (when the physical domain is unbounded); or we can use such a test to decide whether to discard some terms from the difference operator (such as the highest order terms in some regions of a singularly perturbed problem); etc.

It can be shown that the computer work invested in such tests is negligible compared with the solution work itself.

3.3 Results.

The adaptive discretization techniques were applied to a series of test cases which on one hand represent a variety of interesting situations, but each of which, on the other hand, is simple enough to be analyzed in closed forms. (See Section 9 in Brandt [1977]). The following are the basic results of these studies.

A problem is said to have the uniform scale $\eta(x)$ if

$$(3.6) \qquad \tau(x,h,p) \approx t(x) \left[\frac{h}{\eta(x)}\right]^p \qquad (p_0 \leqslant p) \quad .$$

Asymptotically (i.e., for small λ), our automatic discretization will yield, for such a problem,

$$(3.7) \qquad h = \eta e^{-1/d} \quad , \qquad p \approx d \log \frac{Gt\eta^d}{\lambda ed} \quad ,$$

and the error will decrease exponentially as function of work

$$(3.8) \qquad E = C_0 \exp\left[-(ed \int \eta^{-d}dx)^{-1} W\right] \quad .$$

In problems with thin layers (e.g., singularly perturbed problems) the scale η becomes very small in some regions. Fast convergence may then be obtained in two ways:

(i) The function $G(x)$ may be such that no resolution of the thin layer is required. For example, if we are not interested in computing boundary derivatives of the solution, then a suitable error-weighting function is $G(x) = d_x^{m/2}$, where d_x is the distance from x to the boundary and m is the order of the differential equation. For such $G(x)$ no resolution of boundary layers will be either needed or affected.

(ii) When the computation of boundary derivatives is desired (e.g., for drag or lift calculations) and $G(x)$ is accordingly chosen, then our adaptive procedures will automatically resolve the boundary layer. In a suitable coordinate system (see Section 2.3), small mesh-sizes will then be chosen across, but not along, the layer. The typical error-work relation will be

$$(3.9) \qquad E \approx C_0 \exp\left[-CW^{\frac{1}{2}}\right] \quad ,$$

which is still an "infinite-order" rate of convergence.

No degradation of the convergence rates (3.8) or (3.9) is caused by boundary corners, jump discontinuities and other isolated singularities. Finer grids are automatically created near such points (or lines), so that the error contribution of the singularity decreases exponentially as a function of the extra work associated with these refinements.

4. DATA STRUCTURE AND SOFTWARE

The flexible composite grids described in Section 2 are based on a collection of uniform grids, each of which is assumed to be easily extendible (or contractible) to cover a given (changeable, possible disconnected) subdomain. The structure of each of these uniform grids should allow efficient sweeping over it (relaxation, interpolation, etc.). For easy multi-grid programming we should also be able to assign a number to each grid so that we can write routines (e.g., a relaxation sweep routine) in which the grid number is a parameter. The data structure described below (Sections 4.1, 4.2) was developed to meet all these objectives with minimal amount of pointer structure. For simplicity, the description is restricted to two-dimensional grids, which clearly illustrate the general case. Then (Section 4.3) we survey a package of routines which allow the user to generate and manipulate arbitrary (two-dimensional) grids of this structure, reducing for example the task of writing a composite multi-grid program to the writing of a simple relaxation routine. A Fortran preprocessor (Section 4.4) will simplify the programming even further. The data structure and the system were developed in collaboration with Dan Ophir in the Weizmann Institute and with Fred Gustavson, Allan Goodman and Donald Quarles in the IBM T.J. Watson Research Center. They were first reported in Gustavson [1976].

4.1 Definitions.

In the (x,y) plane the lattice $L(x_0,y_0;h_x,h_y)$ is the set

(4.1) $L(x_0,y_0,h_x,h_y) = \{(x_i,y_j) \mid x_i = x_0+ih_x , y_j = y_0+jh_y ;$

i and j are integers$\}$.

A grid $G = G(D;x_0,y_0;h_x,h_y)$ is the intersection of the domain D and the lattice $L(x_0,y_0;h_x,h_y)$. From the data-structure point of view, it does not matter whether this is an independent uniform grid or a subgrid in a composite structure. A grid is organized either by columns or by rows. The column i is the set of grid points of the form (x_i,y) ; the row j is the set of grid points (x,y_j) . The construction order is said to be vertical (horizontal) if the points of every column (row) are stored consecutively. For definiteness we will describe the vertical construction.

Every (non-empty) column i in a grid can be described as a sequence of "point-strings" (or simply "strings" or "intervals") $s_{i1},s_{i2},\ldots,s_{ik_i}$. Each string $s_{i\ell}$ is a sequence of consecutive grid points,

(4.2) $s_{i\ell} = ((x_i,y_{j_{i\ell}}) , (x_i,y_{j_{i\ell}+1}),\ldots,(x_i,y_{\bar{j}_{i\ell}}))$,

where $\bar{j}_{i\ell} < j_{i,\ell+1}$. Normally, the number of strings is kept to the minimum, so that in fact $\bar{j}_{i\ell}+1 < j_{i,\ell+1}$. Similarly, the grid itself can be described as a sequence of column-strings $S_1,S_2,\ldots,S_k$, where each column-string S_ℓ is a sequence of consecutive non-empty grid columns.

(4.3) $S_\ell = (i_\ell,i_\ell+1,\ldots,\bar{i}_\ell)$,

with $\bar{i}_\ell < i_{\ell+1}$ (normally in fact $\bar{i}_\ell+1 < i_{\ell+1}$) .

4.2   The QUAD Structure.

Each grid has a "grid number". All the grids are organized in two general vectors ("garbage-collectors"), the L space for all logical and integer data (mainly pointers), and the Q space for type-real data (mainly numerical values of the grid functions).

The basis of the system is the description of each sequence of strings as a chain of quads (integer quadruples), where each string is represented by a quad of the form

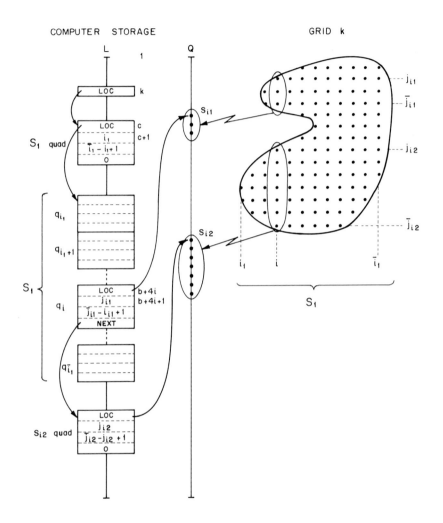

FIGURE 2.   QUAD Structure

Shown is a typical grid, number k, with its computer
storage. The grid has one column-string S_1. Of all its
columns, details are shown only for one typical column i,
which contains two point-strings (s_{i1} and s_{i2}).

(4.4)   QUAD = | LOC | INDEX | LENGTH | NEXT |

LOC is the location where the string is stored (in the L
space if it is a logical string, or in the Q space if it is
a string of numerical values). INDEX and LENGTH describe
the lattice position of the string. INDEX is its first
index ($j_{i\ell}$ for the string (4.2), or i_ℓ for the string
(4.3)) and LENGTH is its length ($\bar{j}_{i\ell} - j_{i\ell}+1$ or $\bar{i}_\ell - i_\ell+1$,
respectively). NEXT is the location (in L) of the next quad
in the chain; NEXT = 0 if the present quad is the last in
its chain. A quad is called a point-quad or a column-quad
according to whether it describes a point-string or a column-
string.

Thus each column in the grid is described by a chain of
point-quads. The first quad in the column i is called q_i .
The q_i quads of the same column-string S_ℓ are stored
consecutively in their natural order $q_{i_\ell}, q_{i_\ell+1}, \ldots, q_{\bar{i}_\ell}$, and
the location in the L space of the first of them (q_{i_ℓ})
appears in the LOC position of the column-quad describing this
column-string. The chain of all column-quads describes the
entire grid, and the first column-quad is accessible through
the grid number N_G ; e.g., its location can be $L(L(N_G))$,
where $L(N_G) = 0$ if the grid N_G has not been defined. Also
directly accessible by N_G are lists of various grid parameters, such as x_0, y_0, h_x, h_y, N_f (number of functions defined
on the grid), a flag showing the construction order, etc.

This QUAD structure of grids is very flexible. Each
string can reside anywhere in the L or Q space and its
length is therefore easily changed, by reconstructing it in a
new location if necessary. After many changes of this type,
many gaps (unused locations) may appear in the Q (or L)
space. When the gaps accumulate to a serious proportion, they
may easily be eliminated by one pass of "grids-compactification"
which is very inexpensive relative to the numerical processes
that create those gaps (e.g., processes of grid adaptation,
involving at least a couple of relaxation sweeps over the
grids).

The QUAD structure is relatively inexpensive since a group of four integers represents a whole string of data values.

Moreover, this structure is very efficient in sweeping over a grid. If the sweep is made in the construction lines (e.g., in columns when the construction is vertical), then it can be made in terms of efficient singly indexed DO loops. To sweep so efficiently in the other direction too, one can transpose the grid (see Section 4.3), which is inexpensive compared with the work of a relaxation sweep. The QUAD structure may be somewhat inefficient in separately accessing a single grid-point (in the unusual situation where several strings are to be scanned in a chain before the desired one is reached), but all MLAT processes are sweep processes and an isolated access to a point is seldom needed.

As a simple example, consider the quite usual case of a single-stringed grid (i.e., a grid with only one column-string, and only one point-string in each column) with one grid function u. The value $u(x_i, y_j)$ will then be stored as $Q(a_i + j)$, where

$$a_i = L(b+4i) - L(b+4i+1) \quad,$$

(4.5)
$$b = L(c) - 4L(c+1) \quad,$$

$$c = L(L(N_G))$$

(cf. Figure 2. Note that $L(c)$ is the address of q_{i_1} and $L(c+1) = i_1$, hence $b+4i$ is the address of q_i). In performing a sweep, the values c, b and a_i are successively determined, and the most efficient access to $u(x_i, y_j)$ is obtained (especially for column-wise sweeps, where throughout a column a_i can be used as a constant rather than a vector, and j can be used as the indexed parameter of fast DO loops).

4.3 GRIDPACK Routines.

Once the data structure of a general uniform grid has been fixed, many grid operations can be programmed once for all. This includes the operation of creating (or defining) grids, extending and contracting grids, transferring or inter-polating value from one grid to another, etc., operations which are common to MLAT and many other grid applications.

A system of such programs, called GRIDPACK, has been developed in the Weizmann Institute and in the IBM T.J. Watson Research Center. The important routines are listed below, sometimes slightly simplified for the sake of clarity.

INIT - Initialization routine. Get parameters from the user and set up the L and Q spaces.

LGRDCR(K,XO,YO,HX,HY,NF,IC,X1,X2,Y1,Y2,CHAR) - create logical grid structure given the characteristic function CHAR(x,y). A logical structure is the collection of quads describing the grid. It does not include allocation of Q space, which can later be done by other routines (QSPACE or POINTO). Thus the LOC positions in the point-quads remain undefined in this routine. The grid whose logical structure is created here is G(D;XO,YO;HX,HY) , and the grid number assigned to it is K. Its domain D is defined by

$$D = \{(x,y) \mid X1 \leqslant x \leqslant X2 , Y1 \leqslant y \leqslant Y2 , CHAR(x,y) = 1\} .$$

NF is the number of functions to be defined on the grid, and IC is the index of construction order (IC = 1 if vertical, IC = 0 if horizontal).

LGRD2F(K,XO,YO,HX,HY,NF,IC,X1,X2,F1,F2) - create logical grid structure given the 2 functions F1(x) , F2(x) . Similar to LGRDCR , except that the domain is defined by

$$D = \{(x,y) \mid X1 \leqslant x \leqslant X2 , F1(x) \leqslant y \leqslant F2(x)\} .$$

DELETE(K) - Delete logical structure K (by setting L(K) = 0).

LCOARS(K,M) - Create logical grid structure (number M) which is the 2:1 coarsening of grid K .

LUNION(K,M,N) - Create logical union of two grids: $N = K \cup M$. It is assumed here, and in the next two routines, that the lattices of grids K and M coincide. In case the routine is called with N = K , it simply serves to extend K , by the (usually small) piece M .

LSECT(K,M,N) - Create logical intersection: $N = K \cap M$.

LMINUS(K,M,N) - Create logical difference: N = K - M. In case N = K , the routine serves to contract grid K . The last three routines, together with LGRDCR and LGRD2F , give us convenient tools to adapt grids.

LTPOSE(K,M) - Create logical transpose: $M = K^T$; i.e., created
    is a logical structure (number M) which describes the
    same grid as number K , but in the opposite construc-
    tion order.

LINNER(K,M,T) - Create the logical structure of grid M which
    is the inner part of grid K relative to the templet
    T ; i.e., a grid-point of grid M is every grid point
    of K such that all its T-neighborhood is in K . Using
    this routine and LMINUS we can create a grid containing
    only the boundary points of K .

QSPACE(K) - Allocate Q storage to grid K , and accordingly
    supply the LOC pointers in its point-quads.

QOFF(K) - Delete Q storage previously allocated to grid K .

PØINTØ(K,M) - Point the logical structure of grid K   (i.e.,
    its LOC pointers) to the corresponding locations in
    the numerical storage of grid M . Usually grid K
    will represent a subgrid of M , created for example
    by calling LSECT(K,N,M)   or   LMINUS(K,N,M)   or
    LINNER(M,K,T) . These routines thus enable us to
    operate on a proper part of a grid. For example, we
    can make partial relaxation (see Section 1.4) using
    our one and only relaxation routine, by supplying it
    with a grid number K which is a subgrid of grid M .

    The above routines deal with pointers only. The amount
of computer work in performing each of them, except for
LTPØSE and LGRDCR, is at most O(q) , where q is the total
number of quads (or strings) in the grids involved. In
LTPØSE the work is O(q log q) since it is necessary to sort
the end points $(i_{jℓ}, \bar{i}_{jℓ})$ of the strings. In LGRDCR the
function CHAR(x,y) should be calculated at all lattice
points in the square [X1,X2] × [Y1,Y2] . The next seven
routines handle the numerical data itself, and the work is
O(q) plus the actual work of data transfer, which is proportional to the number of points receiving the data.

TFER(K,M) - Transfer numerical values from grid K to grid M,
    where the two grids are assumed to be from the same
    lattice and have the same construction order.

TFERTP(K,M) - The same, when the two grids are in t̲ran̲s̲p̲osed order.

PUTSC(K,J,C) - P̲ut̲ the s̲calar c̲onstant C into the J-th grid-function defined on grid K .

PUTSF(K,J,F) - P̲ut̲ the s̲calar f̲unction F(x,y) into the J-th grid-function defined on K .

CTF(K,M) - C̲oarse t̲o f̲ine transfer: transfer from grid K to grid M , where the lattice of K is the 2:1 coarsening of the lattice of M .

FTC(K,M) - F̲ine t̲o c̲oarse transfer.

INTERP(K,M,I) - Perform I-order i̲nterp̲olation from grid K to grid M . This routine is the most difficult to implement. Even in the simplest case of bilinear interpolation (I=2) there are many possible cases to be considered regarding the relative positions of the K points, the M points and the boundary. Abnormal situations may arise, especially with very coarse grids or near special boundary configurations, in which the desired order of interpolation is difficult to achieve because not enough points of K are available. Non-standard (e.g., non-central) interpolation formulas should then be tried in various ways, and at some special points we may be forced to use lower-order interpolation. This routine therefore is, and for some time will continue to be, still in the process of development. In the first stage we program interpolation subroutines that use only grid-function data, without using boundary conditions. This leads to one-sided interpolation formulas near the boundary, which is not much worse than using boundary-conditions, and does not require the user to communicate boundary conditions and boundary locations to the interpolation routine. Also we restrict ourselves in the first stage to the standard case where the coarse lattice lines coincide with every other line of the fine lattice. Thus far bilinear interpolation has been implemented and general-order interpolation is being programmed.

KEYS(K,I1,I2,J1,J2,JR) - Give the user the key to single-
    stringed grid K , by assigning I1 , I2 and the
    vectors J1 , J2 , JR . I1 and I2 are the
    lattice positions of the first and the last column,
    respectively. J1(IR+i) and J2(IR+i) are the
    lattice positions (the row numbers) of the first and
    last grid-points in column i , with IR = 1-I1 .
    JR(IR+i) gives a relative location in Q for
    accessing column i . For example, if only one func-
    tion u is defined on grid K , JR is loaded so that

(4.6) $u_{ij} = u(x_i,y_j) = Q(JR(IR+i)+j)$.

KEYG - Give a similar key, but to general grids. The list of
    parameters is longer than in KEYS , but one easily
    gets used to it and in practice it is as effective as
    (4.6).

PARMG(K,XO,YO,HX,HY,...) - Give the listed parameters of grid
    K . This, together with the KEY routines give the
    user a convenient way to write routines in which the
    grid number is a parameter.

MULTIG(X1,X2,Y1,Y2,CHAR,XO,YO,HXO,HYO,M,TOL,WØRK,LL,ETA,DELTA,
    RELAX,RESCAL) - An example of a driving routine for
    multi-grid solution. X1,X2,Y1,Y2 and CHAR specify
    the domain, as in LGRDCR above. M grids will be
    defined on this domain, the lattice of grid K being

    $L(XO,YO ; HXO*2^{-K} , HYO*2^{-K})$ $(0 \leqslant K \leqslant M-1)$.
    The multi-grid algorithm of Section 1.3 will be
    affected, using the routines RELAX and RESCAL ,
    which should be written by the user. RELAX(K,ERR)
    should be a routine that performs a relaxation sweep
    (and therefore also defines the difference equations,
    including boundary conditions) and outputs the error
    norm ERR . It should be written for a general grid
    number K . By this we mean that grid functions should
    be written in their Q form, as in (4.6), and that the
    corresponding KEYS or KEYG routine is called at
    the beginning. RESCAL(K) is a routine that compute
    the residuals in a fine grid K+1 and transfer them
    to the coarser grid K (cf. (1.16)). Since residuals

are computed in the course of relaxation, RESCAL
can always be written as a trivial variation of
RELAX . The driving routine MULTIG terminates when
the error ERR on grid M is smaller than TOL , or
when the amount of Work Units exceeds WORK . ETA
and DELTA are the switching parameters η and δ ,
respectively, discussed in Section 1.4, and LL is
the order of the differential equation (ℓ) .

DISPLAY(K,...) - Display grid K , or a function defined on it,
as specified by the routine parameters, which also
control the format of the outprinted table. It is
also possible to display several grids, one on top of
the other, to show their relative positions.

DUMPQL - Dump the Q and L collectors, mainly for debugging
purposes.

4.4 Fortran Preprocessor.

With the above GRIDPACK system, grid control (creation
and adaptation) is facilitated, and the programming of multi-
grid solutions is essentially reduced to the writing of a
usual relaxation routine (RELAX). To simplify even further
the task of sweeping over grids (e.g., in RELAX), we plan a
Fortran preprocessor which will allow the user to add to his
Fortran programs certain grid macro-statements, including calls
to GRIDPACK routines. Typical macro-statements are the
following:

DO 5 I = I1,I2,ΔI - The usual DO statement, except that
neither I1 nor I2 , nor the increment ΔI , must
be positive, and they may each be represented by an
arithmetic expression.

DO 5 (I,J) = GRID(K),ΔI,ΔJ,$K_1(I_1,J_1)$,$K_2(I_2,J_2)$,... - The row
index I and the column index J traverse all posi-
tions of grid number K , in its construction order
and in (negative or positive) increments ΔI and ΔJ,
while (I_ℓ,J_ℓ) simultaneously traverse the corresponding positions on grid K_ℓ , $(\ell = 1,2,...)$. K
and K_ℓ may be either particular or general grid
numbers. The preprocessor will replace this statement
with suitable calls to KEY routines followed by

suitable Fortran DO statements.

DO 5 I = COLS(K),ΔI,K$_1$(I$_1$),K$_2$(I$_2$),... - I traverses the <u>colum</u>ns of grid K , in increments ΔI , while I$_\ell$ traverses the corresponding columns of grid K$_\ell$ (ℓ = 1,2,...) .

DO 5 J = ROWS(K),ΔJ,K$_1$(J$_1$),K$_2$(J$_2$),... - Similar.

DO 5 J = COL(I,K),ΔJ,K$_1$(J$_1$),K$_2$(J$_2$),... - J traverses the grid points (X$_I$,Y$_J$) of <u>col</u>umn I in grid K , in increments ΔJ , while J$_\ell$ traverses the corresponding points of grid K$_\ell$.

K(I,J) = K(I+1,J)+K(I-1,J)+K(I,J+1)+K(I,J-1)+K$_1$(I$_1$,J$_1$) - A typical statement (Gauss-Seidal relaxation step for the 5-point Poisson equation, in this example) to appear inside the above DO loops.

IF((I+1,J).IN.K)GOTO 5 - Test whether the (I+1,J) lattice position is <u>in</u> grid K .

IF((I,J).IN(T).K)GOTO 5 - Test whether the T neighborhood of (I,J) is in grid K , where T is a "templet".

T = TEMPLET((0,0),(0,1),(1,0),(-1,0),(0,-1)) - Define the templet (neighborhood) T to be, in this example, the standard 5-points neighborhood.

In addition to these macros, the calls to GRIDPACK routines will be made in a more direct fashion. For example, N = UNION(K,M) will be used instead of CALL UNION(K,M,N) .

REFERENCES

1. A. Brandt [1972], Multi-level adaptive technique (MLAT) for fast numerical solutions to boundary value problems, Proc. 3rd Int. Conf. Numerical Methods in Fluid Mechanics (Paris, 1972), Lecture Notes in Physics 18, Springer Verlag, Berlin, pp. 82-89.

2. _____ [1976], Multi-level adaptive techniques (MLAT). I. The multi-grid method. IBM Research Report RC6026, IBM T.J. Watson Research Center, Yorktown Heights, New York 10598.

3. _____ [1977], Multi-level adaptive solutions to - boundary-value problems, Math. Comp. 31, pp. 333-390.

4. R. P. Fedorenko [1964], The speed of convergence for one iterative process, Zh. vychisl. Mat. mat. Fiz. 4, pp. 559-564.

5. F. G. Gustavson [1976], Implementation of the multi-grid method for solving partial differential equations, 1976 IBM Symposium on Mathematics & Computation - Editor, H. Crowder, October 6-8, 1976. IBM T.J. Watson Research Center, Yorktown Heights, New York 10598, Report RA82 (#26690), 9/24/76, pp. 51-57.

6. Y. Shiftan [1972], Multi-grid method for solving elliptic difference equations, M.Sc. Thesis (in Hebrew), Weizmann Institute of Science, Rehovot, Israel.

7. R. V. Southwell [1935], Stress calculation in frameworks by the method of systematic relaxation of constraints, Parts I and II, Proc. Roy. Soc. (A) 151, pp.56-95.

8. G. Starius [1974], Construction of orthogonal curvilinear meshes by solving initial value problems, Uppsala Univ. Dept. of Computer Sciences, Report No. 61.

9. D.M. Young [1972], Iterative solution of large linear systems, Academic Press, New York, 570 pp.

The research reported here was partly supported by the Israel Commission for Basic Research. Part of the research was conducted at the Tomas J. Watson IBM Research Center, Yorktown Heights, New York. Part of it was also conducted at the Institute for Computer Applications in Science and Engineering (ICASE), NASA Langley Research Center, Hampton, Virginia.

Department of Mathematics
The Weizmann Institute of Science
Rehovot, Israel

ELLPACK: A Research Tool for Elliptic Partial Differential Equations Software

John R. Rice

ABSTRACT

This paper gives the objectives and outlines the technical structure of the ELLPACK project. This project is a cooperative effort to provide a research tool for the evaluation and development of software for the solution of elliptic partial differential equations. The first goal is ELLPACK 77 which is restricted to rectangular geometry in two and three dimensions. ELLPACK 77 has a preprocessor which accepts problems stated in a simple form and it provides a variety of alternatives for operator approximations and linear equation solution. Its structure and the guidelines for the preparation of a module for ELLPACK are discussed. The second goal, ELLPACK 78 is to allow general geometry and provide a variety of enhancements. Finally, the implementation of the ELLPACK preprocessor is described.

1. <u>BACKGROUND</u>. In the summer of 1975, Garrett Birkhoff started discussing the possibility of a cooperative effort to develop and evaluate software for elliptic partial differential equations. In the summer of 1976, James Ortega organized a small meeting of interested parties to explore various viewpoints and possibilities for this idea. Those in attendance were

G. Birkhoff	Harvard University
A. Brandt	Weizman Institute
G. Fix	Carnegie-Mellon University
A. George	University of Waterloo
G. Golub	Stanford University
J. Ortega	Institute for Computer Applications to Science and Engineering
J. Rice	Purdue University
M. Schultz	Yale University
R. Sweet	National Center for Atmospheric Research and University of Denver
R. Varga	Kent State University
O. Widlund	New York University
D. Young	University of Texas.

Two days of discussion showed there was mutual interest in a cooperative effort and a framework was outlined which seemed to accommodate a number of people's work and interests. The two initial projects discussed later were agreed upon and John R. Rice was selected as coordinator and benevolent dictator for the ELLPACK effort.

The ELLPACK organization is completely voluntary. Purdue University will provide the software framework and define the structure precisely. Contributors can prepare programs which fit into this framework and Purdue will incorporate them into ELLPACK. It is assumed that contributors will submit high quality, portable programs to ease the burden of integrating programs into ELLPACK.

1.A. ELLPACK Objectives. The primary objective of ELLPACK is as a tool for research in the evaluation and development of numerical methods for solving elliptic partial differential equations. Various software components can be interchanged and the resulting performance (accuracies, efficiencies, etc.) can be measured. A person primarily interested in one aspect of the problem (e.g. operator approximation, linear equation solution, geometric difficulties) can use other people's software for those aspects where he has less interest and expertise.

ELLPACK's use as a research tool requires its framework
to be convenient, flexible and modular. Thus it will be
suitable for educational use and students will be able to
see how various methods perform on various kinds of problems.
Similarly, ELLPACK may be of considerable use to others who
have easy or moderately difficult problems. It is not
intended that ELLPACK be directly applicable to the very
complex applications (e.g. temperature distribution in a
nuclear power plant or in a rentry vehicle). Nevertheless,
the ability to quickly solve a variety of moderately complex
problems should be valuable in many areas.

It is plausible to expect that if ELLPACK is successful
then someone will use it as the basis for user oriented,
production quality software. That is, someone can select
those components that have proven most effective and build
a software system from them which is more reliable, can
handle larger problems and is more efficient. This even-
tuality is some years in the future.

1.B. Short Term Objectives. The first project is ELLPACK 77
where many of the programs will merely be adaptations of
existing programs. Even so, it will be a complete package
with a reasonable user interface and capable of solving a
range of interesting problems. One of its primary objectives is to test the concept of a modular approach using
interchangeable software parts.

ELLPACK 77 is restricted to rectangular geometry in 2
or 3 dimensions. Anticipated capabilities include:

Operator Approximation

2-Dimensions: 5-point star, 9-point star, Collocation
               and Galerkin with Hermite cubics

3-Dimensions: 7 point star, 27-point star

Special Options: Poisson Problem, Constant Coefficients,
               Self Adjoint Form.

Equation Solution

Direct Elimination (Band or Profile)

Nested Dissection

"Fast" Methods (Tensor Product and FFT)

SOR, Accelerated Jacobi, etc.

Conjugate Gradient

The second project is ELLPACK 78 which is hoped to
contain most of the capabilities of ELLPACK, at least in
some form. The primary extension is to non-rectangular
geometry, an area where some group members are already
active. Other directions which may be followed include:

    a.   Standard, automatic changes of variables

    b.   Enhancement of rectangular domain capabilities

    c.   More operator approximations, e.g.

           HODIE methods, Hermite cubics in 3 dimensions,
           Method of particular solutions, Capacitance
              methods

    d.   More equation solvers, e.g.

           Cyclic Chebyshev, Automated selection of
           SOR parameters

    e. Parallel processor implementation

It is hoped that a significant part of these capabilities
will be implemented by late 1978. At that point the ELLPACK
effort will be evaluated and future efforts, if any,
considered.

1.C. <u>Technical Operation</u>. The framework and ELLPACK
specifications are specified at Purdue University. Careful
attention is given to making ELLPACK compatible with a wide
range of interests and to making it "easy" to contribute to
ELLPACK. On the other hand, success depends on certain
uniform standards and conventions and there is no doubt that
choices will be made which some contributors find inconve-
nient. It is assumed that contributors are experienced in
producing portable, understandable and good quality software.
The main technical document is the <u>Contributor's Guide to
ELLPACK</u> [Rice, 1976] which defines the ELLPACK environment
for a potential contributor. There is also a shorter <u>User's
Guide</u> [Rice, 1977] and a guide to implementing ELLPACK at
locations other than Purdue.

The remainder of this paper outlines the structures and
use of the ELLPACK system. The next section describes the

general structure of ELLPACK. Sections 3 and 4 specifically
consider ELLPACK 77; we describe the user input and how
modules are incorporated into the system. The following
section discusses more briefly the analogous topics as
anticipated for ELLPACK 78. Finally, there is a brief
description of the ELLPACK preprocessor and its implementation.

2. <u>THE STRUCTURE OF ELLPACK</u>. The basic organization of
ELLPACK is illustrated by the diagram in Figure 1.

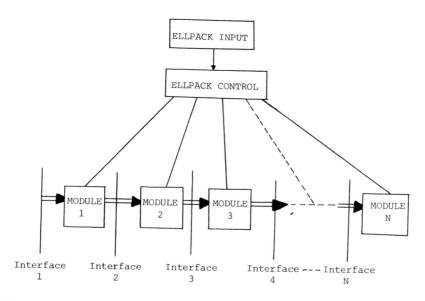

<u>Figure 1</u>. Basic organization of ELLPACK. The interfaces,
         rather than the modules, are the primary struc-
         tural features of ELLPACK.

The INPUT contains the problem description and computational
instructions and they are translated into internal information for the run. The CONTROL actually invokes the requested
ELLPACK modules. As suggested by Figure 1, the simplest case
is straight successive execution of several modules which
result in an approximate solution of the problem. Note,
however, that <u>the interfaces are the fixed points of the</u>
<u>structure</u>. A module may start at one interface and stop at

any later one. The information at any interface is not
destroyed or modified by the execution of any "later" modules.
Thus once one sequence of modules is executed to establish
the interface information, then other modules may be executed
starting at intermediate interfaces. In simple terms this
allows for one ELLPACK run to form a system of equations
once and then use several equation solvers for this system.

We describe three aspects of ELLPACK: the information
structure, storage allocation and execution sequencing.
There are four parts of the information structure of an
ELLPACK run.

Problem Definition: This is a combination of simple variables, arrays (some of variable length) and coefficient functions (embedded in Fortran subroutines) which completely
define the problem under consideration, including the
specification of rectangular grid.

Control Information: This is a small set of variables which
specify various control features. For example, there is an
output level selection and a switch for timing modules.

Workspace: Space is declared which any module may use on a
temporary basis. This storage is safe only during the execution of a single module.

Interface Definitions: This is a combination of simple
variables and arrays (with problem dependent sizes) which
are established by ELLPACK control. This information is
maintained at all times during the run but the content may
be modified with the output from the execution of various
modules.

The allocation of storage is done by ELLPACK control
in three ways:

Standard Fixed Length Information: Many variables must be
available on all ELLPACK runs and these are placed in a
labeled block COMMON which every module may access. This
includes various switches, the number of grid lines, etc.

Variable Length Information: Arrays whose lengths are
problem dependent are declared by ELLPACK control and passed
to modules as arguments. ELLPACK control computes the size
of these arrays for any module from formulas of the module

contributor which are in terms of problem definition parameters. If several modules involve the same interface then
the maximum required storage is allocated for each array.
Workspace Information: This is placed in blank COMMON for
each module to use as it pleases. Each module contributor
must specify the size of the workspace in terms of the
problem definition parameters. The amount of workspace
allocated is the maximum of all the modules' requirements.

The execution of an ELLPACK run occurs in the following
sequence:

1. ELLPACK input: (a)   Read and process the user input.
                     (b)   Print the problem statement plus
                               any diagnostics.
                     (c)   Create Fortran programs for
                               (i)   functions involved in the
                                       problem definition
                           (ii)   ELLPACK control
2. Fortran compiler: Compiles the programs from ELLPACK
                          input.
3. System loader: Loads the compiled programs plus all the
                       modules needed for this run. The modules
                       are already compiled and in the ELLPACK
                       library.
4. Execution of the resulting job.
Note that Fortran programs are created from the ELLPACK input
by inserting statements and values into "template" programs
which already have their structure and form determined.

The execution of a job is essentially done by executing
a sequence of subprograms. Some checking is done by ELLPACK
control to detect illegal sequences of modules, but the
final responsibility rests on the user to specify a valid
computational sequence.

A schematic chart of the processing of an ELLPACK run
is given in Figure 2. Examination of the sample ELLPACK
program in the next section should help clarify the processing.

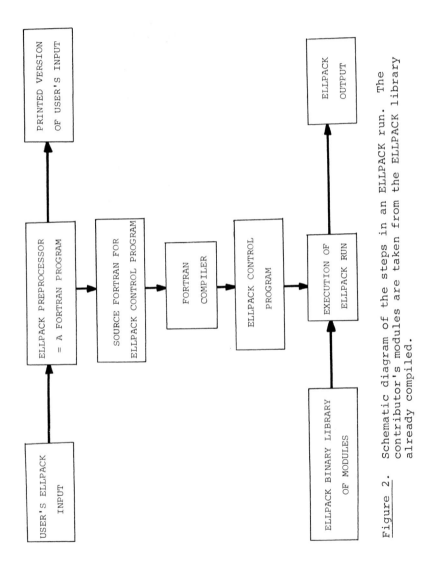

Figure 2. Schematic diagram of the steps in an ELLPACK run. The contributor's modules are taken from the ELLPACK library already compiled.

3. ELLPACK 77 USER INPUT. The user defines a problem to be
solved (including a fixed grid to be used) and then specifies
a combination of modules to be used in its solution. The basic
elements in ELLPACK are segments and we list the segment types
along with a brief indication of their use. An example
ELLPACK 77 program is given at the end of this section.

Group 1: Must appear (only once) and be before any from
Group 2.

EQUATION. Specifies the partial differential equation.

BOUNDARY. Specifies the domain and the boundary conditions
           to be satisfied.

GRID.   Specifies the rectangular grid in the domain.

Group 2: May be used as needed and repeated if desired.

DISCRETIZATION. Specifies the method to discretize the equa-
                 tions and to generate the linear equations.

INDEXING.   Places the equations generated by the
                 discretization module in some desired order
                 for further processing.

SOLUTION.   Actually solves a linear system of equations.

OUTPUT.   Provides various requested information.

Group 3: May appear anywhere and as often as desired.

*   A comment.

OPTIONS. Specifies various options selected.

FORTRAN. Contains Fortran subprogram used by other segments.

Group 4: Must appear after all Group 2 segments.

SEQUENCE. Specifies the sequence for the Group 2 segments
           to be used.

Every ELLPACK program ends with the segment END.

The segments are identified in the input by starting in
column 1. A period in column 1 signals that the previous line
is continued (only 400 non-blank characters are allowed in a
segment). A "C" following FORTRAN is taken as a Fortran
comment and not as signalling a new segment. All the segments
except GRID have abbreviated names. Tags may be added to
Group 2 segments to differentiate segments of the same type.

     Most of the features of ELLPACK 77 input are illustrated
in the example of Figure 3. Note that ELLPACK 77 is heavily
key-word oriented. However, one must be aware that some

```
*                   ELLPACK77 EXAMPLE   -   MARCH 18, 1977
*
OPTIONS.            DEBUG = 2
*
EQUATION. UXX$ +6.UY$ -X**2 UX$ + 1./(X+DUB9(Y))  U = COS(Y*X)
*
BOUND.   X = 0.0      ,  U = 0.0
         Y = 1.0      ,  UY = X
         X = EXP(1.)  ,  U = FXP(Y)
         Y = 0.0      ,  MIXED = (1.2)U  (COS(X+.2))UY = EXP(X)
*
GRID.            UNIFORM X = 7
                 NGRIDY = 11,  0., 0.08, 0.16, 0.24, 0.35, 0.46, 0.575, 0.7, 0.8
                               125, 0.925, 1.0
*
DISCRETIZATION.  5-POINT STAR
*
INDEX(1).        NATURAL
INDEX(2).        RED-BLACK
*
SOL.             SOR1
*
OUTPUT(AA).      PLOT-TRUE   $ PLOT-DOMAIN
OUT(B)           PLOT-ERROR  $ MAX-ERROR
OUTPUT(99).      TABLE(5,5) = U
*
OPTIONS.         TIME  $ MEMORY
*
SEQUENCE. OUTPUT(AA) $ DIS $ INDEX(1) $ SOLUTION $ OUTPUT(B)
                              INDEX(2) $ SOLUTION $ OUTPUT(B)
                              OUTPUT(99)

FORTRAN.
     FUNCTION TRUF(X,Y)
     TRUF = FXP(X+Y)/(1.+DUB9(Y))**2
     RETURN
     END
     FUNCTION DUB9(T)
     DUB9 = T*(T+.5)*EXP(T/(1.+T*COS(T)))
     RETURN
     END

END.
```

Figure 3. A sample ELLPACK 77 program which illustrates the nature
of the language.

(many) modules might not take cognizance of certain key-
words. For example, one might indicate a Poisson problem by
the key-word POISSON and some modules will have no provisions
to take advantage of this fact. Standard naming conventions
are used such as referring to the solution as U and its
various derivatives as UX, UYY, etc. The coordinates are
always called X, Y and Z. See [Rice, 1977] for the
detailed syntax of the ELLPACK segments and further explanation.

4. ELLPACK 77 ORGANIZATION AND INFORMATION. The modules
and interfaces for ELLPACK 77 are shown in Figure 4.

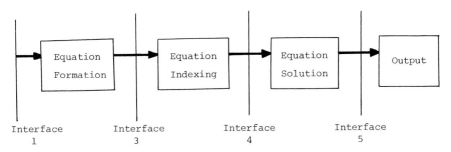

Figure 4.   The basic modules and interfaces for ELLPACK 77.
             Interface 2 will appear in ELLPACK 78.

The items to be specified are:
          General and control information
          Information for each interface
          Workspace
There is a standard framework for the regions illustrated
in Figure 5. Note that the user does not use this framework,
but all the modules do.

4.1. General and Control Information. This information
consists of three types: Fortran functions, variables placed
in labeled COMMON blocks and arrays to be passed as arguments.
This information is described primarily in terms of the
Fortran code that appears. The function supplied for the
definition of the partial differential equation coefficients
is

```
SUBROUTINE PDE(X,Y,CVALUS)
C       TWO DIMENSIONS
C       VALUES OF EQUATION COEFFICIENTS AT (X,Y) IN THE ORDER
C       UXX, UXY, UYY, UX, UY, U, RIGHT SIDE
REAL CVALUS(7)
C
C
SUBROUTINE PDE(X,Y,Z,CVALUS)
C       THREE DIMENSIONS
C       VALUES OF EQUATION COEFFICIENTS AT (X,Y,7) IN THE ORDER
C       UXX,UXY,UYY,UXZ,UYZ,UZZ,UX,UY,UZ,U, RIGHT SIDE
REAL CVALUS(11)
```

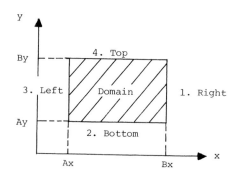

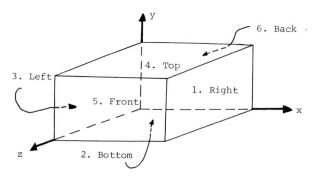

Figure 5.   The standard two and three dimensional domains.
The sides are indexed by the numbers 1 to 6 as
shown and the intervals (Ax,Bx), (Ay,By) and
(Az,Bz) define the domain.

For the self adjoint form of the equations the two functions
p and q in $(p(x,y)u_x)_x + (q(x,y)u_y)_y$ are identified with
UXX and UYY in the subroutine PDE. The subroutine PDE is
constructed even for constant coefficients, however these
constants are also placed in labeled COMMON and modules may
take values from there. These COMMON blocks are, for two
and three dimensions, respectively:

```
COMMON / CPDE / CUXX,CUXY,CUYY,CUX,CUY,CU
COMMON / CPDE / CUXX,CUXY,CUYY,CUX,CUY,CU,CUXZ,CUYZ,CUZZ,CUZ
```

The linear boundary conditions are defined by

```
      FUNCTION BCOND(I,X,Y,BVALUS)
C         TWO DIMENSIONS
C         VALUES OF BOUNDARY CONDITION COEFFICIENTS ON SIDE I AT (X,Y)
C         IN THE ORDER
C             U, UX, UY, RIGHT SIDE
      REAL BVALUS(4)
C
C
      FUNCTION BCOND(I,X,Y,Z,BVALUS)
C         THREE DIMENSIONS
C         VALUES OF BOUNDARY CONDITION COEFFICIENTS ON SIDE I AT (X,Y,Z)
C         IN THE ORDER
C             U, UX, UY, UZ, RIGHT SIDE
      REAL BVALUS(5)
```

Providing both the side index I and the point coordinates x
and y is slightly redundant. It provides for more natural
programming and, more importantly, it is compatible with the
more general domains of ELLPACK 78.

A variety of information about the problem definition
is placed in COMMON/PROB/ as shown below.

```
      COMMON / PROB / DIM2,DIM3,POISON,LAPLAC,CONSTC,SELFAD,CROSST,
     A                DIRICH,NEUMAN,MIXED,AX,BX,AY,BY,AZ,BZ,
     B                NGRIDX,NGRIDY,NGRIDZ,UNIFRM,HX,HY,HZ
C
      LOGICAL DIM2,DIM3,POISON,LAPLAC,CONSTC,SELFAD,CROSST,
     A        DIRICH,NEUMAN,MIXED,UNIFRM
      INTEGER NGRIDX,NGRIDY,NGRIDZ
      REAL HX,HY,HZ,AX,BX,AY,BY,AZ,BZ
C
C         DIM2   = TRUE FOR A TWO-DIMENSIONAL PROBLEM
C         DIM3   = TRUE FOR A THREE-DIMENSIONAL PROBLEM
C         POISON = TRUE FOR THE POISSON PROBLEM
C         LAPLAC = TRUE FOR THE LAPLACE EQUATION
C         CONSTC = TRUE FOR A CONSTANT COEFFICIENTS EQUATION
C         SELFAD = TRUE FOR AN EQUATION WRITTEN IN SELF-ADJOINT FORM
C         CROSST = TRUE FOR AN EQUATION WITH A UXY TERM IN IT
C         DIRICH = TRUE FOR DIRICHLET BOUNDARY CONDITIONS
C         NEUMAN = TRUE FOR NEUMANN BOUNDARY CONDITIONS
C         MIXED  = TRUE FOR GENERAL MIXED BOUNDARY CONDITIONS
C         UNIFRM = TRUE FOR UNIFORM GRID SPACING
C         NGRIDX,NGRIDY,NGRIDZ = NUMBER OF X,Y,Z GRID LINES INCLUDING EDGES
C
C         HX,HY,HZ = X,Y,Z GRID SPACING FOR UNIFORM GRIDS
C         AX,BX,AY,BY,AZ,BZ  = END POINTS OF INTERVALS DEFINING DOMAIN
```

There are two or three arrays from the problem definition
which define the rectangular grid. These are specified below

```
C         ARRAYS THAT DEFINE THE RECTANGULAR GRID
C            GRIDX(I), I = 1,NGRIDX  GRIDY(I), I = 1,NGRIDY
C         THE INPUT MODULE DECLARES THE ACTUAL DIMENSIONS, THE
C         ARRAYS SHOULD BE USED IN THE MODULES AS FOLLOWS
C
      REAL GRIDX(NGRDXD),GRIDY(NGRDYD),GRIDZ(NGRDZD)
```

Finally, there is one array, BCTYPE, which is of fixed
length for ELLPACK 77 (but which becomes variable for
ELLPACK 78) which indicates the type of the boundary condition on the various sides of the domain.

```
C        BCTYPE = INDICATORS OF BOUNDARY CONDITION TYPE FOR I=1,4 OR 1,6
C               = 1 FOR DIRICHLET
C               = 2 FOR NEUMANN
C               = 3 FOR MIXED
C               = 4 FOR SYMMETRIC REFLECTION
C               = 5 FOR NATURAL
C               = 6 FOR PERIODIC
```

This completes the definition of the problem. There
are other variables of a general nature in the common block
CONTRL. One should consult [Rice, 1976] for complete details
of the ELLPACK 77 specification.

4.2. Interface 1: Initial Situation. At this interface all
of the general and control information of Section 4.1 is
defined. Since no module executes in front of this interface,
this information cannot be changed during a run.

In addition, the workspace allocation is specified as
follows.

```
C        WORKSPACE ALLOCATION IS MADE IN ELLPACK CONTROL IN BLANK COMMON.
C            A MODULE MAY USE THIS AS HE PLEASES,  EXAMPLE.
C                      MAIN PROGRAM
      COMMON WORKSP(2000)
C                        MODULE
      COMMON ITABLE(5,5),XLIST(220),PIVOTS(55),REST(2)
```

4.3. Interface 3: Equations Generated. (Interface 2
appears in ELLPACK 78) The equations are generated and
"attached" to the domain (i.e. associated with a particular
mesh point or grid element) rather than placed in some
particular linear algebra format. This specialized sparse
matrix representation makes it reasonable for later modules
to use any procedure for solving the linear equations.

The unknowns that appear in the equations are first
associated with a particular item (grid element or mesh
point), if there is more than 1 unknown per item, they are
then numbered in some systematic way. The left, bottom and
back faces of a grid element are assumed to belong to it.
If the unknown is number L in item IX,IY (or IX,IY,IZ

in three dimensions), then the unknown is represented by the
set (L,IX,IY) or (L,IX,IY,IZ). This representation is
packed into one computer word as follows

IDUNK = L + (MXNUNK+1)*(IX + (NGRIDX+1)*(IY + (NGRIDY+1)*IZ))

where IDUNK = ID of unknown and MXNUNK = maximum number
of unknowns in any one item. This packing requires that

(MXNUNK + 1)*(NGRIDX + 1)*(NGRIDY + 1)*(NGRIDZ)
                       < maximum Fortran integer

which should not be a real constraint on ELLPACK. The
following arithmetic statement functions unpack this representation

```
C      WE GET THE FOLLOWING FROM COMMON / CONST /
C         IPACK1 = MXNUNK*NGRIDX          IPACK2 = IPACK1*NGRIDY
C
       LUNK(IDUNK) = MOD(IDUNK,MXNUNK)
       IXUNK(IDUNK) = MOD(IDUNK/MXNUNK,NGRIDX)
       IYUNK(IDUNK) = MOD(IDUNK/IPACK1,NGRIDY)
       IZUNK(IDUNK) = IDUNK/IPACK2
```

The equations are then represented by their indices
plus a list of coefficients and associated unknown identifiers. The indices are also packed into one word with the same
scheme as for the unknown identifiers. Thus, an equation
is represented by

COEF(1),IDUNK(1),COEF(2),IDUNK(2),---,

    COEF(MXNCOE-1),IDUNK(MXNCOE-1),RSIDE,IDELEM

where MXNCOE = 1 + maximum number of coefficients in any
equations. These representations are placed in two arrays

        COEF(M,N)   M = 1 TO MXNCOE, N = 1 TO MXNEQ
        IDCOEF(M,N) M = 1 TO MXNCOE, N = 1 TO MXNEQ

where MXNEQ is the maximum number of equations. A one to
one correspondence should be made between the equations and
the unknowns in the sense that all the IDCOEF(1,N) are
distinct. This usually allows one to readily associate an
unknown with a position in the domain and to invert the
indexing performed by the equation indexing module.

    An equation formation module should appear as shown
below as far as the definition of Interface 3 is concerned.

```
      SUBROUTINE FORMEQ(GRIDX,NGRDXD,GRIDY,NGRDYD,COEF,MXNCOE,MXNEQ,
     A              IDCOEF)
      REAL GRIDX(NGRDXD),GRIDY(NGRDYD),COEF(MXNCOF,MXNEQ)
      INTEGER IDCOEF(MXNCOE,MXNEQ)
```

4.4. Interface 4: Equation Indexing.

The equation formation module generates the equations in whatever order it pleases. The equation indexing module defines another order of the equations and the unknowns which is appropriate for a specific linear equation solving module. In some cases it is natural to place the equations into another array at the same time.

The four arrays in this interface are NDXEQ,NDXUNK, INVNDX and AMATRX defined as follows

```
      INTEGER NDXEQ(MXNEQ),NDXUNK(MXNEQ),INVNDX(MXNEQ)
      REAL AMATRX(NROWD,NCOLD)
    C
    C       MXNEQ,NROWD AND NCOLD ARE VALUES IN DIMENSION DECLARATIONS
    C       ACTUAL SIZE OF AMATRX IS SPECIFIED BELOW BY NROW, NCOL
    C
      COMMON / EQNDEX / NROW,NCOL,NBAND
```

The array NDXUNK(J) maps the unknown in IDCOEF(1,J) into the new unknown index. The array INVNDX inverts this map, that is

$$IDUNK = INVNDX(NDXUNK(J)) \quad \text{where} \quad COEF(1,J) = IDUNK .$$

The array NDXEQ maps the index J of COEF(N,J) into the new equation index. In many cases one has NDXEQ and NDXUNK the same.

4.5. Interface 5: Equation Solution.

The primary output of the equation solution module is the array UNKNWN of values of the unknowns. Two typical forms of an equation solving module are as follows:

```
    C               TYPICAL SOLUTION BY A DIRECT METHOD
      SUBROUTINE EQSOL(AMATRX,NROWD,NCOLD,UNKNWN,MXNEQ)
      REAL AMATRX(NROWD,NCOLD),UNKNWN(MXNEQ)
      COMMON / EQNDEX / NROW,NCOL
    C
    C
    C               TYPICAL SOLUTION BY AN ITERATIVE METHOD
      SUBROUTINE SOR(COEF,MXNCOE,MXNEQ,IDCOEF,NDXEQ,INVNDX,UNKNWN)
      REAL COEF(MXNCOE,MXNEQ),UNKNWN(MXNEQ),
      INTEGER IDCOEF(MXNC01,MXNEQ),NDXEQ(MXNEQ),INVNDX(MXNEQ)
```

4.6. <u>Output Module Requirements</u>. One facility of the output module is to produce tables or plots of the approximate solution and, if the true solution is available, the error. This requires that a connection must be made between the unknowns obtained by the equation solution module and the approximations made in the equation formation module. Thus every equation formation module must have an associated function to evaluate the approximate solution. In terms of the information available the value of a particular unknown represented by IDUNK is given by

$$\text{UNKNW(NDXUNK(JEQ(IDUNK)))}$$

where JEQ is a function which maps IDUNK into the index (used in the equation formation module) of the equation associated with the unknown IDUNK. In the worst case, one might have to search the array IDCOEF(1,J) for $1 \le J \le$ MXNEQ in order to determine JEQ(IDUNK). In the best cases, this function is trivial. In any case, the output module uses the function provided by the equation formation module contributor. If more than one equation formation module is invoked on a run, then the control module takes care that the correct function is used.

The output module may use the true solution: FUNCTION TRUE(X,Y) if the user supplies it.

5. <u>ELLPACK 78</u>. ELLPACK 78 is expected to have various enhancements compared to ELLPACK 77, but the essential extension is in allowing non-rectangular geometry. An additional module and interfaces is required for ELLPACK 78 as shown in Figure 6.

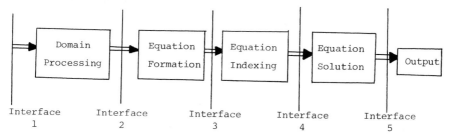

<u>Figure 6</u>. The basic modules and interfaces for ELLPACK 78.

Interfaces 3, 4 and 5 are identical with ELLPACK 77, but the
complexity of the information may be higher. For example,
an equation indexing module that produces the red-black
ordering may take advantage of the fact that the domain is
rectangular for ELLPACK 77, but it must incorporate the
geometric information in ELLPACK 78.

5.1. <u>General and Control Information.</u> The basic geometric
two dimensional situation is shown in Figure 7. The relationship with the rectangular grid is illustrated in Figure 8.
The details of three dimensions are not yet set.

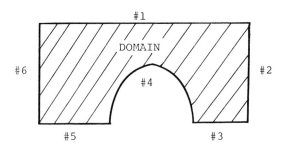

Figure 7.   A typical two-dimensional rectangular domain. The
pieces of the boundary are numbered clockwise and
described parametrically.

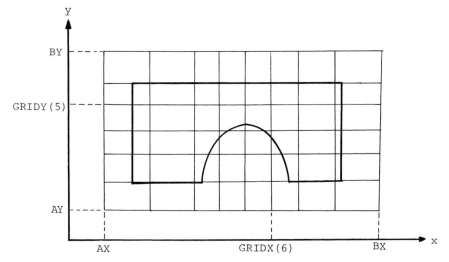

Figure 8.   The domain of Figure 7 with a rectangular grid
overlay. Here we have NGRIDX = 9 and NGRIDY = 7.
In practice one would choose the horizontal and
vertical sides to be mesh lines.

The boundary pieces are described parametrically by functions of the form

$$X = X_i(P) \quad BRANGE(1,i) \le P \le BRANGE(2,i), \quad i = 1,2,---,NBOUND$$
$$Y = Y_i(P)$$

which is implemented in Fortran by the subroutine BCOORD(P,X,Y) which returns the X,Y values for a given value of the boundary parameter P. The index IPIECE of the boundary piece is contained in the COMMON block BNDRY, i.e.

```
      SUBROUTINE BCOORD(P,XVALU,YVALU)
      COMMON / BNDRY / IPIECE,NBOUND
      GO TO(10,20,30,40,...,90),IPIECE
   10 XVALU = P + 1.0
      YVALU = COS(P)
      RETURN
        .....
        .....
   90 XVALU = P*(P-1.)
      YVALU = 3.2*P - 0.4
      RETURN
      END
```

The boundary conditions are still given by BCOND(I,X,Y,BVALUS), but now the index I ranges over the number of boundary pieces.

5.2. <u>Interface 1: Initial Situation</u>. The information of 4.1 and 5.1 is available plus quantities to define the boundary. Three variables are in the common block BNDRY.

```
      COMMON / BNDRY / IPIECE,NBOUND,NBNDPT
C
C
C         IPIECE = VARIABLE INDEX INDICATING CURRENT BOUNDARY PIECE
C         NBOUND = NUMBER OF BOUNDARY PIECES
C         NBNDPT = NUMBER OF BOUNDARY-GRID INTERSECTION POINTS
```

An array of variable size is used to define the parameter ranges for the boundary

```
C      ARRAY TO SPECIFY THE BOUNDARY (ALONG WITH SUBROUTINE BCOORD)
C
C         BRANGE(I,NB)      I = 1,2  FOR FIRST + LAST VALUES OF P
C                           NB = 1,2,...,NBOUND FOR THE DIFFERENT PIECES
```

5.3. <u>Interface 2: Domain Representation</u>. The tasks of the domain processing module are:

a. Locate the domain boundary with respect to the grid.

b. Relate all grid points to the domain (e.g. interior or exterior)

c.   Provide this information in forms convenient for
later processing.

The first type of information is encoded in GTYPE associated with the two dimensional array of grid points:

```
C       GTYPE(IX,IY)  FOR IX = 1 TO NGRIDX, IY = 1 TO NGRIDY
C
C       =   0         GRID POINT OUTSIDE DOMAIN, AWAY FROM BOUNDARY,
C       = INSIDE      GRID POINT  INSIDE DOMAIN, AWAY FROM BOUNDARY,
C                     INSIDE = CONSTANT INTEGER, FOR EXAMPLE 999.
C       = INTEGER     LESS THAN INSIDE, GRID PT = BOUNDARY PT OF INDEX GTYPE
C       = INTEGER     GREATER THAN INSIDE+1 IN ABSOLUTE VALUE
C                     GRID POINT IS NEXT TO THE BOUNDARY. RELATION TO THE
C                     BOUNDARY IS ENCODED BY
C                              GTYPE = INDEX + IPACKB*J
C                     WHERE
C                       INDEX  = SMALLEST INDEX OF NEIGHBORING BOUNDARY PT
C                       IPACKB = CONSTANT FOR PACKING = INSIDE + 1
C                       J      = FOUR BITS FOR DIRECTION TO BOUNDARY PTS.
C                                =1 FOR NOON      = 2 FOR 3 OCLOCK
C                                =4 FOR 6 OCLOCK, = 8 FOR 9 OCLOCK
C                                THUS J = 9 = 1001(BINARY) SHOWS BOUNDARY
C                                POINTS ABOVE AND TO THE LEFT.
C       = POSITIVE FOR GRID POINT IN THE DOMAIN OR ON BOUNDARY
C       = NEGATIVE OR 0 FOR POINT OUTSIDE THE DOMAIN
```

The information about the intersection of the boundary
with the grid lines is contained in a set of 7 linear arrays
of length NBNDPT.   These arrays all have problem dependent
dimensions MAXBND and are used and defined as shown below

```
        INTEGER PIECE(MAXBND),BPTYPE(MAXBND),BNEIGH(MAXBND),BGRID(MAXBND)
        REAL    XBOUND(MAXBND),YBOUND(MAXBND),BPARAM(MAXBND)
C
C       XBOUND(I),YBOUND(I) = COORDINATES OF I-TH BOUNDARY POINT
C       BPARAM(I) = PARAMETER VALUE P OF I-TH BOUNDARY POINT
C       PIECE (I) = INDEX OF BOUNDARY PIECE TO WHICH POINT BELONGS
C                   SMALLEST NUMBER FOR CORNER POINTS
C       BPTYPE(I) = THE TYPE OF THE BOUNDARY POINT
C                 = HORZ    IF POINT IS ON A Y GRID LINE
C                 = VERT    IF POINT IS ON A X GRID LINE
C                 = BOTH    IF POINT IS ALSO A GRID POINT
C                 = CORNER  IF POINT IS A CORNER PT ON A GRID LINE
C                 = INTER   IF POINT IS NOT ON A GRID LINE
C                           HAPPENS ONLY FOR CORNERS NOT ON THE GRID
C                   THE CONSTANTS HORZ, VERT, BOTH, CORNER AND INTER
C                   ARE PLACED BY ELLPACK CONTROL IN COMMON / CONSTS/
C       BNEIGH(I) = IX + 1000*IY  WHERE
C                   IX,IY = INDEXES OF THE X-GRID AND Y-GRID LINES
C                           OF THE FIRST CLOCKWISE INTERIOR GRID
C                           POINT ADJACENT TO THIS BOUNDARY POINT.
C       BGRID (I) = IX + 1000*IY  WHERE THE I-TH BOUNDARY POINT
C                   IS IN THE GRID SQUARE IX,IY. THAT IS
C                      GRIDX(IX) .LE. XBOUND(I) .LT. GRIDX(IX+1)
C                      GRIDY(IY) .LE. YBOUND(I) .LT. GRIDY(IY+1)
C                   (NOTE. IX,IY ARE LIMITED TO NGRIDX, NGRIDY)
```

6.   ELLPACK IMPLEMENTATION AT PURDUE. This section contains
a brief description of how ELLPACK is implemented at Purdue
University. Figure 2 already indicates the general organization as a Fortran preprocessor combined with a library of

already compiled modules.   Thus we make the following assumptions about the environment for ELLPACK.

A.   A standard Fortran compiler is available.

B.   The operating system allows Fortran preprocessors.

C.   The operating system allows a reasonable number of files
     (probably on disks) to be created by a job and simply
     manipulated. Library files of already compiled programs
     are possible.

D.   Certain common utility routines are available. These
     include file copying and concantenation, timing routines,
     and hard copy graphical output. The lack of some of
     these utilities can be circumvented by deleting the
     corresponding features from ELLPACK.

     The basic program flow of the ELLPACK preprocessor is
given by Figure 9. The preprocessor has three types of
subprograms: general utilities, segment processors and
initializing/ending programs. The utilities are

READ	a card
SEGMENT	name identification
BREAK	a line at a special character
KEYWORD 1	right to left matching
KEYWORD 2	left to right matching
MATCH	character pairs
INTEGER VALUE	of a character string
MODULE	name identification

The files created or used by ELLPACK are shown in Figure 10.

     This work was supported in part by Grant MCS76-10225
from the National Science Foundation.

REFERENCES

1.   John R. Rice, ELLPACK: A Cooperative Effort for the
     Study of Numerical Methods for Elliptic Partial Differen-
     tial Equations, CSD-TR 203, Computer Science, Purdue
     University, October 15, 1976, 6 pages.

2.   John R. Rice, ELLPACK Contributor's Guide, CSD-TR 208,
     Computer Science, Purdue University, November 1, 1976,
     44 pages.

3.   John R. Rice, ELLPACK 77 User's Guide, CSD-TR 226,
     Computer Science, Purdue University, March 18, 1977,
     17 pages.

                              Mathematical Sciences
                              Purdue University
                              West Lafayette, Indiana 47907

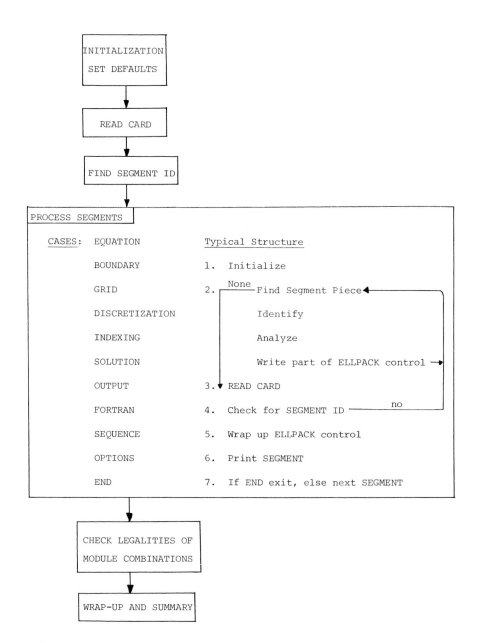

Figure 9.   Basic program organization of the ELLPACK
           preprocessor.

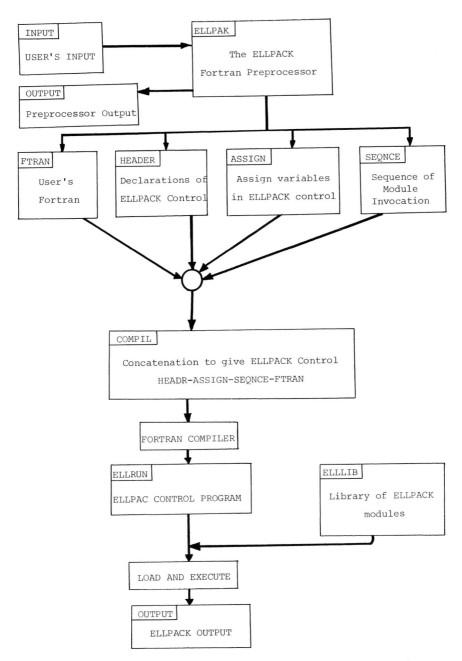

Figure 10.   The file structure of ELLPACK. There are two
             ELLPACK source files: ELLPAK and ELLLIB. The
             other files are temporary or system files.

A Realistic Model
of Floating-Point Computation
W. S. Brown

Abstract

This paper presents a new model of floating-point computation, intended as a basis for efficient portable mathematical software. The model involves only simple familiar concepts, expressed in a small set of environment parameters. Using these, both a program and its documentation can tailor themselves to the host computer.

Our main focus is on stating and proving machine-independent properties of numerical programs. With this in mind, we present fundamental axioms and a few theorems for arithmetic operations and arithmetic comparisons. Our main conclusion is that the model supports conventional error analysis with only minor modifications.

To motivate the formal axioms and theorems, and describe their use, the paper includes numerous examples of bizarre phenomena that are inherent in floating-point computation or arise from the anomalies of real computers. While the use of the model imposes a fairly strict programming discipline for the sake of portability, its rules are easy to remember, and for the most part independently meritorious.

1. Introduction

This paper presents a new model of floating-point computation, intended as a basis for the development and analysis of efficient and highly portable programs for a wide variety of mathematical algorithms. For ease of learning and of use, the model involves only simple familiar concepts of substantial importance to numerical computation. These concepts are expressed in a small set of parameters, which characterize the numerically most significant attributes of a computing environment, and in a small set of axioms, which describe floating-point computation in terms of these parameters.

In writing portable software, one focuses on the model and avoids thinking about the idiosyncracies of any particular machine. Since the parameters of the model may be used freely, a program tailors itself to each environment in which it is installed, and a high degree of efficiency is possible. In writing *about* portable software, one also focuses on the model and its parameters, and thus the documentation is portable too.

343

Although the model is sufficiently tolerant of machine anomalies to encompass a broad range of existing computers, it takes advantage of some properties of computer arithmetic that are normally overlooked. This enables us to prove that conventional error analysis remains valid with only minor modifications. In general, the effects of anomalous behavior on the part of a particular computer are accounted for by adjusting its parameters in such a way as to reduce its purported precision or range. While such a penalty obviously weakens the error bounds or restricts the domains of applicability for portable programs installed on that computer, it does not affect the programs themselves or their portable documentation, nor does it affect error bounds or domains of applicability for other computers.

As presented in this paper, our model is limited to floating-point numbers and floating-point arithmetic. For a library of numerical programs, these may be the most important and complicated aspects of the computing environment, but they are certainly not sufficient. To develop a portable library, one must also be concerned with integer arithmetic, character strings, input, and output. Of course, someone must determine the actual values of all the parameters for each site. Once this is done, there are several possible ways to make them conveniently available, one of which is clearly demonstrated in the rapidly evolving Port library [1].

Section 2 of this paper introduces the parameters of our model, and discusses the representation of floating-point numbers. Section 3 proposes axioms for arithmetic, and discusses some of their implications. Section 4 shows that the model is not restricted to computers of mathematically reasonable design, but can encompass a wide variety of anomalies. The paper reaches its main conclusion in Section 5, which shows that the model supports conventional error analysis with only minor modifications. In the dénouement, Section 6 discusses arithmetic comparisons, and Section 7 examines overflow and underflow.

2. Environment Parameters

Our model includes a few basic parameters and a few derived parameters for short precision and for long precision. The two sets of basic parameters are related by a few very weak constraints. For single-precision arithmetic the basic parameters are:

1. The *base*, $b \geqslant 2$.
2. The *precision*, $p \geqslant 2$.
3. The *minimum exponent*, $e_{min} < 0$.
4. The *maximum exponent*, $e_{max} > 0$.

These must be chosen so that zero and all numbers of the form

$$(1) \qquad x = \pm b^e (x_1 b^{-1} + \cdots + x_p b^{-p})$$

$$0 \leqslant x_i < b; \quad i = 1, \ldots, p$$

$$0 < x_1$$

$$e_{min} \leqslant e \leqslant e_{max}$$

are possible values for single-precision floating-point variables. These *model numbers* are a (possibly complete) subset of all the *machine numbers* that can occur in single-precision computation.

We do *not* assume that the machine actually uses this normalized sign-magnitude representation for floating-point numbers. In fact, the details of the hardware representation are of no concern to us. What we require is simply that the model numbers be possible values for program variables, and that arithmetic operations be at least accurate enough to satisfy the axioms given below.

Note that the model numbers are symmetric under negation, but not under reciprocation. On computers with the implicit b-point on the right, it may be that $|e_{min}| \ll e_{max}$.

Since the model numbers with a given exponent, e, are equally spaced on an absolute scale, the relative spacing decreases as the numbers increase. For error analysis, the maximum relative spacing

(2)
$$\epsilon = b^{1-p}$$

is of critical importance. Also of interest throughout this paper are the smallest positive model number

(3)
$$\sigma = b^{e_{min}-1},$$

and the largest model number

(4)
$$\lambda = b^{e_{max}}(1-b^{-p}).$$

For double-precision arithmetic, we assume the base, b, remains the same, but p, e_{min}, and e_{max} are replaced by P, E_{min}, and E_{max}, respectively. Normally, we have $P > p$, $E_{min} \leqslant e_{min}$, and $E_{max} \geqslant e_{max}$. However, on some machines (see Section 4) it is necessary to set $E_{min} > e_{min}$ to insure full double-precision accuracy throughout the double-precision range. If we were to encounter a computer with no double-precision hardware, and if its Fortran compiler chose not to provide double-precision in software, we could of course set $P = p$, $E_{min} = e_{min}$, and $E_{max} = e_{max}$.

3. Properties of Arithmetic

In the conventional model of floating-point computation [2], one begins by postulating an ideal computer whose machine numbers are exactly the model numbers given above, and whose floating-point operations are as accurate as possible. Suppose x and y are numbers in such a computer, and $*$ is a binary arithmetic operator ($+$, $-$, $\times$, or $/$). Let $fl(x*y)$ denote the result of computing $x*y$ in floating-point arithmetic. Assuming that $x*y$ is in range, it follows that $fl(x*y)$ is equal to the floating-point number closest to $x*y$ (with some simple mechanism for breaking ties). One then proves that

(5)
$$fl(x*y) = (x*y)(1+\delta), \quad |\delta| < \epsilon/2,$$

where ϵ is the maximum relative spacing, given by (2). This theorem is usually taken as the starting point for error analysis, and one never goes back to the original (and much stronger) postulate from which it was derived.

In this paper we take a rather different tack. Instead of assuming that the machine numbers are exactly the model numbers, we require only that they include the model numbers, and instead of assuming that all floating-point operations are as accurate as possible, we adopt a somewhat weaker (and much more realistic) postulate. However, we use our postulate in ways that go well beyond a weakened analog of (5).

We begin the discussion with some definitions and notation. Since error analysis is closely akin to interval analysis [3], it is convenient to formulate our axioms in terms of intervals. In particular, if the end points of a closed interval are both model numbers, we call it a *model interval*.

For any real number x, we say that x is *in range* if $x=0$ or $\sigma \leqslant |x| \leqslant \lambda$, and is *out of range* otherwise. If $0 < |x| < \sigma$, we say that x *underflows*, while if $|x| > \lambda$, we say that it *overflows*.

More generally, we say that a real interval X is *in-range* if x is in range for all $x \in X$; otherwise, X is *out-of-range*. Also, we say that X *underflows* if x underflows for some $x \in X$, and we say that X *overflows* if x overflows for some $x \in X$. Note that any nontrivial interval containing zero underflows.

If x is a real number that does not overflow, we let x' denote the smallest model interval containing x. Thus, if x is a model number, then $x'=x$; otherwise, x' is the closed interval that contains x and is bounded by two adjacent model numbers.

More generally, if X is a real interval that does not overflow, we let X' denote the smallest model interval containing X. It is important to note that $x \in X'$ implies $x' \subseteq X'$.

Since division is sometimes implemented as a composite operation, we replace it by reciprocation in our list of basic arithmetic operations. In the following discussion, we let $*$ denote any *basic binary operation* ($+$, $-$, or $\times$), while we treat the *basic unary operations* (negation and reciprocation) as separate special cases.

Now let x and y be machine numbers, and let

$$(6) \qquad\qquad z = x * y$$
$$\tilde{z} = \mathrm{fl}(x*y)$$

with x, y, and z in range. If x, y, and z are all model numbers, we require that $\tilde{z}=z$; it follows that the basic binary operations on small integers are exact. If x and y are model numbers, but z is not, we require that $\tilde{z} \in z'$; thus any mixture of rounding and truncation (in either direction) will suffice. Finally, if either x or y is not a model number, we do not rely on its extra precision; instead, we broaden it to a model interval and broaden the allowable interval for $\tilde{z}$ accordingly.

Axioms

We shall now present the formal axioms that govern arithmetic in our model, and some theorems to demonstrate that these axioms do indeed meet the requirements discussed above. Note that all operands are required to be in range, and results are not permitted to overflow. Although the axioms permit underflow, they are vacuous if a machine underflow terminates the computation.

Axiom 1

Let x and y be machine numbers that are in range, and let $*$ be a basic binary operator. Then

$$\mathrm{fl}(x*y) \in (x'*y')'$$

provided that the interval $(x'*y')$ does not overflow.

Corollary

Under the same hypotheses,

$$\text{fl}(x \ast y)' \subseteq (x' \ast y')'.$$

Remark

If the prime (′) is regarded as a broadening operator, then in general both the operands and the result must be broadened. However, the corollary shows that no further broadening is required when the result is later used as an operand. It is for this reason that error analyses based on our model require only a single relative error for each operator, even though the axioms at first glance appear to require one when the operator is executed and another when the result is used.

Axiom 2

Let x be a machine number that is in range. Then

$$\text{fl}(x^{-1}) \in ((x')^{-1})'$$

provided that the interval $(x')^{-1}$ does not overflow.

Corollary

Under the same hypotheses,

$$\text{fl}(x^{-1})' \subseteq ((x')^{-1})'.$$

Axiom 3

Let x be a machine number that is in range. Then

$$\text{fl}(-x) = -x.$$

Remark

Negation is always exact, provided that the operand is in range.

Exactness Theorems

The following theorems show that the basic arithmetic operations are exact whenever the operands and results are all model numbers. Although one can conclude that $3 \times 5 = 15$ exactly, it is not necessarily true that $15/5 = 3$ exactly, since division may be a composite operation, and the reciprocal of 5 may not be a model number.

Theorem 1

Let x and y be model numbers, and let $\ast$ be a basic binary operator. If $x \ast y$ is also a model number, then

$$\text{fl}(x \ast y) = x \ast y.$$

Theorem 2

Let x be a model number whose reciprocal is also a model number. Then x is a product of powers of prime factors of b, and

$$fl(x^{-1}) = x^{-1}.$$

Small-Relative-Error Theorems

The following theorems show that the basic arithmetic operations are accurate to within ϵ (see (2)) whenever the operands are model numbers, and the results are in range.

Theorem 3

Let x and y be model numbers, and let $*$ be a basic binary operator. If $x*y$ is in range, then

$$fl(x*y) = (x*y)(1+\delta), \quad |\delta| < \epsilon.$$

Theorem 4

Let x be a model number whose reciprocal is in range. Then

$$fl(x^{-1}) = x^{-1}(1+\delta), \quad |\delta| < \epsilon.$$

4. Machine Anomalies

In this section we show that our model is not restricted to computers of mathematically reasonable design, but can also encompass a variety of anomalies. In general, the effects of anomalies in a computer are accounted for by adjusting its parameters in such a way as to reduce its purported precision or range. Let us begin by discussing the possibility of machine numbers that are not model numbers. In general these come in two classes — those that are *extra-precise,* and those that are *out of range.*

For an example of extra-precise numbers, consider a computer whose working registers are wider (more precise) than its memory registers. Since model numbers must be exactly representable in memory, the precision, p, is determined by the memory registers. However, any number that is representable in a working register is a machine number, since it can arise as the value of a subexpression and then be used immediately as an operand. Most of these machine numbers are extra-precise in the sense that their mantissas (ignoring trailing zeroes) are more than p bits wide. Although it is intuitively clear that wide working registers generally increase the accuracy of computed results, we shall prove only that they (like other extra-precise numbers) are usually harmless. (A situation in which they can cause some limited harm is discussed in Section 5.)

As another example, consider a three-digit decimal computer with no guard digit in its accumulator. If we set $p=3$, then .999 and 1.00 are both model numbers, but

(7) $$fl(1.00-.999) = fl(.100-.099) \times 10 = .01$$

in contradiction to Axiom 1. However, if we set $p=2$, thus designating the last digit of every machine number as a guard digit, then .999 is an extra-precise machine number, not a model number, and Axiom 1, which requires only that

(8)
$$fl(1.00 - .999) \in (1.00' - .999')'$$
$$= (1.00 - [.99, 1.00])'$$
$$= [0, .01]'$$
$$= [0, .01],$$

is satisfied.

On some computers this phenomenon can occur in single precision because of the lack of a convenient way to normalize the double-precision accumulator in which all single-precision results are formed. While it is always *possible* to perform the desired normalization, the compiler writer may prefer to sacrifice a digit of precision rather than to suffer a loss of speed in the object program. Thus, the parameters of our model are not necessarily determined solely by the computer, but may also depend on the compiler that is used.

For an example of out-of-range numbers, consider a computer that maintains and uses machine numbers with magnitudes too small to normalize. To guarantee full precision throughout the range of the model, the minimum exponent must be large enough to exclude these "tiny" unnormalized numbers, which are therefore out-of-range.

For another example, consider a binary computer that uses normalized twos-complement numbers with p bits of precision. Now it is easy to show that a nonzero mantissa, f, satisfies $2^{-1} \leq f < 1$ or $-1 \leq f < -2^{-1}$. If we chose e_{min} to be the smallest machine exponent, then the negative model number with model mantissa -2^{-1} and model exponent e_{min} could not be represented in the machine, since its machine mantissa would be -1 and its machine exponent would have to be $e_{min}-1$, which would be out of range. To avert this disaster, we must increase e_{min} by one, and thus abandon all but one of the machine numbers with the smallest possible machine exponent. This contraction of the range seems a small price to pay to avoid complicating the model with details of the representation.

This collection of anomalies is only a beginning; others are mentioned elsewhere in this paper, and there are still more that could be discussed. However, we hope to have convinced the reader that our model is flexible enough to accommodate a broad range of real computers. Since the choice of parameters for a given computer requires detailed knowledge of its hardware and software, an expert should be involved. If a computer cannot support the model with any reasonable choice of parameters, we suggest that it may be in need of repair or redesign.

5. Error Analysis

The purpose of this section is to show that our model supports conventional error analysis with the following minor modifications:

A.   The unit of error in arithmetic operations is ϵ, not $\epsilon/2$, where ϵ is the maximum relative spacing, given by (2).

B.   Division is considered to be a composite operation, and hence may involve two units of error, rather than only one.

C.   All relevant values must be within the model range, which may be smaller than the machine range.

D.   If an initial datum, x, is not a model number, then it must be broadened to an interval containing the model interval x', and the analysis must take this broadening into account.

E.   If a given expression has a common subexpression, then the subexpression may yield different values for different uses, but the relative difference between any two values is less than ϵ.

Modifications A and B are discussed in Section 3 above, while modifications C and D are necessary to accommodate anomalies such as those discussed in Section 4. The problem of ensuring the validity of Modification C is discussed in Section 7. Modification D treats an initial datum too precise for the model in essentially the same way that conventional error analysis treats an initial datum too precise for the machine. Finally, modification E allows for the possibility of a computer with an extra-precise value of a common subexpression for one use and a stored value for other uses, and as we shall see, this phenomenon can be somewhat harmful.

Let us begin by considering a rational expression, f, with no common subexpressions. Such an expression may be represented graphically by a tree whose leaves are the initial data $x_1, \ldots, x_m$, and whose remaining nodes are basic (unary or binary) arithmetic operators. For example, the expression

$$(9) \qquad f(x_1, x_2) = x_1 + x_2^{-1}$$

may be represented by the tree shown in Figure 1.

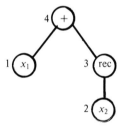

Figure 1. Graph of $x_1 + x_2^{-1}$.

Let each initial datum, x_i, be approximated by a machine number

$$(10) \qquad \tilde{x}_i = \mathrm{fl}(x_i) \in x_i'.$$

If x_i is a model number, then $\tilde{x}_i$ is exact. In any case,

$$(11) \qquad \tilde{x}_i' \subseteq x_i' \subseteq \{x_i(1+\delta_i) : |\delta_i| < \epsilon\},$$

and it follows that

$$(12) \qquad \tilde{x}_i = x_i(1+\delta_i), \quad |\delta_i| < \epsilon.$$

More generally, let f_i be the exact mathematical value of the subtree rooted at node i, and let $\tilde{f}_i = \mathrm{fl}(f_i)$ be the approximate computed value. Also, let δ_i be the relative error introduced at node i, and let η_i be the total relative error at node i.

As noted in the remark following Axiom 1, δ_i includes any perturbation that is introduced into $\tilde{f}_i$ when it is used; however, if node i is an operator that perturbs its operands in the sense of the operand broadening in Axiom 1, those perturbations are assigned to the operand nodes and not to node i. Thus if $f_i = f_j * f_k$, then δ_i is defined by

$$\hat{f}_i = (\hat{f}_j * \hat{f}_k)(1+\delta_i)$$

where $\hat{f}_i \in \tilde{f}_i'$ is the *effective value* of $\tilde{f}_i$.

We are now prepared for the fundamental theorem of error analysis:

Theorem 5

Consider a rational expression $f(x_1, \ldots, x_m)$ represented by a tree with nodes $i=1,\ldots,n$, arranged so that $f_i=x_i$ for $i=1,\ldots,m$, and $f_n=f$. Let $\mathbf{x} = (x_1, \ldots, x_m)$, $\boldsymbol{\delta} = (\delta_1, \ldots, \delta_n)$, and $\|\boldsymbol{\delta}\| = \max|\delta_i|$. Finally, let $\tilde{f}_i = \mathrm{fl}(f_i)$ and $\tilde{f} = \tilde{f}_n = \mathrm{fl}(f)$, and assume that all the f_i and $\tilde{f}_i$ are in range. Then

$$\tilde{f} = f\cdot(1+\eta(\mathbf{x}, \boldsymbol{\delta})), \quad \|\boldsymbol{\delta}\|<\epsilon,$$

where η is a rational function with the relative Taylor series expansion

$$\eta = \sum_{i=1}^{n} \left[\frac{\partial f/f}{\partial f_i/f_i}\right]\delta_i + O(\epsilon^2).$$

The coefficients in this formula are known as *relative* or *logarithmic derivatives*. To compute $\partial f/\partial f_i$, one replaces the subexpression f_i in f by an indeterminate, and then differentiates f with respect to that indeterminate. To obtain the exact rational expression for η, one sets $\eta_i=\delta_i$ for $i=1,\ldots,m$, then works up through the tree using the recurrence formulas in Table 1, and finally sets $\eta=\eta_n$.

Operation	η_i (exact)	η_i (first order)
$f_i = f_j \times f_k$	$(1+\delta_i)(1+\eta_j)(1+\eta_k)-1$	$\delta_i + \eta_j + \eta_k$
$f_i = f_j \pm f_k$	$(1+\delta_i)[1+f_i^{-1}(f_j\eta_j \pm f_k\eta_k)]-1$	$\delta_i+f_i^{-1}(f_j\eta_j\pm f_k\eta_k)$
$f_i = f_j^{-1}$	$(1+\delta_i)(1+\eta_j)^{-1}-1$	$\delta_i - \eta_j$
$f_i = -f_j$	η_j	η_j

Table 1. Recurrence formulas for η_i.

Remark

One can set $\delta_i=0$ in the formula for η whenever the axioms imply that no error is introduced at node i. The following are examples of such situations:

(a)   Node i is an initial datum whose exact value is a small integer or some other model number.

(b)   Node i is the unary negation operator.

(c)   Node i represents multiplication by a power of the base. (If the operand being scaled is a model number, then the operation is exact by Axiom 1; if not, any perturbation in the effective value of that operand is assigned to its root node and not to node i.)

Proof

Let S_i be the index set for the nodes of the subtree rooted at node i; let $\delta^{(i)}$ be the vector of the δ_j for $j \in S_i$; and let $\mathbf{x}^{(i)}$ be the vector of the x_j for $j \in S_i \cap \{1,...,m\}$. We shall prove that

(13) $$\tilde{f}_i' \subseteq F_i \equiv \{f_i \cdot (1+\eta_i(\mathbf{x}^{(i)}, \delta^{(i)})) : \|\delta^{(i)}\| < \epsilon\},$$

where the η_i are the rational functions discussed above, and we shall prove further that

(14) $$\eta_i = \sum_{j \in S_i} \left[\frac{\partial f_i/f_i}{\partial f_j/f_j} \right] \delta_j + O(\epsilon^2).$$

The theorem follows immediately by setting $i=n$.

The proof is by induction on the depth of the subtree. If node i is a leaf, then $f_i = x_i$, and (11) implies (13), with $\eta_i = \delta_i$ in agreement with (14). Otherwise, node i is an operator whose operands may be assumed by induction to satisfy (13) and (14).

First, suppose node i is a basic binary operator, $* \in \{+, -, \times\}$, so that

(15) $$f_i = f_j * f_k.$$

Then

(16) $$\tilde{f}_i = \text{fl}(\tilde{f}_j * \tilde{f}_k),$$

where by induction

(17) $$\tilde{f}_j' \subseteq F_j = \{f_j \cdot (1+\eta_j(\mathbf{x}^{(j)}, \delta^{(j)})) : \|\delta^{(j)}\| < \epsilon\}$$
$$\tilde{f}_k' \subseteq F_k = \{f_k \cdot (1+\eta_k(\mathbf{x}^{(k)}, \delta^{(k)})) : \|\delta^{(k)}\| < \epsilon\}.$$

Now by Axiom 1,

(18) $$\tilde{f}_i \in (\tilde{f}_j' * \tilde{f}_k')',$$

so

(19) $$\tilde{f}_i' \subseteq (\tilde{f}_j' * \tilde{f}_k')' \subseteq (F_j * F_k)'$$
$$\subseteq \{[f_j \cdot (1+\eta_j) * f_k \cdot (1+\eta_k)](1+\delta_i) : \|\delta^{(i)}\| < \epsilon\},$$

where we have used the fact that $\delta^{(i)} = (\delta_i, \delta^{(j)}, \delta^{(k)})$.

If $*$ is multiplication, then

(20) $$f_i = f_j f_k$$

by (15), and

(21) $$\tilde{f}_i' \subseteq \{f_j f_k (1+\delta_i)(1+\eta_j)(1+\eta_k) : \|\delta^{(i)}\| < \epsilon\}$$

by (19). Thus (13) is satisfied with

(22)
$$\eta_i = (1+\delta_i)(1+\eta_j)(1+\eta_k) - 1$$
$$= \delta_i + \eta_j + \eta_k + O(\epsilon^2),$$

in agreement with Table 1. To prove (14), we note that

(23)
$$S_i = \{i\} \cup S_j \cup S_k,$$

so (14) may be rewritten as

(24)
$$\eta_i = \delta_i + \sum_{p \in S_j} \left[\frac{\partial f_i/f_i}{\partial f_p/f_p} \right] \delta_p + \sum_{q \in S_k} \left[\frac{\partial f_i/f_i}{\partial f_q/f_q} \right] \delta_q + O(\epsilon^2).$$

But

(25)
$$\frac{\partial f_i/f_i}{\partial f_p/f_p} = \frac{f_p}{f_i} \cdot \frac{\partial f_i}{\partial f_p} = \frac{f_p}{f_j f_k} \cdot \frac{\partial(f_j f_k)}{\partial f_p} = \frac{f_p}{f_j} \cdot \frac{\partial f_j}{\partial f_p} = \frac{\partial f_j/f_j}{\partial f_p/f_p}$$

for $p \in S_j$, and by induction

(26)
$$\eta_j = \sum_{p \in S_j} \left[\frac{\partial f_j/f_j}{\partial f_p/f_p} \right] \delta_p + O(\epsilon^2).$$

Hence η_j equals the first sum in (24), and similarly η_k equals the second. Thus finally (22) implies (24), which is equivalent to (14).

For the remaining operators the proofs are similar, and we omit the details.

Example

To illustrate the application of this theorem, let us return to (9) and Figure 1. Clearly

(27)
$$f_1 = x_1$$
$$f_2 = x_2$$
$$f_3 = x_2^{-1}$$
$$f \equiv f_4 = x_1 + x_2^{-1},$$

and by Theorem 5 the total relative error in f is

(28)
$$\eta = x_1 f^{-1} \delta_1 - x_2^{-1} f^{-1} \delta_2 + x_2^{-1} f^{-1} \delta_3 + \delta_4 + O(\epsilon^2).$$

More precisely, the recurrence formulas of Table 1 yield

(29)
$$\eta = \delta_4 + f^{-1}(x_1 \delta_1 + x_2^{-1} \eta_3)(1+\delta_4),$$

where

(30)
$$\eta_3 = (1+\delta_3)(1+\delta_2)^{-1} - 1.$$

We emphasize that (29) and (30) are exactly the same as in conventional error analysis, and (28) is the usual (and useful) first order approximation.

Focusing our attention on (28), we see that $|\eta|$ is large if and only if $|f|$ is small compared to $|x_1|$ or $|x_2^{-1}|$, which is true if and only if the two terms of f are nearly equal in magnitude and opposite in sign. In this case, we also see that the "catastrophic cancellation" at node 4 amplifies the errors in its operands, but does not add any important new term. Furthermore, we see that $\|\delta\| < \epsilon$ implies

(31)
$$|\eta| < (|x_1 f^{-1}|+2|x_2^{-1} f^{-1}|+1)\epsilon + O(\epsilon^2),$$

which is our final result.

  If a rational expression has common subexpressions, it cannot be represented by a tree, but it can be represented by a more general directed acyclic graph (dag), and the preceding discussion is essentially unchanged except for Modification E. Instead of reformulating Theorem 5 and its proof in full generality, we shall illustrate the required changes by analyzing the expression

(32)
$$f(x) = x + x^{-1},$$

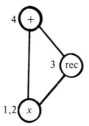

Figure 2. Graph of $x + x^{-1}$.

which may be obtained from (9) by setting $x_1 = x_2 = x$, and may be represented by the dag shown in Figure 2. In numbering the nodes of this dag, we have assigned two node numbers to the leaf x, because it is a common subexpression with two uses, and Modification E requires us to assign a different δ for each use. We now observe that

(33)
$$f_1 = f_2 = x$$
$$f_3 = x^{-1}$$
$$f \equiv f_4 = x+x^{-1}.$$

  For machines that deliver the same value of x for each use, we can set $\delta_1 = \delta_2 \equiv \delta$, and apply Theorem 5 directly to obtain

(34)
$$\eta = (x-x^{-1}) f^{-1}\delta + x^{-1} f^{-1}\delta_3 + \delta_4 + O(\epsilon^2),$$

from which it follows that

(35)
$$|\eta| < \epsilon h_1(x) + O(\epsilon^2),$$

with

$$(36) \qquad h_1(x) = |xf^{-1} - x^{-1}f^{-1}| + x^{-1}f^{-1} + 1$$

$$= \begin{cases} xf^{-1} + 1, & \text{if } |x| \geqslant 1, \\ (2x^{-1} - x)f^{-1} + 1, & \text{if } |x| \leqslant 1, \end{cases}$$

$$= \begin{cases} 2 - x^{-1}f^{-1}, & \text{if } |x| \geqslant 1, \\ 3 - 3xf^{-1}, & \text{if } |x| \leqslant 1. \end{cases}$$

In the more general case when Modification E must be taken into account, we replace Figure 2 by Figure 1 with x_1 and x_2 set equal to x. In this case, Theorem 5 yields

$$(37) \qquad \eta = xf^{-1}\delta_1 - x^{-1}f^{-1}\delta_2 + x^{-1}f^{-1}\delta_3 + \delta_4 + O(\epsilon^2),$$

which is a generalization of (34). However, instead of setting $\delta_1 = \delta_2$, we now impose the weaker condition that $|\delta_1 - \delta_2| < \epsilon$, and thus obtain the weaker result

$$(38) \qquad h_2(x) = \max(xf^{-1}, x^{-1}f^{-1}) + x^{-1}f^{-1} + 1$$

$$= \begin{cases} (x + x^{-1})f^{-1} + 1, & \text{if } |x| \geqslant 1, \\ 2x^{-1}f^{-1} + 1, & \text{if } |x| \leqslant 1, \end{cases}$$

$$= \begin{cases} 2, & \text{if } |x| \geqslant 1, \\ 3 - 2xf^{-1}, & \text{if } |x| \leqslant 1. \end{cases}$$

An interesting fact about this example is that if $\tilde{x}$ is too large, then $\tilde{x}^{-1}$ is too small, and vice versa, so the errors tend to compensate. However, when Modification E is taken into account, the delivered values of $\tilde{x}$ may be different for its two uses, and this compensation may be partially defeated. Nevertheless, the constraint $|\delta_1 - \delta_2| < \epsilon$ has permitted us to retain half of the advantage. Without this constraint (37) would have yielded $h_3(x) = 2 + x^{-1}f^{-1} = 3 - xf^{-1}$, and it is easy to see that h_2 is midway between this and h_1.

We remark that some expressions, such as $f(x) = x - x^{-1}$ do not exhibit the phenomenon of compensation, and in such cases Modification E has no effect on the analysis.

6. Arithmetic Comparisons

Most scientific programming languages permit conditional statements such as

$$\text{if } (x < y) \text{ then } \{action\}$$

where *action* is to be executed or skipped depending on whether $x < y$ is *true* or *false*. We shall refer to the condition $x < y$ as an *arithmetic comparison,* since it compares two arithmetic quantities. The possible *comparison operators* are

$$<, \leqslant, =, \neq, \geqslant, >.$$

In performing an arithmetic comparison, great care is required, since any error in either operand may reverse the result. Nevertheless, the result does convey information, which can be made precise by analyzing the possible error in each operand and then using the axiom and theorems of this section.

When presented with an arithmetic comparison, the computer evaluates the two operands, x and y, and decides whether $x < y$, $x = y$, or $x > y$. The truth value of the comparison is then determined in the obvious way. In discussing the outcome, we shall say that *the computer reports* $x < y$, $x = y$, or $x > y$, and leave it to the reader to consider the resulting truth value.

On many computers a comparison is evaluated by an instruction that compares the bit patterns, and the outcome corresponds exactly to the mathematical relationship between the two machine numbers. Unfortunately, some computers lack such an instruction, and must therefore evaluate the relation by comparing $x - y$ to zero. In this case, the compiler writer has a heavy responsibility to ensure that the subtraction does not cause overflow or underflow. Overflow can be avoided by omitting the subtraction when x and y have opposite signs. Underflow can be avoided by using unnormalized subtraction in this context. To see what can occur when such precautions are not taken, imagine a 3-digit decimal computer with $e_{min} = -99$, and consider a comparison between the model numbers $x = .199 \times 10^{-99}$ and $y = .100 \times 10^{-99}$. Since the normalized difference, $x - y = .99 \times 10^{-100}$, would underflow, the computer might report that $x = y$, even though the two numbers differ by almost a factor of 2.

In applying the axiom and theorems of this section, there is another subtle pitfall to be avoided. Since an expression may yield different values for different uses as discussed in Section 5, the results of different comparisons composed from the same expressions may be inconsistent. For example, consider the program fragment

$$\text{if } (x+y = u+v) \text{ write "yes"}$$
$$\text{if } (x+y < u+v) \text{ write "no"}$$
$$\text{if } (u+v < x+y) \text{ write "no"}$$

and suppose that $x = u$ and $y = v$. If the compiler assigns the first operand to a memory location and the second to an extra-precise working register, then the output may be "no no" instead of the expected "yes", or there may be no output at all. Even a variable may yield different values for different uses, without any intervening assignment, since an optimizing compiler may deliver one value from an extra-precise register, and another from a memory location.

With this background we are now prepared for the axiom of arithmetic comparisons, a theorem, and two corollaries. In each case, we consider an arithmetic comparison between machine numbers x and y that do not overflow.

Axiom 4

If both x and y are model numbers, then the computer reports the mathematically correct result. Otherwise, there are three mutually exclusive cases:

(a)   If x' and y' are disjoint, then the computer reports the correct result.

(b)   If x' and y' are disjoint except for a common endpoint, then the computer may report the correct result or it may report $x = y$.

(c)   If $x' = y'$, then the computer may report $x < y$, $x = y$, or $x > y$, regardless of the actual fact.

Theorem 6

Suppose $x < y$. If there are at least two model numbers in the interval $[x, y]$, then the computer reports $x < y$. If there is exactly one model number in $[x, y]$, then the computer may report either $x < y$ or $x = y$.

Corollary 1

Suppose x and y are positive and in range. If $x(1+2\epsilon) \leqslant y$, then the computer reports $x < y$. If $x(1+\epsilon) \leqslant y < x(1+2\epsilon)$, then the computer may report $x < y$ or $x = y$.

Corollary 2

Suppose x and y are positive and in range. If the computer reports $x < y$, then in fact $x < y(1+\epsilon)$. If the computer reports $x = y$, then in fact $x(1-2\epsilon) < y < x(1+2\epsilon)$.

7. Overflow and Underflow (the *Bêtes Noires* of Portability)

To write a portable numerical program, one must design the algorithm and scale the data so as to permit a *proof* that no overflow will occur. Furthermore, if underflow is not similarly prevented, one must test for it wherever it might occur, since it is imperative to avoid performing any arithmetic operation on any machine number that is out of range.

These rules are easy to remember, but not always easy to follow. This section shows why they are necessary, and discusses how they can be followed. Even if the alternative strategies were conveniently and portably available, we claim that other considerations, such as simplicity and efficiency, would favor the proposed strategy for many purposes.

We begin by reviewing some of the basic facts of overflow and underflow on real computers. When a computer is asked to produce a number that is outside the range of the model, that number may or may not be outside the range of the machine. If not, then a machine number outside the range of the model will be produced, and the computation will continue. Unfortunately, this can lead to loss of precision (see Section 4), or perhaps to a more spectacular disaster, when the number is used. The following examples illustrate some of the hazards:

(a)   If the machine range is not symmetric, then the statement

$$y := -x$$

may cause overflow or underflow.

(b)   If x is the machine's "infinitesimal", then the statement

$$y := 1.0 \times x$$

may cause machine underflow, while the statement

$$\text{if } (x \neq 0) \; y := 1/x$$

may cause division by zero.

(c)   If x and y are both equal to the machine's "infinity", then the statement

$$\text{if } (x = y) \text{ write "yes"}$$

need not produce output, since the difference, $x - y$, may be "undefined" rather than zero.

Since there is almost nothing that can safely be said about operations on out-of-range numbers, the axioms of Section 3 avoid them entirely. However, if the mathematical result, z, of an operation on in-range numbers satisfies $0 < z < \sigma$ (see (3)), then the axioms assert that the computed result, $\tilde{z}$, satisfies $0 \leqslant \tilde{z} \leqslant \sigma$, and similarly if $-\sigma < z < 0$, then $-\sigma \leqslant \tilde{z} \leqslant 0$. These properties of arithmetic permit a disciplined use of underflow (discussed below), since Axiom 4 does not exclude operands in these intervals.

When a computer is asked to produce a number that is outside of its machine range, it will almost certainly recognize the difficulty and take some special action. On some computers, the user may be free to choose between termination and continued computation with a special number ("infinity" for overflow, and zero or some "infinitesimal" for underflow) replacing the unrepresentable number. On other computers, one of these choices may be decreed by the hardware without regard for the user's desires.

If continued computation is permitted, there may nevertheless be a very costly delay while the trap handler thinks about all sorts of irrelevant disasters that might have occurred, and discovers how little it is really expected to do. In any event, the special number that replaces the desired result may be wrong by many orders of magnitude, so any use of this option (even on a mathematically reasonable machine) must be highly disciplined to avoid utterly meaningless results.

Some numerical analysts feel that a well designed algorithm will never produce out-of-range numbers unless unreasonable demands are made on it. Hence they advocate that overflow and underflow should be detected by the computer, and treated as fatal errors. From the viewpoint of a designer of mathematical software, this strategy is attractive because it succeeds in delegating most of the responsibility for overflow and underflow to others without risking incorrect results.

Other numerical analysts feel that this strategy restricts the domain of applicability of an algorithm too severely, and should be modified to permit recovery after an overflow or an underflow. Thus "normal" cases would be handled with maximum efficiency, while testing, scaling, and other costly special actions would be taken only when the most straightforward approach fails.

With regard to program length and complexity, our strategy is generally intermediate between these two alternatives. In efficiency, our strategy handles abnormal cases best, but loses out to the alternatives in normal cases. Since a software designer might well prefer one or both of the alternative strategies to ours in at least some situations, it is regrettable that they cannot be implemented portably (and on some computers, not at all) for the following reasons:

(a)   Machine numbers outside the model range may be produced without detection, and later use of these numbers may be disastrous.

(b)   Some computers are incapable of interrupting the flow of control when an overflow or an underflow occurs.

(c)   Following a trap, there may be no way for the user's program to ask for the return of control, or no way for the operating system to grant it.

Let us now return to the strategy proposed at the beginning of this section. We shall first consider the avoidance of overflow and underflow, and then conclude by discussing the disciplined use of underflow.

An excellent example of an algorithm that rigorously avoids overflow and underflow is J. L. Blue's algorithm [4] for computing the Euclidean norm of a vector. The algorithm makes only one pass over the data — scaling if necessary and accumulating as it goes. If the magnitude of a component is in the "mid-range", it is simply squared and added to an accumulator. Components with larger or smaller magnitudes are scaled toward unity and accumulated separately. The final result is then determined from the values of the three accumulators.

The scale factors and the boundaries of the mid-range are easily determined from the environment parameters introduced in Section 2. Since the scale factors are powers of the base, no error is introduced by the scaling (see the Remark following Theorem 5). Furthermore, since the boundaries of the mid-range are powers of the base, it is possible to bound each accumulator without making any allowance for upward rounding. Rather than going into the details of Blue's analysis, we shall simply present a pair of theorems that are useful in situations of this kind. The second one (Theorem 8) is the key to round-off free bounds.

Theorem 7

Let u, v, and $u*v$ be positive model numbers, where $*$ is addition or multiplication. Let x and y be positive machine numbers that are in range, with $x \leqslant u$ and $y \leqslant v$. Then

$$\mathrm{fl}(x*y) \leqslant u*v.$$

Proof

By Axiom 1.

Theorem 8

Let $x_1, \ldots, x_n$ be machine numbers with $\sigma \leqslant x_i \leqslant b^k$ for $i=1,\ldots,n$, where $n \leqslant b^p$ and $nb^k \leqslant \lambda$. (The environment parameters, b, p, σ, and λ, are defined in Section 2, while k and n are arbitrary integers.) Then

$$y \equiv \mathrm{fl}\left(\sum_{i=1}^{n} x_i\right) \leqslant nb^k.$$

Proof

The proof is by induction on n. If $n=1$, the theorem is trivial. Otherwise, the last step is to compute

$$y = \mathrm{fl}(y_1+y_2)$$

where y_1 and y_2 are computed partial sums. By induction we may assume that $y_1 \leqslant mb^k$ and $y_2 \leqslant (n-m)b^k$ for some $m<n$. Now since $n \leqslant b^p$, Theorem 7 implies that $y \leqslant nb^k$, as was to be shown.

Using Underflow

Rather than rigorously preventing the occurrence of underflow, it may sometimes be easier and more rewarding to elect continued computation (we believe this option is always available in the underflow case), and to avoid using the generated special number. For example, consider an iteration of the form

$$\text{while } (x>a) \ \{action\}$$

where a is in range, and where *action* improves an approximation to a desired result and decreases x. In the last iteration x may underflow, but by Axiom 4 the termination test will succeed anyway. Upon leaving this control structure, one must, of course, avoid using x until a safe value is assigned to it.

8. Acknowledgments

I am grateful to A. D. Hall for calling my attention to the importance of computer modeling. I also thank S. I. Feldman, P. A. Fox, L. Kaufman, and M. D. McIlroy for very helpful comments on an earlier version of this paper.

References

1.   P. A. Fox, A. D. Hall, and N. L. Schryer, "The PORT Mathematical Subroutine Library," *Computing Science Technical Report No. 47*, Bell Laboratories, Murray Hill, New Jersey, September 1976, revised May 1977. To appear in *ACM Trans. Math. Software.*

2.   D. E. Knuth, "Accuracy of Floating-Point Arithmetic," pp. 195-210 in *Seminumerical Algorithms*, Vol. 2 of *The Art of Computer Programming*, Addison-Wesley, Reading, Massachusetts, 1969.

3.   Ramon E. Moore, *Interval Analysis*, Prentice Hall, Englewood Cliffs, N. J., 1966.

4.   J. L. Blue, "A Portable Fortran Program to Find the Euclidean Norm of a Vector," *Computing Science Technical Report No. 45*, Bell Laboratories, Murray Hill, New Jersey, February 1977. To appear in *ACM Trans. Math. Software.*

Bell Laboratories
Murray Hill, New Jersey 07974

The Block Lanczos Method
for Computing Eigenvalues

G. H. Golub

R. Underwood

ABSTRACT

In this paper, we describe a Block Lanczos method for computing a few of the least or greatest eigenvalues of a sparse symmetric matrix. A basic result of Kaniel and Paige describing the rate of convergence of Lanczos' method will be extended to the Block Lanczos method. The results of experiments conducted with this method will be presented and discussed.

1. INTRODUCTION.

Often it is necessary to compute the algebraically greatest or least eigenvalues of a large, sparse symmetric matrix A where r is much less than n, the order of A. In this paper, we describe an algorithm for solving this problem and present the results of experiments in which a program implementing this algorithm was applied to a variety of problems. A theorem describing the rates of convergence of the computed eigenvalues to the true eigenvalues will also be presented along with its proof.

The algorithm we will describe is an extension of the method of minimized iterations due to Lanczos [1]. In this procedure, the elements of a symmetric tridiagonal matrix similar to A are generated by an iterative procedure. Lanczos proposed using these elements to compute the coefficients of a polynomial whose roots are eigenvalues of A

361

and described how vectors generated in the course of the
iteration could be combined to form the eigenvectors corresponding to these eigenvalues. However, due to certain practical difficulties, Lanczos' method was supplanted by Given's
and Householder's methods for solving the general symmetric
eigenproblem.

Paige [9] experimented with Lanczos' method and found
that a few of the least and greatest eigenvalues of the tridiagonal matrix would often converge rapidly to those of A
long before the process was completed. A similar approach
was also suggested by Karush [10].

The method we will describe, the Block Lanczos Method,
is an extension of Lanczos' method in which we iterate with
a block of vectors rather than a single vector. In place of
the tridiagonal matrix generated in Lanczos' method, we generate a _block_ tridiagonal matrix. The Block Lanczos method
can furthermore be used in the manner proposed by Paige.
That is, one can compute a sequence of estimates to the
eigenvalues of A from the block tridiagonal matrix. Our
extension is similar in spirit to the work of Hestenes and
Karush [2] on the method of steepest descent and generalizes
Lanczos' method in the same way that simultaneous iteration
generalizes the power method. It not only enables us to compute several eigenvalues and eigenvectors simultaneously, but
affords us improved rates of convergence.

Several researchers have been instrumental in developing
the Block Lanczos method. In particular, Kahan and Parlett
[3], Cullum and Donath [4], Lewis [5], and Underwood [6]
following a suggestion of Golub. The results and work
reported here are taken in large part from [6].

In the next section we will describe and develop the
Block Lanczos method. In Section 3, we will discuss its
numerical properties and problems associated with its application and in Section 4, we will describe the results of
certain experiments carried out with a program implementing
this method. Finally, in Section 5, we will mention recent
developments and work done with the Block Lanczos method.

2.   A BLOCK LANCZOS ALGORITHM.

Our development of this algorithm follows the path taken

by Lanczos in the development of his method and is described
in greater detail in [6].

Starting from an initial n-by-p orthonormal matrix X,
our goal is to compute a sequence of mutually orthonormal
n-by-p matrices $X_1, X_2, \ldots, X_s$ such that the space of
vectors spanned by the columns of these matrices contains the
columns of the matrices $X, AX, A^2X, \ldots, A^{s-1}X$. To simplify our explanation, we assume that $n \gg 1$, the value of
p is greater than zero and less than or equal to $n/2$, and
s is greater than 1 and less than or equal to n/p . Note
that it will usually be the case that $p \cdot s \ll n$. To start
with, we let $X_1 = X$, compute AX_1 and Z_2 where

$$(2.1) \qquad\qquad Z_2 = AX_1 - X_1 M_1$$

and M_1 is a p-by-p matrix chosen so that the Euclidean
norm of Z_2 is minimized with respect to all possible
choices of M_1 . It can be shown that $\| Z_2 \|$ is minimized
when $M_1 = X_1^t A X_1$. With this choice for M_1 , we have that

$$(2.2) \qquad\qquad Z_2 = (I - X_1 X_1^t) A X_1 .$$

That is, Z_2 is the projection of AX_1 onto the space
orthogonal to that spanned by the columns of X_1 . The
matrix X_2 is then obtained by orthonormalizing Z_2 :

$$(2.3) \qquad\qquad Z_2 = X_2 R_2$$

where R_2 is a p-by-p matrix which is usually but not
necessarily taken to be upper triangular. (X_2 and R_2 are
by no means unique.) Note that R_2 will be singular if Z_2
is rank deficient. In the case that R_2 is upper triangular
rank deficiency means that some of the columns of X_2 can be
chosen arbitrarily. To make the algorithm go through, it is
necessary only to choose these columns so that they are
orthonormal to X_1 . In any event, we have that X_2 is
orthogonal to X_1 . From (2.2) and (2.3), it is easily seen
that the space spanned by X_1 and X_2 contains the columns
of X and AX .

The remaining matrices in the sequence $X_1, X_2, \ldots, X_s$
are computed as follows: Given $X_1, X_2, \ldots, X_i$ for

$i \geq 2$, we compute AX_i and Z_{i+1} where

(2.4) $\qquad Z_{i+1} = AX_i - X_1 B_{i,1}^t - X_2 B_{i,2}^t - \cdots$

$$- X_{i-1} B_{i,i-1}^t - X_i M_i$$

and $B_{i,1}, B_{i,2}, \ldots, B_{i,i-1},$ and M_i are chosen so that the Euclidean norm of Z_{i+1} is minimized with respect to all possible choices of these matrices. It can be shown that $\| Z_{i+1} \|$ is minimized when

$$B_{i,j} = X_i^t AX_j$$

and

$$M_i = X_i^t AX_i .$$

and hence,

(2.5) $\qquad Z_{i+1} = (I - X_1 X_1^t - X_2 X_2^t - \cdots - X_i X_i^t) AX_i .$

Thus, Z_{i+1} is the projection of AX_i onto the space orthogonal to that spanned by the columns of $X_1, X_2, \ldots, X_i$. We now compute X_{i+1} by orthonormalizing Z_{i+1} :

(2.6) $\qquad Z_{i+1} = X_{i+1} R_{i+1}$

where R_{i+1} is a p-by-p matrix and X_{i+1} is orthonormal. Since Z_{i+1} is orthogonal to $X_1, X_2, \ldots, X_i$, we have that X_{i+1} is orthogonal to all previous X_j . As before, if Z_{i+1} is rank deficient, we choose the additional columns of X_{i+1} so that they are orthonormal to the columns of $X_1, X_2, \ldots, X_i$.

By equations (2.4) and (2.6), we have that

$$AX_i = X_1 B_{i,1}^t + X_2 B_{i,2}^t + \cdots + X_{i-1} B_{i,i-1}^t$$

$$+ X_i M_i + X_{i+1} R_{i+1} .$$

From this last equation, we conclude from the orthogonality of the X_j that

$$B_{i,j} = 0$$

for $j = 1, 2, \ldots, i-2$, since AX_j is a combination of $X_1, X_2, \ldots, X_{j+1}$. Thus, we have

(2.7) $$AX_i = X_{i-1}B_{i,i-1}^t + X_iM_i + X_{i+1}R_{i+1} \cdot$$

It can be easily shown that

$$B_{i,i-1} = R_i \cdot$$

Equations (2.1), (2.3), and (2.7) can therefore be written as follows:

(2.8) $$AX_1 = X_1M_1 + X_2R_2$$

(2.9) $$AX_i = X_{i-1}R_i^t + X_iM_i + X_{i+1}R_{i+1}$$

for $i = 2, 3, \ldots, s-1$, and

(2.10) $$AX_s = X_{s-1}R_s^t + X_sM_s + Z_{s+1} ,$$

or

$$A\bar{X}_s = \bar{X}_s\bar{M}_s + \bar{Z}_{s+1}$$

where

$$\bar{M}_s = \begin{pmatrix} M_1 & R_2^t & \Theta & . & . & . & \Theta \\ R_2 & M_2 & R_3^t & . & & & . \\ \Theta & R_3 & M_3 & . & & & . \\ . & . & . & . & & & . \\ . & . & . & . & & & . \\ . & . & . & . & & & \Theta \\ & & & . & & M_{s-1} & R_s^t \\ \Theta & . & . & . & \Theta & R_s & M_s \end{pmatrix}$$

$$\bar{X}_s = (X_1, X_2, \ldots, X_s)$$

and

$$\bar{Z}_{s+1} = (\Theta, \Theta, \ldots, \Theta, Z_{s+1}) \cdot$$

Since Z_{s+1} is orthogonal to $X_1, X_2, \ldots, X_s$ we have that

$$\bar{X}_s^t\bar{Z}_{s+1} = \Theta$$

and

$$\bar{X}_s^tA\bar{X}_s = \bar{M}_s \cdot$$

From (2.5) and (2.6), it can be shown [6] that the space spanned by X_1, X_2, $\ldots$, X_i contains the columns of the matrices X, AX, A^2X, $\ldots$, $A^{i-1}X$ for all $i = 1, 2, \ldots ,s$.

Using equations (2.8), (2.9), and (2.10), we define the following <u>Block Lanczos Algorithm</u>: Given p and s where $1 \leq p \leq n/2$ and $1 \leq s \leq n/p$, and X, an n-by-p orthonormal matrix, compute sequences of matrices X_1, X_2, $\ldots$, X_s , M_1, M_2, $\ldots$, M_s, and R_2, R_3, $\ldots$, R_s satisfying equations (2.8), (2.9), and (2.10) as follows:

Step 1.   Let $X_1 = X$. Compute AX_1 and $M_1 = X_1^t AX_1$.

Step 2.   For $i=1, 2, \ldots , s-1$, do the following three steps:

Step 2a.   Compute
$$Z_{i+1}= \begin{cases} AX_1 - X_1 M_1 & \text{if } i=1 \text{ , or} \\ AX_i - X_i M_i - X_{i-1} R_i^t & \text{if } i>1 \text{ .} \end{cases}$$

Step 2b.   Compute X_{i+1} and R_{i+1} such that X_{i+1} is orthonormal, R_{i+1} is upper triangular and
$$Z_{i+1} = X_{i+1} R_{i+1} \text{ .}$$
If Z_{i+1} is rank deficient, choose the columns of X_{i+1} so that they are orthogonal to all previous X_j .

Step 2c.   Compute AX_{i+1} and
$$M_{i+1} = X_{i+1}^t AX_{i+1} \text{ .}$$

Because of the numerical properties of this algorithm (cf. Section 3), it will be necessary to modify step 2b to ensure that X_{i+1} is orthogonal to all previous X_j even when Z_{i+1} is <u>not</u> rank deficient. This point will be discussed further in Section 3.

Note that $\overline{M}_s$ is a symmetric block tridiagonal matrix and since the R_i are chosen to be upper triangular, it is also a band matrix with half-band width $p+1$. If it were the case that $p \cdot s = n$, then $\overline{M}_s$ would be similar to A and the eigenvalues of $\overline{M}_s$ would also be eigenvalues of A . In general, because of the numerical properties of the Block Lanczos Algorithm mentioned above, it is not practical to carry the method through to completion. The value of the algorithm lies in the fact that some of the least (and greatest) eigenvalues of $\bar{M}_s$ will closely approximate the corresponding eigenvalues of A for values of s such that $p \cdot s \ll n$, as the following theorem indicates.

Theorem 1 [6]. Let $\lambda_1 \le \lambda_2 \le \ldots \le \lambda_n$ be the eigenvalues of A with orthonormalized eigenvectors $q_1, q_2, \ldots, q_n$. Assume that $\lambda_p < \lambda_{p+1}$. Let $\mu_1 \le \mu_2 \le \mu_3 \ldots \le \mu_{ps}$ be the eigenvalues of $\bar{M}_s$. Let

$$W \equiv \begin{bmatrix} W_1 \\ W_2 \end{bmatrix} \equiv Q^t X$$

where

$$Q = (q_1, q_2, q_3, \ldots, q_n)$$

and W_1 is a p-by-p matrix composed of the first p rows of W. Suppose that W_1 is nonsingular so that σ_{min}, the smallest singular value of W_1, is greater than zero.

Then for $i = 1, 2, \ldots, p$,

$$\lambda_k \le \mu_k \le \lambda_k + \varepsilon_k^2$$

where

$$\varepsilon_k^2 = \frac{(\lambda_n - \lambda_k) \tan^2 \theta}{T_{s-1}^2 \left(\frac{1 + \gamma_k}{1 - \gamma_k} \right)}$$

$$\theta = \arccos \sigma_{min}$$

$$\gamma_k = (\lambda_k - \lambda_{p+1})/(\lambda_k - \lambda_n) \text{, and}$$

T_{s-1} is the (s-1)st Chebyshev polynomial of the first kind.

Proof. We will only outline the proof here. For complete details, see [6].

By the Courant-Fischer theorem [7], it can be shown that

(2.11)
$$\lambda_k \le \mu_k \le \lambda_k'$$

where

(2.12)
$$\lambda_k' = \max_{\substack{y \in E_k \\ y \ne \theta}} \frac{y^t A y}{y^t y}$$

where E_k is any k-dimensional subspace spanned by k independent vectors in $L(s,X,A)$, the space spanned by $X_1, X_2, \ldots, X_s$. We will show that there are p vectors $g_1, g_2, \ldots, g_p$ in $L(s,X,A)$ such that if E_k is the space spanned by the first k of these vectors, then

(2.13) $\lambda_k^{\prime} \leq \lambda_k + \varepsilon_k^2$.

By combining (2.11) and (2.13), we have Theorem 1.

The vectors g_i are chosen as follows: Let P be the polynomial such that

$$P(\lambda) = T_{s-1}(z)$$

where

$$z = 1 - 2(\lambda_{p+1} - \lambda)/(\lambda_{p+1} - \lambda_n) .$$

By the properties of Chebyshev polynomials,

$$P(\lambda_1) \geq P(\lambda_2) \geq \ldots \geq P(\lambda_p) \geq 1$$

and

$$\left| P(\lambda_i) \right| \leq 1$$

for $i = p+1$, $p+2$, ... , n . Let Λ be the diagonal matrix of eigenvalues whose ith diagonal element is λ_i . Similarly, let Λ_1 and Λ_2 be diagonal matrices of orders p and n-p respectively, whose ith diagonal elements are λ_i and λ_{p+i} respectively. It follows that

$$AQ = Q\Lambda$$

and

$$P(A)Q = QP(\Lambda)$$

where $P(A)$ and $P(\Lambda)$ are matrices computed by evaluating P at A and Λ . Now, let

$$G = (g_1, g_2, \ldots , g_p) \equiv P(A) X W_1^{-1} P(\Lambda_1)^{-1} .$$

It can be easily seen that each column of G is a combination of the columns of X, AX, A^2X, ... , $A^{s-1}X$. Since $L(s,X,A)$ contains the columns of the matrices X, AX, ... , $A^{s-1}X$, each g_i is in $L(s,X,A)$. The remainder of the proof involves showing that with E_k chosen to be the space spanned by $g_1, g_2, \ldots , g_k$, the value of $\lambda_k^{\prime}$ defined by equation (2.12) satisfies equation (2.13).

This theorem is an extension of a result due to Kaniel [8,9], and, indeed, reduces to Kaniel's theorem when $p=1$. A similar theorem can be given for the largest eigenvalues.

Example. Suppose A is of order 1000 and $\lambda_1 = 0.0$, $\lambda_2 = 0.1$, $\lambda_3 = 0.5$, and $\lambda_{1000} = 1.0$. Suppose further that

X is such that $\sigma_{min} = 0.04$. If we then apply the Block Lanczos method to A and X with p=2 and s=10, we will find that the two least eigenvalues μ_1 and μ_2 of $\bar{M}_{10}$ will satisfy

$$\lambda_1 \leq \mu_1 \leq \lambda_1 + 2.6_{10}-8,$$

and

$$\lambda_2 \leq \mu_2 \leq \lambda_2 + 3.6_{10}-7.$$

Thus for the relatively small cost of computing $\bar{M}_{10}$ (of order 20) and its two least eigenvalues, we are able to obtain very accurate approximations to the two least eigenvalues of A.

As is the case with the simultaneous iteration method, there is no need in the Block Lanczos method to explicitly modify the matrix A. Rather, all that is needed is a procedure for multiplying a vector x by A. This is what makes it especially valuable for sparse matrices. In contrast to the simultaneous iteration procedure, however, one can get either the largest or smallest eigenvalues of A automatically with the Block Lanczos method regardless of whether they are of largest modulus or not.

Note that, as we have defined it, the Block Lanczos method is not a method for computing eigenvalues and eigenvectors per se. Rather, it is a procedure for computing a block tridiagonal matrix which is similar to A. To produce a complete algorithm for computing eigenvalues and eigenvectors, we need to combine it with a technique for computing the eigenvalues μ_i and eigenvectors y_i of $\bar{M}_s$. In [6], the QR method is used.

Given an eigenvector y_i of $\bar{M}_s$ corresponding to μ_i, the vector $\bar{q}_i$ will be a good approximation to q_i where

$$\bar{q}_i = \bar{X}_s y_i.$$

It can be shown that $\bar{q}_i$ and μ_i satisfy

(2.14) $\qquad A\bar{q}_i - \mu_i \bar{q}_i = r_i = \bar{Z}_{s+1} y_i = Z_{s+1} w_i$

where w_i denotes the vector of order p composed of the last p components of y_i. We see from equation (2.14) that the eigenvalues of $\bar{M}_s$ will be exact eigenvalues of A if we have $Z_{s+1} = \Theta$. While we might normally expect that the eigenvalues of $\bar{M}_s$

might not bear any relationship to those of A unless all the
elements of Z_{s+1} were very small or zero, it will turn out
to be the case that the elements of the vector $Z_{s+1}w_i$ for the
least and greatest eigenvalues of eigenvectors of $\overline{M}_s$ will be
very small.

In practice, it usually is the case that the number of
steps s of the Block Lanczos method that can be carried out
must satisfy p·s $\leq$ q where q is a value dictated by the available memory on the computing system and in most instances, q
will be much less than n. After carrying out these maximum
number of steps, we may find that the eigenvalues μ_i have
not converged to the desired accuracy. The result of Theorem
1 suggests that more accurate approximations may be computed
by re-applying the Block Lanczos method to A and the matrix
X composed of the eigenvector approximations $\overline{q}_i$. In fact, one
may apply the procedure repeatedly starting each iteration
after the first with a matrix X composed of the eigenvector
approximations computed during the previous step. This idea
leads us to the following <u>Iterative Block Lanczos Algorithm</u>:
Let X be an arbitrary orthonormal n-by-p matrix where
$1 \leq p \leq n/2$. Let s be an integer value such that $1 \leq s \leq n/p$.
Compute approximations to the p least eigenvalues and eigenvectors of A as follows:

Step 1.   Apply the Block Lanczos Algorithm to X computing
          $\overline{M}_s$ and $\overline{X}_s$.

Step 2.   Compute the p least eigenvalues μ_i and eigen-
          vectors y_i of $\overline{M}_s$.

Step 3.   Compute $\overline{q}_i = \overline{X}_s y_i$ for i = 1, 2, ... , p.

Step 4.   If $\mu_1, \mu_2, \ldots , \mu_p$ are sufficiently accurate,
          then stop. Otherwise, return to step 1 with
          X replaced by the matrix $(\overline{q}_1, \overline{q}_2, \ldots , \overline{q}_p)$.

It may be the case, however, that the number r of eigenvalues
and eigenvectors that we need is not equal to p, the block
size. Furthermore, once a few eigenvalues and eigenvectors
have converged, one need not iterate with them any longer.
However, it is necessary to maintain the orthogonality of the
matrices $X_1, X_2, \ldots , X_s$ computed during each iteration with
respect to eigenvectors already computed. This may be conveniently carried out in the context of step 2b of the Block

Lanczos Algorithm. For a complete description of an Iterative Block Lanczos Algorithm incorporating this concept and allowing the computation of an arbitrary number r of eigenvalues and eigenvectors subject only to memory limitations, see [6].

3. IMPLEMENTATION.

In this section, we will consider certain properties of the Block Lanczos Algorithm and problems associated with its implementation and application.

By the way in which the X_i were defined in Equations (2.1), (2.2), (2.5), and (2.6), it would seem that they should be mutually orthogonal. In practice, however, because of the loss of figures when Z_{i+1} is computed, they rapidly lose orthogonality so that after a few steps of the Block Lanczos process, the current X_i will no longer be orthogonal to the initial blocks in the sequence $X_1, X_2, \ldots ,$ X_i. It is this phenomenon that makes the Lanczos algorithm unsuitable for the general symmetric eigenproblem. To maintain the stability of the process requires costly reorthogonalization of each X_i with respect to all previous X_j, making the method relatively more costly to apply in relation to, say, the Givens or Householder methods for tridiagonalizing a matrix.

When used as described in the previous section, however, loss of orthogonality is a mixed blessing. As Paige [9] pointed out in his thesis, loss of orthogonality goes hand-in-hand with convergence of some of the eigenvalues of $\overline{M}_s$ to eigenvalues of A. That is, at the very point that the process is about to go awry, we have achieved our desired goal of computing accurate approximations to a few of the eigenvalues of A. The difficulty in using the Lanczos method in this way lies in reliably and efficiently determining at what point orthogonality is being lost. If the process is continued beyond this point, then it in essence restarts and we may recompute eigenvalues that have already been computed. That is, a simple eigenvalue of A may appear more than once among the eigenvalues of $\overline{M}_s$ even though its multiplicity is one. One is then faced with the task of determining whether an eigenvalue of $\overline{M}_s$ which

appears more than once is truly a multiple root of A or
whether it is a simple root which has been computed more than
once. To this date, there is no completely reliable solution
to this problem. Kahan and Parlett [3] examined this problem
and concluded that not enough is known at the present time
to design a universal Lanczos program although the process
can often be tailored to a particular problem with considerable success.

    In our work we have chosen to include a reorthogonaliza-
tion step. In particular, we replace step 2b in the description of the Block Lanczos Algorithm with the following modified step:

      Step 2b'.   Reorthogonalize Z_{i+1} with respect to all
                 previous X_j and compute X_{i+1} and R_{i+1}
                 such that $Z_{i+1} = X_{i+1} R_{i+1}$.

It should be pointed out that this modification preserves
the stability of the algorithm at a considerable cost. The
reorthogonalization process not only requires a large number
of arithmetic operations but requires that each of the X_j
be in memory during each step of the method as opposed to
only the previous two blocks in the basic process. However,
our experiments indicated that even with a reorthogonalization step it was competitive with the simultaneous iteration
algorithm, one of the best techniques for solving large,
sparse symmetric eigenproblems.

    The Iterative Block Lanczos method described in the last
section provides a convenient method for estimating the
accuracy of the computed eigenvalues and eigenvectors. It
can be shown [6] that the ith column of the matrix Z_2 (cf.
section 2) computed in each iteration after the first will
be the residual vector for the ith eigenvalue μ_i and eigenvector $\bar{q}_i$ computed in the previous iteration. One may then
determine at the start of an iteration the accuracy of the
eigenvalues and eigenvectors computed at the end of the
previous iteration and discontinue iterating with those that
have converged.

    We end this section with a few suggestions on how to
choose the block size p . If possible, it is usually best

to choose p equal to the number r of eigenvalues and
eigenvectors we are attempting to compute. It seldom pays
to iterate with more than r vectors since this will mean
that we will be able to carry through fewer steps due to
memory limitations. If one is afforded some a priori information on the spectrum of A , Theorem 1 suggests that a good
choice for p is one for which the gap between λ_p and
λ_{p+1} is fairly large. Also, it is best to choose the block
size at least as large as the largest multiplicity possessed
by any eigenvalue of A . Note that if A has an eigenvalue of multiplicity m and m > p , then we can compute at
most p of these eigenvalues at a time.

4. EXAMPLES.

In this section we report on experiments conducted with
a Fortran program implementing the iterative Block Lanczos
Algorithm described in [6]. The results reported here were
computed on an IBM 370/168 computer and are also taken from
[6].

Example 1 [6, ch. 4, ex. 1]. The matrix A is a diagonal matrix of order n=454 with eigenvalues λ_1 = -10.00,
λ_2 = -9.99, λ_3 = -9.98, λ_4 = -9.00, ... , λ_{454} = 0.0. We
used the program to compute the three least eigenvalues and
eigenvectors (r = 3) with an initial block size of three
(p = 3). A total of fifteen vectors were allowed for storing
the X_i (q = 15 and p·s $\leq$ 15) and an accuracy of eps =
$1.0_{10}-8$ was requested. In 11 iterations, the program computed μ_1 = -9.9999 99999 99996, μ_2 = -9.9899 99999 99994 ,
and μ_3 = -9.9799 99999 99991 with relative errors less than
$1.0_{10}-8$ in all three cases. Note that the error is the
error in the eigenvectors and that the eigenvalues, since
they are Rayleigh quotients, are approximately twice as
accurate as the eigenvectors.

Example 2 [6, ch. 4, ex. 2]. The matrix in this example
is the same as in example 1 except that the spread in the
eigenvalues has been reduced by a factor of 10. That is,
λ_1 = -10.00, λ_2 = -9.999, λ_3 = -9.998, λ_4 = -9.900, ... ,
λ_{454} = -9.000. As in example 1, the three least eigenvalues
were computed to an approximate accuracy of $1.0_{10}-8$ using
fifteen working vectors. In this case, the program took 10

iterations to compute the desired eigenvalues to about the same accuracy as in example 1. This example together with example 1 serves to illustrate the point that the rates of convergence of the Block Lanczos Algorithm depend on the relative spread of the eigenvalues as Theorem 1 suggests.

Example 3 [6, ch. 4, ex. 4]. In this example, A is of order 180 with eigenvalues $\lambda_1 = \lambda_2 = 0.0$, $\lambda_3 = \lambda_4 = 0.1$, $\lambda_5 = .25$, ... , and $\lambda_{180} = 2.00$. We computed the four least eigenvalues and eigenvectors to a relative precision of $1.0_{10}-4$ using ten working vectors (q = 10). In this case we tried block sizes of p = 1, 2, 3, and 4. The program took the fewest iterations with p = 2 and the greatest number with p = 4. Even though the rates of convergence were better with the larger block size, the program could carry through more steps of the Block Lanczos Algorithm with p = 2. This example demonstrates that the program often has no difficulty computing multiple eigenvalues and that the least eigenvalues need not be the eigenvalues of greatest modulus as is the case with the simultaneous iteration method.

Example 4 [6, ch. 4, ex. 5]. The matrix A is of order 300 with $\lambda_1 = 0.0$, $\lambda_2 = \lambda_3 = \lambda_4 = 0.1$, $\lambda_5 = 0.25$, ... , $\lambda_{300} = 1.0$. Block sizes of p = 1, 2, and 3 were tried with p = 3 requiring the fewest iterations. In particular, with p = 3, the program took four iterations to compute the three least eigenvalues to an approximate precision of $1.0_{10}-3$ using 12 working vectors. Note that with p = 3 there is no gap between λ_3 and λ_4 and in spite of this, the algorithm worked very well. Theorem 1 therefore clearly does not tell the whole story regarding the convergence of this method. We suspect that in this example λ_5 plays a role but we have discovered no way of proving this.

Example 5 [6, ch. 4, ex. 7]. In this example, we compute the twelve smallest eigenvalues of the discrete biharmonic operator H [11] of order 1024. Rather than compute the eigenvalues of H directly, we compute those of A = $-H^{-1}$ where the matrix vector product Ax = y required by the Block Lanczos procedure is obtained by solving

$$Hz = x$$

for z using the method of Buzbee, Dorr and Golub [16], and then setting

$$y = -z .$$

This serves to illustrate an important point mentioned previously regarding the Block Lanczos method. Namely, it is not necessary to explicitly modify the matrix A. Rather, all that is required is a procedure for computing the matrix-vector product Ax given x .

Using 16 working vectors (q = 16) and an initial block size of p = 3, the program took 19 iterations to compute the required number of eigenvalues and eigenvectors to precisions which varied from $1.0_{10}-3$ to $1.0_{10}-6$.

Using the eigenvalues of A , we can compute those of H which are in turn related to the frequencies of vibration of a square, clamped elastic plate. The frequencies computed using our program compare favorably with those reported by Bauer and Reiss [11] and the rough plots of the eigenvectors indicate that they accurately describe the fundamental modes of vibration of clamped plates.

We note, finally, that this program has been successfully applied to the eigenproblem of the Laplace operator over arbitrary bounded plane regions by Proskurowski [12].

A listing of the program used in the above examples is contained in [6] and copies of the program are available from the authors upon request.

5. EXTENSIONS.

Although the emphasis of the paper has been on computing the least eigenvalues, we note that the technique applies equally well to the problem of computing the greatest eigenvalues of A . One could easily construct a program for computing the greatest eigenvalues and eigenvectors directly or apply the ideas in this paper to the matrix -A .

Golub, Luk and Overton [13] have developed a program for computing a few of the largest singular values of a matrix using a variant of the Block Lanczos method. The basic idea is to use several vectors to generate a block bidiagonal matrix which has band structure.

The Block Lanczos method can also be used for generating a band matrix with a given eigenvalue structure. In parti-

cular, suppose one is given the eigenvalues of the first
p+1 leading principal minors of a symmetric matrix. This
information is sufficient to compute the first p elements
of the eigenvectors of the matrix. From these vectors, it
is possible to generate a symmetric matrix which has a half
band width p+1 . Details of this algorithm are given in
[14].

Finally, it is well known that there is a close theoretical connection between the Conjugate Gradient method and
Lanczos' method. Underwood [15] has developed a Block Conjugate Gradient method which extends the Conjugate Gradient
method in the same way that the Block Lanczos method extends
Lanczos' method. That is, using a program based on this
method, he has been able to solve several systems of equations with the same matrix simultaneously with improved rates
of convergence over those afforded by the standard Conjugate
Gradient method.

REFERENCES

1. C. Lanczos (1950), An iteration method for the solution
    of the eigenvalue problem of linear differential and
    integral operators, Journal of Research of the
    National Bureau of Standards, 45, pp. 255-282.

2. M. R. Hestenes and W. Karush (1951), A method of grad-
    ients for the calculation of the characteristic roots
    and vectors of a real symmetric matrix, Journal of
    Research of the National Bureau of Standards, 47,
    pp. 45-61.

3. W. Kahan and B. N. Parlett (1976), How far should you go
    with the Lanczos process, Sparse Matrix Computations,
    J. Bunch and D. Rose, eds., Academic Press, New York,
    pp. 131-144.

4. J. Cullum and W. E. Donath (1974), A block generalization
    of the symmetric s-step Lanczos algorithm, Report
    RC 4845 (21570), IBM Thomas J. Watson Research
    Center, Yorktown Heights, New York.

5. J. Lewis (1977), Algorithms for sparse matrix eigenvalue
    problems, Ph.D. dissertation, Stanford University,
    Stanford, California.

6. R. R. Underwood (1975), An iterative block Lanczos method
    for the solution of large sparse symmetric eigen-
    problems, Ph.D. dissertation, Stanford University,
    Stanford, California.

7. J. H. Wilkinson (1965), *The Algebraic Eigenvalue Problem*, Clarendon Press, Oxford, England.

8. S. Kaniel (1966), Estimates for some computational techniques in linear algebra, *Mathematics of Computation*, 20, pp. 369-378.

9. C. C. Paige (1971), The computation of eigenvalues and eigenvectors of very large sparse matrices, Ph.D. dissertation, The University of London, London, England.

10. W. Karush (1951), An iterative method for finding characteristic vectors of a symmetric matrix, *Pacific Journal of Mathematics*, 1, pp. 233-248.

11. L. Bauer and E. L. Reiss (1972), Block five diagonal matrices and the fast numerical solution of the biharmonic equation, *Mathematics of Computation*, 26, pp. 311-326.

12. W. Proskurowski (1976), On the numerical solution of the eigenvalue problem of the Laplace operator by a capacitance matrix method, Internal report, Lawrence Berkeley Laboratory, University of California, Berkeley, California.

13. G. H. Golub, F. Luk, and M. Overton (1977), A block Lanczos algorithm for computing the largest singular values and associated vectors of a matrix, Computer Science Department Technical Report, to appear, Stanford University, Stanford, California.

14. D. Boley and G. H. Golub (1977), Solving the inverse eigenvalue problem for band matrices, to appear in the Proceedings of the Dundee Conference on Numerical Analysis.

15. R. R. Underwood (1977), A block generalization of the conjugate gradient method, to appear.

16. B. L. Buzbee and F. W. Dorr (1973), The direct solution of the biharmonic equation on rectangular regions and the Poisson equation on irregular regions, Report LA-UR-73-636, Los Alamos Scientific Laboratory, Los Alamos, New Mexico.

The authors were supported in part by the National Science Foundation under Grants GJ35135X, GJ29988X, and MCS75-13497-A01, by the Atomic Energy Commission under Grant AT-(04-3)-326-PA30, and by the Energy Research and Development Administration under Grant E(04-3)-326-PA30.

Computer Science Department   Nuclear Energy Division
Stanford University   General Electric Company
Stanford, California 94305   San Jose, California 95127

Index

A

Aasen, J. O., 142
Absolute stability, 127, 137
Accuracy, 3, 223, 239, 242
   and order, 263
ACM transactions on mathematical software,196, 201
Adaptation techniques, 302
Adaptive, 226, 238, 239, 246, 247
   discretization, 278, 302, 304
   techniques, 226, 239
Additive model, 142
Affine transformation, 89
Aiken relay calculator, 200
Aird, T. J., 223
Akima, H., 163, 164, 191
Akritas, A. G., 36, 39, 56, 67
Algebraic numbers, 35
Algorithm analysis, 36
Algorithmic foundations, 203
Anomalies
   arithmetic, 348
Anselone, P. M., 17
a–posteriori analysis, 226, 228, 243
Approximation–Order, 302, 305
Arbitrarily placed data, 110
Arithmetic, 343, 344, 345, 346
   anomalies, 348
   comparison, 355
   model, 349
Aronofsky, J., 224
Asymptotically correct
   estimator, 260
Aziz, A. K., 253

B

Backward error, 129
   analysis, 3
Bailey, C. B., 274
Bakhvalov, N. S., 254
Banded systems, 9

Barker, L. E., 138
Barnhill, R. E., 161, 163, 164
Barrodale, I., 28, 31
Barwell, V., 142
Barycentric coordinates, 85, 88
Base, 343
Basic linear algebra subroutines, 11
Basili, V., 254
Battiste, E. L., 220, 223
Bauer, F. L., 14
Bauer, L., 375
Bengtsson, B. E., 163
Bentley, J., 223
Berlekamp, E. R., 43, 66
Bicubically blended patch, 73
Bicubic patch, 76
Biharmonic operator, 374
Bilinear
   form, 234, 236, 237, 245
   interpolant, 73
Birkhoff, G., 91, 92, 164, 317, 319
Bisection, 40, 45, 53
Bivariate forms, 226
BLAS, 11, 12, 13, 14
Block
   elimination, 246
   Lanczos algorithm, 366, 372
   Lanczos method, 361, 363
   tridiagonal matrix, 362
Block, N., 161
Blue, J. L., 360
Boley, D., 377
Boolean sum, 71, 75, 95, 103, 113
Boundary, 337
   approximation, 299, 303, 305
   condition, 237, 248, 331, 337
      normal, 237
      nonnormal, 237
   curved, 296, 300
   layer, 279, 299, 302, 306
   relaxation, 291
   – value problems, 277

Bounds on variables, 31
Boyle, J. M., 221, 222
Brandt, A., 254, 320
Brown, B. E., 85
Brown, J. H., 75, 81, 91, 104
Brown, K., 222
Brown, W. S., 41, 66
Buell, W. R., 254
Bunch, J. R., 142
Bush, B. A., 254
Businger, P. A., 14
Buzbee, B. L., 370, 375

C

Capacitance methods, 322
Cauchy–Riemann equations, 248
Caviness, B. F., 41, 66
Certification, 209
Chebyshev polynomial, 48, 49, 54, 367
Chinese remainder theorem, 41
Choice of formula, 271
Cholesky factor, 10
Chou, T. J., 36, 68
Circle criterion, 178, 179, 180
Clarke, L., 206, 221
Clough, 171
Clough–Tocher
   element, 171
   triangle, 88
Coarse–Grid
   amplification
      factor, 289
   correction, 283, 284, 298
Cody, W. J., 221, 222
Collected algorithms of the ACM, 201
Collins, G. E., 36, 49, 54–59, 66, 67
Collocation, 321
Column
   –quad, 310
   scaling, 9
   –string, 308
Common subexpression, 354
Communications of the ACM, 201
Comparison
   operators, 355
   value, 144
Compatibility conditions, 71, 78, 79, 96
Compatibility corrected bicubic patch, 78
Compiler effects, 12
Compilers IBM, 13
Complete
   factorization, 39, 42, 43
   pivoting, 8

Complexity, 292, 306, 313
Composite grid, 294, 307
Computational
   analysis, 229
   goals, 228
   model, 124
Computer algebra, 36, 67
Concurrent processes, 247
Condition
   estimator, 4
   number, 2, 3
Confirmatory data analysis, 140
Conjugate gradient, 322
   method, 376
      block, 376
Consistency, 204
Construction order, 308
Continuation, 304
Contour
   C^1 continuity, 161
   plotting, 161, 162
      example, 173, 174
Control system, 124
Converged edge, 190
Convergence
   factor, 282
   rate, 286, 292, 298, 306, 307
Convex hull algorithms, 164
Coons patches, 69
   rectangular, 72
   triangular, 92
Coons, S. A., 72
Correction
   scheme, 283
   term, 78, 79, 80, 96
Cost, 197, 211, 213, 216, 217
   control, 248
Courant–Fischer theorem, 367
Cowell, W. R., 221
Cullum, J., 362
Curtis, A., 14
Curved
   boundary, 296
   domains, 312, 322, 335

D

Damping, 135
Data
   analysis, 139, 140
   fitting, 16
   structure, 307
Davenport, S. M., 273

Davis, P. J., 81
Debug, 12
Degeneracy, 18, 24
Degenerate elliptic, 282
Delay, 125
  reduction, 131
Delayed
  Euler method, 128
  trapezoidal rule, 136
Denby, L., 156
Dennis, J. E., 158
Derivative sequence, 54, 55
Descartes' rule of signs, 36, 55–58
de Vries, G., 255
Diagnostic plot, 144
Differential equations, 126
Dimensional reduction, 232
Discretization, 74, 96, 277, 302, 321, 327
  adaptive, 278, 304
  control, 304
  high order, 302
  optimal order, 303
  optimization, 303, 305
Display, 141, 156, 316
DO, 316
Documentation, 2, 203, 204, 343
Domain representation, 337
Dominance, 43, 44, 58
Donath, W. E., 362
Dongarra, J. J., 12, 13, 222
Dorr, F. W., 375
Double–precision, 345
Douglis–Nirenberg
  system, 233, 246
  type, 233, 246
Downdating, 9, 10, 11
Dritz, K. W., 222
Dube, R. P., 72
DuCroz, J. J., 223
Dynamic residuals, 286

E

Eddy, W. F., 164
Editing session, 76, 77, 115
EDSAC library, 198
Effects, 142
Efficiency, 203
Efron, B., 167
Eigensystem computation, 208
Eigenvalue, 361
  problem, 234
Eigenvalues
  inverse problem, 375

EISPACK, 208, 211
Element
  bilinear, 248
  plate, 229
  trilinear, 232
Elliptic, 278, 282
  equations, 319
  systems, 282
ELLPACK, 319
  file structure, 341
  preprocessor, 332, 339, 340
  structure, 323
Embedding, 304
Emulation, 123
England, R., 261
Enright, W. H., 221, 274
Ensign, M. G., 103
Environment parameters, 343, 344
Equation indexing, 334
Equations of motion, 131
Error
  analysis, 343, 347, 349, 351
  control, 127
  estimate, 232, 236, 246, 247, 259, 268
  estimator (E), 270, 303
  norm, 239
  smoothing, 282
  – weighting function (G), 303, 306
Errors, 3, 7, 9, 218
  in integration, 129
Estimating
  derivatives, 171
  partial derivatives, 170
Euler method, 127
  delayed, 128
Ewing, D. J. F., 85
Exact arithmetic, 35, 39
Exchange algorithm, 16
Exciting research area, 118
Explicit methods, 127
Exploratory data analysis, 139, 140
Exponential fitting, 134
Extrapolation, 134
Extra–precise arithmetic, 348

F

Factorization, 4, 5, 7, 9, 17, 30
Fast
  Fourier transform, 321
  Solver, 278, 292
Fateman, R. J., 60
Fawkes, A. J., 119

Federenko, R., 254
Fedorenko, R. P., 318
Fehlberg, E., 261
Feldman, S. I., 360
Fellen, B. M., 274
File structure, 341
Finite
  −difference equations, 277, 297, 300
  −differences, 277, 281, 321
  element, 80, 88, 225
    mesh, 238
    software, 225, 226, 227, 228, 229, 238,
        243, 245, 248
    solver, 226, 248
  field, 41
Fisherkeller, M. A., 158
Fit, 141
Fix, G., 320
Flat spots, 75, 111, 112
Floating−point
  arithmetic, 345
  computation, 343
  numbers, 344
Ford, B., 222, 223
Form *see* bilinear form
  bilinear, 226, 228, 234, 236, 245, 248
  proper, 236, 237, 238, 246
Forrest, A. R., 164
Fortran preprocessor, 339
Foshee, G. L., 223
Fourier analysis, 281, 283, 287
Fox, P. A., 359
Franke, R. H., 112, 114, 116, 163
Friedman, J. H., 158
Fulkerson, D. R., 43, 67
Full-approximation scheme, 284, 298
Function approximation, 31, 208
FUNPACK, 208

G

Gaisaryan, S., 223
Galerkin, 321
Gallagher, R. H., 254
Garbow, B. S., 221, 222
Garrett, R., 161
Gaussian elimination, 5, 7, 9
Gauss−Seidel relaxation, 281, 282, 288, 292
Gear, C. W., 274
George, A., 142, 320
Gill, P. E., 17
Gill, S., 199, 260

Global error, 129
Goldenviezer, A., 254
Golub, G., 14, 158, 320
Goodman, A., 307
Gordon, W. J., 74, 91, 92, 110
Graham, R. L., 164
Graphics, 141, 152, 156
Greatest common divisor, 39, 41, 42, 50, 62, 67
Greenberger, M., 224
Gregory, J. A., 71, 78, 89, 91, 102, 103, 104, 113
Grid, 308
  composite, 294
  data structure, 308, 309
  macro−statements, 316
  non−uniform, 294
  operations, 312
  refinement, 294, 299
  representation, 308, 309
  sequence, 278
  software, **GRIDPACK**, 311
  transpose, 313
  triangular, 161, 164, 165, 171
  variable−size, 302
GRIDPACK, 311
  macro−statements, 316
  preprocessor, 316
Griffiths, J. R., 119
Grisvard, P., 254
Growth factor, 7, 8, 9
Gustavson, F. G., 292, 307

H

Hague, S. J., 223
Hall, A. D., 360
Handles, 75, 76, 77, 94, 107, 108, 115
Hanson, R., 11, 158, 161
Hat matrix, 154
Heindel, L. E., 36, 38, 46, 51, 54, 55, 67
Helicopter simulation, 125, 137
Helmholtz equation, 283
Hensel's lemma, 43
Hermite
  basis, 74, 95
  cubics, 321
Herron, G. J., 72, 85
Hestenes, M. R., 362
Hetzel, W. C., 221
Hiebert, K. L., 274
High
  −leverage point, 155
  −order discretization, 302

Hillstrom, K., 222
HODIE method, 322
Hong, S. J., 164
Horner's method, 47
Ho, S.–B. F., 223
Householder, A. S., 14
Householder tridiagonalization, 142
Huber, P. J., 158
Hull, T. E., 221, 274
Hyperbolic, 278, 282, 291

I

Ikebe, Y., 221, 223
Ill-conditioning, 3, 10, 19, 29
ILLIAC, 198, 199
Implicit, 126
    function problems, 163
IMSL, 215
Information structure, 324
Initial
    errors, 8
    –value, 126
Injection, 283
Inner point, 295, 296
Instability, 10
Integration, 126
Interactive design, 69, 70
Interfaces, 323
Interpolation, 71, 88, 91, 103, 110, 289, 300, 311, 314
    C^1, 162
    in a triangle, 171
    multi-grid, 289
Interval arithmetic, 35, 39, 59–63, 345
Inverse eigenvalue problem, 375
Irreducible factors, 39
Isolation of roots, 38, 42
Iteratively reweighted least squares, 156
Iterative methods, 247

J

Jarvis, R. A., 164
Jones, R. E., 274

K

Kabanov, M., 223
Kaganove, J. J., 224
Kahan, W., 362, 372

Kaniel, S., 361, 368
Karush, W., 362
Kaufman, L., 142, 360
Kernighan, B. W., 220
KEY routines, 315
Kincaid, D., 11
Kirchhoff hypotheses, 229
Klema, V. C., 222
Klucewicz, I. M., 75, 81, 82, 112
Knuth, D. E., 44, 67, 360
Krogh, F., 11
Kronmal, R. A., 159
Kutta, W., 260

L

Lagrange multiplier method, 246
Lanczos
    algorithm
        block, 366, 372
        iterative block, 370
    method
        block, 361
Lanczos, C., 361
Languages, 200
L_1 approximation, 28
Lattice, 307
Lawson, C., 11, 88, 158
Least squares, 5, 6, 7, 9, 10, 114
    method, 247
Leverage, 158
Lewis, J., 362
Library, 200, 213, 216
Linear
    algebra, 201
    equations, overdetermined, 15, 19
    programming, 15, 23, 28, 30
    regression model, 157
    system, 1, 2, 5, 7, 211, 278, 321, 326
Line relaxation, 282
LINPACK, 1, 7, 9, 10, 11, 12, 13, 211
Little, F., 72, 75, 79, 83, 91, 104, 105, 107, 112, 162, 188
Livingston, H. M., 221
L_1 norm, 143
Local
    coordinate transformations, 299, 306
    error, 129
    extrapolation, 259
    mode analysis, 282, 283, 287
    optimization procedure, 183
    refinement, 300

Locally optimal edge, 184
Loop optimization, 13
Loos, R., 36, 38, 49, 54–59, 67
L–shaped domain, 248, 297
LU factorization, 4, 5, 7
Luk, F., 373
Lyness, J. N., 224

M

Machine
  anomalies, 343
  –independent properties, 338
  number, 343
Madsen, K., 29, 30
Maintenance, 203, 204
Mallows, C. L., 156
Man-machine interaction, 125
Mansfield, L. E., 116, 163, 164
Marshall, J. A., 101, 120
Massy, W. F., 224
Mathematical
  formulation, 226, 228, 229, 233, 235
    weak, 228, 236, 237
  model, 124
  model, 229, see Mathematical formulation
Matrix, 361
  block tridiagonal, 362
  eigenvalues, 361
  factorizations, 17
  inverses, 17, 26, 29, 201
Maude, A. D., 163
Maude's method, 116
Max–min angle criterion, 168, 176, 178, 179,
    180
McIlroy, M. D., 360
McKenney, J. L., 224
McLain, D. H., 114, 163, 164, 187, 191
McLain's triangulation, 187
Measures of quality, 262
Median polish, 125
Membrane, 233
  deflection, 233
Menus, 93
Merson, R. H., 261
Mesh, 238, 239, 336
  data structure, 309
  generator, 239
  non–uniform, 293
  –ratio, 299
  refinement, 239, 242, 246, 250
  sequence, 278

Mesh (cont.)
  –size, 294, 302, 305
  –size ratio, 288
  variable–size, 302
Mesztenyi, C., 254
Mignotte, M., 40, 42, 66
Minimax solution of equations, 16
Minimum root separation, 42, 46
Minkoff, M., 222
MINPACK, 211
Mixed type, 278, 292
MLAT, 277, 302
  error estimator, 303
  tests, 306
  work functional, 303
Model
  arithmetic, 349
  interval, 345
  numbers, 344
  of floating–point, 343
Modularity, 323
Moler, C. B., 8, 12, 221, 222
Moore, R. E., 360
Movie, 69, 72, 107, 120
MTAC, 201
Multi–grid
  algorithms, 281, 285, 315
  convergence rate, 286
  data structure, 307, 309
  difference equations, 297
  interpolation, 289
  parameters, 288, 290
  relaxation, 281
  routines, GRIDPACK, 311
  software, 307
  storage, 287, 301
  tests, 292
Multi–level adaptive technique, 277, 302
  GRIDPACK, 311
  tests, 306
Multiplicity, 35, 39, 52, 55
Multirate methods, 136
Murray, W., 17
Musser, D. R., 43, 67
Myers, G. J., 221

N

NAG, 212
NATS, 207
Nazareth, L., 222
Networks, 218

Neumann boundary conditions, 279, 290, 291, 292
Newbery, A. C. R., 220
Nicolaides, D. A., 254
Nielson, G. M., 91, 101, 102, 163
Nonlinear
    least–squares, 154, 156
    optimization, 211
Nonoptimizing compiler, 13
Non–uniform grids, 278, 293, 294, 296, 299
Nordbeck, S., 163
Norm, 41
    vector, 358
Normal equations, 10
Normalization, 338
Norrie, D. H., 255
Numerical
    linear algebra, 1, 154
    stability, 18, 30
    tests, 292, 298

O

Oden, J. T., 255
Ophir, D., 307
Optimization software, 211
Ortega, J., 319, 320
Orthogonal triangularization, 10
Osborn, J., 253
Osterweil, L. J., 221, 223
Outer point, 295, 296
Overflow, 4, 346, 356, 357
Overhead, 266, 268
Overton, M., 375

P

Paige, C., 361, 362, 371
Parallel processing, 283, 322
Parlett, B. N., 142, 362, 372
Partial
    derivatives, 170
    differential, 319
        equations, 277, 281
            curved domains, 312
        equation software, 307
    pivoting, 8, 9
    relaxation, 290, 311
Partition of unity, 240, 241
Patch, 72, 76, 77, 78, 92
Pereyra, V., 158

Perspective
    plot, 161, 173, 175, 176
Perturbation, 6
Petrowski
    system, 233
    type, 233, 248
PFORT, 218
Phillips, C., 31
Pilkey, W. B., 255
Pinkert, J. R., 36, 38, 41, 50, 51, 65–67
Pivoting, 7, 8, 9
Pivots in linear programming, 30
Plate, 229, 232
    model, 229, 232
    thin, 232
Plauger, P. J., 220
Poeppelmeier, C., 110, 113
Point
    –quad, 310
    –string, 308
Poisson
    equation, 282, 288, 291, 292, 298
    problem, 278, 291
        L–shaped domain, 298
        relaxation, 282
Polynomial zeros, 35–68
Pool, J., 222
Portability, 200, 210, 213, 216, 343
Portable arithmetic, 358
Port library, 344
Powell, M. J. D., 161, 164, 178
Precision, 71, 81, 103, 118, 344, 348
Predictor–corrector, 133
Preparata, F. P., 164
Preprocessing, 75, 82
Preprocessor, 226, 246, 327, 339
    GRIDPACK, 316
    partial differential equations, 316
Principle of argument, 36, 49, 63–66
Production
    process, 196
    tools, 207, 210, 218
Program
    proofs, 206
    testing, 209, 218
    transformation, 210, 218
Programming
    languages, 226, 247
    style, 200, 205
    systems, 247
Proskurowski, W., 375
Publication of algorithms, 200, 202

Q

QR
  factorization, 9, 10
  method, 369
QUAD structure, 279, 308
Quantifier elimination, 55, 67
Quarles, D., 307

R

Radial projector, 101
Ramamoorthy, C. V., 223
Range, 345, 358
Raynaud, H., 167
Real–time, 122
  constraints, 131
  simulation, 123
Rectangular
  domains, 330
  grid, 336
Red–black (checkerboard) ordering, 292
Reddy, J. N., 255
Refereeing process, 201
Reference, 16
Registers, 348
Reid, J. K., 14, 142, 158
Reinsch, C., 222
Reiss, E. L., 375
Reitwiesner, G. W., 49
Relative
  error, 3
  truncation error, 284
Relaxation, 281, 285, 288, 292, 311, 315, 316
  schemes, 292
  smoothing, 282
    factor, 288
Reliability, 202, 204, 226, 227, 228, 238
Renyi, A., 167
Reorthogonalization, 371, 372
Residual, 141, 148, 156
  equation, 283
  vector, 5, 6
  weighting, 289, 297
Resistance, 141
Resistant line, 147, 149
Rhynsburger, D., 178
Rice, J. R., 21, 220, 320
RKF45, 257, 273
Roberts, F. D. K., 28
Rojtberg, J. A., 255
Rolle's theorem, 36, 52–55

Root
  bound, 44
  squaring, 50
Rosenzweig, M. B., 254
Rounding
  error, 7
    analysis, 7, 8, 9
  errors, 19
  unit, 5, 7
Rump, S., 46, 68
Runge–Kutta, 198, 257
  accuracy, 263
  efficiency, 265
  estimator, 260, 268, 269
  explicit formulas, 258
  fifth order formulas, 264, 267
  formulas, 271
  fourth order formulas, 264, 267
  implementation, 257
  method, 138
  overhead, 266, 268
  stability, 270
Ryder, B. G., 223

S

Sabin, M. A., 164
SAC–1, 39, 50, 67
Sacralski, K., 255
Sard, A., 163
Sayers, D. K., 222
Scaling, 7, 8, 9, 359
  of variables, 17
Schaeffer, H., 255
Schatz, A. H., 254
Schrem, E., 255
Schryer, N. L., 360
Schultz, M., 320
Schumaker, L. L., 110, 114, 164
Schwing, J. L., 120
Second order differential equations, 136
Sedgwick, A. E., 221, 274
Segmental refinement, 301
Selective relaxation, 282
Share, 200
Shell model, 232
Shells, 232
Shepard, D., 112, 162
Shepard's Formula, 110, 113, 114, 116, 117
Shiftan, Y., 292
Shintani, H., 261
Sibson, R., 161

Siemieniuch, J. L., 223
Sikorsky method, 138
Simulation, 122, 123
Single-precision, 344
Singular
    corner, 298, 307
    perturbation, 279, 282, 305, 306
    problems, 279, 306
    value decomposition, 4
    values, 375
Singularity, 239, 250, 251, 279, 307
Smith, B. T., 221, 222
Smooth, 71
Smoothing, 282, 288
    factor, 288
    rate, 288, 290, 292
Snyder, F. E., 220
Sobolev space, 237
Software
    constraints, 122
    cost, 197, 211, 213, 217
    development, 320
    distribution, 199, 216, 217
    engineering, 206
    library, 212, 215
    needs, 154
    package, 1
    production, 196, 198, 202, 207, 212, 213,
        215, 217
    projects, 206
    reliability, 202, 206
    symposia, 196
    testing, 5, 6
Solution
    optimal, 228, 241, 242
    weak, 236
SOR, 322
Southwell, R. V., 283
Sparse, matrices, 17, 332, 334, 360
Spider, 75
Squarefree factorization, 40, 41, 53
Stability, 2, 3, 5, 6, 7, 130, 270
    boundary, 135
    improvement, 131
Starius, G., 300
Statistical software, 139
Steepest descent, 362
Steppel, S., 158
Stewart, G. W., 222
Stiefel, E. L., 16, 17, 18
Storage, 200, 203, 246, 266, 268, 278, 287,
        301, 302, 311, 324
    multi-grid, 287

Stresses, 232, 243
Strictly convex quadrilateral, 178
Structural analysis, 225, 243
Structured programming, 205
Stucki, L. G., 223
Sturm sequences, 36, 45–51, 66
Sturm's theorem, 36, 45, 50
Styan, G. P. H., 158
Style, 200, 201, 203
Subexpressions, 354
Subresultants, 46
Subroutine library, 199
Sulanke, R., 167
Summary points, 148
Surface
    C^1, 161, 162
    fitting, 164
    interpolation, 161
        algorithm, 164
    irregular data, 163
    plotting, 162
Surfaces, 69, 97, 98, 99, 100
SURFED, 69, 72
Sweet, R., 320
Switching parameters, 286, 290, 298
Symmetric
    indefinite system, 142
    matrix, 361
Systematized collection, 208

T

TAMPR, 210, 218
Tarter, M. E. 159
Taylor, G. D., 17
TEMPLET, 317
Tensor products, 74, 75, 321
Testing, 218
Thiessen
    neighbors, 179, 185
    proximity regions, 180, 186
    region criterion, 178, 180, 181
    triangulation, 173, 177, 184, 185
Timings, 142
Timing tests, 12
Timoshenko, S., 253
Tocher, J. L., 171
Todd, J., 221
Transformation, 141, 144, 300
    local, 299
Transonic flow, 286, 292
Transportability, 2

Trapezoidal
  method, 127
  rule, 127
    delayed, 127
Traub, J. F., 220
Triangular
  Coons patch, 92
  grid, 171
    construction, 165
Triangulation, 82, 83, 97, 98, 99, 161, 164,
    165
  algorithm, 169
  circle criterion, 178, 179
  complexity, 167, 170, 190
  converged edge, 188, 189, 200
  criteria, 176, 180
  data structure, 165
  locally optimal edge, 184
  max-min angle criterion, 168, 176, 179
  McLain, 187
  method of McLain, 189
  optimal, 84, 181, 183, 185
  preferred, 167
  software, 166
  storage, 191
  Thiessen, 184, 187
    criterion, 178
    region criterion, 180
Tridiagonal matrix, 361
Truncation error, 284, 303
Tukey, J. W., 140, 158, 159
Twelve parameter patch, 77
Twists, 75, 78
Two-way table, 142

U

Uncertainty, 7
Underflow, 4, 346, 357, 359
Uniform scale, 306
UNIVAC programming, 200
Unrolled loop, 13, 14
Updating, 10

User
  groups, 200
  input, 327
Users, 217
Uspensky, J. V., 36, 55-61, 68

V

Varga, R., 320
Variational principle, 238
Verification, 1
Vincent's theorem, 57, 68
Voevodin, V., 223

W

Washizu, K., 255
Wegstein, J., 201
Welsch, R. E., 158
Wheeler, D. J., 199
Whiteman, J. R., 255
Widlund, O., 320
Wilfe, P., 14
Wilkes, M. V., 199
Wilkinson, J. H., 3, 6, 9, 222, 224, 275
Wire frame data, 78
Wirth, N., 221
Wolfe, P., 18, 31
Work
  functional (W), 303
  -unit, 298

Y

Young, D., 281, 320

Z

Zienkiewicz, O., 255
Zlamal, M., 255
Zonneveld, J. A., 261

A
B 7
C 8
D 9
E 0
F 1
G 2
H 3
I 4
J 5